British and Irish Art
1945-1951

D.M.

MAURICE COWLING

BRIAN WORMALD

COLL. DIV. PET. CANTAB. SOCIORVM

QVORVM ACVMEN ET DILIGENTIAM VALDE MIRATVS

PRIMVM COGNOVI

QVANTI ESSET MOMENTI HISTORIAM SCRIBERE

QVAMQVE DIFFICILE

Time which antiquates Antiquities, and hath an art
to make dust of all things,
hath yet spared these minor monuments.
Sir Thomas Browne, *Hydriotaphia*, 1658

Ther's nothing simply good, nor ill alone,
Of every quality comparison,
The only measure is, and judge, opinion.
John Donne, *The Progresse of the Soule*, 1601

British and Irish Art
1945-1951
From War to Festival

Adrian Clark

Hogarth Arts

2010

First published by Hogarth Arts 2010

ISBN 978-0-9554063-4-8

Distribution by Paul Holberton Publishing
89 Borough High Street London SE1 1NL

Design and production David Hodgson

Printed in Cornwall by TJ International

Contents

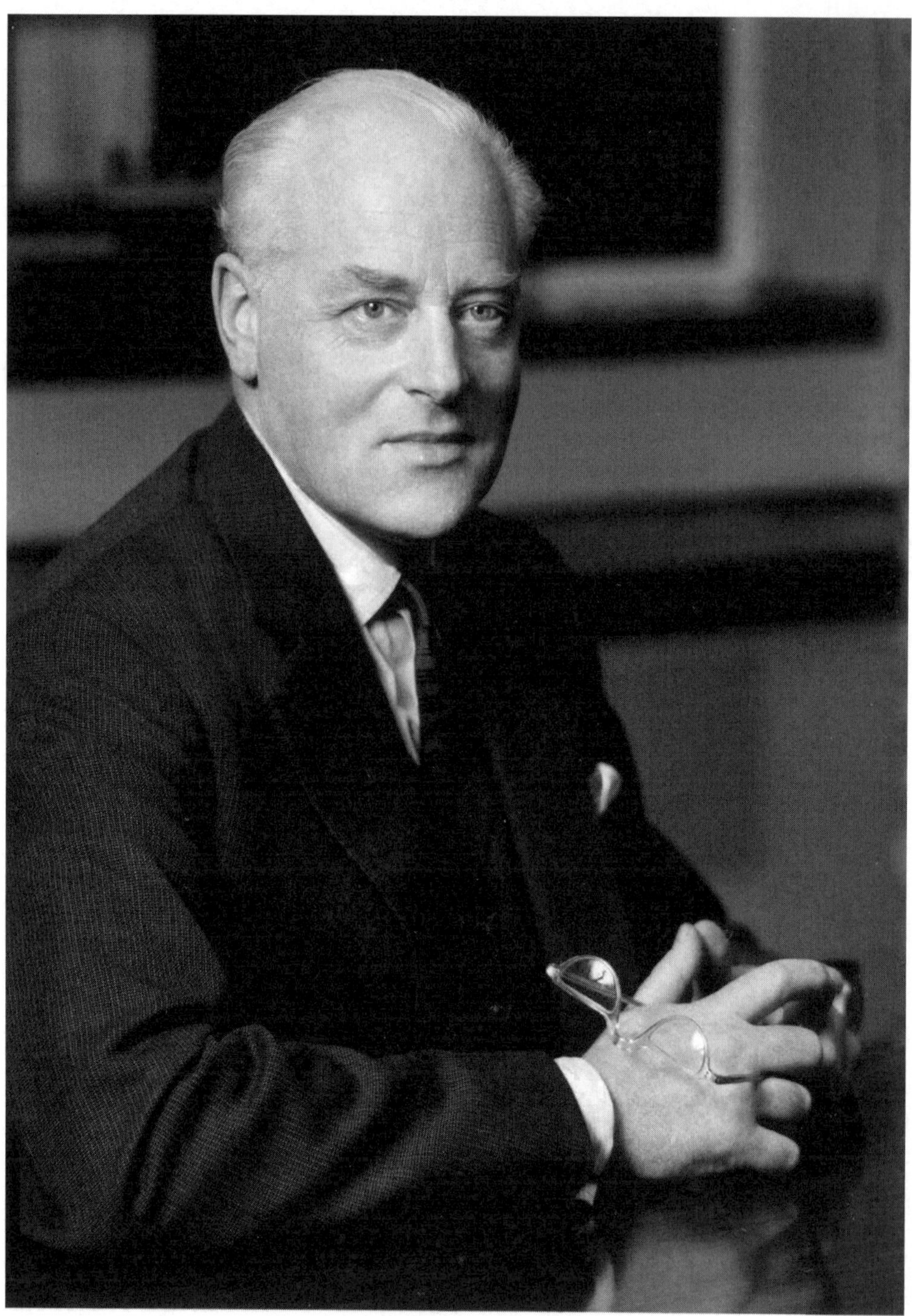

Sir Colin Anderson (1904-80)

Introduction

Artists of the British Isles in the 20th century are sorely in need of a balanced assessment. Monographs devoted to them have presented stories into which no word of criticism has been allowed to intrude. The artist in question never paints a poor picture and usually makes an apparently inexorable progress from modest beginnings to an astonishing level of skill and significance. At the same time, artists whose lives and reputations have, for whatever reason, ceased to be known or appreciated by later observers, or who have fallen into disrepute, may well need to have their reputations rescued. The work of such artists has to be reconsidered together with that of their more celebrated contemporaries: only such a synthesis can approach a more accurate assessment.

Critics writing in the 1940s, having emerged from a past in which art criticism could be learnt almost as a science, and a picture analysed according to pre-selected tests and attributes, were always going to struggle with the freer creations of the painters of the mid-century. Even those artists whose work was basically representational did not necessarily paint according to the rules which had applied to their predecessors. Some aspects of their work could be judged by critics using the old critical apparatus, but there were many others that could not be judged in the same way. Once an artist's work moved towards the abstract, contemporary judgments were bound to come adrift from their moorings in accepted art criticism. Critics tended to struggle with abstract work[1] – perhaps understandably – and they even struggled to cope with artists such as Sutherland and Bacon, whose subjectivity made them hard to assess. That great critic, Eric Newton, writing in the *Sunday Times*, frequently wrestled with the problem of making judgments on contemporary artists. On 28 March 1948 he wrote:

> The artist of today has inherited no tradition of craftsmanship that is of any use to him. Existing forms, existing techniques, stifle his intentions instead of releasing them. What the truly creative artist of today wants to impart is so new and so personal to himself that a traditional mode of expression has not yet been evolved to fit it. Consequently he has to grope ineffectually for the painterly equivalent of his vision.

In Ireland, Edward Sheehy, writing in the July-September 1946 issue of the *Dublin Magazine*, made a related point in trying to compare modern art with that of the past:

> The artist in a stable society could see life steadily, whole and orderly. His vision was the intensification of the whole contemporary social vision. The artist today gives expression merely to the momentary, immediate and individual attempt to make some kind of personal order out of chaos.

The successful reassessment of the artistic works of the whole century would be a wonderful book, unimaginable in its scope and complexity. It would take a greater stamina than mine. But by concentrating on one key period, 1945-51, an attempt can be made to describe the circumstances in which artists in the British Isles operated and to analyse how their reputations came to exist.

The accuracy of a description of what happened in the past cannot be verified, for the past cannot be reconstructed. It has left behind bits and pieces of often unrelated evidence, which may enable fragments to be pieced together with a tentative degree of confidence; but the whole picture is and always will be lost. What happened in the past and why it happened cannot be known. Writers about the past who wish to piece together their fragments into a coherent narrative therefore have no choice but to invent what they think happened or what they want to have happened. Whether subconsciously or deliberately, they will be selective about their use of the evidence that survives. Above all, their judgments will necessarily be affected by hindsight. In 1945 those observing and commenting on the contemporary art world saw a present full of possibilities. The present is always full of possibilities. In identifying those artists whom they considered to be significant, they too were affected by hindsight: but the judgments they made on the past and the present were no more right, or accurate, than those which we make, either on their past or on our own. Judgments made in 1945 were as likely to be as fallible as contemporary judgments made in any era: and yet, in an important sense, those judgments shaped the future.

The focus of this book will be a detailed study of the facts available from a comparatively short period of British art history, in the belief that it can provide a glimpse into the way artists' lives and reputations developed and formed, and the background against which this took place. It assumes that the simplifications of art history, in concentrating on just a few British artists who later became well known, are unlikely to create an accurate analysis of what actually happened. It also assumes that the modern focus especially on Francis Bacon and Lucian Freud has to some extent been manufactured by their admirers and proselytisers. In fact, the effect of promotion and self-promotion by and of certain artists – one thinks of 'St Ives' and the Euston Road School – leads to a suspicion that a distortion is being wilfully attempted on the modern public about the shape of the mid-20th-century British art world. It is a distortion that this book sets out to analyse and, if necessary, to correct.

Certain artists seem to me, for various reasons, to have been given too much emphasis by art historians: Pasmore, Heron, Gear, Wynter, Clough and Herman are examples. Meanwhile, certain artists have received too little attention, such as the Northern Irish artists, Michael Rothenstein, Robert Colquhoun and Kenneth Rowntree. To my mind, Pasmore and Heron[2] were so obsessed by self-promotion that it is difficult now to assess the quality of their work in comparison with that of their contemporaries, whereas some artists of great thoughtfulness and sensitivity – Dillon, Luke, Underwood[3] and Rowntree spring to mind – simply got on with producing serious and thoughtful work. Revealingly, they have never received a similar degree of attention or respect from art historians of their period.

A particular challenge, which all historians face, is to try to use the available facts to explain changes that have occurred over time. There is a temptation to seek to identify historical 'turning points', which may be held out as explaining change. In political history there may be turning points, although they usually have to be treated with caution, or even suspicion, as being simplifications and distortions of a series of events which may well have had no actual beginning, middle or end. Indeed, they may have been chosen by the historian who purports to have identified them, or who uses them, out of laziness, or from a desire to generate an illusory impression of drama. The Second World War may have been a turning point in some respects, although there were many others in 20th-century Britain. In fact, the way that historians view past events such as the War varies not only according to deliberate choices about the use of evidence, but is also dependent upon when and from where the historian is viewing the past. An English historian's view of the significance of the War will have been different in 1945 from what it would be to an historian in 2010; and a German historian's view of the War will also have altered over the years (although not necessarily in the same way).

The same complex shifting of perspective, conscious and unconscious, applies to the views of art historians as they look back, although how much British art historians have allowed for this shifting focus – or even recognized it – is debatable. Those writing in 1945 about the immediate past were, of course, doing so in ignorance of the way that British art would actually develop and therefore in a state of ignorance about many fundamental things which were in fact going to happen: changing attitudes towards abstract art; the ongoing influence of Picasso; the changing relationships between London and Paris; the introduction of New York as an international art centre; the novelty of pop art; and so on. Art has had its historical changes, just like all forms of history, but it has had few obvious turning points, although there are respected commentators who believe that the War was one such turning point for British art. Here, for example, is Sir John Rothenstein,[4] for a long time director of the Tate, writing towards the end of the third and final volume of his autobiography, *Time's Thievish Progress* (1970):

> The Second World War had a transforming effect on the entire art world. Not only was the influence of the old Establishment eroded until it ceased to exist, but a new public and new critical attitudes came into being – attitudes which before long were the exact opposite of those which had previously prevailed.[5]

Clearly it is possible to argue like this that world events can have a major effect on the course of art. It is probably not correct – who can prove it either way? – but it is, at least, arguable. What is less arguable is the attempt to explain change by identifying artistic, as distinct from political, turning points. One can only read so many times about the impact on British art of the later 1950s of the arrival from America of Abstract Expressionism before realising how misleading this emphasis is. The slightest attention to the detail of the artistic events of the century immediately destroys any idea that the arrival of this particular type of painting was anything other than a thread in a very elaborate tapestry. It clearly had an effect on such insignificant painters as Patrick Heron, but what material effect did it have on Bacon or Freud, Hockney or Sutherland, Le Brocquy or Vaughan? Theorising about 'developments' in art – or sudden 'changes', to use a less judgmental word – almost never makes any sense once such suppositions are subjected to testing by a few facts, and indeed is almost as doubtful an approach as one based upon any presumption of progress in art.[6]

In this book I shall attempt, in so far as I can, to let the surviving facts speak for themselves,[7] and see if they can be made to tell us something of interest about that lost world of which they can now only provide glimpses. For, although mountains of paper survive from the past to tempt historians looking back at the mid-20th century, the mountains are only molehills when compared to what existed at the time, and whatever paper existed – then or now – was only ever a fragment of what would be required to recreate past time in any detail.[8] Furthermore, documents surviving from the past, which the historian chances upon and grasps with a sense of relief and gratitude, may themselves be slippery things. They may be contemporary evidence, but they are quite likely to contain lies, in an historical sense. For example, the writers of diaries give one a contemporary glimpse of the past; but it is a glimpse which the writer of the diary has deliberately created. It therefore has to be treated with caution before the historian can risk relying on it as an accurate record of something that actually happened in the way described. The writer of the diary will have filtered and sifted the information that he was able to, or chose to, recall in deciding what to represent about his day and how to present himself in the context of that day and, to that extent, the reliability of the evidence delivered to the future by the diary is less than absolute.[9]

Similarly, the mere contemporaneity of art criticism is not something that should encourage blind reliance on the part of historians. John Berger, Patrick Heron and David Sylvester were clever, knowledgeable art critics, but they cannot be said to have been unbiased in certain respects (which writer can?) and they certainly each had blind spots and areas of ignorance. Critics cannot in any way be treated as representing the 'truth' other than, of course, a kind of truth about criticism of the time. In any event, the emphasis on the survival or otherwise of paper evidence is itself misleading, in that large tracts of a life, and of the events that link together different lives, are inevitably unrecorded on paper. Here the spoken recollections of contemporaries are necessary to fill in some of the gaps, and of course, those recollections themselves may have to have been recorded on paper or on tape, if they are to provide any assistance, since reliance now on the memories of those people still alive with contemporary recollections is bound to be of varied quality. It hardly needs to be pointed out that, where the spoken word is concerned, the scope for mischief or the possibilities of simply being misled are at least as great.

The Bacon 'interviews'

Some contemporary commentators appear to have gone out of their way deliberately to have manipulated records of the spoken word in such a manner as to offer the result as if it were 'documentary evidence', when it clearly is not. A well-known example is the Sylvester interviews with Francis Bacon.[10] These have been treated by the large community of writers who like to analyse Bacon as though they were great historical sources that can afford us an unparalleled insight into Bacon's apparently highly developed and sophisticated thoughts on art. They are supposed also to fill us with wonder and gratitude for Sylvester's clever interviewing technique. He appears, on the face of it, to have had remarkable skill in drawing out Bacon's thoughts, which the artist then uttered in a remarkably coherent fashion, which Sylvester delivered verbatim to a hungry audience.[11] But even at the basic level of the construction of these interviews (ignoring, for these purposes, their actual content), there is a problem with them of which any historian ought immediately to be aware.[12] For in his description of how the different interviews were constructed and 'edited', Sylvester reveals that a very great deal of editing was conducted, and that the final published form differs considerably from the spoken word. The 'interviews', presented as such, are very far from being transcripts; indeed, so it appears, they are not really even interviews. This may not matter, because Sylvester may genuinely have been simply tidying up Bacon's unprepared words, without altering the sense of whatever Bacon may have meant by them, but the historian will have an alarm bell ringing in his ear. How much do these writings embody Bacon's words and meaning? Or how much do they merely reflect what Sylvester wanted the public to think that Bacon had said?[13]

The reality is that these 'interviews' are as much by Sylvester as they are by Bacon. This is made clear in the book's introduction, although Sylvester is at pains to claim that they 'present Bacon's thought clearly and economically':

> What is preserved here amounts to no more than about a fifth of the material in the transcripts – out of choice, not because of any arbitrary limitation on length. Furthermore, since the editing has been designed to present Bacon's thought clearly and economically – not to provide some sort of abbreviated record of how the taped sessions happened to develop – the sequence in which things were said has been drastically rearranged. Each of the interviews, apart from the first, has been constructed from transcripts of two or more sessions, and paragraphs in these montages sometimes combine things said on two or three different days quite widely separated

> in time. In order to prevent the montage from looking like a montage, many of the questions
> have been recast or simply fabricated. The aim has been to seam together a more concise and
> coherent argument than ever came about when we were talking, without making it so coherent
> as to lose the fluid, spontaneous flavour of talk.[14]

The process of 'adjusting' whatever Bacon may originally have said to Sylvester was to continue when another of Bacon's great friends and supporters, Michel Leiris, translated the interviews into French.[15] According to Bacon himself, when talking to Michel Archimbaud,[16] the Leiris translation was, curiously, 'possibly better than the original'. Leiris 'managed to give it a much more profound meaning than I had been able to express. It's extraordinary; I felt myself to be much more intelligent when I read it. I didn't think I had said such things'. In other words, Leiris presumably decided that he could do even better than Sylvester had done in putting across the thoughts of the master – a perfectly acceptable thing for an admirer to do, but not under the guise of translating an interview. One senses that even Bacon thought Leiris had gone a little beyond his remit and Leiris's French text needs to be treated with considerable caution by any historian struggling towards 'the truth'.

With these extraordinary examples of manipulation in mind, it will be seen that art historians need to proceed cautiously, as much with what appears to be spoken evidence as with written evidence. I shall try to do so without seeking to make those facts that do survive prove some predetermined theory about the past, and without trying to create a narrative thread that purports to link events which themselves may or may not have happened.[17] It is also the purpose of this book to proceed without undue emphasis on English artists. Art historians who seek to write synthetically, bringing together different artists and developments, have to make choices about geography. Which artists do they include in their study? Do they decide to include or exclude artists on the basis of place of birth; place of work; political boundaries; geographical boundaries; apparent artistic boundaries? All such decisions can be challenged. I believe that that there is no justification in seeking to distinguish between artists working in different parts of the British Isles during the period covered.[18] There is, no doubt, some sort of gap, however imprecise, between painters of the British Isles and those of France, or between those of the British Isles and those of Germany, but not necessarily between those born in Scotland and those born in Dublin or Belfast.[19] It needs to be stated that the book will not attempt to use a structure based upon the political events of the years 1945-51, nor to build up a picture of the social or general cultural situation in the British Isles during this period. There are many modern studies that seek to do this (although in many cases they are based on England or Ireland, for example, but not both at the same time). While in some contexts it may be necessary to try to understand the mood of the people (at least the people of England) who rejoiced at the end of the War or voted in the Labour party (whose period in power neatly coincided with the years of this book), or who lived with the continuation of rationing long after the end of the War, who suffered in the terrible winter of 1947, and who, at various stages, worried gloomily about the increasingly tense and threatening world political situation or even the difficulties suffered by the British upper classes, none of that is the subject of this book.[20]

The War in Europe finished on 8 May 1945 and the Festival of Britain opened on 3 May 1951. We shall look at the artists working in the British Isles during that six year period and the art world in which they operated. How they lived, interrelated, worked, developed; how taste and reputations formed; who flourished. Above all, why and how some grew in stature and others did not.[21]

The artistic scene

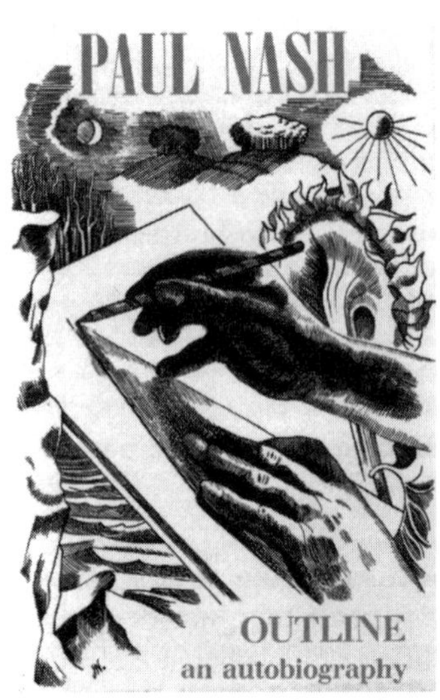

The elasticity and arbitrariness of the periods which historians choose to study must always be emphasised. Meaningful historical periods often turn out not to exist on closer study and a determination to identify such periods may not be the best use of an historian's time. Certainly, historians who insist on the significance of apparently arbitrary periods of time based on decades or centuries, for example, may be treated with some scepticism. The history of the 19th century has, for example, been given a particular flavour by late 20th-century historians, but it had a different resonance for historians writing earlier in the century and, in any event, it can have no meaning as a period worthy of study in any absolute sense.[1] Important people were not generally born in 1800 and did not then generally die in 1900. So it is with artists. The choice of 1945 therefore cuts through the art-historical continuum at an arbitrary moment and unwittingly gives credence to the possibility that the end of the War had a particular significance for the development of British art, which is not necessarily the case. It in fact, as one would expect, left some artists about to die, full of years, their work finished; others about to die young; others in between. Examples present themselves easily and forcefully. In the first category we might put Frances Hodgkins, who was to die in 1947, at the age of 78. In the second category falls Tom Hennell, caught up in the aftermath of the War and dying tragically in the Dutch East Indies in late 1945 at the age of 42, after the War in Europe had finished. In between could we put Paul Nash, dying in 1946 at 57, his work apparently still evolving?

The starting date also throws into relief certain artists who were already well set in their careers, but who were to live for some time, perhaps unfashionable, perhaps just very old. In this category is Augustus John (to die in 1961 at the age of 83); David Bomberg (dying in 1957 at 67); the Irish painter Paul Henry, born in 1876 and not to die until 1958, but in fact largely incapacitated by illness from 1946 onwards; and perhaps the utterly Edwardian-seeming Sir William Nicholson, who did not in fact die until 1949 at the age of 77; and Charles Spencelayh, who had been born in 1865 and was to die in 1958.

The year catches some artists who could perhaps be described as being in mid-career. Here we might put Edward Burra, many of whose uniquely strange pictures had been produced by 1945, but who carried on painting for the next 30 years; and David Jones, who carried on painting until 1963 (dying in 1974). Then comes a category of those already seeing some success, although younger. Robert Colquhoun's first solo exhibition had been at the Lefevre in 1943; Minton's was in 1945; and Vaughan's in the same year. Finally came those already working, but so far largely failing to register on the wider art world of the British Isles, such as Bacon, Le Brocquy (yet to arrive in London from Dublin), Davie (his first small one-man exhibition was to be at an Edinburgh bookshop in 1946) and Freud, who took part in various shared exhibitions in the 1940s, but who had no real prominence until well into the 1950s. It is essential to recognise that, whatever their modern reputations, in 1945 they were of no material importance in the wider artistic community.

THE PAINTERS

Where they can be established, facts provide the armature upon which some sort of historical structure can be created. Without facts, theorising about the state of British art in 1945 would be interesting, depending upon one's view of the writer, but it would not mean anything as history: no facts, no history. A basic factual starting point for this study is to consider which artists were working in 1945. As should have been made clear already, grouping artists does not help much; instead, one has to start with a blank mind and see what the facts reveal. Choosing by date of birth, those who were at the time regarded as among the most significant living artists[2] are set out here in List 1:

LIST 1 Artists by date of birth

1869	Frances Hodgkins	1897	Edward Wolfe	1910	Colin Middleton
1871	Jack Yeats	1898	William Gillies	1911	Josef Herman
1872	Sir William Nicholson	1900	Edward Ardizzone	1911	Roger Hilton
1876	Paul Henry	1901	Fred Uhlman	1912	Keith Vaughan
1878	Augustus John	1901	Norah McGuinness	1913	Robert MacBryde
1879	Matthew Smith	1903	Ceri Richards	1913	William Scott
1882	Wyndham Lewis	1903	Edward Bawden	1914	Robert Colquhoun
1885	Duncan Grant	1903	Richard Eurich	1915	William Gear
1887	Laurence Lowry	1903	Thomas Hennell	1915	Patrick Hennessy
1889	Paul Nash	1903	Graham Sutherland	1915	Kenneth Rowntree
1889	Christopher Nevinson	1903	John Piper	1915	Bryan Wynter
1889	Edward Wadsworth	1903	William MacTaggart	1916	Louis le Brocquy
1889	Cedric Morris	1905	Edward Burra	1916	Gerard Dillon
1890	David Bomberg	1905	Tristram Hillier	1917	George Campbell
1890	Leon Underwood	1905	John Aldridge	1917	John Minton
1891	Bernard Meninsky	1905	Gerald Wilde	1918	Kyffin Williams
1891	Stanley Spencer	1906	John Luke	1918	Peter Lanyon
1892	Gilbert Spencer	1908	Cecil Collins	1919	Prunella Clough
1893	John Nash	1908	William Coldstream	1920	Alan Davie
1893	Winifred Nicholson	1908	Victor Pasmore	1920	Patrick Heron
1893	Ivon Hitchens	1908	Michael Rothenstein	1920	Daniel O'Neill
1894	Ben Nicholson	1908	Carel Weight	1921	Michael Ayrton
1895	William Roberts	1909	Francis Bacon	1922	Lucian Freud
1895	David Jones	1910	Rodrigo Moynihan	1922	John Craxton
1895	Jankel Adler	1910	Julian Trevelyan		

The list shows that there were 74 artists of some note and working or living in the British Isles at the end of the War. By 1951, Adler, Hennell, Hodgkins, Meninsky, Paul Nash, Nevinson, Sir William Nicholson and Wadsworth had died. Only just over half of the artists who could be considered to be significant in 1945 were born in England.[3] The variety of geographical backgrounds is striking and it will be a particular ambition of this book to seek to avoid the Anglo-centric nature of such synthetic works as there have been on this period. Although many of the artists mentioned in this book worked or lived in London at some part of their careers, they were often not English. It is, in my view, essential to respond to this fact. Some were not from the British Isles (Freud, Hodgkins, Uhlman), but worked here for a long time. A proper synthesis of the period's artistic activity would not, therefore, restrict itself to those working in the British Isles; it would have to cover the whole painting world. But that cannot be contemplated in a short book and it has to be accepted as a weakness. Instead, by expanding what might be thought to be the 'usual' emphasis on English artists, by extending our coverage at least to Welsh, Irish and Scottish born artists, perhaps some progress may be made towards a unified, coherent history of art in the period concerned. List 2 shows which art schools they went to, if any (some went to more than one and some attended only briefly).

LIST 2 **Artists by place of training**

The Slade
    Bomberg, Coldstream, Eurich, Heron, Hillier, Hilton, John, Lewis, Meninsky, Moynihan, P. Nash, Nevinson, B. Nicholson, Roberts, Rowntree, Smith, G. Spencer, S. Spencer, Underwood, Wadsworth, Williams, Wolfe, Wynter

Royal College of Art
    Bawden, Burra, Collins, Piper, Richards, G. Spencer, Underwood, Yeats

Central
    Ardizzone, Craxton, Rothenstein

Camberwell
    Jones, G. Spencer

Westminster
    Ardizzone, Craxton, Grant

South Kensington
    G. Spencer

London Polytechnic
    Hennell

Goldsmiths
    Sutherland, Weight

Chelsea
    Clough, Rothenstein, Wilde

Chelsea Polytechnic
    Burra, McGuinness

Hammersmith
    Weight

Royal Academy Schools
    Hitchens, Scott

St John's Wood
    Ayrton, Hitchens, Minton, Nevinson

Regent Street Polytechnic
    Underwood

Byam Shaw School
    W. Nicholson

Plymouth
    Collins

Salford
    Lowry

Cambridge
    Bawden

Bradford
    Wadsworth

Richmond
    Piper

Ruskin School
    Rowntree

Dublin
    McGuinness

Belfast
    Henry, Luke, Middleton, Scott

Glasgow
    Colquhoun, MacBryde

Edinburgh
    Davie, Gear, Gillies, MacTaggart

Dundee
    Hennessy

Swansea
    Richards

Out of 74 artists, 23 had been to the Slade, easily the largest group attending one school of art. Interesting, too, however, is the number of different schools of art which were attended. Twenty-seven different schools around the British Isles appear and no doubt there were others. It is also noticeable how some developing artists attended two or even three of the schools, often for comparatively brief periods.

CENTRES

In order to give the reader an account of the full breadth of the artistic scene in the British Isles, it would be necessary to take a wide-ranging tour. It can be no surprise that artists were working in a large number of places, although it is also no surprise that we can capture quite a number of them by focusing on a few large cities, where many of them tended to congregate, simply because that is where they had some chance of selling their pictures, wherever they would have preferred to live.[4]

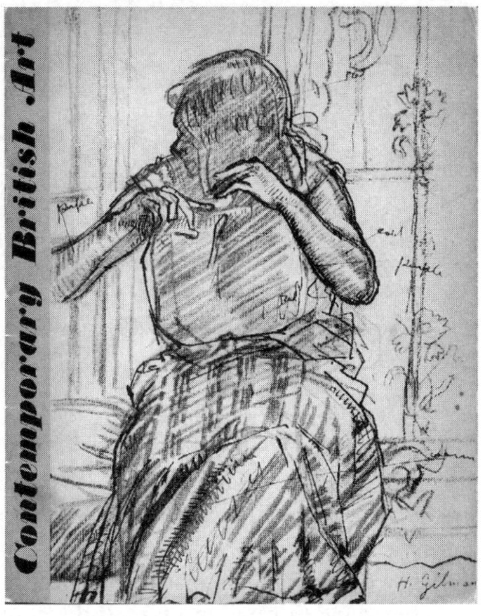

Clearly, in this study no substantial mention will be made of foreign artists who showed in London but did not live in the British Isles, nor of the many dealers and exhibitions which focused on art from earlier periods, although it is as well to remember that this was the constant backdrop to the activities described here. The visitor to London or Dublin, for example, would have been able to see the great national collections at the National Gallery in London or in the National Gallery of Ireland in Dublin. The likelihood of seeing large public displays of contemporary British art would have been much less and really dependent on occasional exhibitions at the Tate, for example, or at the Royal Academy in London or the Royal Hibernian Academy in Dublin or the Irish Exhibition of Living Art, or at private galleries, or on great occasions such as the various shows associated with the Festival of Britain. The reader may feel that the art-lover was surrounded by the works and activities of contemporary artists, but this would have been far from the case, especially in Dublin, Belfast, Edinburgh and Glasgow, but also in London. What follows can only be an impressionistic account of the artistic life amongst those focused on modern art in the different centres.

London

At this period London was undoubtedly a magnet for all artists in the British Isles seeking to make their careers; perhaps it always had been. It was one of the world's great art capitals, its only real challenger being Paris at this time. We have seen that it had many art schools, including the dominant Slade. It also had many dealers and more potential buyers, both institutional and private, than any alternative centre in the British Isles. It also had the galleries and museums where important exhibitions were likely to be held of the contemporary foreign artists whose works were influential to varying degrees. Once reputations were made, artists could risk moving away, but many of them who did not necessarily start in London had their London 'phase', earlier in their careers, and some had a very long phase indeed. Even those artists who did not live in London often had to visit it regularly to get materials, visit exhibitions, see friends or visit their dealers. A good example of this is Sutherland, who was living in Kent, but seems to have been regularly in London – for instance visiting Bacon – in

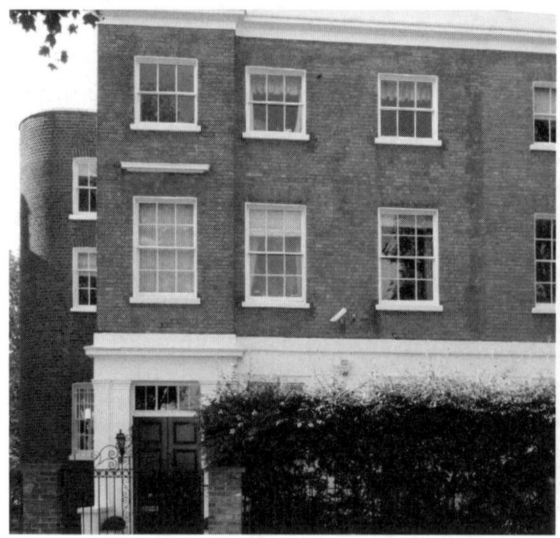

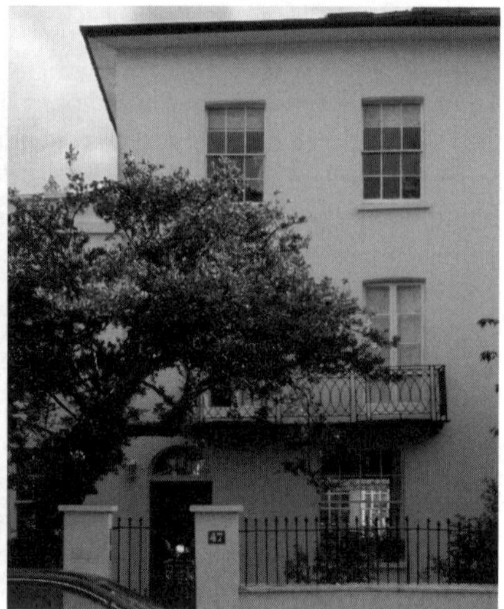

37 Hamilton Terrace NW8 home to
John Minton and Keith Vaughan from August 1946

47 Downshire Hill NW3
home of Fred Uhlman

the years immediately following the War. Others went in the opposite direction. Born in London, Hitchens responded to the bombing of his Adelaide Road, Hampstead studio by moving out to Lavington in Sussex, where he had a studio for working and a gypsy caravan to live in, together with six acres of woodland which was to inform so much of his work thereafter.[5] He kept away from London as much as possible and seems to have been happy leading a comparatively isolated painter's life in the depths of Sussex.

They came to London from all directions, with some born there and staying there, and others arriving from far and wide.[6] Some had got to know each other well, socialising together regularly. In this category we can put the often described 'group' – Bacon, Freud, Colquhoun, MacBryde, Vaughan, Minton, Wilde and Craxton (and perhaps Clough) - who met in the pubs of Soho and other places. They lived in various parts of West London, sometimes sharing studios.[7] Number 77 Bedford Gardens in Kensington had been built as a block of studios in the 19th century. Colquhoun and MacBryde showed up there in 1941; Minton joined them in the same studio in 1943. Adler arrived in the same block in 1943. Edward Wolfe was there at some point and Ronald Searle arrived in July 1946, after returning from the War.[8] There has been some confusion and misleading information published as to how long Colquhoun and MacBryde stayed in Bedford Gardens. It has often been said[9] that 'the Roberts' left for good in 1947 to go to stay in Lewes in Sussex with those strange sisters, Frances Byng Stamper and Caroline Lucas, never to return.[10] It is also said that this 'ejection' contributed to their later decline. But the facts we have suggest that although they undoubtedly did leave London in 1947 to live at Westgate House in Lewes (home of the sisters), they then returned quite regularly to Bedford Gardens and wrote many letters from there, [11] right through to at least October 1950, when another phase of living outside London – this time in Essex – began.

The interaction between the Roberts, Minton and Adler while they were all living in the block casts an interesting light on the life of these artists at the time.[12] Minton stayed in the same studio as the Roberts from some time in 1943 to 1946. He slept in the small back bedroom and the Roberts slept in the main studio room, in which all three artists used to work. Minton's inherited money was welcome to the Roberts, but it may be that, if they could ever be said to have been financially solvent, it was during this period. Adler also arrived (at least in a different studio) in 1943. His life had been torn apart by the War. He was a Pole from Lodz who had worked in 1931 alongside Klee in Düsseldorf, but had then fled and come, via various intervening adventures, to Dunkirk with some part of the Polish army. From there he arrived in Glasgow, where he was reunited with Herman, who had reached Glasgow in the early 1940s. They both came to London and Adler to Bedford Gardens. He played an important part in the artistic development at least of Colquhoun, MacBryde and Minton during the next few years, although it is not easy to establish that he had a wider influence, except perhaps on Le Brocquy. (A picture entitled *Child with doll, hommage à Jankel Adler, 1949*, the year of Adler's death, was sold at Whyte's in Dublin in 2008.) He seems to have had a strong personality and clearly

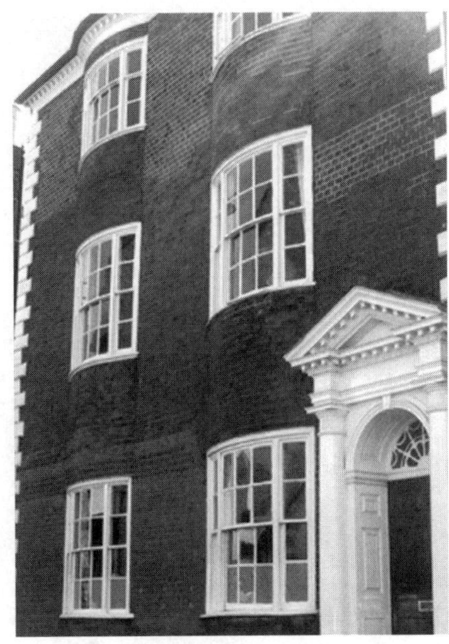

Westgate House, Lewes, where 'the Roberts' stayed from 1947

introduced elements of Cubism which the younger artists may not otherwise have found easy to encounter at first hand (especially during the War). He certainly acted as an antidote to the influence of Sutherland, which had glanced upon Colquhoun[13] immediately prior to Adler's arrival. In any event, Minton could not carry on living with the Roberts forever and in 1946 he moved out. The Roberts then seem to have fallen out with Adler and at some stage he ended up in a cottage in Aldbourne in Wiltshire, provided for him by Jimmy Bomford (whose position in the art world will be dealt with later). The tendency of artists in London at this time to live together is well illustrated by following what happened next in Minton's life, for in August 1946 he set up home with Keith Vaughan in a maisonette at 37 Hamilton Terrace, NW8. They had a floor each and led largely separate lives.

In 1945, there had until quite recently been more artists fairly nearby in Hampstead and Belsize Park. But by the end of the War, Ben Nicholson and Barbara Hepworth, Naum Gabo and Mondrian had departed for Cornwall. Fred Uhlman was still there at 47 Downshire Hill. He was a German refugee, trained as a lawyer in Germany and only lately turned to painting, his work seemingly heavily influenced by that of Utrillo. The Surrealist artist and collector Roland Penrose was also living in Downshire Hill at this time. Other refugees, or Jewish artists, also chose to live in the area. Gotlib[14] lived in Fellows Road in Hampstead; Bomberg in Rosslyn Hill; and Kestelman[15] at 27 Belsize Park Gardens (although they did not necessarily all live in the area at the same time, they were all there in about 1950). Craxton was by this time beginning his travels, but his family base – he was only 22 when the War ended – was in Hampstead.[16] Coldstream returned to London from the War in July 1945 and moved into his parents' flat in Marlborough Mansions in West Hampstead. His friends in the art world at this time included Anthony Blunt and Adrian Stokes (when he was in London). He himself was, of course, to become the artist-

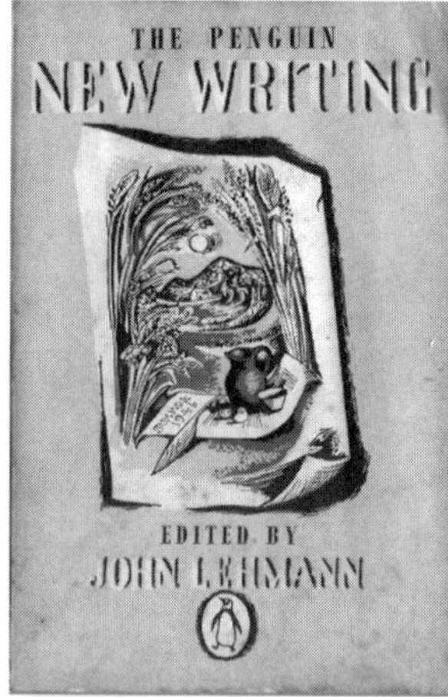
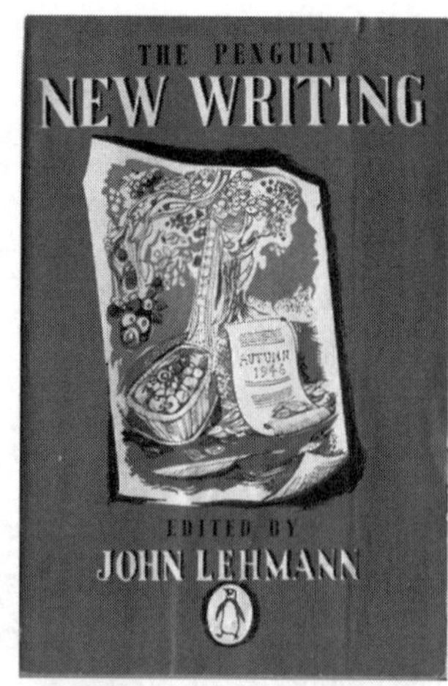
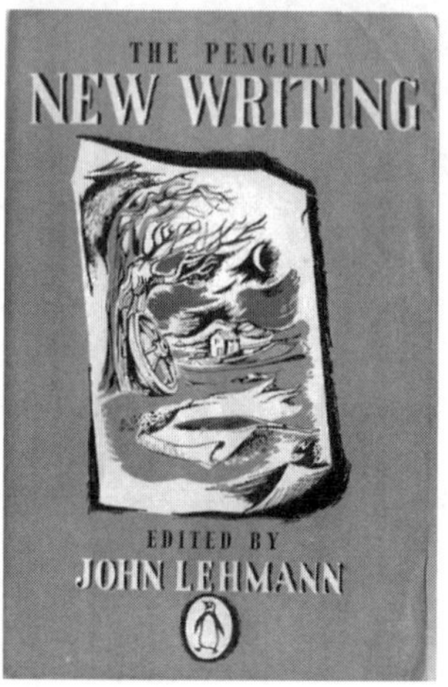
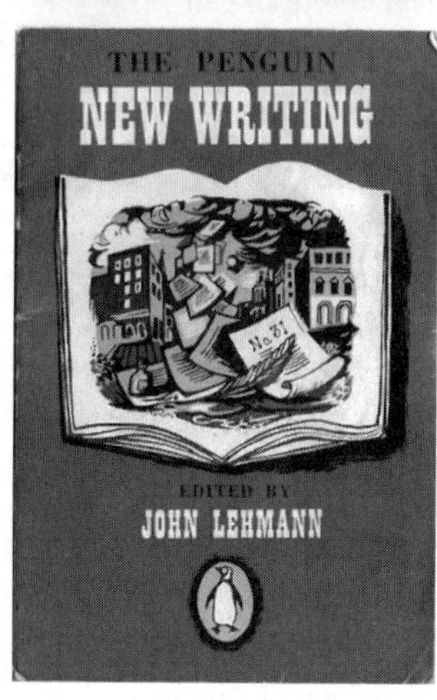

committeeman par excellence, being appointed a trustee of the National Gallery in April 1948 and in January 1949 joining the boards of the Tate and the Whitechapel. In July 1949 he became Slade Professor of Painting.

Artists whose lives overlapped in part with Coldstream's were Rodrigo Moynihan and his wife, Elinor Bellingham-Smith.[17] They moved into a large bomb-damaged house at 155 Old Church Street in Chelsea in the autumn of 1945. They stayed there throughout our period. Their painter friends Anthony Devas and Robert Buhler lived nearby (as did Anthony Gross) and the Chelsea Arts Club was almost next door. It was at No. 155 in 1946 that Moynihan received the Queen and Princess Elizabeth in order to do a portrait of the latter, indicating the great status he had achieved in portraiture at this time. (For example, a commission to paint the Labour Prime Minister, Clement Attlee, followed in 1947.) Proximity to the Chelsea Arts Club meant that visitors arrived from there without warning. One of these was Sir Alfred Munnings, President of the Royal Academy, who was permanently at war with some aspects of 'modern' art. Although Munnings' visits were not necessarily welcome, it is hard to imagine them being even possible with, for example, that group of artists busy socialising in Soho, and this gives an indication of the gaps between these artistic enclaves, however much the artists themselves occasionally overlapped.[18] While at No. 155, Moynihan also, for at least part of the time, maintained a separate studio in Chelsea at the Carlyle Studios off the King's Road.

Bacon, in the meantime, spent the period covered by this book renting the studio at 7 Cromwell Place in South Kensington which had formerly belonged to Millais. He shared this on and off with his older lover, Eric Hall, and they ran an illegal gambling establishment from it for a while. (Bacon preferred this area of London. He had been at 1 Glebe Place in Chelsea from 1936 to 1943, when he moved to Cromwell Place, where he stayed until 1951. He was later to have the famous studio at 7 Reece Mews, just off Old Brompton Road, for the last 30 years of his life.) He socialised with those artists who favoured the Soho pubs and clubs, but also with people like the Sutherlands, who didn't particularly, but with whom he was, at this time, personally and professionally close.[19] This closeness led to Bacon's meeting highly influential people in the British art world, such as Clark, Anderson and Rothenstein, with whom Sutherland was already friendly, and there is no doubt that this furthered Bacon's growing reputation (for instance by Anderson's purchase of a Bacon on behalf of the Contemporary Art Society in 1946). Sutherland also introduced Erica Brausen to Bacon, which was to have a considerable impact on the growth of Bacon's reputation (as will be seen later). On the other hand, Bacon also spent large parts of this period living

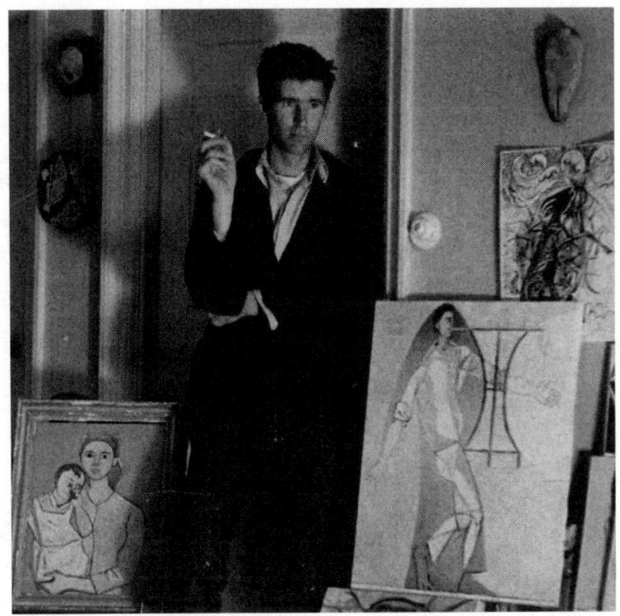

John Craxton in his London studio *c.*1951

in or around Monte Carlo, gambling at the casino there. Some artists naturally lived quite separately from others. Matthew Smith took a tiny flat at 762 Chelsea Cloisters in Sloane Avenue, while paying the rent on one of his mistresses' flats at 15 Cheyne Place and retaining a separate studio in Clarendon Gardens. He seems mostly to have mixed outside the artistic community of younger painters (he was 66 at the end of the War), although keeping in touch with Epstein and Augustus John and the novelist Henry Green.

Ceri Richards (born in Wales) returned to London as soon as he could after the War finished, and took a bomb-damaged house on Wandsworth Common West Side.[20] Le Brocquy arrived from Dublin in November 1946 and lived in a flat in York Street, off Baker Street. He then moved nearby to a studio in Crawford Street in 1947 and met Adler.[21] In the same year he took up a post at the Central School[22] and by 1950 he had a studio in Holly Hill in Hampstead.[23]

Geographically close to Hampstead is St John's Wood. There in 1945, not far from Vaughan and Minton in Hamilton Terrace, was to be found a curious and increasingly important (although completely unrelated) centre of artistic activity at 102 Abbey Road. The Belfast artist Gerard Dillon shared a part of a house which his sister Molly had acquired there and he stayed there, on and off, for the best part of the next 20 years. His artist friends from Northern Ireland (such as George Campbell and Arthur Armstrong) soon started coming to stay there as well and it is interesting to come across works by Dillon clearly painted around the area when so much of his work is of the West of Ireland. There is, for example, a picture called *Demolition* which dates from around 1950 and which clearly represents men at work on exactly the sort of thing which Dillon was employed to do in the area – demolishing bomb-damaged London buildings.[24] Other London-based artists at this time had little social contact with the groups so far mentioned, although no doubt they knew of each other and their paths crossed from time to time.[25]

Belfast

The position in Belfast at this time has been shamefully overlooked both by English art historians writing about British art of the mid-century and by Northern Irish and Irish art historians, who cover the painters of the time, but who narrow their significance by simply looking at them in the context of Irish art which, at this time, did not necessarily have a significant individuality. In fact there were a number of artists either working there or originating from there and revisiting during the period who should be looked at in the wider context of the work going on in the British Isles at the time. We might consider, for example, a number of artists who were born or grew up in Belfast, and who all now have considerable reputations as Irish artists, with their work selling for significant sums at auction. One of the most pre-eminent was John Luke (1906-75), whose mature work is truly astonishing.[26] He attended the School of Art there and then the Slade. His first one-person show was at the Belfast Museum and Art Gallery in 1946[27] and his reputation grew from that. Gerard Dillon (1916-71) spent only the briefest period at the College of Art there and was in reality self-taught. Although he was living in London in 1946, he was very much an Irish artist and he was given a one-person show by CEMA in Belfast in 1946 and again in 1950 (his reputation as an artist will be considered in more detail in Chapter 6). Colin Middleton (1910-83) also attended the College of Art. In 1945 he was given a show in Belfast. He moved briefly to England in 1947 and then back to Northern Ireland. He died in Belfast and the Ulster Museum holds a large collection of his work. George Campbell (1917-79) was not actually born in Belfast but grew up there and was first shown there in 1944. He had a CEMA one-person show there in 1949, but much of his later life was spent away from Northern Ireland (latterly in Spain). Arthur Armstrong (1924-96) was very young during this period, but had his first show (in Dublin) in 1950, having spent only six months at the College of Art. Daniel O'Neill (1920-74) had a brief spell at the College of Art. By 1946 he was showing with Victor Waddington in Dublin and his reputation rapidly grew.

The real problem for all these artists was that there were very few established places in Belfast where they could show their work,[28] almost no dealers, and a minute number of modern art buyers.[29] This left the artists with little choice but to explore the slightly more developed scene in Dublin, where Victor Waddington's gallery operated almost as a one-man modern art market[30], or London, where there were far more opportunities for shows and sales. Thus, for example, Gerard Dillon had been to London before the War, but had been effectively trapped in Ireland when the War began because of the severe travel restrictions which were imposed. At the end of the War he returned to London and obtained work with local builders beginning the long task of restoring London's bombed buildings. As already mentioned, he lived in Abbey Road and other Irish artists joined him there from time to time, including Armstrong, Campbell and James MacIntyre.

One of the more helpful developments for local young artists to occur during the War had been the creation of the Northern Irish part of CEMA. This began with effect from 1 February 1943 and, in its first year, held a loan exhibition called 'Living Irish Artists'. Eight of the 19 participating artists could be said to have been Northern Irish (not including, for example, Norah McGuinness, who was born in Londonderry, but was regarded as a Dublin-based artist). The next CEMA exhibition was of fourteen resident watercolourists and in the summer of 1944 it held a show called 'The Collection of Zoltan Frankl'. Frankl's rôle as a serious Belfast collector of modern art will be mentioned later and it is not to be underestimated at this period. Many exhibitions organised by the Belfast Art Gallery followed, including shows for comparatively unknown Northern Irish artists. But during the

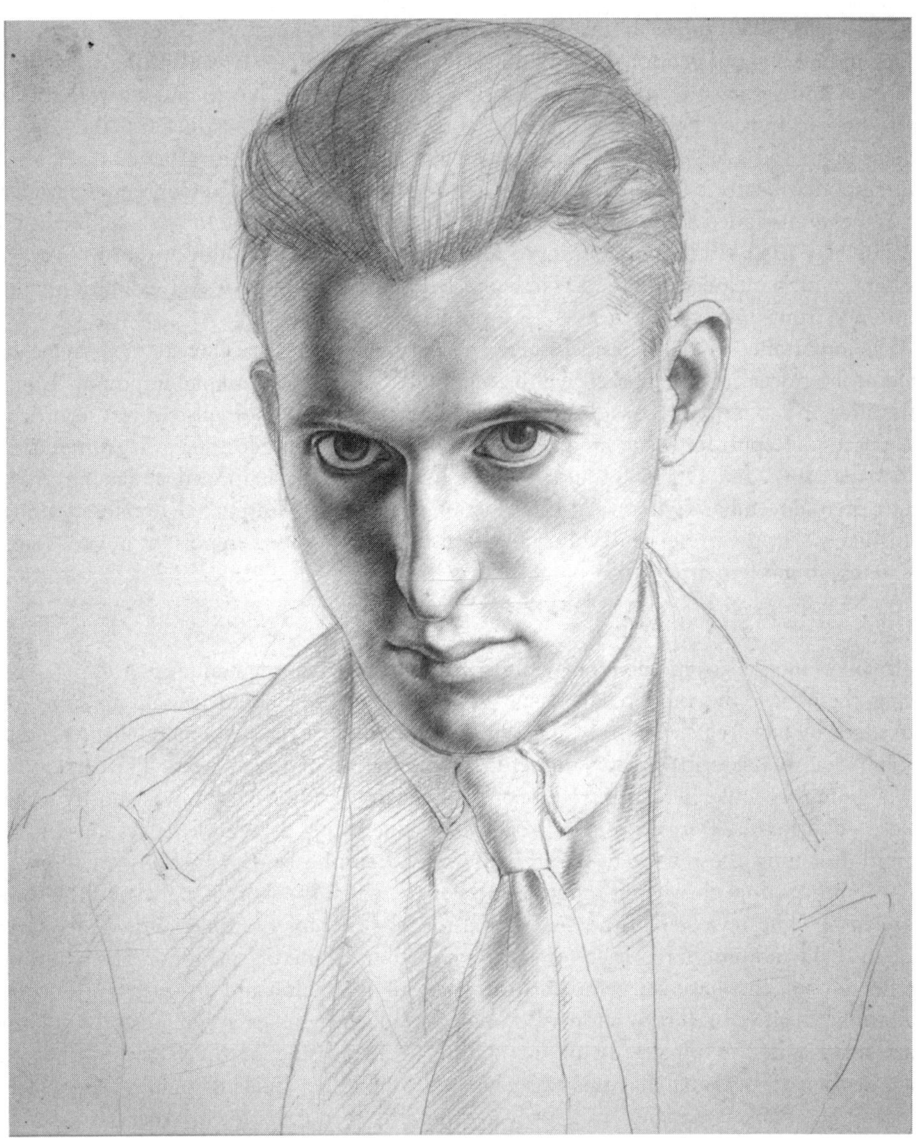

Self-Portrait by John Luke (1906-75). Ulster Museum

War the real excitement was starting to focus on the work of Campbell, Dillon and O'Neill. Their work was included towards the end of the War in a CEMA exhibition called 'Works by some Ulster artists', and thereafter their work became more widely known outside Belfast. At this time there were no obvious commercial outlets at all for modern art in Belfast, so that CEMA shows were invaluable (as was the fact that CEMA also bought works from artists, albeit on a small scale). The Arts Society was the only body of its kind in Ulster. It held annual exhibitions at the Belfast Museum and Art Gallery, which gave an outlet for a variety of local artists, both amateur and professional. However, it had no premises, no endowment and no property, and so its position was not likely to prove decisive in any way in the promotion of local talent. In 1950, the Cultural Relations Committee set up by the Ministry of External Affairs in Dublin arranged for an exhibition called 'Contemporary Irish Painting' to be shown in Boston and Ottawa. Of the 73 exhibitors, 11 were from the North and all were resident somewhere in Ireland. As part of the Festival of Britain celebrations in 1951, the City Art Gallery organised a large Lavery retrospective and a show of the Arts Council collection of Contemporary Scottish Paintings; and CEMA organised a show called Contemporary Ulster Art and commissioned a book on 'The Arts in Ulster' and a mural by John Luke for the City Hall. In May 1951 Waddington arranged for the London gallery, Tooths, to show 'Five Irish Painters', which included Dillon, O'Neill and Middleton (reviews of that exhibition will be mentioned from time to time).

The importance of the Belfast Museum and Art Gallery as a place where modern local art could at least occasionally be seen will be mentioned later. For example, important English authorities on modern art occasionally gave lectures there. John Rothenstein was recorded in the Museum's Report for the year ended 31 March 1946 as having lectured on 'Contemporary British Painting' and David Baxandall (see Chapter 7) was mentioned as having given a lecture on 6 November 1946 on 'An Introduction to Modern Painting'. Generally speaking it seems likely that the presence of John Hewitt at the Museum was important in encouraging an interest in modern art.

Dublin

As Ireland emerged from the strange and painful experience of maintaining its neutrality during the War,[31] the modern art scene in Dublin in 1945 could be said to have been dominated by Jack Yeats.[32] On 11 June 1945 there opened at the National College of Art in Dublin what was described as a National Loan Exhibition of Yeats's work. The catalogue to this large retrospective had an introduction by Earnan O'Malley,[33] who was shortly to have a piece published in *Horizon* on Le Brocquy. An interesting aspect of the response to this exhibition among the reviewers was the attempt to emphasise the Irishness of the work; many commentators clearly felt proud of the stature which the work had, beyond the shores of Ireland.[34] The reviewer in the *Irish Times* for 12 June, for example, said: 'Yeats has let loose his wild and unfettered Irish romanticism in all its dramatic splendour. His painting is a reflection of the national temperament with all its faults and its merits.' Once the exhibition finished in July, Victor Waddington published an essay on Yeats by Thomas MacGreevy and it is illustrative of the stature of Yeats (and of the friendship between MacGreevy and Beckett) that this was reviewed by Samuel Beckett for the *Irish Times*.[35] Interestingly, Beckett had no time for a nationalistic interpretation of Yeats's work: 'The national aspects of Mr Yeats's genius have, I think, been overstated, and for motives not always remarkable for their aesthetic purity.'

Yeats was, by this time, well-known in London as well as in Dublin.[36] John Rothenstein, as director of the Tate, visited him in Dublin on 6 December 1945 (apparently at the instigation of O'Malley) and chose one of his pictures for the Tate collection.[37] In the spring of 1946 this picture was shown in London at a one-man show at Wildenstein's, and in July he was given the honorary degree of Doctor of Letters by Dublin University. While he was badly affected by the death of his wife in 1947, this did not affect his work output and in 1948 he produced 80 canvases, the most prolific year of his whole life as an artist.[38]

The Irishness of Irish art of this period is a subject which needs to be dealt with.[39] It is often possible to identify the Irishness of an artist of the mid-century by the subject-matter of his work.[40] In particular, the landscape of the West of Ireland drew many artists[41] who were of Irish birth or family (Yeats was, after all, born in London). The romantic overtones of the unspoilt landscape and people of the West is a vast topic in Irish cultural studies and is not confined to painters. The West was seen as the part of Ireland least affected by the centuries of English rule and also as the most genuinely Celtic part of the island. The miserable economic hardships which the small population of the country districts of the West had endured, and which had discouraged the sort of developments in building and commerce which had begun to affect those parts of Ireland nearer England, meant that the West did indeed resemble a different place from elsewhere in the British Isles, both socially and physically, and painters (as well as poets and other writers) sought to capture its essence.

But, as regards technique or style, Irishness is not a feature which one finds easy to identify in mid-20th century 'Irish' painters. Yeats in his later style was not part of any sort of Irish pattern (he is tellingly described in the *Irish Times* of 31 October 1946, reviewing a show at Waddingtons, as belonging 'in spirit to the Celtic renaissance of 40 years ago'), and the same would apply to other leading Irish artists such as Le Brocquy and O'Neill. One of the great cultural commentators, at least of Northern Ireland, was John Hewitt. In 1951[42] he wrote, 'Until this decade, no-one would have been rash enough to claim that there was, or ever had been, an easily identifiable school of Irish painting, even worth numbering among the lesser schools of European art.' In a similar vein, Arthur Power, the art critic for the *Irish Times*, in reviewing an Oireachtas Exhibition on 4 November 1947, noted that Irish artists may paint Irish subjects, but in doing so they used a French or English technique. He thought there was no sign of any Irish school of painting. On the other hand, there is no arguing that the idea of the Irishness of Irish art was in the air during the 1940s. In 1943 the 'Irish Art Handbook' had been published,[43] followed by 'Irish Art' in 1944.[44]

Arthur Power had this to say on the subject to his Irish audience on 5 October 1948, in reviewing the 'Oireachtas Art Exhibition'. In noting that it was difficult to find works among the 111 exhibits with any discernible Irish character, he said that 'this question of nationality in art is a vexed one. Most artistic nations have enjoyed age-old sovereignty, and are unconsciously national in their art and literature. But we, having until recently been subjected to strong influences from outside, our nationality still sits uncomfortably upon us, and we are still groping towards its full realisation'. Another great commentator on, and supporter of, modern Irish artists was the Irish writer James White. He had an occasional 'Letter from Dublin' column in *Art News and Review*, which is particularly interesting in showing an Irish writer writing about Irish painters in a magazine published in England for what must have been a largely English audience. On 12 March 1949 he was prepared to touch upon the subject of how contemporary Irish artists were handling their 'Irishness':

> Those of our painters who remain in Ireland tend… to formalise their conceptions and render them in the arid terms of any-mans-land; whereas our exile artists seem to hanker after some quality picturesquely associated with home. Gerard Dillon, for instance, becomes almost stage-Irish in rendering the bawneen-clad figures and whitewashed cottages of the west, while Louis le Brocquy is preoccupied by the tinkers and gypsies who still pursue their vicarious existence in the lanes and byways of our island. [The point being that Dillon and Le Brocquy were by this time firmly established in London.]

When John Russell, writing in the *Listener* on 10 May 1945, reviewed an exhibition at the Arcade Gallery in London of the work of Young Irish Artists, he felt bound to say that 'there is little that would strike an English eye as peculiarly Irish'. Similarly, M.H. Middleton, writing in the *Spectator* on 18 October 1946 on the Irish pictures on view at the Leicester Galleries said 'it would hardly be possible to speak of a 'school' as being revealed by the work shown'.

When the exhibition of five Irish painters was shown at Tooth's in London in 1951 the review in the *Times* noted (on 1 June) that 'they do not have much in common and there is little to suggest that the school of painting which is flourishing in Dublin today has any very pronounced regional character'.[45] Even in 1965 Miriam Hederman, writing in the *Irish Times*[46] could say that 'there is a vigorous Irish tradition in literature but none in the visual arts'.

Apart from Yeats, who was something of an isolated figure in the Dublin art world, the 'official' side of the modern scene was represented by the Royal Hibernian Academy, with its annual exhibition (somewhat mirroring the position of the Royal Academy in London). Here we find a number of competent artists, often said to be following in the traditions of Sir William Orpen, who had died in 1931. The most interesting and important of these was perhaps Sean Keating. He had a highly successful career, in a variety of comparatively traditional styles, and was another Irish artist strongly influenced by his experience and perception of the West (in his case, the Aran Islands). He became President of the RHA in 1949, in succession to another significant figure from the 'traditional' side of the modern scene, James Sleator. He had been PRHA since 1945. The third significant artist of this type worthy of mention in this context was Leo Whelan and slightly younger was Maurice MacGonigal.[47] Brian Fallon[48] rather harshly says that the art of these painters 'often resembles Soviet propaganda art', in that there was a slight tendency for them to depict the honest Irish folk of the West in a somewhat stylized and romanticized fashion. Even so, there is no doubting their artistic skills.

'The Irish Exhibition of Living Art' (the IELA) had been created in 1943, partly as a result of dissatisfaction with the cautious attitude towards artistic development of the RHA.[49] In May 1943, with Mainie Jellett as chairman, a committee had been formed comprising Evie Hone, Louis le Brocquy, Jack Hanlon, Norah McGuinness, Margaret Clarke, Ralph Cusack, Laurence Campbell and Elizabeth Curran. One of the triggers for the establishment of this group had been the rejection by the RHA in 1942 of Le Brocquy's picture *The Spanish Shawl* and Le Brocquy and his mother seem to have had a lot to do with the establishment of the new group. In contrast to the RHA exhibitions, those of the IELA were intended to provide a platform for modern artists. The first show, which opened on 16 September 1943 in the National College of Art in Kildare Street, was restricted to artists of Irish birth, but the limitations of this in a small country were apparent, so that thereafter the work of foreign artists was included.[50] So, for example, Picasso, Braque and Matisse were to be included, as well as Colquhoun and MacBryde,[51] Adler and Minton (all in 1947).[52] It is important to realise that the IELA was not hostile to the RHA and Academicians were invited to, and did, participate from the beginning. The first show received about 500 works and 168 were selected. Open from 16 September to 9 October, over 5,000 people (of whom approximately 2,000 were schoolchildren) attended and the far from lavish sum of £289 was apparently raised from sales of about one third of the exhibits.[53]

Another key figure in Dublin at this time was Norah McGuinness (1901-80). She was born in what later became Northern Ireland, attended the Dublin Metropolitan School of Art (also studying later at the Chelsea Polytechnic in London) and studied in Paris. After living in London from 1931-37, she returned to Dublin in 1940. She had become President of the IELA in 1944 following the death of Mainie Jellett and exhibited in Dublin and at the prestigious Leicester Galleries in London. She and Nano Reid were chosen to represent Ireland on the first occasion that the country participated in the Venice Biennale, in 1950.

Louis le Brocquy is now – rightly in my view – treated as a painter of considerable importance both in the context of the smaller pool of Irish artists of the second half of the

20th century, but also in the far larger and more competitive group of 'British' artists of that period. But in our period he spent most of the time in London, where he moved in late 1946, and we should not expect to find him dealt with in a Dublin context at this time.

Mention should be made – if only in passing – of the White Stag Group.[54] It had been founded in London in 1935 by Basil Rakoczi and Kenneth Hall and they had moved to Ireland in 1939 to escape the War. They arrived in Dublin in 1940 and held occasional shows throughout the War. There was no very rigorous selection policy of those wishing to exhibit at these shows and the impression forms that quite a wide variety of not necessarily talented individuals came and went, displaying their works at some shows, but not others.[55] Something of the flavour of what they may have been trying to achieve by their studied modernity can be seen from the title of one of their better known exhibitions, in January 1944, which was 'Exhibition of Subjective Art'. A book came out about them in 1945 – *Three Painters* – which was blessed with an introduction by Herbert Read. The ending of the War saw the members of this group split up and go their separate ways.

In terms of commentators on contemporary Irish art from within Ireland, the efforts of the *Irish Times* will be noted in a later chapter, as will the contribution of the key journal, *The Bell*. This had been founded in 1940 by Sean O'Faolain and was edited from 1946 until its demise in 1954 by Peadar O'Donnell[56]. Other cultural magazines were *Commentary* and *Envoy*. There was also the *Dublin Magazine*, with regular art columns from Edward Sheehy. Outside Dublin, it should not be overlooked that *Horizon* had occasional items on Irish art.[57] Apart from O'Malley's well known article on Le Brocquy in 1946,[58] there had also been an article by Margot Moffet called 'Young Irish Painters' in April 1945 and Cyril Connolly himself had written about an exhibition of work by the White Stag Group in April 1946. When Irish artists were shown in London, the art journalists sometimes covered the shows in the English papers. For example, on 11 October 1946, the *Times* noted a show at the Leicester Galleries called 'Modern Irish Painters'. This included work by Le Brocquy, Dillon and Nano Reid and drew the following comment: 'There is evidently at the present time a school of considerable vitality and professional ability. Whether by reason of the influence of Yeats or because it is a national characteristic, many of the artists have a distinctively romantic outlook and show a marked interest in character.' Similarly, both the *Sunday Times* and the *Observer* art critics noted Irish art when it appeared in London, often favourably.

One thing which is clear from contemporary reviews is that there were a number of galleries available in Dublin where shows could be held. Apart from the two leading commercial galleries, which were Waddington's and the Dawson Gallery,[59] the Shelbourne Hotel was on occasion used, there was the Grafton Gallery in Harry Street, the White Stag Gallery in Lower Baggot Street, The Gallery in St Stephen's Green, the Dublin Painters' Gallery, a gallery at 13 Merrion Row, a gallery at 6 Baggot Street, and so on. It is also worth noting that links between Ireland and America may have meant that an avenue more open to some Irish artists than to their English contemporaries was to exhibit in America. For example, Le Brocquy was included in exhibitions of Irish paintings in March 1947 in the Associated American Artists' Galleries in New York and in the Institute of Contemporary Art in Boston in February 1950.

It should also be mentioned that some parts of the rest of Ireland showed an interest in modern Irish art, a notable example being the opening of the Limerick City Gallery of Art in 1948. This had been supported by local artist, Sean Keating, and it was hailed as the first gallery in Ireland devoted exclusively to Irish art. The *Irish Times* celebrated its opening with

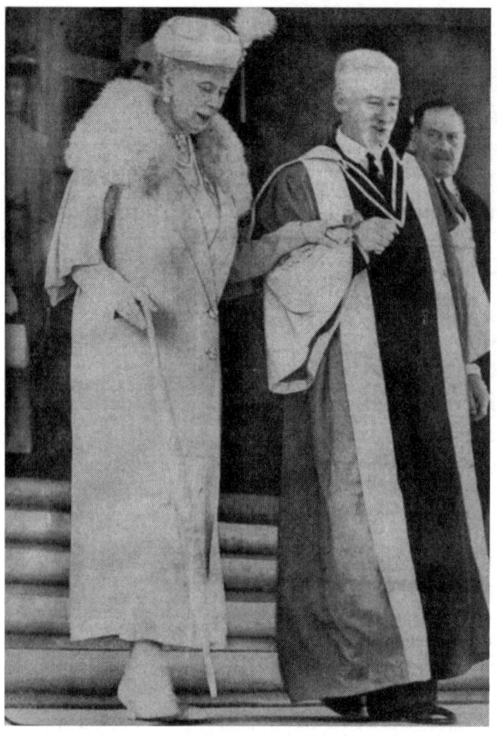

Thomas Bodkin in academic robes,
with Queen Mary on the steps of
the Barber Institute, Birmingham, 1939

a large piece on 23 March, noting that it held 120 modern Irish pictures and that its first curator was Robert Herbert. Limerick also had the Goodwin Galleries, which dealt in modern Irish art.[60] Alfred Goodwin was a friend of Victor Waddington, who gave him advice on contemporary artists. In the 1940s alone the Goodwin held exhibitions of work by Dillon, Henry, Keating, Le Brocquy, Letitia Hamilton, Markey Robinson, George Campbell, McElvey and Kernoff, amongst others. Goodwins held a Yeats exhibition in September 1945.

As the period studied in this book progressed, the Irish State began to consider whether it should develop a more coherent policy towards the arts generally than it had so far formed.[61] In this it had an eye on developments in England, where first CEMA and then the Arts Council had been developing throughout the 1940s. In 1948 Sean MacBride, Minister for External Affairs, nominated the first Cultural Relations Committee, which was to be responsible for a number of important travelling exhibitions of Irish art in the 1950s. Then, in 1949 the Prime Minister, John Costello, who had come to power in place of de Valera in 1948, commissioned a well-known but not universally popular Irishman, Professor Thomas Bodkin to prepare a report on the state of the arts in Ireland.[62] Bodkin spent the period from 16 July to 31 August making his enquiries and delivered his report to the Government on 4 October 1949. Entitled *Report on the Arts in Ireland*, its 70 pages were none too complementary about that state. Relevant chapters were devoted to The National Museum, the National Gallery, the National College of Art, Provincial Art Schools, the RHA and School and University Education and the Arts.[63]

Generally, he could find little to say in favour of existing arrangements at any of these institutions. The National Gallery, for example, was described as being in a 'stagnant, if not moribund, condition', various unfavourable comparisons being made with the Gallery under its present regime and how it had been when he had been its Director. Among the provincial art schools, Cork got a rare bit of praise, but the efforts of the small schools at Clonmel, Limerick and Galway were not to his liking. He calculated that the total number of full-time art teachers in all the art schools of Ireland was no more than twenty-five. Art was neglected in Irish schools and 'negligible' and 'precarious' in its Universities.

The *Report* ended by proposing the establishment of some sort of government-sponsored body for the Fine Arts, effectively an Irish Arts Council, with 'powers similar to those vested in the Arts Council in England'. After quite a lot of toing and froing, a draft Arts Bill was produced in late 1950, meeting generally negative reactions in the Irish press.[64] While the draft, which Bodkin had not seen prior to its publication,[65] was being considered, Bodkin's report was published on 11 January 1951 and the Bill was enacted on 8 May 1951 as the Arts Act, setting up a rather feeble Arts Council, with limited powers, limited funding and, most importantly, limited clarity of purpose. The preamble to the short Act (of only eight sections) stated that it was 'An Act to stimulate public interest in, and to promote, the knowledge, appreciation, and practice of, the arts and, for these and other purposes, to establish an Arts Council, and to provide for other matters in connection with the matters aforesaid'. Costello's Government fell a month later and de Valera returned as Prime Minister. As a result, the first Director of the new Arts Council was Paddy Little,[66] who had been actively promoting its establishment long before Bodkin got involved. Little was sent by de Valera to Paris and London to see how their official arts policies worked. In London, for example, he met officials of the Arts Council and also the President of the Royal Academy, Sir Gerald Kelly. De Valera then chose the first members of the Arts Council, who were: Alfred Chester Beatty (an American philanthropist), Monsignor Patrick Browne (Chairman of the Dublin Institute of Advanced Studies), John Maher (former Comptroller and Auditor General), R.J.Hayes (Director of the National Library), Thomas MacGreevy (Director of the National Gallery) and the Earl of Rosse (an Anglo-Irish aristocrat). Their appointment took effect on 4 December 1951, which is regarded as the official date of the establishment of the Irish Arts Council.

Edinburgh and Glasgow

In 1945 there were four art schools in Scotland, at Edinburgh, Glasgow, Aberdeen and Dundee, as well as the centre for graduate art students at Hospitalfield, near Glasgow. The dominant schools were those of Edinburgh and Glasgow and their dominance alternated, so that, while Glasgow had been pre-eminent in the earlier years of the century, some of the more noteworthy Scottish artists who were actually working in Scotland at the end of the War (as distinct from those working elsewhere), were based in Edinburgh, namely Gillies, Maxwell, MacTaggart and Redpath.[67] Just as London acted as a magnet for English art students and young painters, so did Edinburgh and Glasgow for Scottish artists. So, for example, none of the four artists just mentioned originated in Edinburgh. In Glasgow, in the meantime, the most important artist was J.D. Fergusson (although he was originally from Edinburgh), who gathered about him a number of young artists. He was also the art editor of *Scottish Art and Letters*, a journal which appeared intermittently from 1944-50 (and which will be considered in Chapter 5). Fergusson's group of artists had formed the New Art Club in 1940, in opposition to the old-established Glasgow Art Club. This new club was from 1942 to hold exhibitions under the title of the New Scottish Group. Two significant artists associated with Fergusson were William Crosbie and Donald Bain[68], but one of the most significant artists to emerge from Glasgow was the English artist, Joan Eardley.[69]

Commentators seeking to define Scottish art in some way which can distinguish it from the work of other artists working in the British Isles in 1945 have to wrestle with the usual issues.[70] Writers about Scottish artists have to make the usual challenges to our credulity. So, for example, Joan Eardley, born and brought up in England, has to be treated as Scottish, because she spent her working life as a painter there. Colquhoun and MacBryde were the other way round, but they too are taken as Scottish when it suits the writer's vision of Scottishness to claim them. The other game at which the writer on Scottish art has to be proficient is emphasising the place of Scottish art in the wider European (or even, occasionally, international) scene. Scottish art, we are told, has closer links to French art than other, sometimes unnamed but impliedly English, artists. (The links of English artists to French art were equally strong, but that is not noted by these writers.) Sometimes France is not enough of a distinguishing feature and we are asked to believe that Scottish artists were particularly close to north European expressionists (for example, Munch in the case of MacTaggart, perhaps because he had a Norwegian wife), or even American contemporaries (the later influence of Abstract Expressionism on Davie is often cited). The reality is, I suspect, different and too subtle for easy explanation. It seems to be the case that those artists who were subjected to Scottish art schools came under the influence of what may almost be called Scottish propaganda about the status of Scottish art and artists as against that of other parts of the British Isles. Students were certainly led to think that they were, in some indefinable way, more

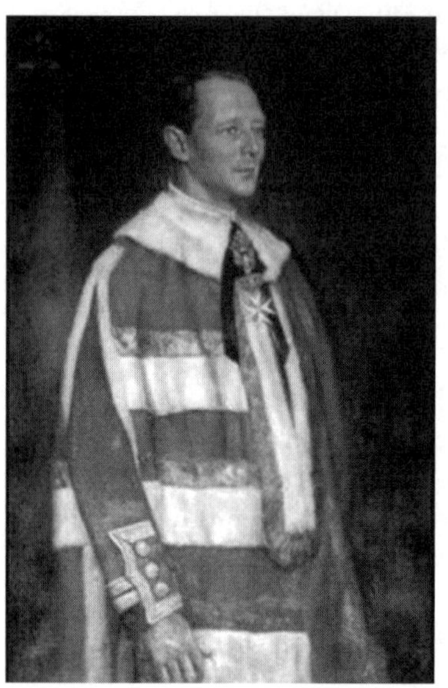

Evan Morgan, 2nd Viscount Tredegar

influenced by French art than by other art, and this may have led to an emphasis on colour which can characterise a Scottish-trained artist. Certainly in the period covered by this book, the influence on local artists of the Scottish Colourists, who were indeed heavily dependent on French work, remained strong in some cases. J.D. Fergusson, the last of the Colourists, had come back from France to live in Glasgow in 1939. He brought with him a strong Francophile attitude towards painting, putting this into print with his book '*Modern Scottish Painting*' in 1943. The attitude of Scottish artists to France and to their own home-grown artists is neatly illustrated by a quote from Donald Bain in the fourth issue of *Scottish Art and Letters*. In a review of a Bonnard and Vuillard show, he found himself drawn to writing of the Scottish Colourists, which led him into the following rather bold statement: 'We are indeed lucky that these men survived to make paintings that place Scotland beside France as leaders in world painting.'

Within the art schools themselves, Hugh Crawford was an influential teacher at Glasgow from 1925-48, when he moved to become Head of the School of Art at Aberdeen. Douglas Percy Bliss was director of the Glasgow School of Art from 1946-64. He was joined there in the late 1940s by Gilbert Spencer as Head of Painting (after Spencer's unceremonious removal from the RCA). Gillies, MacTaggart, Maxwell and Redpath were influential at Edinburgh, where they were joined by the English-born Robin Philipson[71] in 1947. Gillies took over from David Alison[72] as Head of the Drawing and Painting School in 1946.[73] Maxwell was on the staff at Edinburgh from 1935-46 and then again from 1955-61. Alberto Morrocco[74] studied at Aberdeen and taught part-time there from 1946-49. He was then appointed Head of the Painting School at Dundee in 1950. James Cowie[75] was Warden of Hospitalfield from 1937-48 and he was followed there by Ian Fleming from the Glasgow School of Art, who was Warden from 1948-54.

Apart from the annual show of the Royal Scottish Academy, there were a number of other annual events, either in Edinburgh or Glasgow, at which the Scottish artistic community could exhibit its works. There was, for example, the annual exhibition of the Royal Glasgow Institute of Fine Arts and of the Society of Scottish Artists; the Scottish Society of Women Artists and the Royal Scottish Society of Painters in Watercolours.[76] There was also a

Scottish Modern Arts Association, whose chairman in 1947 was Henderson Blyth. On 30 April 1947 the *Scotsman* reported that the Association, which owned about 300 pictures, was considering opening its own gallery. This was not in fact opened and a lot of pictures were given to the City Art Centre in Edinburgh in 1964.

The Scottish art scene after the War gradually received more outside influences. The Edinburgh Festival began in 1947,[77] bringing with it opportunities to have exhibitions at times when the City was increasingly full of potential visitors. So the Society of Scottish Artists held an open exhibition in 1947 of modern Scottish painting (inevitably including Colquhoun and MacBryde). The Picasso/Matisse show which had opened at the V&A in London in December 1945 and which may have been influential on many of those artists who saw it there, reached Glasgow in 1946 (its impact on the Scottish art community will be dealt with in Chapter 2).[78] There was also an important Van Gogh show in Glasgow in 1948. In 1948 Eric Newton, writing in the *Sunday Times*, began the process of writing one week about the Royal Academy Summer Exhibition in London and the next week about the Royal Scottish Academy Exhibition in Edinburgh.[79] He was pleased to note many good pictures, picking out Gillies, in particular, saying that no-one in England could paint a big still-life 'with the combination of dash and discipline shown by Gillies', and also commenting very favourably on works by MacTaggart, Redpath and David Donaldson.

The following year (on 8 May) he revisited Edinburgh and noted that 'after officialdom and mediocrity have been served, the residue in Edinburgh is a good deal more interesting than in London'. He particularly liked the work of Henderson Blyth, Ian Fleming, Sinclair Thomson and the inevitable MacTaggart and Gillies ('the most assured pictures in the show'). In 1951 the Royal Scottish Academy was to show works by contemporary English artists, namely Smith, Weight, Spear, Hitchens, Clough, Burra, Scott, Minton, Richards, Sutherland, Tunnard, Vaughan, Heron, Moynihan, Nicholson and Hepworth.

Wales

The Welsh art scene immediately after the War is not easy to define or to describe. A number of practising artists had been born in Wales: Augustus John, Ceri Richards, Sir Cedric Morris, Kyffin Williams, John Elwyn and Merlyn Evans are examples. Others, while not born there, had connections there (David Jones and Allan Gwynne-Jones, for example) or they painted there regularly (Sutherland being the obvious example, together with Herman and Piper). Some went to Welsh art schools, either at Cardiff, Swansea or Carmarthen, but many, if not most, who achieved wider fame did so by moving to London or to other parts of England. Williams was taught at the Slade and then moved to become art master at Highgate School in London, only moving back to Wales in later life; Morris spent a long period of his life in Suffolk and so on.[80]

As with other areas of the British Isles, a consciousness that local art was to be encouraged also developed in Wales.[81] The Contemporary Art Society for Wales was established in 1937. There were 12 founder members of the executive committee, who were all still in place by the end of the War. Lord Howard de Walden was the first chairman, from 1937-46. He was succeeded as chairman by Augustus John (1946-60), who was already on the committee. The other committee members in 1945 were Sir Cyril Fox, Geoffrey Crawshay, Brynmor Anthony, Frances Byng Stamper, Gwendoline Davies, Margaret Davies, Sir Leonard Twiston-Davies, Sir Wynne Cemlyn-Jones, James Manson and Viscount Tredegar. During our period they were joined or replaced by Ralph Edwards,[82] Grant Murray, John Steegman and Russell Thomas. The first post-war meeting was held in Cardiff in July 1946, at which Augustus John was elected chairman. At the first distribution of paintings, 47 works were presented, principally to the National Museum and the art galleries at Swansea, Newport and Merthyr, with the remainder going to colleges in Wales. A similar procedure was adopted in the 1951 distribution.

Of the buyers, Ralph Edwards covered 1944-5 and bought work by Richards, Spear, Gwynne-Jones and Kyffin Williams, among others. John Steegman took over from 1946-8 and his purchases included work by Colquhoun, MacBryde, Herman, Richards, Williams, Rowntree, Smith and Grant. In 1949 Cemlyn-Jones bought work by John Elwyn, Merlyn Evans, Williams and Cedric Morris and in 1950-51 David Bell's purchases included works by Herman, Piper, Elwyn, Spear, Suddaby and Weight. By the end of 1951 the Welsh CAS had bought just over 100 works in total.

In April 1944 CEMA had opened a regional office in Cardiff and in 1945 an Advisory Panel had been set up to administer CEMA funds and to carry out its policy with regard to Wales. The Welsh Committee of the Arts Council came into existence in 1946. Relevant exhibitions organised in Wales by the Arts Council in our period included a number which focused on Welsh art: 'Welsh Landscape in British art' (1947); 'Some Pictures from a South Wales town: drawings and paintings by members of the Merthyr Art Society' (1949); 'Selection from the South Wales Group' (1949);[83] 'Some purchases of the Contemporary Art Society for Wales' (1950); and 'An exhibition of pictures for Welsh schools' (1951). The two principal galleries where modern art might be seen were the National Museum of Wales in Cardiff (which had been founded in 1907) and the Glynn Vivian Art Gallery in Swansea (1911).

GROUPS

The work of some contemporary artists influenced others directly and obviously. It is even possible to discern the makings of occasional, loose groupings amongst British artists from time to time. But these groups – the most egregious being those christened 'neo-Romantics' – never really existed so as to have any substantive coherence or significance and an analysis of the art world which attempts to use and rely upon the shorthand which such group headings provides is probably worthless and certainly in danger of being risible. Most British artists of the time simply cannot comfortably be put into groups.[84] A good illustration of the difficulties facing the critic or historian who is determined to squeeze artists from a particular decade into convenient categories is provided by the heroic efforts of the catalogue for the Whitechapel show in 1972 called 'Painting, Sculpture and Drawing in Britain, 1940-1949'.

The catalogue is divided into sections. The first is called 'Independents'. These are presumably those strange painters who simply could not be categorised, however much of a strain the definition of the categories was put under. It included Adler, Bomberg, Gillies, Herman, Hitchens, Lewis, Lowry, Maxwell, Roberts, Smith and Spencer. Curiously, Jones and Collins are not to be found; neither is Bacon, Auerbach or Burra. The second category is 'Realists: the Euston Road School'. They are easier to trap: Coldstream, Gowing, Hill, Martin, Moynihan, Pasmore, Rogers, Tibble and Townsend. None of those are, in my opinion, of the first rank. Then comes a particularly striking category: 'After Surrealism', and here we find Bacon and Burra, together with Evans, Medley, Paul Nash and Richards. (It is particularly pleasing to find Nash in with Bacon). Then the tired (and tiresome) category of 'Neo-romantics': Ayrton, Clough, Colquhoun, MacBryde, Craxton, Freud, Minton, Piper, Sutherland and Vaughan. Then 'Before and After Abstraction', which has Davie, Gear, Heron, Lanyon, Nicholson, Scott, Tunnard and Wynter and, finally, 'The War Artists', which is probably the easiest group to be sure about, since they all painted pictures of the effects of the War, as a paid job. Here we discover Ardizzone, Bawden, Gross, Coldstream, Moore, Nash, Piper, Ravilious, Roberts and Sutherland. An alternative effort at grouping artists emerges from Anthony Bertram's book *A Century of British Painting 1851-1951* (1951). Here his last chapters attempt to categorise some contemporary artists into the heading of 'Post-Impressionist', where he places Lewis, Smith, Roberts, Grant, John Nash, Bawden, Jones and Ben Nicholson; and others under the headings of 'Romanticism, Surrealism and the Neo-Romantics'. For the latter he tries Augustus John and Stanley Spencer for Romanticism, Armstrong and Burra for Surrealism and Sutherland and Piper for Neo-Romanticism. To show how careful one has to be in applying the expectations of today to the judgments of contemporaries, the modern reader may be interested to know that his final chapter picked out and emphasised two artists whom he regarded as among the most important artists of the recent past: Wadsworth and Paul Nash. Let us look then at the 'groups' which may have been identified in 1945 and see what survives of them after they have been subjected to some critical scrutiny.

Neo-Romanticism

I do not believe that it would be possible, in the context of British art of the 1940s, to define Romantic art in a meaningful way, such that any reliable conclusions would be drawn from categorising artists as Romantic or otherwise. The term is simply too diffuse. The artists who have been touched with this brush by later art historians are therefore inevitably a diverse bunch. They need a great deal of ex-post facto scrubbing-up by historians working to achieve their own agendas before they can even begin to be identified and, even then, they fall apart as a group before they have even been made to stand together to have their photograph taken. Claims made for this group have to work on a basis in landscape and they tend to focus on the influence of Blake and Palmer and particularly on the similarities of Sutherland's early wood engravings to the work of Palmer. Unfortunately for users of the group's name, a focus on landscape had been an attribute of a wide range of British artists for a very long time indeed by 1945. Taking the landscape rather than, say, the human form as a starting point, was not confined to those later identified as neo-Romantics.

The next problem is to find any real common thread between those artists who from time to time exhibited tendencies which could be called Romantic.[85] David Jones was an utterly Romantic painter. As a painter[86] he often seemed to inhabit a strange Romano-British past of his own imagining. Cecil Collins was similarly as 'Romantic' a painter as one could wish to encounter, with his multiple renderings of 'fools' of different types and the extraordinary spirituality of many of his pictures.[87] Yet neither artist suits the main modern identifier of this strange neo-Romantic group, who is Malcolm Yorke. Perhaps they are a bid odd for his liking; for whatever reason, he excludes them. Instead, he exaggerates the material that is there. [88] The vagueness and artificiality of this whole area may be illustrated by comparing Yorke's artists with those used in the 1987 exhibition at the Barbican called 'A Paradise Lost. The Neo-Romantic imagination in Britain 1935-1955'.[89] Here, the painters chosen were Collins, Vaughan, Richards, Piper, Craxton, Jones, Colquhoun, Minton, Ayrton, Sutherland, Wilde and Hurry. The concept was made to extend to contemporary British poetry and films. The dates chosen were undoubtedly arbitrary, the concept used as a way of reacting against a modern style of art which no doubt needed challenging by the 1980s. For there can be a reasonable point made that the work of Sutherland of a certain period (until, perhaps, his style altered under the influence of Bacon and the South of France); the non-abstract middle and later work of Piper (partly driven by a nostalgia for a Britain damaged by bombs, which wasn't particularly something which was a mainspring of Sutherland's 'romantic' work); a few scraps from Colquhoun's easel – after he had got to London, but before Adler got to him and toughened him up; a few bits from the maverick and multi-talented Ayrton; early Craxton, when he was very young and strongly influenced by Sutherland and Palmer; some early Minton, which had some similarities with early Craxton; and so on, all these did perhaps amount to a coherent mood for certain artists for a couple of years. But no attention needs to be paid to this passing phenomenon.

Abstract art

Many of the great figures in the British art world of the time – Kenneth Clark, John Rothenstein, Anthony Blunt, Wyndham Lewis, Alfred Munnings – were not keen on abstract art. In fact, to a greater or lesser extent, they hated it.[90] Maurice Collis, the *Observer*'s art critic in the first part of our period, reviewed an exhibition of work by Agar on 19 January 1947, thankfully noting that she had emerged from what he called a 'Parisian' non-representational style. This abstract style 'leads at last to no more than the reshuffling of forms and colours and becomes a decoration without significance'. He was particularly pleased to note that there were, in his opinion, a number of British painters – noting Tunnard and Richards – who were beginning to shake off the influence of Paris and – by contrast, 'to develop an imaginative statement which is related to life, literature, romance, emotion and even comedy'. The art critic of the *Times*, writing on 16 October 1945, made the following comments about Ben Nicholson's abstracts:

> The effect, especially in the bigger pictures, is to make one wonder whether this surrender of almost everything which painting has meant in the past, in favour of a sort of tidy cleanliness which reminds one, somehow, of the bathroom, is worth while. Mr Nicholson has obvious natural good taste, of a restrained kind, in colour, he has neatness, and his arrangements of form must need ingenuity – though not, one would guess, a very high degree of ingenuity. Are these things enough? Most people, it is to be presumed, would answer 'No'.

Sir William Nicholson, that most highly skilled of 'traditional' artists, was also quite happy to debunk his son's abstract work. After a reviewer in the *New English Weekly* described the son's work as 'a lavatory artform', the father was apparently in the habit of goading Ben by asking him 'done any more of them awful lavatory seats, Ben?' One of the leading Irish art critics of the time, Edward Sheehy, was also unimpressed by abstract art. Writing in the *Dublin Magazine* in the July-September 1947 issue, he said: 'If I am somewhat intolerant of abstract painting it is not that I do not enjoy its contemplation; but that I am inclined to look on it in the light of an exercise.' Similarly when Pasmore started to show his abstract work in 1949 the critics were not necessarily impressed. The *Times* described it as an extraordinary development. What would happen to artists experimenting with abstraction once they had exhausted all possible theories? Presumably then they would have to return to paint and nature?

One of the great destructive polemics against abstract art came a little outside our period. Although Wyndham Lewis published 'The Demon of Progress in the Arts' in 1954, a lot of it is backward-looking, to the period following the War.[91] He praised the work of Ayrton, Bacon, Colquhoun, Craxton, Minton, Moore, Pasmore (in his earlier style), Richards, Sutherland and Trevelyan, but he excoriated abstract art. He couldn't see how those British artists who tended towards abstraction would be able to improve upon the work of Mondrian or Kandinsky, which had been produced many years earlier. A young artist could go so far in the direction of abstraction, but by the middle of the 20th century the paths were few and well-trodden; there was nothing new to discover. He saw the abstract artist as 'a slave of the great god Progress, who is a very jealous god indeed'.

There were, of course, critics who supported abstract art, of which Herbert Read was the most prominent. He, for example, chaired a debate organised by the ICA in March 1950 on the subject of 'The Strange Case of Abstract Art', with Pasmore and Kenneth Martin supporting abstraction. He also published an essay shortly afterwards on 'Realism and Abstraction in Modern Art'. The other leading critic who particularly promoted abstract art, slightly outside our period, was Laurence Alloway. His *Nine Abstract Artists: their work and theory* came out in 1954.

The views of artists on abstract art occasionally come to the surface. Bacon was notoriously rude about abstract art, as about so many other things. Here he is, at the end of his life, talking on the subject to Michel Archimbaud:

MA Apart from Surrealism what else don't you like in painting? Abstraction?

FB Yes, abstract art seems to me an easy solution. Painting materials are in themselves abstract, but painting isn't only the material, it's the result of a sort of conflict between the material and the subject. There's a kind of tension there, and I feel that abstract painters eliminate one of the two sides of this conflict right from the start: the material alone dictates its forms and its rules. I think that that is a simplification. I also find that the human figure with its constant changes is very important. Abstraction has never been enough for me; it has never satisfied me. It seems to me that abstraction basically reduces painting to something purely decorative.[92]

Against that view, which artists tried their luck in that direction? The 'leader' of this style was indeed Ben Nicholson and the artistic community of St Ives came to be particularly closely associated with it. Their position will be dealt with shortly. Outside St Ives, Gear went in an abstract direction quite early in his career and, indeed, he was to be one of the five winners of a prize at the '60 Paintings for '51' show at the Festival of Britain, to the horror of the British public, many of whom wrote to the newspapers to complain.[93] Another artist whose work developed abstract elements and was occasionally completely abstract was Scott. Both Gear and Scott had international reputations which at least in part owed something to the fact that, to an international audience of the mid-century, 'abstract' was a style which they took to be an international rather than a domestic style.

There is a borderline in some types of abstract art between painting and sculpture and it is important to recognise the serious artists who worked in this area, partly coalescing around the converted Pasmore and partly reaching abstraction through their own researches and developments. In our period, the important ones to mention are Kenneth and Mary Martin, Robert Adams, Adrian Heath and Anthony Hill.[94] Much of their work postdates our period, but they had been starting to appear in public since the late 1940s. The work of this loose group appeared together for the first time at the London Group exhibition in February 1951 and this was followed by the more ambitious show at the AIA gallery in May 1951 of 'Abstract Paintings, Sculptures, Mobiles'. Problems of defining 'abstract' art always come quickly to the surface. At this show, for example, there were also works by Ben Nicholson, Paolozzi, Barns-Graham and Richards.

In Dublin there had been a period before the War when Mainie Jellett and Evie Hone had practised the rather debased Cubism which they had learnt in Paris, initially from Lhote and then from Glezies, but Jellett died in 1944 and Hone's talents were somewhat diverted into designing stained glass, so that there were no major artists based in Dublin after the War who were practising abstract artists. Nor were there any in Belfast or Scotland, although Scottish artists working outside Scotland, such as Gear, Davie, Paolozzi, Barns-Graham and Johnstone were, to a greater or lesser extent, inclined to abstract.

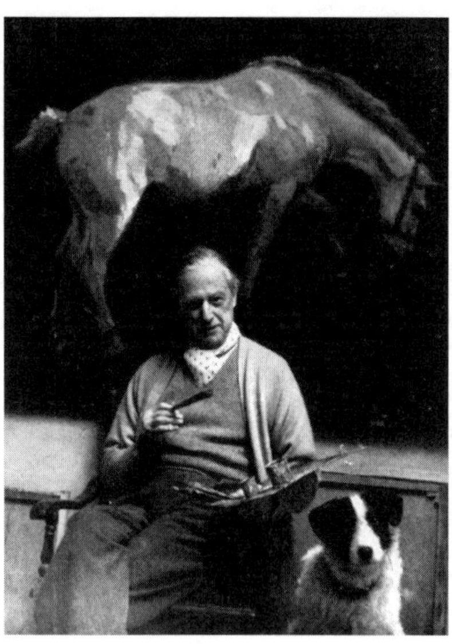

Alfred Munnings in his studio

St Ives

By 1945, Ben Nicholson and Barbara Hepworth had been settled in Cornwall since before the beginning of the War. It is too simplistic to describe Nicholson as merely an abstract artist; the variety of his painting is extensive. In his book on the artist,[95] Norbert Lynton illustrates five pictures dating from 1945, all in different styles, and Nicholson was certainly capable of a largely representational style of landscape and still-life (and often both together) which he seems to have turned to throughout his working life and which he seems not to have regarded as inferior or antithetical to his abstract work. He was, in any event, at least initially regarded as the king of the local modern artists who gathered in the area. The specific reason that Nicholson and Hepworth had come to St Ives in 1939 to escape London (apart from the fact that it was well away from any serious risk of heavy bombing) was an invitation from Adrian Stokes[96] and his Scottish painter wife Margaret Mellis. They were also friendly with Patrick Heron, who had married just before the end of the War and was living in London. Each year the Herons spent part of the summer in Cornwall. Apart, however, from his vague 'modernity', no-one could suggest that the coincidence of Heron's occasional presence in Cornwall could in any way be said to link him with the work of Nicholson, particularly because at this time Heron's work was largely influenced by Braque (and, to a lesser extent, by Picasso and Matisse).

Peter Lanyon was the artist most clearly associated with the area, because he was actually born there. He also became friendly with Adrian Stokes and was especially influenced by Stokes's written works on aesthetics, especially *Colour and Form* of 1937. At Stokes's suggestion, Lanyon (only 21 at the time) had taken lessons with Nicholson shortly after the latter's arrival in Cornwall. In a letter to Herbert Read in about 1940, Nicholson said that Lanyon 'has immediately a simple and profound understanding of the new ideas and has already made some interesting discoveries of his own'. In other words Lanyon was now making 'constructions', and it is clear that his work was also influenced by that of Gabo. On returning to Cornwall after the War, Lanyon painted some striking images, in part influenced by Gabo, in part by concepts gleaned in some way from the writing of Sigmund Freud. Some of the works are abstract, others an unusual combination of abstract and representation (such as *The Yellow Runner* of 1946 and *Landscape and Cup (Annunciation)* of the same year).

After the War, Ben and Barbara began to extend their influence over the St Ives Society of Artists in a way which ultimately was to lead to a severe clash with the area's non-abstract artists (that is, most of the local artists) and, indeed, a clash among the artists who might be said to be influenced, in a variety of ways, by Nicholson's personality and, sometimes, by his work. In February 1949 he engineered a split in the Society and formed a new local group called the Penwith Society of Arts. Herbert Read agreed to be its president. The Penwith Society was itself, however, soon to be riven by dissent, in this case that of Lanyon and Sven Berlin. The latter clashed with Nicholson by writing a book about Alfred Wallis which implied that Nicholson had been able to benefit financially from his relationship with Wallis. This

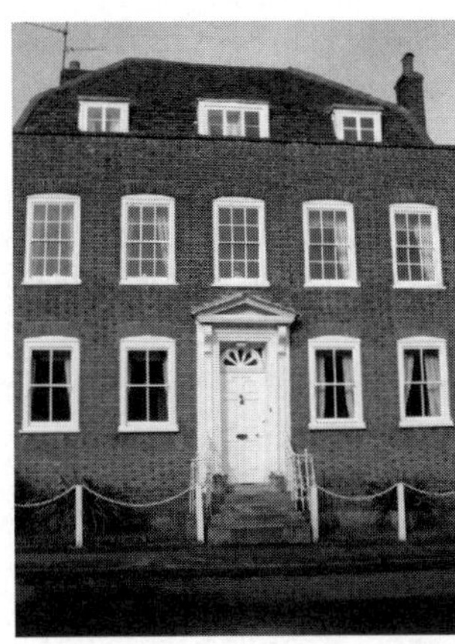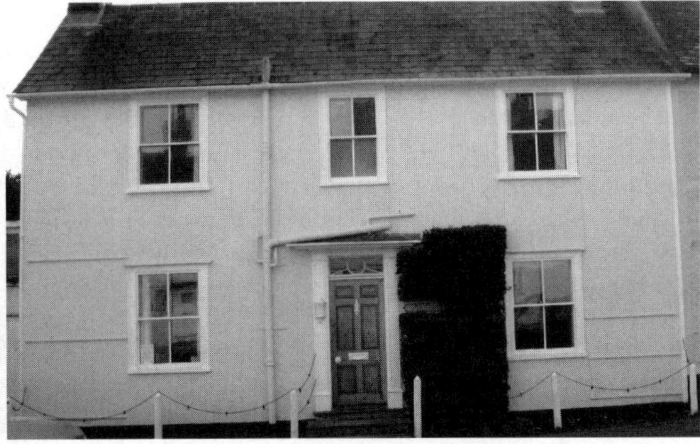

(left) Edward Bawden's house at Great Bardfield
(above) Michael Rothenstein's house at Great Bardfield

produced a violent Nicholson reaction and various elaborate art politics were used to discredit Berlin. At this time, Nicholson was encouraged by the 'conversion' of Pasmore from realism to abstraction and Pasmore was delighted to be invited to Cornwall to visit Nicholson.

1949 was a crucial year for the creation of an environment in which British abstract art could be taken a little more seriously. On 30 April the well-known speech by Sir Alfred Munnings, PRA, at the Royal Academy annual dinner was given. In the presence of Winston Churchill – himself not keen on abstract art – and live on the radio, Munnings attacked abstract art in a tirade which is said to have had the effect of encouraging some listeners to react by taking abstract art more seriously (although at the time Munnings claimed to have had thousands of letters in support of his position). Another artist who arrived in the area as a friend of the Stokes's was Wilhelmina Barns-Graham, who had known Margaret Mellis in Scotland before the War and who reached St Ives in March 1940.[97] By the end of the War she was exhibiting regularly with local artists and her style also varied at this stage in her career, from fairly representational landscapes to more abstract works, a style which gradually came to dominate in later years.

Great Bardfield

In 1925 Ravilious and Bawden had come across the Essex village of Great Bardfield and taken a lease over part of a house called the Brick House. This began an artistic association with the village, and the surrounding area, which was to continue in one form or another until the 1980s.[98] During that long period, artists came and went. To Bawden and Ravilious (who died on active service in 1942) were added, at different times, Michael Rothenstein,[99] Kenneth Rowntree and John Aldridge, together with a number of other, lesser figures such as Walter Hoyle, George Chapman, Sheila Robinson, Bernard Cheese, Audrey Cruddas, Clifford Smith and David Low. If the longest period and the widest geographical area are taken, one can bring in Michael Ayrton (1921-75), who moved into an old house just outside the village of Toppesfield[100] in July 1952.[101] But whatever the accumulation of friends and connections who coalesced around the area at various points, there wasn't much sense of them during the period covered by this book as a group or school, except geographically. Later, from the end of our period, there began to be mention of a Great Bardfield 'school' of artists. Hoyle, Cheese and Robinson had been students of Bawden at the RCA and one of their reasons for coming to the area was his presence there. They sometimes helped him on large commissions and the sheer density of artists in the village of about 700 inhabitants certainly distinguished it from most other villages. An open house event to show people what went on in these artists' houses had been held as part of the Festival of Britain and the next one, on a larger scale, was held in 1955. The Great Bardfield Artists Association was formed in 1959. On the other hand, the handsome figurative work of Bawden, early Rothenstein, Aldridge and Rowntree (together, of course, with the earlier and very beautiful work of Ravilious), represents what may now be seen as a golden era of mid-20th-century British painting of a traditional type and their achievements have perhaps been under-trumpeted for too long.

Euston Road

What later came to be known as the Euston Road School had an extremely short formal life of less than two years and that life finished before the War began. In October 1937 a 'School of Drawing and Painting' had been established by Coldstream, Pasmore and Rogers at 12 Fitzroy Street in W1. This moved in February 1938 to 314-6 Euston Road, nearby, and the school closed in the summer of 1939, never to re-open. It published a prospectus in 1937, anonymously paid for by Kenneth Clark. Indeed, he was generally involved with the founding of the school and encouraged wealthy friends like Samuel Courtauld to support it as well. Apart from the three artists mentioned, others involved were Bell, Tibble, Gowing, Moynihan, Devas and Lynton Lamb (and others even less well-known today).

Various efforts were made at the time and later to describe what the School stood for. Pasmore said that it 'began as a positive attempt to 'start again' by retrieving a determinate and basic objective standpoint both in the visual object and on the picture plane'. If that isn't particularly clear, no clearer statement is readily identifiable. The War put a stop to it, in any event, and one of its key figures – Bell – was killed in the War. The only reason for including it here is that by 1945 it was still enjoying a sort of strange half-life, this time informally at Camberwell. What happened was that when Pasmore arrived there to teach in 1943, he found some old Euston Road types (including Gowing) and he then deliberately brought in Rogers and Coldstream. Off they went again, showing what has been described as a 'spirit of open, unprejudiced enquiry into the philosophy of painting the visible world'.[102] In fact by this time there was less coherence and the term was starting to be used by others in an unflattering way. An example comes from the *Sunday Times* art critic, Eric Newton, on 4 May 1947, reviewing the Royal Academy Summer Exhibition. He noted that many of the pictures fell into the category of being 'Euston Road' pictures, a term which had by then, in his view, outgrown its usefulness. He saw it as a 'healthy but limited tradition. It is incapable of the grand manner. It is neither gay nor sensuous. It is incompatible with what is usually called imagination'. By 5 September 1948 he was noting that almost all contemporary British painting fell into one or other of three categories, one of which was 'Euston Road'. Of pictures painted in this style, 'the best of them will be to posterity what the petits maîtres of the Dutch seventeenth century are to us. The rest will be forgotten'. In his *A Century of British Painting 1851-1951* Anthony Bertram felt that he was too close, chronologically, to Euston Road to come to any conclusions as to its importance. Was it 'a late epilogue to Impressionism, or a prologue to a new revival'? Knowing what we know now, it would have to be said that it did not fall into the latter category. Townsend provided a sort of conclusion to its activities by organising a large-scale retrospective exhibition called 'The Euston Road School' in 1948 and this turned into a more limited Arts Council touring exhibition of the same name in 1948-49. Pasmore was not pleased at this reminder of his earlier style, as his work had by now become wholly abstract.

CHAPTER 2

SELLING, BUYING AND EXHIBITING

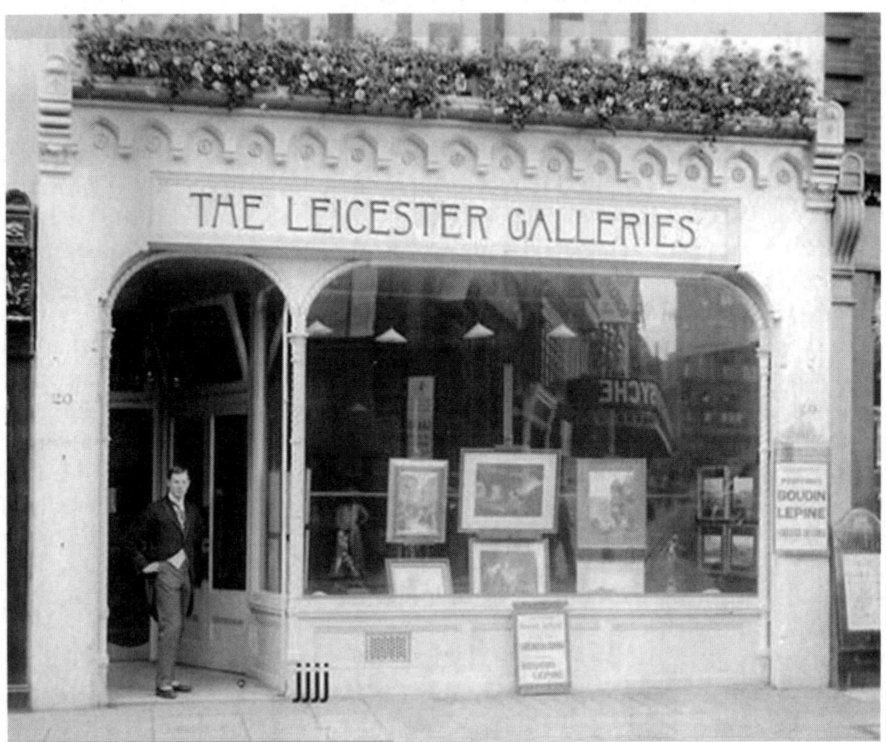

GALLERIES

During the period covered by this book, the main galleries in London which were prepared to show modern British artists on anything like a regular basis were the Leicester Galleries, the Lefevre, the Hanover, the Redfern, the Mayor, Gimpel Fils, the Marlborough, Roland, Browse and Delbanco and the London Gallery.[1] In Dublin, Victor Waddington was the leading gallery for modern art; in Edinburgh, Aitken Dott. In Glasgow the leading galleries seem to have been the Simpson Gallery, Pearson and Westergaard and James Connell & Sons. There seem to have been no specialist dealers in Belfast.

Leicester Galleries
The Leicester Galleries were one of the most important venues for young British artists to show their works in London during our period. They had opened just off the corner of Leicester Square in the summer of 1902 and ever since had held a series of shows of the

work of foreign and British artists. Despite bomb damage, they kept going during the War, resuming their exhibitions in 1940, and holding exhibitions of Moore, Hitchens, Piper and Sutherland. They were run by two well-known dealers, Cecil Phillips and Oliver Brown.[2] The memoirs of the latter contain the address given by Kenneth Clark at Brown's memorial service in 1967. In this, some hint of the great influence of Brown (and the Leicester Galleries) on the contemporary British art market is given by the following quote:

> I suppose that in those years when the Leicester was the chief exhibition gallery in London – and remember that before 1945 there were no Arts Council exhibitions, no special exhibitions at the Tate, no adventurous policy at the Whitechapel – in those years Oliver Brown must really have had considerable power in the art world.

In order to illustrate the extent of the activities carried on at the Leicester Galleries, it is worth considering the details of the exhibitions held there during our period. It is hard to imagine how they could possibly have squeezed any more shows in to their galleries. And so, in 1945, as they struggled to recover from their bomb damage, they nevertheless held at least 10 shows, including Piper, Roberts and Peake, and also the well-known shows entitled 'Artists of Fame and Promise'. These were held each year, sometimes in two parts, in about July or August. They consisted of works by well-known and less well-known artists and thereby gave an opportunity, often very gratefully received, for young artists to show their work in circumstances in which there was at least some chance that it would catch the eye of a potential buyer. It was, in many respects, a brilliant concept on the part of the gallery. Well-established collectors were lured in, both by the prospect of seeing work by artists they knew and also by the possibility of getting a bargain by an artist who might soon become well-known, since the mere fact of being included in the show gave a young artist some possibility of developing his reputation. One hardly dares to say it in connection with the art market, but it was something like a virtuous circle, especially as, by all accounts, the Leicester was known for its reasonable prices and the comparatively reasonable commission of 33.3% which it took from its artists for selling their work.

By 1946 the gallery was starting to operate at full speed again. Bearing in mind how long shows must have taken to organise, the fact that they held 25 in the year was surely a tremendous achievement.[3] The exhibitions ranged from solo shows, such as Lucien Pissarro, Moynihan, Robin Darwin, Gilbert Spencer, Rowntree and Weight, through group shows such as 'Living Irish Art' in October and back again to the usual 'Artists of Fame and Promise' in July/August. 1947 saw the trend of ever more exhibitions continue. They held another 25 shows in the year. Nevinson, Wolmark, Hitchens, Epstein, Hill, Burra, Gross, Aldridge, Devas, McGuinness, Coxon and Lord Methuen featured in various different shows; and 'Artists of Fame and Promise' spread over two parts, right through July, August and September. By 1948 the number had risen to 26. These included Appelbee, Ardizzone, Gowing, Augustus John, Le Brocquy, Bellingham-Smith, Scott and Piper, amongst others and so on. Twenty-six more in 1949 included the annual Irish contribution, on this occasion from Sine Mackinnon,[4] although I have no idea if that was a policy: Norah McGuinness[5] was to get another solo show in 1951. Burra had a one-man show; and Roberts, Bawden, Evans, Gilbert Spencer and Hitchens were amongst the group shows. The same pattern of 25 shows followed in 1950 and so on.

There were, over these years, occasional shows of non-British artists, such as Pissarro in 1946 and 1947, Rouault in 1949 and 'Notable French contemporary artists' in 1950, for example, but most of the exhibitions of specific artists were of British artists. Another feature of the Leicester at this time was its habit of showing the collections of (sometimes deceased) collectors: Sir Hugh Walpole's collection in three parts in 1945; Sir William Rothenstein's in 1946; Hugh Blaker's and Sir Louis Fergusson's in 1948; that of Howard Bliss in 1950; and Sir Augustus Daniel's in 1951.

Lefevre

The merged firm of Alex Reid and Lefevre opened in London in 1926 and specialised in French artists until the War.[6] In 1943 its King Street premises were bombed and at the end of 1944 the gallery reopened at 131 New Bond Street, moving to 30 Bruton Street in 1950. One of the directors, the Scottish Duncan MacDonald (who had previously worked for Aitken Dott and Alex Reid), moved back from New York in 1944 to re-establish the gallery, and the exigencies of the War meant that he had little choice but to concentrate on British artists. And so Moore, Colquhoun, MacBryde, Sutherland, Bacon, Lanyon and Vaughan, among many others, got shows. (For example, the gallery showed 'Recent Paintings by Francis Bacon, Frances Hodgkins, Henry Moore, Matthew Smith and Graham Sutherland' 1–30 April 1945 and 'Recent Paintings by Ben Nicholson, Graham Sutherland and Francis Bacon [an interesting linking of their names], Robert Colquhoun, John Craxton, Lucian Freud, Robert MacBryde and Julian Trevelyan' in February 1946).

The Lefevre series of exhibitions in our period makes for an interesting comparison with the Leicester. 1945 saw 'The School of Paris' and one or two foreign artists, but mostly British artists filled the galleries: Lowry, Armstrong, Mackinnon, Ben Nicholson, Collins and Katherine Church[7] being examples. 1946 saw a French show ('Delacroix to Dufy'), solo shows for Adler and Hepworth, as well as the important group show mentioned previously and another interesting grouping of Minton, Trevelyan and Vaughan. 1947s French show was 'Bonnard and his French Contemporaries'; Colquhoun, Tunnard, Sutherland and Ben Nicholson got solo shows. While 1948 appears not to have had a French exhibition, this was compensated for in 1949, which opened with 'Contemporary British and French Artists' and included '19th century French Painters' later in the year, as well as 'Selected works by French 20th century masters' in November. In fact, 1949 may have marked a slight change in direction (as noted above, it was the year in which Macdonald suddenly died), as there was only one solo show for a British artist, John Minton. The emphasis on French work continued in 1950, with solo shows for Degas and Dufy, '19th Century French Masters' and '20th century French pictures' leaving less room for British artists. Minton was really one of the main British Lefevre artists by this stage, appearing in 1950 with Paintings of Spain and in 1951 with Paintings of Jamaica. Otherwise, 1951 continued the French trend: presumably a deliberate reversion to their pre-War policy.

Redfern

The Redfern had been founded in September 1923 at Redfern House, 27 Old Bond Street as a small artists' co-operative. The founders were two wealthy individuals, the exotically named Arthur Knyvett-Lee and Anthony Maxtone Graham, but the most famous proprietor, who had joined in 1925 and who took over in 1931, was another dealer with a notable name, Rex Nan Kivell. The gallery moved to 20 Cork Street in 1936. As the War ended, the Redfern started its programme with a mixed exhibition of three artists of whom the British representative was Hurry. In fact, French artists featured regularly at the Redfern over the next few years and living British artists did not feature so highly.

Pasmore got solo shows in 1947, 1948 and 1949. Wyndham Lewis had a solo exhibition in 1949, as did Richards, Vaughan and Heron during 1950. Otherwise a limited number of living British artists appeared from time to time in group shows: Ayrton and Heron in 1947; Ironside, Uhlman, Barns-Graham, Suddaby, Jones, Wynter, Hill and Richards in 1948 (amongst others); Gore, Rothenstein, Eurich and Ayrton were included in 1949; Suddaby, Gore, Smith, Wynter, Pasmore and Jones in 1950; Rothenstein, Suddaby, Smith, Ayrton, Richards, Heron, Uhlman, Sutherland, Vaughan and Clough in 1951.[8]

St George's

This gallery re-opened shortly before the War ended with 'Paintings and Watercolours by Twenty Masters'. It had had a particular rôle in helping in the creation of an English reputation for Frances Hodgkins when it had held an important show for her in 1930, and its owner, Arthur Howell, later wrote a book about her. She was given a posthumous show in 1949 and there were occasional shows for British artists, such as a mixed show in 1947 and shows for Sven Berlin and Rosoman in 1948.

Mayor

Founded in 1925 in Sackville Street by Freddie Mayor,[9] the Gallery re-opened after the War (in October 1946) at 14 Brook Street with an exhibition of French and English Paintings and Drawings. Not many exhibitions were held in a year at the Mayor Gallery, but British artists got their chances: for example, Paolozzi, Ithell Colquhoun and Sickert in 1947; Paolozzi again in 1948 and 1949; Smith in 1949; Craxton in 1950 and Wolfe in 1951.

Gimpel Fils

The gallery was founded in London towards the end of 1946[10] by brothers Charles and Peter Gimpel, in homage to their father René, who had died during the War in a German concentration camp. With its French family connections, it is not surprising that Gimpel was weighted towards French and other artists, rather than British artists. In fact, English (as distinct from British) artists featured very rarely at this gallery. Adler appeared in 1947 and, after his death, in 1950; Gear in 1948 and 1951, and Le Brocquy from time to time, but the first sign of an English artist being given any prominence (they may, of course, have been included in the occasional Summer exhibitions), was when Trevelyan appeared in March 1950.

Hanover

The Hanover opened in 1948 with a solo show by Sutherland. Thereafter it tended to have either French or British artists and Wilde and Ayrton got a joint show later in that year, followed by a solo show for Agar in 1949. The first Bacon show (shared with Ironside) was in November 1949. Vaughan was in a group show in 1950 and Freud's first show there was in April 1950. Sutherland and Agar reappeared in 1951, but really very few British names appeared at the Hanover, although it could be said that covering Bacon, Freud and Sutherland indicated a high degree of far-sightedness.

Marlborough

Marlborough Fine Art was founded in London in 1946 by Frank Lloyd and Harry Fischer, both of whom had emigrated from Vienna. In 1948 they were joined as a partner by David Somerset,[11] who was only 20 at the time.

London

The London Gallery at 28 Cork Street had been founded in 1936 and in 1938 it was bought by the wealthy Surrealist painter, Roland Penrose, with help from Anton Zwemmer, as a centre for Surrealist work. The Belgian E.L.T. Mesens was employed as the manager and the gallery had reopened under its new ownership with an exhibition of Magritte. By the time of the War, the British Surrealists were no longer a particularly coherent group and the gallery had been closed since the beginning of the War. It reopened in 1946, now at 23 Brook Street, with Mesens living in a flat above, but its life was troubled by the fact that Penrose was at loggerheads with Mesens, and was in any event more focused on formulating what later became the Institute of Contemporary Arts.

By the time it closed in 1950, after suffering heaving losses, the London Gallery had held an exhibition for Craxton (hardly a Surrealist) and for Desmond Morris, who was (and still is) a Surrealist artist. For British artists its most significant post-War event was a joint Freud/Craxton show in 1947. The post-War daily life of the gallery is very well captured by George Melly,[12] who began work there in 1946 as an assistant at £3 a week. His greatest moment was in forcibly ejecting Douglas Cooper from the gallery after he had annoyed Mesens by dissuading a customer from buying a Craxton. He also describes well the silently conducted sale of the gallery stock after its closure to its participants, Mesens, Penrose, Zwemmer, Peter Watson (who was a director of the gallery) and Melly himself. Mesens bought most for minimal sums, Penrose and Melly a few things and Watson nothing, rolling his eyes and groaning as each unsold piece (often of obscure Surrealist provenance) was brought out. No-one competed for any item and all items were simply transferred at whatever price was named.

Roland, Browse & Delbanco

Roland, Browse and Delbanco opened at 19 Cork Street at the end of the War.[13] It was formed by two German academically trained art historians and Lilian Browse, who was South African and had worked before the War at the Leger Galleries. Their first show was a loan exhibition of English drawings, from the 17th century to John Minton and Leslie Hurry. This illustrates neatly the dilemma faced by most, if not all, London galleries at the time, which was that, however much they might have preferred to concentrate on modern pictures, it was generally thought to be economically difficult, or impossible, to focus on these to the exclusion of older pictures, since the buying public, private or institutional, simply was not large enough, or prepared to pay enough money, for modern pictures. More recent 'British' artists whom they took on included Sir William Nicholson (in his last few years); the Polish immigrants, Gotlib and Herman; Sickert (who had died in 1942); the Irish born Roderic O'Conor (who had died in 1940); and the later Joan Eardley.

Some of the gallery's records from our period are now in the Tate Archive. They provide the material for the sort of close, factual analysis of certain aspects of the British art market at this time which I believe has not been attempted. For amongst the papers are a number of leather-bound handwritten ledgers, consisting of the gallery 'stock books' and 'sale books'. From these it is possible to work out at least the following aspects of the gallery's business: which pictures a gallery of this type was buying; how much they paid; how much profit they made when they sold; where they bought from; who they sold to; how long it took to sell the pictures; how many pictures the proprietors kept for themselves; and so on. From our period, the gallery stocked, at different times, work by Sickert, Hurry, Smith, Paul Nash, Pasmore, Minton, Sutherland, William Nicholson,

John and Gotlib. Other artists started to appear with the passing of time. A Piper appeared on 14 August 1946, bought from the Mayor Gallery for £150 and sold three months later for £250. The same year saw Scott's first appearance (a picture bought for £20 and sold to the Redfern for £27); Colquhoun appeared in 1947; Clough in 1948. Some examples of costs and profits are evident from this account and it might be possible to work out if there was a standard mark-up for pictures, although I have not tried to do that. Other facts emerge. A Smith bought for £180 was sold for £290; a Paul Nash was bought for £23.12.6d and sold for £31.10; a Pasmore was bought for £80 and made £99.15; the Colquhoun was spectacularly profitable, being bought from a private vendor for £23 and sold to Delbanco himself for £63.

Occasionally a picture was obviously not a success in profit terms (there were also some struck through and marked 'fake', but they were older works). A Sutherland bought on 14 August 1946 for £85 was sold on 23 October 1947 for £84 and another Sutherland bought for £15 was apparently then sold for £15. (One needs, even here, to remember the degree of caution which has to be applied when analysing apparently reliable historical evidence. Books of account in any business do not always mean what they say, especially if, for example, the tax authorities are ever likely to want to review them. I suspect that the laconic entries in some instances mask some sort of more complicated transaction based on exchanging a group of pictures at deemed values, without cash necessarily changing hands, usually between dealers — what a stockbroker might recognise as an 'agency cross'.)

Then there is the question of where they bought from. Sometimes artists sold directly to them, but not just their own works. The Sutherland, for example, which seemed to come in and out at £15, came from Ayrton. Then, other galleries sold to them: Tooth's, the Redfern and the Mayor Gallery, for example. Other individuals also sold to them. And then we may ask, to whom did they sell? The books contain fascinating information here. Many of the characters who feature so regularly in this book were occasional buyers: Clark, Watson (he bought a Moore *Family Group* on 8 October 1948 for £126), Anderson (including a Sickert and a Sutherland), Evill and Mortimer (a Sickert), for example. Institutions, too, were buyers: the Whitworth Art Gallery in Manchester (a Hurry), the Arts Council (a Minton), the British Council (another Hurry), the Leicester Art Gallery (a Paul Nash), the CAS and so on. All three proprietors bought in their own names (Roland bought a Moore, for example, and Delbanco a Minton). Artists sometimes bought — Pasmore bought a Sutherland in 1947 and Ayrton a Minton. Famous people bought — George Melly and Vivien Leigh, for example. Other galleries also bought from the gallery: the Redfern and the Mayor. Many sales went to private buyers. Pictures by earlier artists were sometimes sold through the saleroom, often at Sotheby's.

Victor Waddington

Waddingtons is still a major London gallery, but for the period covered by this book it was not in London, but in Dublin. Victor Waddington had been born in London, but had moved to Ireland in the 1920s. By the beginning of the 1930s he was dealing in art and during the War he set up in Dublin at South Anne Street.[14] His particular good fortune was to have Jack Yeats as his principal contemporary artist, holding his first Yeats show in 1943. Nevertheless, by the time Waddington gave up in Dublin and moved the gallery to London in the later 1950s, he claimed that he had been losing money ever since the end of the War at the rate of £80 per week, or about £4,000 a year, which shows how difficult it was in Ireland at this time to establish a business dependent on contemporary art. Waddingtons, of course, as the main commercial gallery in Ireland in our period, had the pick of Irish artists wishing to show in Ireland, but it also showed English and foreign artists, including[15] Picasso, Bonnard, Matisse, Braque, Rouault, Kokoschka, Masson, Ben Nicholson, Hitchens, Spencer, Moore and Hepworth, a remarkable achievement for a gallery in a small country not known at the time for its cultural sophistication in terms of modern art-buying.[16]

Aitken Dott (the Scottish Gallery)

This was Scotland's premier gallery. Founded in 1842, it is still going. During the War, it had a connection with the Lefevre through its former employee Duncan Macdonald, for example borrowing a Lowry show from there in 1944. From about 1940-50 it was under the control of Beatrice Proudfoot.[17] Although in a sense part of the historic Scottish arts establishment, it was prepared to hold one-man shows for new artists. Earl Haig and Gillies got their first one-man shows there, for example, in 1945; Adam Bruce Thomson followed in 1946. In 1947 they held their first Festival exhibition (Peploe) and in 1950 Redpath had her first solo show there. They were also prepared to show English artists. For example, in 1951 they held an exhibition of 'Forty contemporary English paintings', which included work by Sickert, Hitchens, Ben Nicholson, Vaughan, Minton, Vanessa Bell, Burra and Tunnard.

INSTITUTIONS

The Council for the Encouragement of Music and the Arts (CEMA)

CEMA had been created early in the War by the Government, with the help of financial support from the Pilgrim Trust (which administered a bequest of £2 million left by the American, Edward Harkness). A Scottish Committee was established in 1943, as was CEMA (Northern Ireland). As its name indicates, this was not an organisation aimed solely at painting. Its initial objectives were stated as:

(a) the preservation in wartime of the highest standards in the arts of music, drama and painting;
(b) the widespread provision of opportunities for hearing good music and the enjoyment of the arts generally for people who, on account of wartime conditions, have been cut off from these things;
(c) the encouragement of music-making and play-acting by the people themselves;
(d) through the above activities, the rendering of indirect assistance to professional singers and players who may be suffering from a wartime lack of demand for their work.

From the above, it will be seen how closely linked to wartime conditions were its ambitions. CEMA's Art Panel was under the control of Kenneth Clark and it had a board consisting of Samuel Courtauld, William Emrys Williams, Duncan Grant,[18] Henry Moore and John Rothenstein. Very little of CEMA's annual budget went to support art. Shortly after the end of the War, CEMA turned into the Arts Council, largely due to the influence of Lord Keynes, with the background assistance of Kenneth Clark. The pictures purchased during CEMA's short existence will be covered in the next section.

The Arts Council

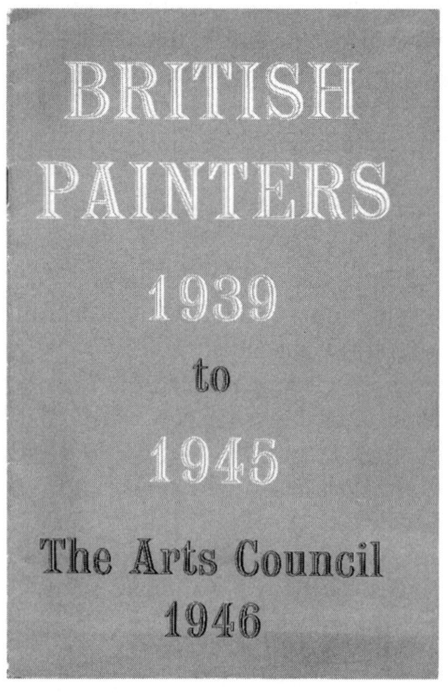

This came into being in 1945. Lord Keynes made a broadcast on the Home Service, which was published in the *Listener* on 12 July 1945 under the heading 'The Arts Council: its policy and hopes'. In this he remarked upon the development of state patronage of the arts. He also noted the growth in popular interest in fine art, partly due to the War, but also to the work of the BBC. He concluded by saying that 'the purpose of the Arts Council of Great Britain is to create an environment to breed a spirit, to cultivate an opinion, to offer a stimulus to such purpose that the artist and the public can each sustain and live on the other in that union which has occasionally existed in the past at the great ages of a communal civilised life'.

The Arts Council received its Royal Charter in 1946. The recital to the Charter stated that the Arts Council was established 'for the purpose of developing a greater knowledge, understanding and practice of the fine arts exclusively, and in particular to increase the accessibility of the fine arts to the public'. The first Council members included Kenneth Clark. Mrs Cazalet-Keir[19] was also a member. As discussed elsewhere,[20] she owned a limited number of modern British pictures, and had recently ended her political career as an MP in the position of Parliamentary Secretary to the Board of Education, the body which had been administering CEMA during the War. It was more likely to have been this connection than her picture collection which recommended her for the job on the Council. Separate Arts Council committees were established at the beginning of 1947 for Scotland and Wales.

The key part of the Arts Council for our purposes was its Art Panel. This body was so important to the development of contemporary British Art that its progress has to be followed in some detail. As we shall see, the members of this Panel could exert considerable influence over decisions which could directly affect the development of an artist's career. Its first meeting (bearing in mind that it was, in many ways, simply a continuation of CEMA's Art Panel), was held on 16 August 1946 at the then head office of the Arts Council at 9 Belgrave Square. Kenneth Clark was in the chair and Sir Ernest Pooley was in attendance.[21] Similarly, the Labour MP, Mrs Ayrton Gould,[22] was there. The actual members of the Panel, apart from Clark, seem to have been Leigh Ashton, Duncan Grant, Henry Moore, John Rothenstein, Major Alfred Longden, Tom Monnington, Samuel Courtauld and Philip Hendy, the latter three being absent from this first meeting. Edward O'Rorke Dickey was present at this meeting, but perhaps in an administrative capacity. He is better known for having been the first secretary, 1939-1942, of the WAAC. A large secretariat was also present: the well-known Mary Glasgow (secretary-general), Philip James (director of art), Gabriel White (assistant director of art), Eric White (deputy secretary) and Mrs Rodgers (art assistant).

The business of meetings such as this ranged across a wide variety of subjects connected with the arts in England and so matters for discussion might include such topics as which proposed exhibitions to support financially; whether or not to raise the hiring fees paid to artists when their works were borrowed for exhibitions (they were raised, at the first meeting, from £5 per annum for oils to £10); whether to create a picture collection (the decision to do that was taken at the second meeting, held on 7 November 1946); whether to support the work of the ICA once that got going (it was decided to donate £500 at the meeting on 2 February 1948 and at the meeting on 9 May 1950 £1,500 towards the ICA's Festival contribution – the exhibition called 'Ten Decades'); and, in due course, how to respond to the need to organise events for the Festival of Britain (see Chapter 7).

Once the decision had been taken to buy contemporary British art, an extremely important question for our purposes was who should be authorised to make the purchases and how should they be made? Whoever it was would have great power and influence over the way in which certain artists would flourish, because this fund at the disposal of the Art Panel – they initially (on 16 January 1947) gave themselves a grant of £4,500 – represented an important source of contemporary state patronage.

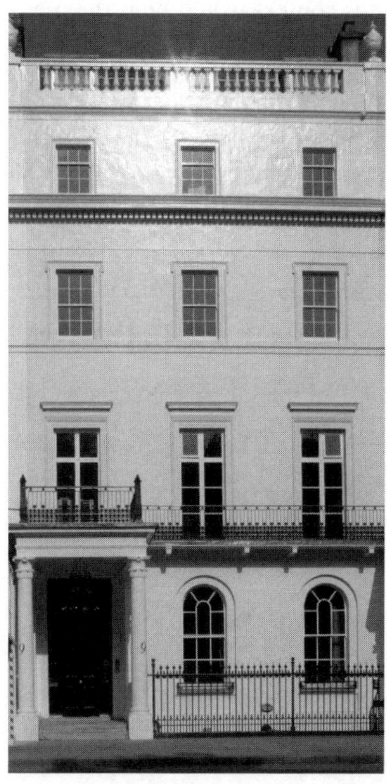

9 Belgrave Square, in 1946 the first home of the Arts Council

Their thought at the time was that this sum should enable them to buy, say, 60 oils at an average of £60 each and perhaps 30 watercolours and drawings at an average of £25 each. Nothing indicates so clearly the enormous power of certain people in the British art world at the time as the fact that the three members of the Panel chosen as the initial buyers were Clark, Anderson and Philip James. They promptly went to work on their programme of buying and the nature of their tastes was quickly revealed. At the next meeting (on 21 March 1947) it was reported that they had bought drawings by Minton and Ayrton and, at the following meeting (on 25 June) the Panel was told that works by Vaughan and Ben Nicholson had been acquired. One senses these may have represented Anderson's taste more than Clark's. In any event, it was too much for the Panel, and Duncan Grant and Tom Monnington were drafted onto the purchasing sub-committee, the latter, at least, no doubt with a view to balancing up the more avant-garde tastes with a healthy dose of conservatism. However, the question still arose as to how this sub-committee was supposed to exercise its rather dangerous powers.

The minutes contain various references to changes in personnel of the sub-committee and, more crucially, debates about how many people on the sub-committee needed to be involved in actually making purchases. Clearly it was extremely cumbersome, in a market context, for five busy people to get together in order to confirm that pictures, presumably initially spotted by one of their members, could indeed be bought. A quorum was needed. Even so, one suspects that the only way even a quorum system could work in practice in this context would be if the members of the sub-committee basically trusted each other's judgment. The introduction of the formal requirement for a quorum no doubt operated to calm the wilder extremes of enthusiasm which each member on his own might have had for the work of certain artists, since he would have in each case either to persuade fellow members of the worth of his choice before the purchase was completed or, presumably, risk buying it and having it rejected. It is interesting to see how this restraint

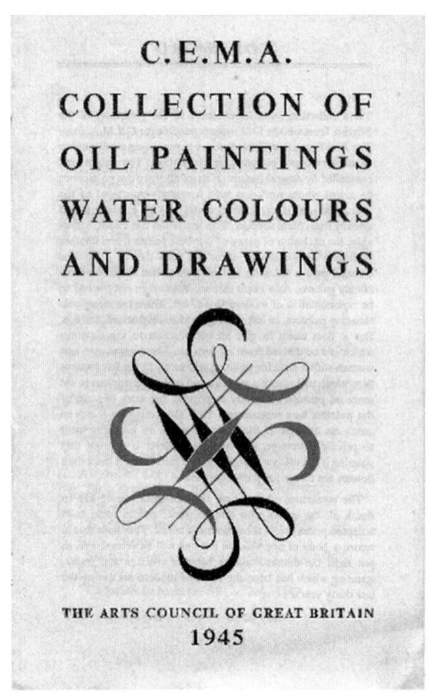

had an influence in practice. Colin Anderson is the pivotal figure here. He seems to have been on the purchasing subcommittee for some time (although it is not possible from the minutes to be sure of this, since the members of the sub-committee were usually only mentioned when changes to the membership were being made). We know that he was one of the earliest people to select a picture by Bacon for 'official' purchase, when he selected an early work for the CAS when he was its buyer in 1946. But, of course, the CAS had a different purchasing method. Perhaps because of its organisation as a private society rather than the Arts Council, which had been created by statute and was more of an official body, the CAS allowed one of the members of its committee to be the sole buyer for the year, his or her purchases being unchallenged by the members of the committee. Anderson was later to state publicly that he thought this method of purchasing far superior to any method which required a committee decision and, while he did not say so at the time (in the Introduction he wrote in the catalogue to the Arts Council

sponsored exhibition in 1949 to 'Some Recent Purchases of the Contemporary Art Society'), it must be the case that he was contrasting CAS methods with those of the Art Panel. There were certainly no purchases of pictures by Bacon by the Art Panel at this time.

Membership of the Art Panel did change quite a lot over the period, although the position is complicated by the absence of certain members from each meeting and by the occasional attendance of people acting in some temporary capacity. There is a file in the Arts Council archives[23] which contains copies of letters sent by Mary Glasgow to people inviting them to become members of the Art Panel. If the assumption were made that this was a complete file, it would be possible to piece together exactly who became a member and at what date. The first letter went out on 22 August 1946: curiously, after the date of the first meeting. Here mention will only be made of particular changes. For example, it was obviously a key change that Colin Anderson appeared as a member for the second meeting, which was held on 7 November 1946. He had been invited by letter dated 19 October and had accepted promptly, on 22 October. A new name in the British art world of the time was that of Miss G.V. Barnard, from the Norwich Museum and Art Gallery. She also joined for the second meeting. The art critic Eric Newton appeared for the first time on 16 January 1947 (the third meeting) and on 24 October 1947, at the sixth meeting, Francis Watson, described as the Director of Visual Arts at the British Council, appeared, in place of Major Longden. We know from a separate Arts Council file[24] that in 1948 Clark wanted to resign as Chairman of the Art Panel. He wrote on 31 March to Pooley asking to resign and Pooley replied saying that he would prefer him to go at the end of the year, which he did. The meeting held on 9 December 1948 was therefore supposed to be Clark's last as Chairman, to be replaced by Bill Williams. However, not many meetings passed before Clark was back. He next attended on 24 October 1949, perhaps because the focus on the Festival of Britain drew him back. He certainly attended the next, key, meeting in relation to the Art Panel's preparations for the Festival and, while the minutes do not make clear exactly what happened, the resignation of Bill Williams was mentioned at the meeting on 23 January 1951 and Clark was back in the chair for the next meeting, on 10 April.

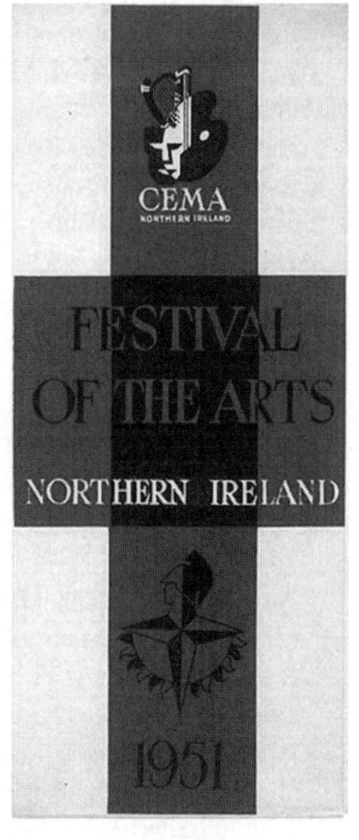

Another important addition to the membership was that of Herbert Read.[25] Oliver Brown of the Leicester Galleries also appeared for the first time on 28 February. One wonders about the possibility for conflicts of interest in having an art dealer on the Panel, especially one of the most prominent art dealers in the very area of art which the Panel was focused on – contemporary British art. As will be seen shortly, there were inevitably many purchases by the Panel from the Leicester Galleries.

William Coldstream first attended on 28 February 1950. He was another friend of Clark's. He promptly joined the purchasing sub-committee. Just as the members of the Panel changed, so did membership of the purchasing sub-committee. Clark came off when he resigned the chairmanship at the end of 1948 and Le Bas and Newton joined as replacements for him and Allan Walton, who had died. By early 1950 the members of the purchasing sub-committee were Anderson, Le Bas, Hendy and Coldstream and, significantly, this group had become Clark, Anderson, Coldstream and Moynihan by the beginning of the following year.

It is worth looking in detail at the purchases made by CEMA and the Arts Council, so as to give an indication of the contemporary choices which were being made as to which artists were worthy of 'official' support in the period up to 1951.[26] All the purchases by CEMA during the period 1942-1944 were made directly from the artists themselves. Thereafter, various galleries got involved and they have been indicated where known. It is particularly important to illustrate the range and number of purchases made by these institutions, because this is the period when it is sometimes asserted that state patronage of contemporary British artists increased so as to fill a gap which had apparently arisen in the number of private buyers of such works. Clearly it is easy to use these details to establish that more modern work was being bought by institutions, for the simple reason that CEMA and the Arts Council had not previously existed. Whether there was a corresponding decline in private patrons and collectors is not, however, provable and I do not think that any correlation can be established.

CEMA purchases
1942
Aldridge, Appelbee, Armstrong, Walter Bayes, Keith Baynes, Vanessa Bell, Nadia Benois, Burra (2), Thomas Carr, George Charlton, Katherine Church, Colquhoun, Coxon, Devas, Evelyn Dunbar, Dunlop, Georg Ehrlich, Clifford Ellis, Leila Faithfull, Margaret Fisher Prout, James Fitton (2), Gerhard Frankel, Ginner, Gowing, Grant, Gwynne-Jones, Archibald Hartrick, Hennell, Hitchens, Hodgkins, Percy Horton, R.K. Jamieson, Basil Jonzen, Mary Kessell, Eve Kirk, Le Bas, Vincent Lines, Augustus Lunn, Robert Lyon, Frances Macdonald, Kenneth Martin, John Maxwell, Meninsky, Lord Methuen, Arthur Middleton Todd, Harry Morley, Moynihan, Charles Murray, Susan Palmer, Pasmore, Maresco Pearce, Roland Pitchforth, Patricia Preece, Geoffrey Rhoades, Richards, Claude Rogers, Rosoman, Rothenstein, Rowntree, Albert Rutherston, Rupert Shephard, Beryl Sinclair, Alan Sorrell, Spear, Gilbert Spencer, Suddaby, John Tunnard, Ethel Walker, Audrey Waterfield, Weight, Kenneth Wood and Underwood.
1943
Lowry
1944
Graham Bell, Gillies and Rogers.

Arts Council purchases
From 1947 it is worth indicating, where known, where the pictures were being acquired from, as various galleries got involved:
1947
Aldridge (Leicester Galleries), Ayrton (Redfern), Colquhoun (Lefevre), Hepworth (Artist), Lamb, Maxwell (Artist), Minton (Roland, Browse and Delbanco), Nicholson (Lefevre), Rogers (Leicester Galleries), Trevelyan, Vaughan.
1948
Appelbee (Leicester Galleries), Ardizzone (Leicester Galleries), de Grey, du Plessis (London Group), Gowing (Leicester Galleries), Harold Grisham (Leicester Galleries), Jones (Redfern), Medley (Lefevre), Meninsky, Moore (2), Nash (private donor), Sir William Nicholson (CAS), Scott, Sickert, Spear, Kyffin Williams, Wynter.
1949
Bawden (Leicester Galleries), Keith Baynes (Thomas Agnew), Vanessa Bell (Agnew), Coldstream (Leicester Galleries), Ginner (Artist), Grant (Mayor Gallery), Hayes, Herman (Lefevre), Hitchens (Leicester Galleries), Innes, Lewis (Redfern), John Nash, Paul Nash (Family), Winifred Nicholson (Agnew), Margaret Thomas (Leicester Galleries), Tibble (Arthur Tooth).
1950
Barns-Graham (Artist), John Berger (Artist), Buhler (Royal Academy), Clausen (Artist's son), Craxton (Mayor Gallery), Hepworth (Lefevre), Heron (Redfern), Hill (Leicester Galleries), Jones (Redfern), Kessell (Leicester Galleries), John Luke (Mayor Gallery), Lynton Lamb, MacBryde (Redfern), de Maistre (Adams Bros), Minton (Lefevre), Moynihan, Nicholson (Leicester Galleries), Mary Potter (Leicester Galleries), Richards (Redfern), Roberts (2) (Leicester Galleries), Scott (Howard Bliss), Sutherland (Hanover Gallery), Wilde (Artist).
1951
Beryl Sinclair (2) (British Institute of Adult Education), Stokes (Leger), Weight

(Leicester Galleries), Collins (Leicester Galleries), Hill (Leicester Galleries), Grant (2) (Artist/Leicester Galleries), Paolozzi (Artist), Ardizzone (Leicester Galleries), Le Bas (Artist), Bellingham-Smith (Artist), Seabrooke (Leicester Galleries), Sutherland (Hanover), Piper (7) (British Institute of Adult Education), Kit Lewis (London Group), Lowry (London Group), Mary Potter (Leicester Galleries), Nigel Lambourne (Colnaghi), Clough (Artist), MacBryde, Moynihan (Artist), Spear (Leicester Galleries), Stella Steyn (Leicester Galleries), Pasmore (2) (Artist/Redfern), Gillies (Artist), Gear (Gimpel Fils), Townsend (Leicester Galleries).

The Arts Council organised exhibitions of contemporary British art from time to time. For example, in 1946 it showed 'British Painters 1939 to 1945'. This consisted of 70 works, by the following artists: Appelbee, Colquhoun, Gillies, Gowing, Grant, Hitchens, Hodgkins, A. John, Moynihan, P. Nash, Pasmore, Piper, du Plessis, Rogers, Smith, Spear, Sutherland and Tunnard. (A few of the pictures were for sale.) It also sponsored an exhibition called 'Four Young British Painters' (Ayrton, Minton, Scott and Vaughan) and in 1947 it was the turn of Appelbee, Rogers, Spear and Weight. Yeats got a retrospective in 1948, as did the Euston Road School, Herman, Hennell and a 'Selection of Paintings and Drawings acquired by the Contemporary Arts Society'. A Hodgkins exhibition was supported in Swanage and a Ravilious in Eastbourne. In November 1949 it joined with the British Council to celebrate the reopening of the New Burlington Galleries with an exhibition of 'Contemporary British Art from the collections of the Arts Council and the British Council'. (Curiously, in view of the title of the exhibition, the catalogue cover showed a drawing by Gilman, who had died in 1919.) The introduction to the catalogue was by Philip James, who lamented the fact that work by Henry Moore and Paul Nash was unavailable because it was already being exhibited abroad by the British Council. 74 works were shown. From 1945 Philip James was supported by Gabriel White as his assistant Director of Art. White eventually succeeded Philip James as Director of Art in 1958. He had studied drawing at the Westminster School of Art under Meninsky and there he met fellow student Ardizzone, marrying the latter's sister in 1928. (He was to publish a book on Sickert's drawings in 1952 and one on Ardizzone in 1979.)

The British Council

Originally called 'The British Committee for Relations with Other Countries', the British Council had been founded in 1934 with the aim of encouraging cultural relations with other countries. Its work was not restricted to the promotion of artists, although the fine arts were soon considered an integral part of its activities. On 16 October 1935 a meeting had been held – inevitably attended by Kenneth Clark (and Eddie Marsh) – to consider the formation of a Fine Arts Advisory Committee and the first meeting thereof was held on 7 November of the same year. Sir Eric Maclagan was at that meeting and, by the time our period starts, he was in the chair, where he was to remain throughout the period. Some attention will be paid to the composition of this Committee and to the way in which it operated in relation to the promotion of contemporary British art. The first meeting after the War[27] was held at 43 Portland Place on 28 June 1945. Apart from Maclagan, it was attended by Makower, Marsh, Herbert Read, John Rothenstein, the Earl of Sandwich, Viscount Tredegar, the Duke of Wellington, William Montagu-Pollock (representing the Foreign Office), Major Longden (the Director), Lilian Somerville and Miss L. Harvey. Apologies were received from the Earl of Crawford, Lord Harlech, Sir Owen Morshead and Campbell Dodgson.

The first thing that strikes one about this group is its aristocratic composition. None of the other bodies concerned with the arts had this sort of representation, which is partly perhaps due to the fact that the British Council's committee was not solely or particularly aimed at the promotion of contemporary art, but was instead concerned with a vast range of artistic activities. The other interesting thing is the overlap with other committees of individuals like Marsh, Read and Rothenstein.

The width of the agenda of this Committee is well illustrated by what the Director chose to cover in his report for this meeting. He mentioned existing British Council supported exhibitions in South America, Cairo and Canada; an arts and crafts exhibition in the US; an exhibition of children's paintings in South America;[28] an exhibition of graphic art in the Middle East and Turkey; artists' colour prints in Tehran; graphic art in Russia and China; and caricature in Sweden. The report then moved on to exhibitions from other countries held in the UK that the British Council was supporting: Peruvian architecture, Brazilian art, Yugoslav textiles and Chinese painting. The report concluded with potential new exhibitions. The topic which the Committee seems to have found irresistible – children's painting – was considered for Paris and South Africa and, rather more importantly, the possibility of arranging exchange exhibitions with France was considered. This may have been an early reference to the exhibition that was to cause such furore when it opened at the V&A in December 1945: the infamous Picasso/Matisse show. But at this stage the proposal was for Picasso/Bonnard for one show, Braque/Matisse for another, Léger/Dufy for a third and perhaps Rouault/Miró for a fourth. It was mentioned that Leigh Ashton had offered the use of the V&A for these shows, perhaps because the Tate was still completely out of action following War damage. In return, Rothenstein was pushing for the British Council to sponsor a big show in Paris of the modern British collection from the Tate, which was otherwise languishing in storage while the Tate was being repaired. For some reason, which is hard to decipher from the minutes, this seems to have provoked a lot of debate as to whether or not it was an appropriate exhibition for the British Council to sponsor. The gist of the opposition was perhaps caused by a concern that what the Tate was offering – and lists of potential pictures were circulated to the members of the Committee – was not representative enough, since it simply consisted of what the poorly funded Tate had been able to scrape together from occasional deliberate purchases, occasional unpredictable gifts and legacies, and random, often unwanted, dumps from the Chantrey gift.

The debate about this rumbled on for a number of meetings and when the show did eventually hit Paris in 1946, under the heading 'Tableaux Britanniques modernes appartenant à la Tate Gallery', it was reported back to the Committee's 32nd meeting (27 July 1946) that the show had been poorly received. This was in contrast to the reception given to the Picasso/Matisse show, which was said to have been seen by over 150,000 people over five weeks in London, by 88,952 people in Glasgow and by 73,500 in Manchester. This was in addition to the innumerable people who must have heard on the radio one of the three talks about the exhibition given on different bits of the BBC.

There were occasional changes made to the membership of the Committee. Gerald Coke appeared for the first time on 27 September 1945 and, at the meeting held on 24 January 1946, Clive Bell and John Witt were present. Hendy first attended on 28 March 1946 at a meeting at which it was reported that Leigh Ashton and Professor Boase had agreed to join the Committee. Philip James from the Arts Council attended on 12 September 1946; Allan Walton became a member in 1948 shortly before his death. By 1948, Tom Honeyman was being invited to join, as was Anthony Blunt and Basil Taylor. Gordon Russell was invited to join later in 1948. Ellis Waterhouse joined in 1949 and John Steegman in 1950.

Kenneth Clark appears to have had little to do with the British Council in later years. He was a member of the Committee at some stage, but his resignation was noted at the meeting on 24 January 1946. He makes nothing of this in his autobiography, but we know this to be the case because there are letters in the Clark archive in the Tate[29] which make it clear that in late 1943 he tried to resign. It would be interesting to know quite what happened between Clark and the British Council. A letter dated 16 January 1952 from Sutherland to Clark makes the following, rather tantalising, comment: 'I know you don't like the British Council and nor, in fact, do I. At least I am most suspicious of their activities. I have watched their Fine Arts Directors in various capitals. For the most part they are social climbers with little – or no – interest in art.' Whatever Clark's attitude may have been, the timing of this comment from Sutherland has to be seen in the context of a note in the minutes of the Committee on 29 January 1952, in which it was reported that Clark had offered to lend to the British Council a long list of contemporary British pictures.

The way in which the British Council went about promoting contemporary British art outside Britain was to arrange exhibitions in foreign countries. In the Winter of 1945-1946, nine British artists were shown in Paris[30] ('Quelques contemporains anglais')[31] and in 1946, as we have seen, a selection of modern British art from the Tate – 'Tableaux Britanniques modernes appartenant à la Tate Gallery' – travelled to Paris[32] and then on to Athens, Berne, Brussels, Rome, Stockholm and Vienna. In 1947 Australia received 'Contemporary British Paintings and Drawings', selected from the British Council's Wakefield Collection.[33] Included in this exhibition in the watercolours and drawings section were works by Collins, Colquhoun, Hennell, Hodgkins, Augustus John, Minton, Paul and John Nash, Piper, Roberts and Gilbert Spencer. South Africa got 'Contemporary British Art' in 1947-48. The pictures for this exhibition were selected by Maclagan, Coldstream, Gwynne-Jones and Rothenstein and Coldstream wrote an introduction to the catalogue. At this time, towards the end of 1947, the minutes started to identify groups of people who were to be asked to form a selection committee for particular overseas exhibitions. Significantly, those asked did not have to be members of the Committee and were often chosen as well-known experts in the field.

Sweden got 'Contemporary Art' at the beginning of 1947 and again at the beginning of 1948. The Committee had asked Clark (or, failing him, Anderson), Rothenstein and Clive Bell to select the pictures for Sweden. At the same time Read, Hendy and Mortimer (later replaced by art critic Michael Middleton) were asked to select pictures to go to four European centres during 1948-49. Greece, Italy, France and Czechoslovakia got an 'Exhibition of Modern British Painting (1942-1947)' in 1947-48. Paris and Brussels got another opportunity to see the work of young British artists with 'La Jeune Peinture en Grande – Bretagne' in 1948-49.[34] 'Contemporary British Drawings' then went to Canada in 1948. Philip James in the catalogue introduction repeated the often repeated line that interest in art was increasing:

> It is no exaggeration to say that in the last decade, not excluding the war years, a vast new public
> has discovered the rich experience to be gained through an enjoyment of the arts.

There is no way of checking exactly how much of this statement does, in fact, represent an exaggeration. It probably simply meant that he had the impression that there were a lot of exhibitions going on and a lot of people attending them.[35] Whether there were more than previously is unknown. It is also possible that he said it because it was an

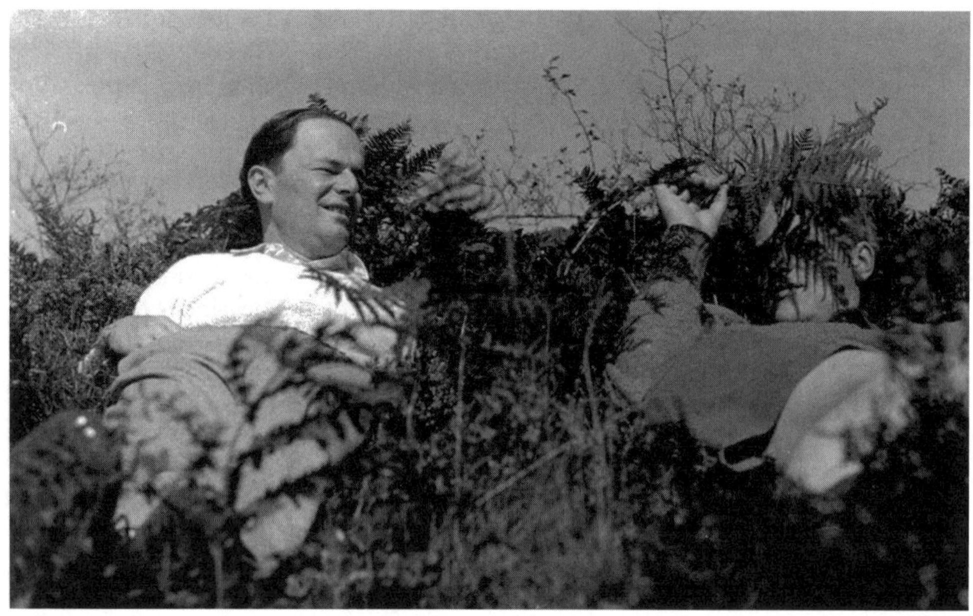

impression which he wanted to create, whether or not he actually believed it. What is undoubtedly a rashly unverifiable statement is the idea that those new crowds were, in some way, discovering a new or rich experience. Today large numbers of people go to 'blockbuster' art exhibitions, but what they experience at them is hard to tell.[36] In any event, this exhibition had many of the usual favourites: including Bawden, Colquhoun, Gillies, Hodgkins, John, Jones, Lewis, Lowry, Maxwell, Minton, Paul Nash, Ben Nicholson, Paolozzi, Piper, Stanley Spencer, Sutherland, Turnbull and Vaughan.[37]

Next it was Australia's turn again, in 1949, with 'Eleven British Artists'. They got a truly bizarre grouping: Gowing, Hitchens, Le Bas, Ben Nicholson, Pasmore, Hillier, Hodgkins, Lowry, Sir William Nicholson, Piper and Tunnard. The catalogue introduction was by A.J.L. McDonnell and without interest apart from the fact that he was to appear two years later as one of the judges for '60 Paintings for '51'. The exhibition visited Perth, Adelaide, Melbourne, Sydney, Brisbane, Hobart and Launceston. Then it was back to Canada in 1949-1950 with Paul Nash, then Germany got a dose of English culture in 1950-1951 with 'Moderne Englische Zeichnungen and Aquarelle', selected by Geoffrey Grigson. His introduction was in German and those shown included another permutation of those who by this time must be regarded as the sort of artists always chosen to represent the British Council abroad: Burra, Colquhoun, Craxton, Hodgkins, Jones, Lewis, Minton, Ben Nicholson, Stanley Spencer, Sutherland, Vaughan, Wadsworth and Wynter. 1950 saw Craxton, Freud and Hitchens featured in a show called 'British Painting and Sculpture 1925-1950', which was held at the Academy of Fine Arts in Pennsylvania.

Finally it was back to Canada and on into the US in 1951 for some more cultural nourishment, with an exhibition called '21 Modern British Painters'. This travelled to Vancouver, Seattle, San José, San Francisco, Salt Lake City and Portland. The selection committee was named in the catalogue (although this had not been done previously), as

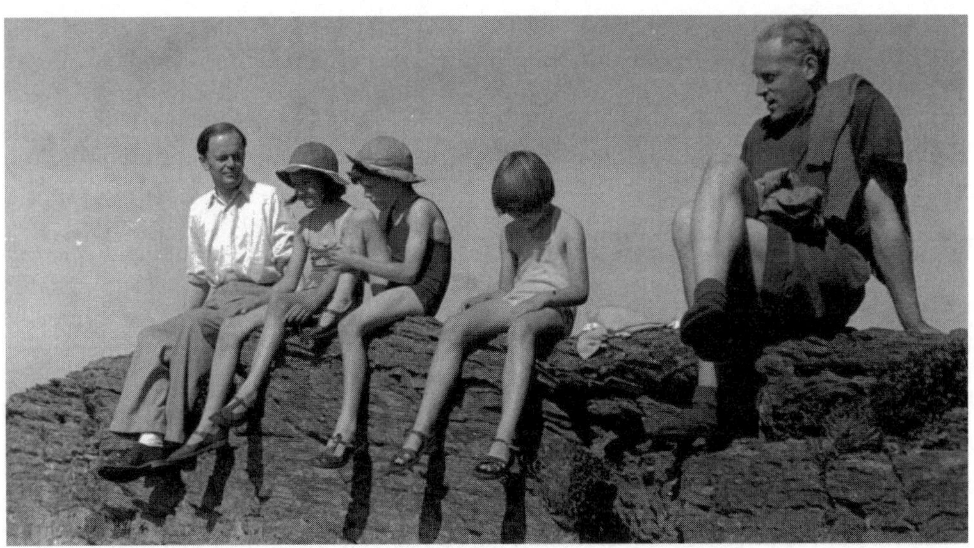

Family pictures (above and opposite) of Kenneth Clark and Colin Anderson

Mrs Horace Somerville,[38] Basil Taylor[39] and Denys Sutton.[40] The catalogue had an introduction by Doris Shadbolt, the education director of the Vancouver Art Gallery. Interestingly, she noted that contemporary British artists were little known in North America, with the exception of Moore and Sutherland, especially on the West Coast. Again she chose to remind us of what someone like Philip James must have told her, namely that it was 'common knowledge that during the War the arts in Britain witnessed a tremendous upsurge of activity'. Another novelty for this exhibition was that the 37 pictures were for sale (see 'Money' in Chapter 4).

It is an indication of the stature of Henry Moore, as the pre-eminent British sculptor during this period, that he got British Council sponsored solo shows in Australia in 1947-1948; in Mexico in 1949-50; in Hamburg and Düsseldorf in 1950; and in Greece in 1951. He was, moreover, chosen as the British representative at the first Venice Biennale to be held following the end of the War, in 1948. The painters represented were Ben Nicholson and Tunnard. Arranging the British contribution to the Biennale was another function of the Committee. In preparation for the 1948 show, the minutes of the meeting held on 2 September 1947 noted that Bell, Clutton-Brock, Le Bas and Read had been chosen as the selection committee. By the time of the next Biennale, to be held outside our period in 1952, the selection committee[41] was Hendy, Read, Rothenstein and Basil Taylor.

The other activity which the Committee increasingly focused on during our period was buying contemporary British pictures. This first came up at the meeting on 29 May 1946 when £1,000 was allocated towards the purchase of such art. A sub-committee of two, initially Bell and Read, was established for the first year, with instructions that no work was to cost more than £200 without the approval of the whole Committee. It was assumed that this grant would enable the purchase of approximately 20 pictures at an average of £50 each. The first purchases mentioned thereafter were at the meeting on 12 September 1946 when works by MacBryde, Kenneth Martin, Paul Nash, Ben Nicholson and Smith were noted. At the next meeting (on 22 November) another work by Ben Nicholson was added, together with works by the rather safer Coldstream and Gowing.[42] There was then a very long gap for some reason until the next meeting (on 18 April 1947), by which time the Committee found it had acquired pictures by Colquhoun, Collins, Minton, Tunnard and Hennell, although these purchases were made using the money from the Wakefield bequest.

The pattern then changed for the second purchasing year. Philip Hendy was appointed on his own (presumably the sub-committee concept had proved cumbersome, as it did with the Arts Council, and the CAS method of sole purchaser was preferred), although he was allowed to decide himself if he needed someone else to be his co-purchaser. His first purchase was of a picture by Sutherland and there were Wakefield purchases of works by Sutherland, Colquhoun, Bateson Mason, Hurry and Wood. Then, at the meeting on 2 September 1947, there was an unexplained mention of a surprise one-off amount of spending money. Somebody had given the Committee £4,800 to spend. Hendy was allocated £800 of this, while a group consisting of Anderson, Rothenstein and Bell were given £2,000 to spend and another group consisting of Hendy, Michael Middleton and Read were given the other £2,000. As if in celebration, the Committee promptly approved the purchase of a Pasmore for £250 from the Redfern. Not surprisingly, by the time of the next meeting (on 25 February 1948), a big chunk of the bonanza had been spent, as follows:

Pasmore	(2 works, one for £250, the other £175)
Sutherland	£250
Tunnard	£160
Hepworth	£18 (a drawing)
Ben Nicholson	£175
Ayrton	£150
Lowry	£160
Moore	£150 (a sculpture).

Things had calmed down by the time of the next meeting (26 May) when only works by Gowing and Hepworth were recorded. At this point the Committee clearly felt it was time to take stock and see what they did actually own.[43] The whole collection was listed and there were found to be works by Appelbee, Aldridge, Ayrton, Coldstream, Colquhoun, Craxton, Gilman, Gore, Gowing, Grant, Hepworth, Hitchens, Hodgkins, Lowry, MacBryde, Martin, Moore, Paul Nash, Ben Nicholson, Pasmore, Piper, Roberts, Sickert, Smith, Sutherland, Tibble and Tunnard. Of these, the most expensive had been the following:

Sickert	£850
Smith	£675
Smith	£500
Smith	£325
Smith	£300
Moore	£300 (sculpture)
Paul Nash	£250
Pasmore	£250
Sutherland	£250.

The purchasing continued to be recorded as follows:

22 September 1948
Jones, Gertler, Ben Nicholson, Stanley Spencer, Sickert, Hodgkins, Hitchens, Lowry, MacBryde, Sutherland and Tunnard

8 December
Craxton, Winifred Nicholson, Moore and Ginner

16 February 1949
Ben Nicholson, Freud, Vaughan, Hitchens, MacBryde, Colquhoun, Smith, Paul Nash and Sutherland

27 April
Baynes, Burra, Grant, Hayes, Hitchens, Hodgkins, Gwen John, Paul Nash, Winifred Nicholson, Schwabe, Sickert and Spear

29 June
Ayron, Connard, Jones, Lewis, Moore, Moynihan, Paul Nash, Richards, Gilbert Spencer

8 September
Steer, Wynter, Piper

1 February 1950
Clough, Gilman, Gross, Lewis, Minton, Moore, Ben Nicholson and Tibble

11 July
Appelbee, de Maistre, Grant, Hepworth, Heron, Stanley Spencer and Ethelbert White

12 September
Barns-Graham, Burra, Craxton, Etchells, Ginner, Gwen John, Lewis, Sutherland, Wadsworth, Wood and Wells

13 February 1951
Ben Nicholson

8 May
Nothing.

Perhaps by this point the Committee felt that it had spent enough money and had a sufficiently representative collection for sending on its seemingly innumerable overseas exhibitions without drawing too heavily on the generosity of lenders.

The Contemporary Arts Society (the CAS)
The CAS had been founded in 1910 in order to acquire paintings and sculptures which were not more than 20 years old. These were to be acquired, exhibited as widely as possible, and then presented as gifts to national and municipal collections.[44] Funds were to come from these municipal galleries, in expectation of receiving gifts, and from individual members, of which there were said to have been 297 in April 1946, about 1,100 in April 1947 and approximately 1,750 in 1950. Until 1946 the CAS was physically located within the Tate and run by young Tate curators such as H.S. Ede and Robin Ironside, who acted as its Assistant Secretary. The CAS was able to make more adventurous purchases of modern British art than the more cautious Chantrey bequest, which was controlled by the Royal Academy. As with other institutions at around this time, the influence of Kenneth Clark on the CAS was considerable.[45] He was a committee member 1937-53[46] and his taste for certain types of contemporary British art influenced some of its acquisitions during the 1940s.[47] As will be seen in the section on him in Chapter 3, he gave a lot of pictures to the CAS by way of gift. There were other

committee members who made considerable contributions, such as Colin Anderson, a member 1945-65, who purchased the Society's first Bacon in 1946. (The fact that no galleries wanted the Bacon was not Anderson's fault. Rather perversely it ended up at the Art Gallery in Batley in Yorkshire after six years when no-one who was offered it by the CAS, including the Tate, wanted it.)

Towards the end of the War a part-time assistant was employed by the CAS for the first time in the form of the painter Denis Mathews. He was to stay until 1956 and is remembered for starting a programme of exhibitions at the Tate and for rapidly increasing the number of individual members. Each year a committee member was invited to be the Society's purchaser, and they exercised their personal taste to buy as many pictures as possible within their budget. This method of allowing an individual to exercise his discretion, as distinct from trying to make purchases by committee decision, was an unusual characteristic of the CAS and contrasts with the way in which the more public bodies, the Arts Council and the British Council, went about their purchasing. Every three or four years the CAS purchases were put on exhibition and directors of the member galleries were invited to submit their choices. These were then rationalised as well as possible and the pictures distributed. During our period, the buyers and the amounts which they had at their disposal to spend (where known) were:

1945	Lowinsky
1946	Anderson (£500)
1947	Le Bas (£700)
1948	Mortimer
1949	Ironside
1950	**Lord Methuen**
1951	Evill

The figures stated were from what was called the General Fund, and the buyers in this period also had a sum of money (£150) from the Prints and Drawing Fund. (There was also, at least at the beginning of the period, a separate Pottery and Crafts Fund). What the buyers bought is sometimes noted, especially as the procedure seemed to require them to place the pictures before the Committee for their approval, presumably before the purchases were confirmed. Anderson bought pictures by Bacon, Colquhoun, Weight and Le Brocquy (and maybe others). Le Bas bought two by Weight and one by Ginner. Ironside somehow managed to acquire works by Bacon (*Laughing Man* for £125), Margaret Kaye,[48] a Picasso lithograph, three by Craxton, Freud, Richards, Wilde, Jones, Brian Robb,[49] Winifred Nicholson, Pasmore and E. Box.[50] There was an exhibition at the Tate in September 1946 of 'Select Acquisitions of the Contemporary Art Society'. The *Times*[51] thought this to be a very appropriate venue for such an exhibition, because without the CAS it thought that the Tate 'could have made no claim to have any representative collection of 20th century paintings and sculpture'. Douglas Cooper was, of course, not so flattering. Writing in the *Burlington Magazine* in the December 1946 issue, he thought the system of allowing one person to exercise sole control over the year's purchases was too undisciplined and had led to poor decisions being made. For once it is hard to disagree with him that purchases of works by artists such as Ironside and Lowinsky (both, in fact, also buyers doing our period) were not up to the standards of works by more prestigious artists.

Apart from Kenneth Clark and Colin Anderson, it is highly instructive to note the members of the Committee during the 1945-1951 period because many of the names occur in various different guises in other parts of this book and the comparatively small number of names helps to illustrate one of our key themes: the tight concentration of the British art world of the time. Lord Keynes, who was to die in 1946, and whose influence on CEMA and the Arts Council is mentioned elsewhere, was a member of the committee from 1932 to his death. Thelma Cazalet-Keir (whose years on the committee were 1938-1956), John Rothenstein (1938-1965), Edward le Bas (1945-1956), Raymond Mortimer (1945-1965), Philip Hendy (1946-1957), Robin Ironside (1946-1952), Lord Methuen (1946-1953), Wilfrid Evill (1947-1963) and Howard Bliss (1950-1957) are all dealt with elsewhere as significant collectors (a pre-requisite, in any event, for getting on to the committee in the first place). That leaves a few slightly less well-known names (Arthur Hind, Tom Lowinsky, Vincent Massey, Lady Sempill, Alan Ward, Hugo Pitman and A.E. Popham) as the remainder of those serving on the committee at some point between 1945 and 1951.

The Artists' International Association (the AIA)

Founded in 1933 at a time of growing European political unrest and concern about fascism, the AIA was, in the years following the end of the War, to struggle to maintain its raison d'être. This had been to organise visual artists 'so as to enable them to express their commitment to social responsibility in art and to support radical, political ideas directly in terms of their practice as artists'.[52] Whatever its ideals, it had never had many members (not many more than 1,000 at its peak). Nevertheless, it had some claim to be the body which artists of the period turned to when they wanted to operate politically. It was also concerned with the occupational conditions of the working artist and designer and with trying to extend an interest in visual art to parts of the community not normally associated with it. All this meant that those artists in Britain who were actually Communists in Britain also saw the AIA as the body for them, even though its members and participants were far from all being Communists or even – especially after the War – particularly political in their outlook.

After the War the political scene changed. Fascists were largely irrelevant and the extreme wickedness of Soviet Communism in Eastern Europe was starting to become apparent to the West, as were the horrors of Stalinism. The Welfare State and the Labour Government changed the social environment in the UK and many ideas of popularising art, which the AIA had fostered before the War, were now taken over by the Arts Council. Accordingly, the members of the AIA were not sure whether they should still have a predominantly political purpose or if they were now just another art association with vaguely popularising ambitions. Chairmen came and went during the period. Morris Kestelman in 1945 was followed by Maurice de Sausmarez in 1946, Beryl Sinclair in 1947 and Richard Carline in 1950. One theme which did seem to have survived the War and the changed circumstances was the idea of encouraging popular art and, particularly, untrained artists. So an exhibition in 1945 was given over to a pavement artist, David Burton, and in 1948 there was a show which included the work of George Poole (a Battersea carpenter) and Eric Thornton (a foundry-man). In 1950 an exhibition called 'The Coalminers' was held.

In April 1947 premises were taken at Lisle Street, close to Leicester Square, and many shows were to be held there. Of note was the interesting combination of Lowry, Minton,

Rothenstein, Trevelyan, Uhlman and Weight in October 1949 and the challenging show of 'Abstract Art' during the Festival of Britain, including works by Frost, Heath, Hepworth, Hilton, B. Nicholson, Paolozzi, Pasmore and others. But gradually the characteristics which had, before the War, made the AIA the body through which they might operate when they wanted to be overtly political changed. Those members, including artists, who still wanted to be 'political' in the AIA were perceived by others as Communists and that was not acceptable to others who simply wanted to use the AIA as

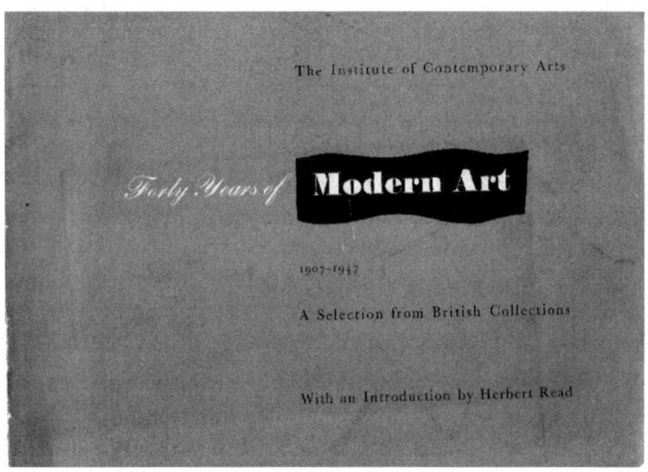

an artistically radical group and exhibition centre. Various confrontations took place in the second half of the 1940s, until in October 1949 the committee published a policy statement which stated that 'no action on any issue which could have a political interpretation will be taken without consultation with the membership.' So it was that when, in 1950, Leslie Hurry, Minton, Herman and Pasmore urged the members to complain about the threat to world peace posed by the campaign in Korea, the members were suspicious and divided. By the time a similar group (together with Rowntree, Spear, Weight and Rogers, among others) wanted the AIA to support the 'Peace movement' in the early 1950s, it was all over for the AIA as a politically motivated body and the three 'Artists for Peace' exhibitions organised by some of those artists in the period 1951-53 were organised outside the AIA.

The Institute of Contemporary Arts (the ICA)

In January 1946 Herbert Read met Roland Penrose and Edward Mesens to consider the creation of a London-based Museum of Modern Art, in emulation of the one in New York. Whilst the original intention was to attract 500 subscribers at £100 each, so as to have sufficient capital to have permanent premises, with theatre and library, the reality, which came into existence during 1947, was rather more modest. Its ambitions, influenced particularly by Surrealism, were to create an experimental and international artistic organisation, independent of the State and State control. It was partly enabled to struggle into life by the support of the reasonably newly created Arts Council, which saw the Institute of Contemporary Art, as it was now called, as relieving some of the pressure on the Arts Council to hold exhibitions of avant-garde work. Philip James, director of the Arts Council's Art Department, was a great supporter of the ICA and the Arts Council gave it £500 in 1947. Although the idea seems to have originated at least partially in the mind of Herbert Read, the other constituting members need to be mentioned. An important participant was Peter Watson, who had a clear understanding of contemporary European art in his capacity as a highly refined collector himself. Eric (Peter) Gregory was another founder, as were the critics Robert Melville and Geoffrey Grigson, the film maker, JB Brunius, George Hoellering, proprietor of the Academy Cinema in Oxford Street, JM Richards,[53] editor of the *Architectural Review*, and, very briefly, Douglas Cooper, who soon fell out with everyone.[54] By February 1947 the Committee had been increased to fifteen people, now including Alex Comfort,[55] actress Peggy Ashcroft, Jack Beddington[56] and Michael St Denis, who was Director of the Old Vic. The first public announcement of the existence of the ICA was made by a letter from Read to the *Times* on 26 June 1947. The first exhibition was held in Hoellering's basement from 10 February to 6 March 1948 and was called 'Forty Years of Modern Art, 1907-1947. A Selection from British Collections'. 127 works were shown[57] from a wide variety of British and foreign artists, including 3 Braques, 5 de Chiricos, 2 Dalis, 3 Matisses, and 5 Picassos and the inevitable Colquhoun, MacBryde, Nash, Nicholson, Sutherland, Craxton and Moore, as well as the rather less well-known Freud and Bacon (who are likely to have been promoted by Watson). Paolozzi also made an early appearance and there was the inevitable range of reactions in the press. About 16,000 people attended. The catalogue reproduced a portrait of Dora Maar by Picasso, which had been lent to the exhibition by Arthur Jeffress. He was also noted as one of the people, alongside Kenneth Clark, Philip James and Basil Burton (together with the

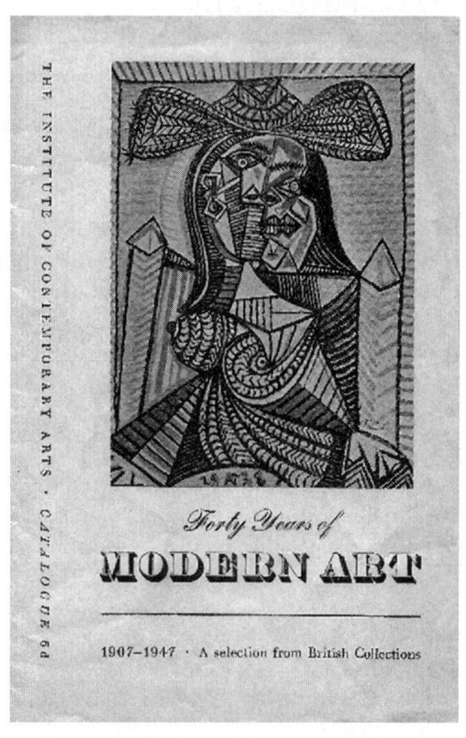

Southampton Art Gallery) who had financially supported the show as well as lending pictures.

There was a long list of lenders. Peter Watson lent works by John Banting, Gris, Klee and a piece of sculpture by Henry Moore. Clark lent pictures by Matisse, Rouault, Sutherland and Tchelitchew and a bronze by Maillol. The 'Organising Committee' of the ICA for this first exhibition was listed as Herbert Read (Chairman), Frederic Ashton, Jack Beddington, JB Brunius, Edward Clark, Alex Comfort, Michael St Denis, Eric Gregory, Geoffrey Grigson, GM Hoellering, Robert Melville, ELT Mesens, Roland Penrose, JM Richards, Peter Watson and Bill Williams (with Ivo Jarosy[58] as secretary). Later in the same year (opening on 21 December) the ICA came up with the rather more provocatively titled '40,000 years of Modern Art', which ranged from ancient sculptures (often highly abstract) to Picasso's *Les Demoiselles d'Avignon*, appearing in Britain for the first time. Unfortunately, the size of Picasso's work had not been appreciated, and part of the wall had to be knocked down to get it in. The Arts Council donated £400 to the show, which met with more mixed reviews, even among the more learned critics such as Sylvester (in the *New Statesman*) and Eric Newton (in the *Times*), as well as the inevitably critical Douglas Cooper (in the *Observer*).

In April 1950 the ICA moved into its first permanent home, a gallery on the first floor of 17 Dover Street. T.S. Eliot opened the first exhibition held there, which was called 'James Joyce, his life and work'. As its contribution to the Festival of Britain, the ICA came up with 'Ten Decades. A Review of British Taste 1851-1951', for which the Arts Council gave £1500 (for this exhibition see Chapter 7 below).

The Thomas Haverty Trust

Established under the will of Thomas Haverty, son of the Galway painter Joseph Patrick Haverty (1794-1864), an endowment produced an annual sum (from about 1928 onwards) which was to be spent on encouraging the development of art in Ireland. As such, it was the largest endowment to which contemporary Irish artists could look for patronage.[59] Paintings were selected by the trustees, who initially consisted of the President of the Royal Hibernian Academy, the Director of the National Gallery of Ireland, the Lord Mayor of Dublin, the Lord Mayor of Belfast, the Curator of the Belfast Museum and Art Gallery, and three other representatives from the National Gallery of Ireland and the RHA. Once purchased, paintings were donated to appropriate museums or galleries.[60] Unfortunately this did not guarantee an absence of controversy, right from the beginning of the Trust's activities. The first picture purchased, in 1930, was, needless to say, by Yeats, as the leading Irish contemporary painter of the time. While the trustees no doubt thought they were being particularly up to date by purchasing *The Liffey Swim*, the artist himself decried their choice: 'I hoped they would have taken something wilder, but there were some cold feet.' Then it was impossible to give it to its natural home – the National Gallery of Ireland – because it was not at the time permitted to hang the work of living artists. The painting was then offered to the Municipal Gallery of Modern Art (the Hugh Lane), but was refused. Eventually it was taken in by the Crawford Gallery in Cork before finally finding its way into the National Gallery's collection.[61] The Ulster Museum has a number of works by the prominent Irish artists of the period mentioned in this book which it received from the Trust, often surprisingly early on in the life of the artists' reputation. For example, it received two works by Le Brocquy through the Trust as early as 1945 and a picture by Luke as early as 1941. An O'Neill picture arrived by this route in 1951, as did a Dillon, but Campbell was not picked up in this way until 1957.

ART SCHOOLS

In 1945, the main London art schools were the Slade, the Royal College of Art, the Central and Camberwell. The Slade had been founded in 1871 as part of University College, London. During the War the school had been evacuated to Oxford, where it had shared the premises of the Ruskin School of Art. Its Professor, Randolph Schwabe, died in September 1948 and, after not inconsiderable manoeuvrings behind the scenes, Coldstream was eventually appointed, following an early intervention in his favour by the ubiquitous Kenneth Clark, in July 1949. This long delay, following the disruption of the War years, taken together with the dilapidated buildings and lack of funding, meant that Coldstream inherited a famous but now rather dispirited institution. He calculated that the ratio of teaching days by staff to student days was 1 to 20 at Camberwell and the Royal College of Art, but 1 to 62 at the Slade, thereby justifying some new teaching appointments. Among those appointed to the staff were Aldridge and Freud and many well-known names were added as 'Visitors', including Ardizzone, Léger, Moore, Pasmore, Piper, Sutherland and Vaughan. None of the staff inherited by Coldstream were well-known painters in their own right.

The Royal College of Art, founded in 1837, had spent the War in the Lake District. It had a Professor (Gilbert Spencer 1938-48 and Moynihan 1948-57) and also a Principal, who was Percy Jowett from 1935 to the end of 1947 and Robin Darwin 1948-71. We know from Moynihan's well-known picture *Portrait Group (the Teaching Staff of the Painting School at the Royal College of Art 1949-1950)* (Tate) painted in 1951, that the staff by the end of the decade (assuming, of course, the accuracy of the picture) consisted of Minton, Moynihan, Rowntree, Burn, Buhler, Hays, Mahoney, Weight and Spear. In fact, Moynihan, Minton, Spear and Buhler had only recently arrived from the Central School, Darwin having, in modern terminology, 'poached' them, much to the disgust of William Johnstone, the aggrieved Principal of the Central at the time.

The Central School had been founded in 1896. In the second half of the 1940s Morris Kestelman, Bernard Meninsky and William Roberts taught there. William Johnstone became Principal in 1947 and, by the early

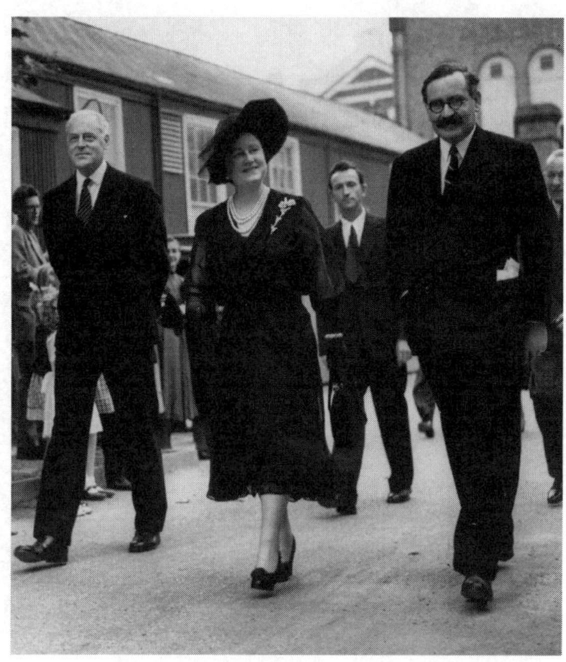

Robin Darwin (right), Principal of the Royal College of Art with Colin Anderson and Queen Elizabeth (the Queen Mother), 1952

1950's, Collins and Peake had arrived. As we have seen previously, a number of members of the teaching staff moved over to the RCA in 1948.

The Camberwell School of Arts & Crafts opened in 1898. The clustering of former Euston Road artists who gathered there around Pasmore at the end of the War has been described earlier. Camberwell seems to have found itself particularly swamped by ex-servicemen enrolling on one or other of its courses.[62] As such, it was quite a difficult place to administer. Until his departure to the Central School in 1947, William Johnstone was the Principal[63] and matters were apparently not helped by tension between him and Coldstream. He was followed by Leonard Daniels who held the position of Principal from 1948-1975. Daniels was responsible for introducing to the teaching staff the German artist, Martin Bloch.[64] Other well known artists who had a period teaching at Camberwell included Ardizzone, who taught illustration there 1948-51; Eurich; Minton, who taught illustration, composition and perspective 1943-47; Peake; Rosoman, 1946-48; Rothenstein, teaching in the print-making and graphics section 1948-58; Gilbert Spencer, who became Head of Painting in 1950; and Vaughan.

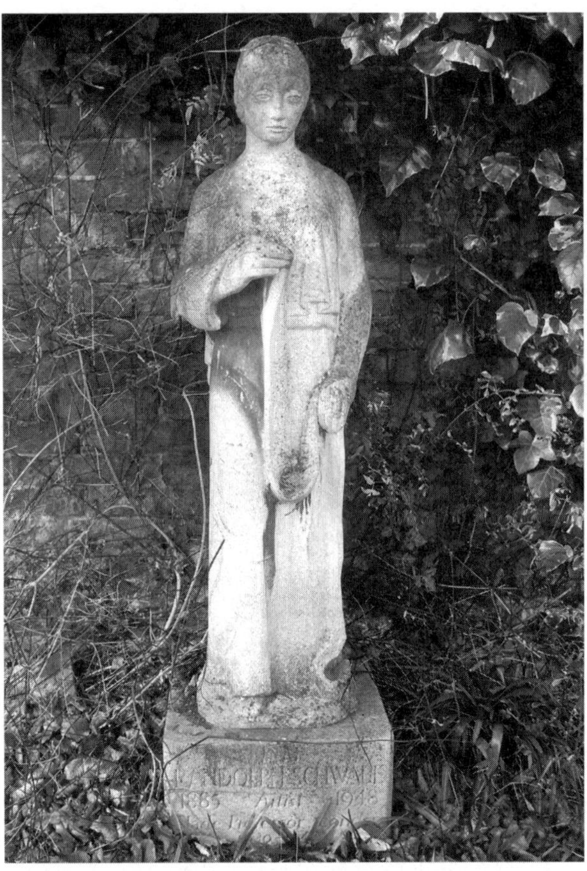

Memorial to Randolphe Schwabe,
Hampstead churchyard

There were many other schools of all sorts scattered around London and in other parts of the country and particularly worthy of mention is Corsham in Wiltshire. This was the Bath Academy of Art, moved in 1946 by Clifford Ellis from Bath to Corsham Court, the home of the painter Lord Methuen. William Scott was appointed first Senior Painting Master, Kenneth Armitage joined as head of sculpture, and later teachers to arrive included Frost, Lanyon and Wynter. Another rural art school was the East Anglian School of Painting and Drawing at Benton End in Suffolk. This had been established by Cedric Morris and Arthur Lett-Haines at Benton End in 1940, having been located at other places in Suffolk before then. The elaborately cultivated garden at Benton End was particularly important to the atmosphere of the school, which was kept quite deliberately away from and outside the more commercial imperatives of the London schools. As a consequence, teaching was not driven towards the generation of commercially successful artists and the intention of the founders was to enable their students to develop their own skills at their own pace. One of its prospectuses described it as 'an oasis of decency for artists outside the system'. Many artists benefited from this unique system (including the young Freud and, at a later date, Maggi Hambling), which survived as long as its founders were able to manage.

Mention has been made of the Scottish schools in the section on Edinburgh and Glasgow. In Dublin, the College of Art had been founded in the 18th century and the Cork (or Crawford) School of Art in the 19th century. The Belfast College of Art also had its origins in the 19th century.

Public galleries and museums

For our purposes, the key questions facing public galleries and museums in the British Isles in 1945 were whether they had any interest in purchasing modern art of any kind and, if so, were permitted by their constitutions and whether they could afford to do so. For modern British art, a great deal turns on the position of the Tate in respect of these key questions and here, needless to say, the position was complicated. Although modern art was supposed to come to the Tate, there was an inevitable difficulty about defining what was modern and about when it should cease to be regarded as modern. There was also the small problem that the Tate had absolutely no public funding whatsoever before 1946. In light of this, a committee had been set up on 28 April 1944 under the chairmanship of Vincent Massey 'to examine the functions of the National Gallery and the Tate Gallery and, in respect of paintings, of the Victoria and Albert Gallery, with special reference to their relations with one another and to the further representation of British art; and to consider the working of the Chantrey Bequest'. The membership of the committee[65] reads like a roll-call of the great and the good of the London art world at this time: Leigh Ashton, Kenneth Clark, Eric Maclagan, Sir Jasper Ridley and John Rothenstein.[66] This committee met for the first time on 6 July 1944 and reported its findings to the Chancellor of the Exchequer on 29 December 1944. The 28-page report which resulted was published on 28 May 1946.[67] Most of its recommendations inevitably related to the Tate, the most prominent being that the Tate should be split into two departments: a national gallery of British art of all periods; and a national gallery of modern art.[68] 'Modern' should be work of not more than 100 years old. As regards the wretched state of the Chantrey Bequest, the best thing, according to the report, would be for the Tate to be given control of this in future (it amounted to about £2,100 p.a.) together with public funding from the Treasury of £3,000 p.a. (The total sum from public funds was to be £5,000 p.a. if the Chantrey money was not able to be handed over.) Needless to say, it is not clear whether any of the committee's recommendations were adopted, save that the Tate did start to get public funding (of £2,000 p.a.) from 1946 onwards.

The Tate Gallery

By the end of the War[69] the Tate had suffered very serious bomb damage and was largely unusable. After extensive repairs, a small part re-opened in April 1946, but the remainder was not back in use until 24 February 1949. In the gap between the end of the War and the partial re-opening, the Tate organised an exhibition of Klee at the National Gallery (opening on 22 December 1945). This means that at the end of the same year as the War had finished, the London public was able to see Picasso and Matisse at the V&A and Klee at the National Gallery. So much for the idea that the British public was unable to see modern pictures in the mid-1940s. When six restored galleries opened on 10 April 1946, there were three small exhibitions (curiously, promoted by three separate institutions): an Arts Council show of Cézanne watercolours; a British Council exhibition of Braque oils and Rouault aquatints; and the collection of British art of Vincent Massey, which he was soon to donate to the National Gallery of Canada.

The complexity of affairs at the Tate following the War is an illustration of the elaborately inter-linked nature of the British art world at this time (and perhaps at many other times). To begin with, John Rothenstein, as the surviving pre-War director, had to cajole government departments to organise repairs to the building as quickly as possible, and a lot more quickly than would otherwise have happened in those austere and sobering months which followed the brief euphoria which marked the end of the War. Pictures had to be recovered from their wartime hiding-places out of London. A small and badly-paid staff had to wrestle with the extremes of their bomb-damaged building and transitional circumstances.

The director had to keep his trustees happy. In 1945 there were ten trustees: Sir Muirhead Bone, Kenneth Clark, Allan Gwynne-Jones, Henry Lamb, Vincent Massey, Henry Moore, Hugo Pitman, Sir Jasper Ridley (the chairman), Sir Donald Somervell and Charles Wheeler. Later additions to this group were Philip Hendy and John Piper in 1946; Sutherland in 1948; Coldstream in 1949; and Edward Bawden and Sir Osbert Sitwell in 1951. (A number of those listed also retired during the period.) It was important for Rothenstein to maintain decent relations with the chairman of the trustees – Sir Jasper Ridley throughout our period – and he had somehow to apportion the absurdly low purchase grant which was available to him between British and foreign paintings and sculpture, a balancing act which simply could not be successfully achieved, in the sense that it could not be done in such a way as to keep the different constituent parts of the British art world happy. A number of controversies flourished in the small world of mid-20th century art occupied by the Tate – small to the point of claustrophobia – and it is difficult now to see who was to blame for too many British pictures being purchased at the expense of foreign pictures, or too few, or pictures of the wrong period or quality, or at the wrong price. Every decision taken was scrutinised internally (for example by the trustees, with their differing standpoints) and externally (for example by the ever-irascible Douglas Cooper). In addition, seemingly endless strife took place between the Tate and the Royal Academy,[70] which administered the Chantrey Bequest and which seems to have taken some pleasure, or at least pride, in using the Chantrey money to buy British art of the type and period which the Tate director was none too keen on (no agreement on the purchases, which ended up at the Tate, having to be made with the Tate).[71] Although there was a 'Recommending Committee', it had two representatives of the Tate and three of the Royal Academy on it, so that the RA could always outvote the Tate. Even if the Committee agreed on a purchase, the ultimate say was with the President and Council of the Royal Academy, who were able to turn down works supported by both parts of the Recommending Committee, such as the surely utterly innocuous work by Tristram Hillier rejected in 1946, a year in which apparently, only £50 of the £2,100 p.a. available from the Chantrey Bequest was actually spent.[72]

Smarting from this sort of treatment, and its view of the generally low quality of works bought over the years with the Chantrey money and imposed upon it,[73] the Tate encouraged the Royal Academy to put on a display at the RA of all of the Chantrey pictures in January 1949 (there were 437 exhibits and many, if not most, had to be brought out of the Tate's storage). This was accompanied by the extraordinary spectacle of the director of the Tate publishing an article on the leader page of The *Daily Telegraph* on 20 January 1949 headed 'Why the Tate does not show its Chantrey pictures'. Many reviews appeared, some alleging that vast sums of money supposedly spent over the years for the public good had, in fact, been wasted on work not of the highest quality, and others viewing the collection calmly and not without at least qualified support. An anonymous reviewer in the *Sunday Times* on 9 January saw the exhibition not as a field-day for the critics but as a 'nostalgic feast' for the general public.

He made the point that many of his generation had grown up with reproductions of many of the pictures shown, and they were likely to receive a much warmer welcome than a great deal of modern art. Writing a week later on the same subject, the paper's usual art critic, Eric Newton, in a piece entitled 'Chantrey afterthoughts' said that it was not so much an exhibition of British art as a commentary on British taste. The pictures were 'monuments to the mutability of taste'. Wyndham Lewis, writing in the *Listener* on 13 January, had no hesitation in indicating which side of the debate he was on: 'It would have been better to leave the Tate completely empty, rather than hang any of the Chantrey pictures.' He concluded with the helpful suggestion that the RA might like 'to keep this collection of ghastly junk itself'.[74] The *Listener* followed this up on 17 February with a piece taken from a show on the Third Programme, in which Sir Gerald Kelly had made what he could of the case for the RA; John Rothenstein had presented the case against and an unnamed King's Counsel had given a legal interpretation of the proper application of the Chantrey funds.

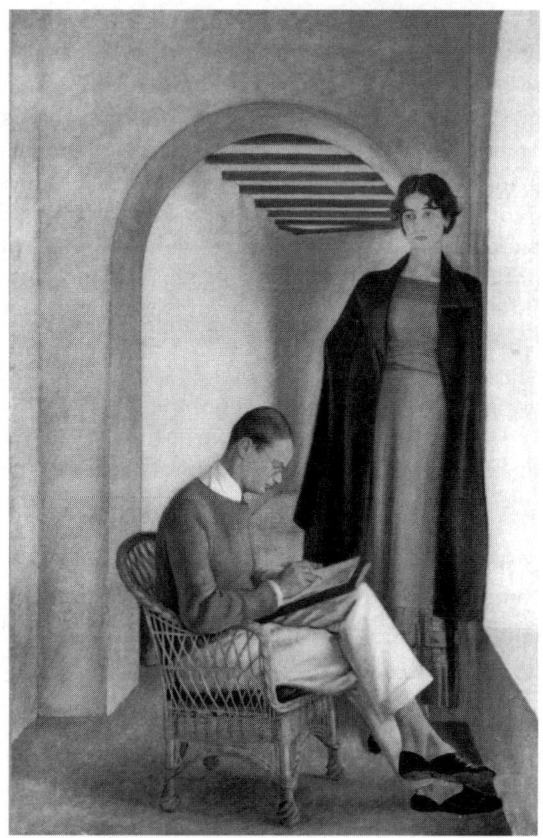

The young John Rothenstein and his wife
by William Rothenstein (1872-1945)

It can be highly illuminating when the cool spotlight of legal analysis is applied to the affairs of the art world, then as now. (One thinks of the later case brought by the Bacon Estate against the Marlborough Gallery, with its many fascinating insights into the relationships between galleries and their artists.) Here, the KC, instructed by the BBC and, of course, ignoring the competing demands of taste and fashion, was able to say that, in his view, it would not be easy to sustain an allegation that the RA had behaved in breach of the terms of the will in administering the Chantrey Bequest. The original purpose of the Bequest was not, in fact, to build up a great representative collection of modern art; it was more limited than that.[75] Sir Gerald Kelly made a particularly telling point in his defence of the RA, pointing out – no doubt correctly – that if, as had been suggested, the RA acted in breach of the will trust and handed control of the funds to the Tate, the result would simply be 'a new series of purchases which would be just as unacceptable to posterity as the Collection now on view at Burlington House is to so many of us today'.[76]

The *Times* paid full attention to the opening of the exhibition as well, with a long review and also a long leader article on 8 January. The reviewer thought it was important to try to understand this extraordinary collection, particularly as it had been assembled in the period up to 1922, when the Tate had started to be involved in the selection process. In view of the original terms of the bequest, which required those purchasing paintings with it only to buy works 'of the highest merit… that can be obtained', it was quite hard to understand how the pictures chosen could ever have satisfied this requirement. The writer of the leader noted, astutely, that 'no doubt the Tate expects the present exhibition to demonstrate that most of these works should not be exhibited'. Interestingly, the apparent controversy either did not stir up as much interest in *Times* letter writers as one might have expected or the editor chose not to print many on the subject.77 The only letter of substance seems to have been from Charles Wheeler who was later to become President of the Royal Academy. His letter was published on 29 June and it was an extremely judicious and balanced piece (he being at the time both a member of the RA and a trustee of the Tate). He gently pointed out that perhaps both sides had shown a lack of 'the need to appreciate more fully the ephemeral nature of present values, as well as a slight over-confidence in our estimate of ultimate values'. He particularly emphasised that, from his personal knowledge as an insider on both sides, he could confirm that all those involved in selecting the pictures to be bought by the fund had discharged their responsibilities seriously and properly. Raymond Mortimer, writing in *The New Statesman and Nation* on 15 January 1949 under the heading 'The Tate versus the Academy', came down on the side of the Tate, but not before he had noted that even some of the purchases made under the shared influence of Tate representatives had been a little odd. 'Deeply as I respect the Tate Board, I fear that their representatives have been accomplices in many perplexing purchases.' (He said that he had in mind works by Dame Laura Knight, Harold Knight and Meredith Frampton.) Some of his comments were dryly sarcastic. 'Among living painters the one on whose work it has been thought wise to spend most money is the present President of the Academy.' This was, of course, Munnings. He also thought it shocking that, at a time when the Tate had virtually no grant of its own to spend on purchases, the £2,000 p.a. available from the Chantrey money had only been spent as to £186 in 1941; £45 in 1942; and £90 in 1946. He concluded by saying that 'The public, I fancy, will decide that in this contest the Tate Board have won, hands down.' Whatever the controversy (or perhaps because of it), the exhibition seems to have been a financial success and Sir Charles Wheeler records in his autobiography78 that when the RA sent all the works back to the Tate at the end of the exhibition, no doubt to be put back into storage, it sent the Tate a cheque for £1,000 towards their purchase funds.

Not content with regularly falling out with the Royal Academy, the Tate also had from time to time to do battle with the National Gallery. From its foundation in 1897, the Tate had in formal terms been an annexe of the National Gallery (its original full title being The National Gallery of British Art), whose trustees owned the Tate's collection. Because of the confusion over which gallery was supposed to hold British/foreign/modern art (and the evolving definition of 'modern' over time), there were awkward tensions between the Tate and the National Gallery as to which of them should have certain works. With the director of the National Gallery inevitably feeling superior in rank to the director of the Tate, demands were made at various stages after the War by the National Gallery for the Tate to transfer some of its French pictures to the National Gallery. Rothenstein resisted these demands (from Philip Hendy, who had taken over from Kenneth Clark at the National Gallery in 1945), but eventually in 1950 he could resist no longer and 14 French pictures were moved to the National Gallery against the wishes of the Tate.[79]

There was great potential for strife with his own trustees – later to escalate so spectacularly into the so-called 'Tate Affair', thankfully outside the period of this book – and Rothenstein maintained the practice of appointing artist trustees, with Piper in 1946, Sutherland in 1948, Coldstream in 1949 and Bawden in 1951.[80] Unfortunately, the effect seems to have been mixed in that some, at least, of the artist trustees (especially Sutherland) not only had strong and dogmatic views on which pictures should and should not be acquired, but also had a propensity for a level of mischief in achieving their wishes which matched that of any of the non-artist trustees.

None the less, amid the different arguments and intrigue, there were highlights. Many fine British pictures were acquired, including the pick of the work which had been produced during the War under the supervision of the War Artists Advisory Committee. In 1945 seventy-three pictures were obtained from this source, followed by a further 90 in 1949. In addition, exhibitions of various types continued to be held in the Tate, among those of modern artists being Chagall in 1948, as well as Paul Nash and Jack Yeats. Léger arrived in 1950 and Wadsworth in 1951.

Victoria & Albert

In April 1945 the tenure of long-serving Director, Sir Eric Maclagan, came to an end. He was followed by Leigh Ashton, who was Director until 1955. One of the frequently repeated views by later art historians on the period covered by this book is that the Picasso and Matisse exhibition held at the V&A in late 1945[81] was a major turning-point for British artists of the period, starved, as they must have been, of recent experience of that greatest of modern artists, Picasso. We have already questioned whether these great 'turning-points' should be permitted to carry so much weight and emphasis in an objective analysis of earlier artistic periods, and some examination of this particular exhibition is therefore crucial for a variety of reasons. According to the *Times*, the exhibition had been arranged by something called the *Direction Générale des relations culturelles* in Paris, in co-operation with the French Embassy in London and the British Council. The precise involvement of the latter was not altogether clear and certainly caught the attention of some who wanted to attack the showing of the pictures. There were 24 pictures by Picasso, all from the period 1942-45 while he had remained working in occupied Paris. They were:

Woman with Mandolin
Nude
Seated Woman
Pigeon and Child
Woman and Rocking Chair
The Window
The Sailor
Woman in Arm Chair
Woman on Sofa
Portrait of a Lady
Woman with Green Dress
Child with Crawfish

Woman – Grey Composition (x2)
Small Child with Flower
Still Life – Skull with Leeks
Seated Woman
Royan
Window and Bullock's Head
Still Life – with saucepan
Paris – La Cité
Basket and Flower Vase
Woman with Fish Hat
Still Life – white background.

The works by Matisse were less controversial and generally seemed to fare rather well in the eyes of the British public compared with the Picassos.

An illustration of the impact of the exhibition can be gleaned from the *Times*. It first seems to have been mentioned there on 5 December, when some of the pictures were reproduced, and ten days later a letter was printed describing the Picassos as 'monstrosities'. This started an avalanche of correspondence (although of course one never knows how many letters the editor had, what percentage he chose to print and whether he allowed those printed accurately to reflect the balance of opinions of those received). First to reply was the well-known BBC man Harman Grisewood. On the same day those inveterate troublemakers, Thomas Bodkin (who was Irish) and D.S. MacColl (who was Scottish), wrote a joint letter condemning the exhibition as being of 'highly disputable merit' and querying how the V&A had come to be used for such an exhibition. This was on 17 December and now letters were printed almost daily, often from distinguished or well-known people. On 18 December Norman Wilkinson, President of the Royal Institute of Painters in Watercolours, said that 'the time has come when someone should come into the open and challenge the movement which was crystallized in the exhibition now on view at South Kensington. Fostered by a clique, backed by the British Council and supported by Government money, this exhibition is an insult both to artists and the intelligent public'. Next day, Lord Ivor Churchill's[82] letter was published and also one from Lord Brabazon of Tara, [83] which was also highly critical of the British Council. (This provoked a reply on behalf of the British Council pointing out that there had been no cost to the Council.) There were three other critical letters that day. On the next day Evelyn Waugh had his turn, of course highly critical of Picasso, whose 'painting cannot be intelligently discussed in the terms used of the civilised masters'. And so it went on, with more letters published on 21, 22 and 24 and then on 27, 29 (from Topolski, curiously criticising Picasso for being a representative of a style which was itself now well out of date), 31 December, 2 January 1946 (from MacColl again – this time thumping Herbert Read as 'our most distinguished lover of bad painting' and also taking the opportunity to take a swipe at Paul Klee, whose major show at the National Gallery had opened on 22 December, an exhibition dismissed by MacColl as 'doodles'), 4 January (a reply from Read), 7 (Sir Edward Marsh) and on 8 January a rather interesting letter from Cyril Asquith.[84] He reviewed some of the earlier correspondence and particularly felt drawn to comment on what he saw as two fallacies coming through the letters. The first was that later opinion of works of art almost always turned out to be sounder than contemporary opinion. A number of the correspondents who had denigrated critics of the exhibition had done so by noting that contemporary commentators were unlikely to be as perceptive as later critics. 'Is not a decline in public taste a frequent phenomenon?' Secondly, and relatedly, he thought it was another fallacy for some letter-writers to assert that works of art condemned by contemporary opinion often went on to be approved by later writers. In fact, he said, most art which contemporaries thought to be rubbish was actually rubbish and remained so.

By now the saga was almost exhausted. The great Picasso scholar (and another determined controversialist) Douglas Cooper had his say on 9 January and the editor obviously decided that enough was enough on 12 January, when he printed the last letter on the subject, appropriately enough from MacColl again (his third). There were various other reactions from regular art journalists, sometimes strongly hostile. Ayrton was very rude about the Picassos in the *Spectator* on 14 December. In *Apollo*, 'Perspex' said (in the January 1946 issue), 'I confess that for me this stuff means precisely nothing and I refuse to be bludgeoned into dishonesty by the vogue for it.' He went on to say, 'This exhibition is monstrous nonsense trading on a widespread dishonesty of opinion and fear of not being in the swim.' Philip James, on the other hand, writing in the *Listener* on 13 December 1945 was very impressed, particularly by the Picassos, and Roger Marvell in the *New Statesman and Nation* of 15 December said the pictures were 'very welcome and exciting'.

Whitechapel

The Whitechapel sits curiously between the City of London and the East End, properly neither one nor the other. We tend now to look back to its glory days as being under the directorship of the Australian Bryan Robertson, but he falls outside the scope of this study, at least so far as his Whitechapel period was concerned, because he did not arrive there until 1952. Before then, Hugh Scrutton had been the director since 1947. He, together with Lord Bearsted as Chairman of the Trustees from 1943-48, had been responsible for reviving the gallery after the War (when it had suffered bomb damage) despite very difficult financial circumstances.[85] A look at the list of exhibitions held at the gallery from 1945-51 shows a certain dedication to local issues and to general exhibitions of well-known artists, but it also shows that the pre-Robertson years were very far from being devoid of the sort of artists later to be particularly promoted by Robertson. So, for example, in 1949 under the heading 'Pictures for Schools' there appeared Lowry, Weight, Hilton, Uhlman and Tunnard; and in 1950 'Painter's Progress: Lives and Work of some living British painters' included Grant, Lowry, Hitchens, Clough and Armstrong.[86] The gallery's contribution to the Festival was 'Black Eyes and Lemonade', which was an exhibition of popular and traditional art.

National Gallery

The National Gallery is not directly relevant to our study. Philip Hendy took over from Clark in 1945 as Director and he was sympathetic to modern British art but hardly in a position at the National Gallery to promote it directly.[87] Although damaged in the War[88] the National Gallery was in a considerably better state than the extensively damaged, and indeed unusable, Tate. As a result, the National Gallery was able to start bringing back its stored pictures from Wales shortly after the War ended. While Kenneth Clark was still in charge, it held an exhibition (in June 1945) of 86 pictures that the Tate had acquired since 1942, including works by Grant, Spencer, Gertler and Smith. (The *Times* critic noted 'the

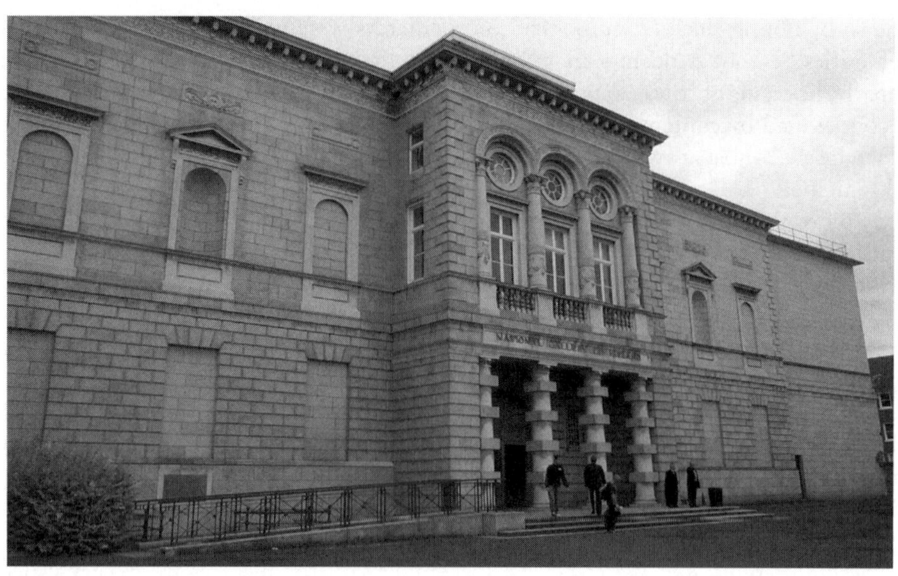

catholicity of the list is evidence of a singularly wise, discriminating and unprejudiced policy on the part of the Gallery's administrators'.) Then on 22 December 1945 the National Gallery (now under Hendy) held an exhibition of Paul Klee, which had been organised by the Tate.

Royal Academy

Every year the Royal Academy Summer Exhibition, which opened in Burlington House in May, got extensive and almost invariably adverse reviews in a wide range of newspapers and journals. It was perhaps inevitable that its awkward position, as some sort of official body in a world of modern art which had already started to lose touch with its inherited ways of thinking, would be difficult to sustain. Year after year the critics attacked the contents of the Summer Exhibition as being in some harmless, but irrelevant, mode of art which, of course, was often popular with the less advanced segment of the art-buying public than any 'modern' works by 'advanced' painters would ever be. Ayrton, writing in the *Spectator* on 10 May 1946, is at the extreme end of the spectrum of enlightened opinion on the Summer Exhibition, but his views are not so far away from the norm as to be ridiculous: 'The same qualities of meaningless vulgarity, decadence, incompetence and juvenile sentimentality are displayed in the vast majority of the exhibits.' Nevertheless, in among the humdrum were works by artists who were acknowledged to be respectable even by the most critical of modern writers. Stanley Spencer's work was often noted, for example, as was that of Augustus John. Among younger artists, Ruskin Spear was often picked out for approval and by 1951, for example, work by Bawden, Buhler, Eurich, Moynihan, John Nash, Aldridge, Minton, Gilbert Spencer, Roberts and Wadsworth was being shown. This indicates that, while there was never the degree of overlap which was present in a smaller jurisdiction, such as Ireland (where so many of the artists showing at the RHA also showed at its supposed antidote, the IELA), between the RA and the rest of the artistic world, there was overlap. Perfectly respectable 'modern' artists were prepared to show at the RA, indicating that its reputation was never so debased that artists would rather not show there at all.[89]

Various controversies dogged the RA in our period. As we have seen, relations were not good with the Tate under Rothenstein, and this culminated in the unseemly spectacle of the Chantrey Exhibition at the beginning of 1949 (whose details are set out here in the section on the Tate). In particular, the President of the Royal Academy at the time, Sir Alfred Munnings, whose paintings in a traditional mode of foxhunting and portraits sold for (and still sell for) prodigious amounts of money, was always spoiling for a fight with the world of modern art. His notorious, allegedly drunken, speech (mentioned earlier) at a Royal Academy Annual Dinner in front of Sir Winston Churchill, in which he launched a violent attack on modern art,[90] attracted a lot of press and public attention, not least because it was broadcast live on the radio. Needless to say, he later claimed that a large proportion of the letters he received from ordinary members of the public were supportive of what they must have seen as a refreshing dose of honesty on a subject which so often welcomed obfuscation.

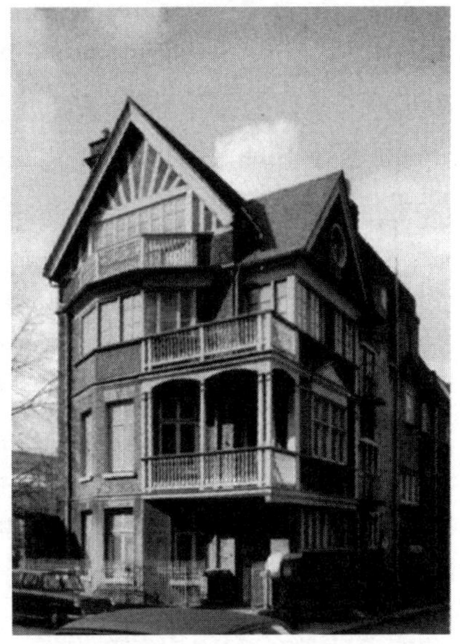

The Royal Hibernian Academy, 1951
(above)
The National Gallery of Ireland, Dublin
(opposite)

Royal Hibernian Academy

Founded in 1823, this royal institution survived the creation of the Irish Free State and Republic and continues to this day, in Ely Place in Dublin. Its main interest to this study is because the alleged limitations of its vision in selecting pictures for its annual public exhibition led, in 1943, as has been noted earlier, to the creation of the 'Irish Exhibition of Living Art'. In fact, it would be dangerous to distinguish the two bodies in all respects, partly because the small size of the Irish art world meant that artists took the opportunity to show their work at both exhibitions, but also because, under the goad of the IELA and perhaps in response to the constant criticism of its shows in the Irish press, the Academy tried a few tricks to widen its appeal. So, under its new President, Sean Keating, who had taken over in 1950 following the death of his predecessor, James Sleator, the Academy in 1951 asked three Irish artists resident in London to select works by English artists to appear alongside the indigenous offerings. Two of the three were Sir Gerald Kelly and Le Brocquy and one can imagine that it was more likely to have been the latter who chose to show Bacon's *Painting 1950* at the Academy – a work which must have contrasted rather sharply with some of the gentler pictures on display.

The National Gallery of Ireland

The National Gallery of Ireland was in 1945 not unduly interested in modern Irish art, or indeed in modern art of any kind. Trapped like so many institutions of its kind at the time by a tiny purchase grant, and with a small staff, with very few visitors, its main objective seems to have been to maintain and gradually develop its inheritance. In 1945 the Director was George Furlong, who had been elected in 1935. Although he was Irish, and as such his succession was preferred to an English candidate, it is significant to note that, prior to his election, he had been an Assistant Keeper at the National Gallery in London 1930-35, overlapping for a few years with Kenneth Clark. As a result, Clark supported his candidacy for the Irish post and perhaps that support was not insignificant to the Board which elected Furlong. The influence of Clark clearly extended in some circumstances even to Ireland.

The only modern Irish artist whose work attracted serious attention from the Gallery at this time was, of course, Yeats. Three pictures were acquired during Furlong's tenure, but by gift, in 1941 (presented by the Haverty Trust), 1945 (presented by the Jack B. Yeats National Loan Exhibition committee) and 1947 (presented by Father Senan, editor of the *Capuchin Annual*). During the second half of the 1940s Furlong's attention to his duties in Dublin seems to have wandered and he made no secret of his preference for being in London, where he moved following his resignation in February 1950.[91] For the rest of the period which concerns us the Director in Dublin was Thomas MacGreevy, as from June 1950, and he remained Director until 1963. No significant attempt was made to focus on or to purchase modern Irish art, although gifts were occasionally received. The real event which was to transform the Gallery's finances happened outside our period: the receipt of huge sums of money, by the standards of the time, from the will of George Bernard Shaw.

The Hugh Lane Municipal Gallery of Modern Art

Whereas the National Gallery of Ireland is housed in a building built in 19th-century museum style, the Hugh Lane has been housed (since 1933) in an exquisite Georgian town house in an area of Dublin which is rather off the beaten track for tourists: Charlemont House in what is currently known as Parnell Square (formerly Rutland Square). The origins of this gallery's collection rest with that of the eponymous Sir Hugh Lane, who drowned in the sinking of the *Lusitania* in 1915. The appalling complexity of the story whereby part, but not all, of his collection turned up in Ireland, whereas the rest stayed in London, does not, thankfully, need to be re-told here.[92]

Belfast Museum and Art Gallery[93]

During the 1940s, a decision was taken to build up a permanent collection of good-quality works by artists associated with Ulster. This, together with a wide variety of works by other Irish artists, means that the museum now houses one of the finest collections of 20th-century Irish art. It claims, for example, to hold works from every stage of the career of Lavery, Henry, Scott, Middleton, Jellett and Le Brocquy.[94] In addition, many works by 20th-century British artists are in the collection, including work by Sickert, Smith, Paul and John Nash, Stanley Spencer, Bacon, Davie, Hitchens, Hilton and Pasmore. Much of this was acquired from the 1930s onwards. Details of what happened to the Gallery during our period come from the annual Reports of the Committee. A composite edition, covering the five years ended 31 March 1945, was published in 1945, followed by annual editions. Various interesting facts emerge. John Hewitt, for example, so important to the encouragement of young Ulster artists,[95] was noted as 'Chief Assistant' at the Gallery in 1945, but thereafter had risen – or been redesignated – to Keeper of the Art Division. He was no doubt at least partly responsible for the series of one-man shows of contemporary Ulster artists which began with Colin Middleton in 1944 and included Luke (one of Hewitt's favourite local artists) in 1946, William Gordon[96] and Morris Harding[97] in 1947, Frederick Hull[98] in 1949 and then Kathleen Bridle[99] in 1950.

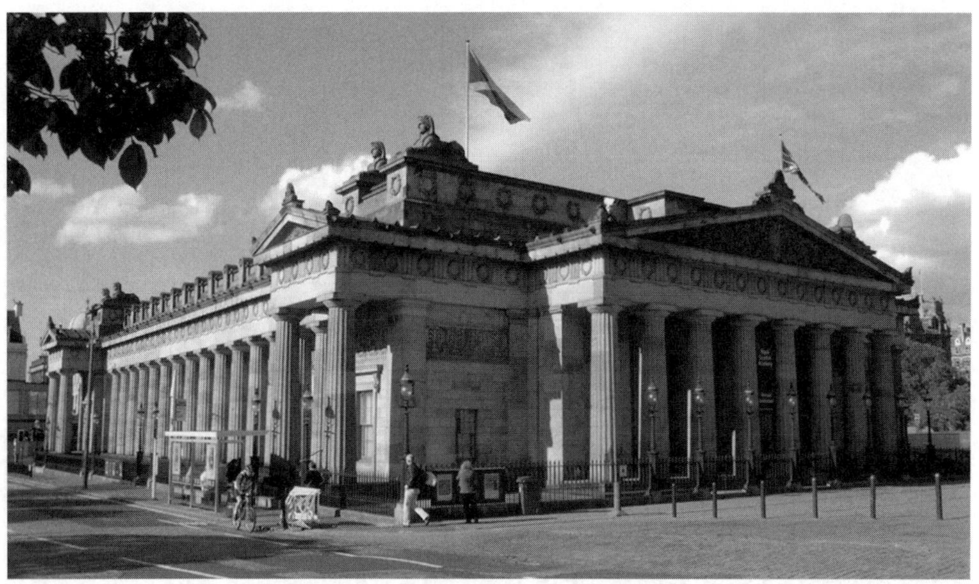

The Royal Scottish Academy, Edinburgh

Acquisitions, by purchase and donation, were listed. Some arrived occasionally from the Haverty Trust (for example, works by Keating, MacGonigal and Luke arrived by that route during the War) and others through the CAS (works by Moynihan, Daintry and Jones during the War). The limitations of the purchasing budget are, however, all too apparent. During the five, admittedly wartime, years covered by the first Report, nine oils had been purchased which at least included modern artists such as Middleton, Conor, Olive Henry and Campbell. In the year ended 31 March 1946, four oils are recorded as having been bought (one by Luke) and a Yeats arrived from the CAS and two pictures by Le Brocquy from the Haverty Trust. Few purchases are mentioned thereafter (although this may be because the lay-out of the Reports changed). The 1951 Report mentioned that gifts from the Haverty Trust included works by O'Neill, Dillon, Friers and Cooke-Collis.

Royal Ulster Academy
This was called the Ulster Academy of Arts until 1950. It held an annual exhibition at the Belfast Museum and Art Gallery. Its President from 1944-1947 was John Hunter and Morris Harding[100] from 1947-1957.

Royal Scottish Academy
Founded in 1826 as the Scottish Academy it had as its first objective 'an Annual Exhibition open to all artists of merit'. It became the RSA in 1838. By 1945 its President was the pioneer of Scottish planning, Frank Mears. From 1948 it began to hold a series of special exhibitions for the newly-created Edinburgh Festival. Its annual exhibition received a long and detailed review in the *Scotsman* and was also occasionally reviewed in the English newspapers, usually being favourably compared with the Royal Academy Summer Exhibition.

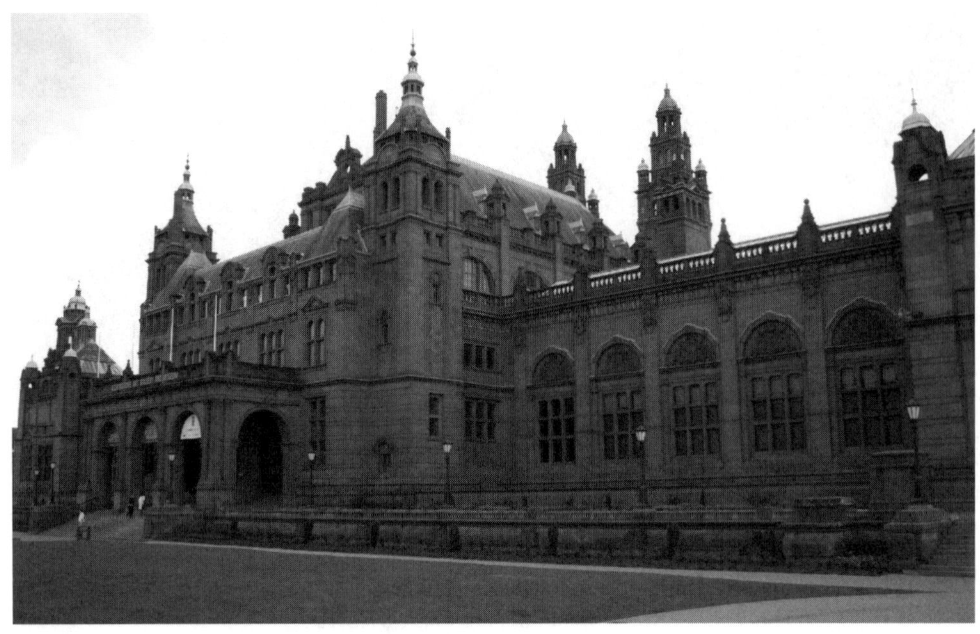

Kelvingrove Art Gallery, Glasgow

National Gallery of Scotland

Although holding the largest collection of art by Scottish artists, it was not, as an institution, particularly relevant to modern art in mid-century. Its modern pictures were transferred to the Scottish National Gallery of Modern Art when that was established in 1960. Its director from 1930-48 was Stanley Cursiter.[101]

Glasgow Art Gallery (Kelvingrove)

Founded in 1901, the collections during our period included the fabulous Burrell Collection, which had been given to the City in 1944 by Sir William Burrell. The Director from 1939-54 was Tom Honeyman and one of the big events of his tenure was the arrival at the Gallery of the controversial Picasso and Matisse exhibition from the V&A in January 1946. The reader will recall the controversy which the V&A show had aroused in the English press. The Glasgow show hit the *Scotsman* on 26 January, with a positive review and a series of comments from various people who had attended the private view on the previous day. Stanley Cursiter thought it 'excellent', and a number of practising artists, such as J.D. Fergusson, Hugh Crawford and William Crosbie, were supportive. Others were less so. Sir John Stirling-Maxwell, for example, said he saw 'no sense or value in Picasso's works' and so on. Needless to say, the arguments then moved into the letters columns, as they had done in London. The first letter appeared in the *Scotsman* on 29 January; two followed on 31 January; four on 1 February; four more on 2 February and so on.[102] The arguments either way were similar to those in London. A more interesting way of gauging the popularity of the show was that when Honeyman gave a lecture on Matisse (according to a review in the *Scotsman* on 4 February) all 500 seats were taken early and large crowds had to be turned away. Moreover, at the end of the first week of the exhibition 53,000 people were recorded as having attended.

CHAPTER 3

PRIVATE PATRONAGE AND COLLECTING

PATRONS

In the context of the period we are describing, what definition of private patrons should be used? They were certainly not simply great collectors.[1] Many more wealthy people collected contemporary pictures in Britain than that much smaller number who could be characterised as patrons. We will deal with the principal collectors shortly.[2] Patronage here will mean an act of support for a number of artists; probably, but not necessarily, financial in nature; and including a wish to help an artist's development, without necessarily benefiting the patron in any way. The term does not have to involve the commissioning of pictures from the artists concerned, nor indeed buying their work to any particular extent. But it does imply a degree of selflessness on the part of the patron.

The sweeping generalisation which one sometimes reads, to the effect that, after the War, or even earlier in some accounts, private patronage gradually, or abruptly, ceased to exist and that the rôle of private patrons was gradually, or even abruptly, taken over by the Arts Council and so on, is no more than a generalisation. It merits neither confirmation nor disproof; one does not have to react to every half-baked statement which has tried to seep into the historical mainstream – especially where, as one suspects, it has suited some writers to purport to identify this particular trend through some desire to diminish the supposedly aristocratic, or merely money-based, concept of private patronage so as to replace it with state-based, and therefore more egalitarian, and therefore, better, patronage.

It would probably be fairly accurate to notice that private patronage, of the type evinced by those who are about to be described, did change over the course of many years, but gradually and subtly over time, as has the whole notion of what artists are for and how they are to be treated by the societies which shelter them. It is also important to note that the decisions taken by the public patrons of art – the Arts Council, the British Council, the CAS – to purchase contemporary British art were not made by bureaucrats or civil servants. Throughout this study – and particularly in the Appendix – the reader is assailed in footnotes by details of the schools and universities which many of the non-artists attended. From this it will have been noticed that when the great State patrons turned their attention to buying contemporary art after the War they did so through the medium of people like the old Etonian Colin Anderson or the Wykehamist Kenneth Clark (both, coincidentally, attending the same Oxford college). For evidence of this the reader would simply have to look through the names of the nominated buyers for these bodies. They were, in very many cases, public school and Oxbridge educated; they were often important patrons and collectors in their own right. Further details of this are contained in the Appendix. So much for the post-War collapse of private patronage.

Considered here in some detail will be the activities of the four most prominent patrons of contemporary British art of our period, followed by a brief description of the more significant collectors.[3]

Colin Anderson

Colin Anderson (1904-1980) was educated at Eton and Trinity College, Oxford, where in October 1923 he found himself on the same staircase as Kenneth Clark[4] (who had arrived a year earlier from Winchester), starting a long friendship which undoubtedly had an effect on the development of Anderson's artistic interests.[5] However, before then there had already been signs of his artistic interests. He painted at school and his name appears on a list of

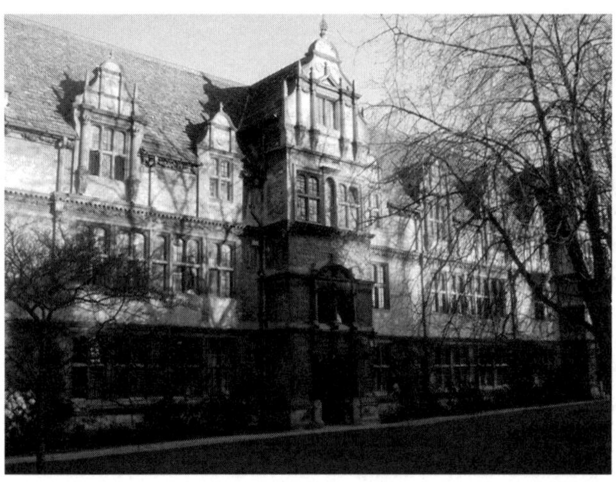

Trinity College, Oxford, the Jackson building.
Colin Anderson and Kenneth Clark were on the same staircase in 1923

boys, many of whom were later to achieve considerable significance in the cultural life of Britain. These were the founders of the Eton Society of Arts in February 1922. The list included Brian Howard,[6] Henry Yorke,[7] Harold and William Acton,[8] Robert Byron,[9] Alan Clutton-Brock,[10] Hugh Lygon[11] and Anthony Powell.[12]

Leaving Oxford without taking his degree[13] in 1925, Anderson joined his father's company, Anderson Green, which managed the Orient Line (later part of P & O). He became a director in 1930. Here he was in a position to commission artists to complete works for the ships.[14] From the launching of the *Orcades II* in 1937, when John Armstrong and Ceri Richards received commissions, through the *Orcades III* in 1948 (Bawden, Minton, Winifred Nicholson, John Nash and Rowntree), the *Oronsay II* in 1951 (Bawden and MacBryde), the *Orsova* in 1954 (Richards, Trevelyan, Colquhoun and MacBryde) and the *Oriana* in 1960 (Piper), Anderson was fully involved in finding artists to produce things for the new ships.[15] One of his earlier friendships with artists was with Sutherland, whom he met in 1934 through Kenneth Clark.[16] (Sutherland did not get anything into any of the ships, but he did design a poster in 1939.) That friendship was to last all his life, and there is a famous letter written by Sutherland to Anderson, which was later published in *Horizon* in April 1942 under the heading 'Welsh Sketchbook'.[17] This attempted to describe the influence which Wales, and particularly Pembrokeshire, had had on Sutherland's painting. A number of pictures by Sutherland were bought, but there were no indications that the relationship between them was other than friendship.

Another early example of Anderson's patronage was the case of Ceri Richards. Here the small, thoughtful ways in which Anderson sought to help Richards cast Anderson in a very attractive light and illustrate the subtle process whereby artists could be encouraged. So, for example, when War broke out, Anderson arranged for Richards and his wife to rent a house in Suffolk at a low rent. Since the Richards had no income whatsoever at this point, this was very welcome. Before then, in 1935, Anderson had commissioned Richards to design a booklet advertising a new liner in the Orient Line fleet and in 1953 another commission arrived, this time for a mural for another ship. In 1954 Anderson wrote the foreword to Richards' exhibition catalogue at King's College, Durham University.[18] In 1964 he gave the address, as Chairman of the Tate Trustees and as an old friend and collector of Richards' work, at the opening of a large exhibition at the Glynn Vivian Gallery in Swansea. The text of this address is glowing in its admiration for Richards' work and in Anderson's affection for him as a friend. In fact, throughout their long acquaintance, Anderson bought works and visited the artist's studio and exchanged long letters about what Richards was trying to achieve. There is, for example, an important nine-page letter of 19 December 1941 in which Richards discusses his work in detail.

Anderson helped Richards to become a trustee of the Tate and in 1959 there were a number of letters between Anderson and the Bishop of Llandaff, in which he sought to persuade the Bishop to purchase a large *Deposition* which the artist had done. Also in 1959 Anderson donated a Richards' construction to the Tate and he frequently agreed to loan his pictures by the artist to exhibitions. In 1960, Bryan Robertson's Preface to the catalogue for Richards's

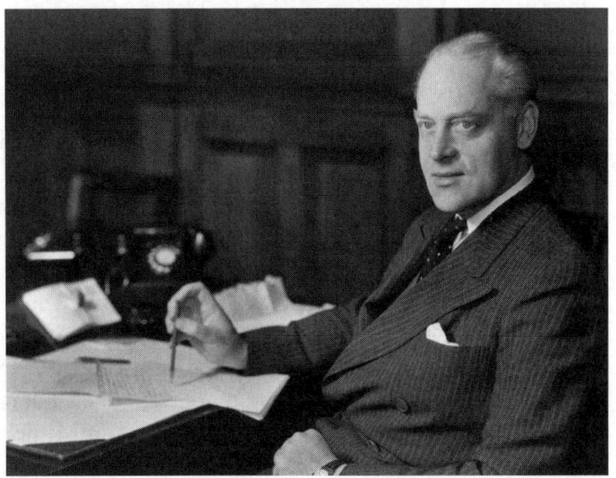

Colin Anderson at his desk at the family firm of Anderson Green which managed the Orient Line, later part of P&O

retrospective at the Whitechapel made an honourable mention of Anderson: 'He has not lacked supporters, notably in the amiable and unfailingly discerning patronage of Sir Colin Anderson, to whom English painting owes far more than is generally realised.'

After the artist's death and shortly before Anderson's own death in 1980, Frances Richards wrote to him (on 18 April) and the last paragraph of this last letter perhaps expresses perfectly the relationship which Anderson created with his artist friends: 'I am always grateful for the encouragement and support you gave to Ceri and myself in difficult times. Not enough importance, to my mind, has been given to the help and assistance you gave to the good artists before and after the Second World War.'

In the 1930s Anderson and his family moved into 81 Bedford Gardens in London's W8. Next door (77) was a purpose-built block of artists' studios and there arrived Colquhoun and MacBryde in 1941. Somehow a friendship developed between 'the Roberts' and Colin Anderson. This does seem unlikely: Colquhoun and MacBryde were soon drinking a lot and were already fastening on to the homosexual milieu of artistic London, which must have been distinctly alien to Anderson. Indeed, he describes in his unpublished memoirs briefly attending a party given by the Roberts sometime in the 1940s. Anderson had by this time also got to know John and Myfanwy Piper and, as they were staying at number 81, with Graham and Kathleen Sutherland, the six of them, including Anderson's wife Morna, visited the party. He describes the alien surroundings and the cultural clash was obviously severe.[19]

In 1947 the Roberts moved out of the studio, at least for part of the year, to Lewes[20] and later that year the Andersons moved to Hampstead. There began a long correspondence between them – many of the letters remaining in the possession of the Anderson family. These start in 1947 and end, poignantly, with a sad letter from Robert MacBryde of 1962, describing Colquhoun's recent death. There are 60 surviving letters in all, 48 from MacBryde and 12 from Colquhoun. In many of the letters they beg for money and, written across the letters before they were filed, Anderson records his reaction. In July 1948 he noted that he had given them £125; in September 1948 £120; in January 1949 £30 and so on.[21] At certain points he can take no more, in 1955 for example, writing 'Refused – the last straw' at the top of a letter. These gifts of money were never repaid. They did not amount to a huge sum, although no doubt they were substantial amounts of money by the normal standards of the time.

It is apparent from other artists' letters retained by the Anderson family (there are 11 letters from Bacon dating from 1945 to 1979)[22] that considerable sums were being disbursed to others. Thus, in June 1947, Francis Bacon, who was in Monte Carlo, begged for and received £300; in October 1947 (still in Monte Carlo) another £300; and in February 1952 (although, curiously, Bacon mis-dated the letter to 1951), he wrote: 'My dear Colin, I am in a desperate state could you lend me £400.' Anderson obviously demurred at this point and queried exactly what the money was for. He clearly wondered whether, by chance, the money was in some way supporting Bacon's notorious appetite for gambling (for it had not been a coincidence that the earlier begging letters had arrived from Monte Carlo). Bacon obliged, acknowledging that Anderson would not want to encourage the gambling, and established his impecunious bona fides by sending him bills from Muriel Belcher (£182),[23] his tailor (£90)[24] and his artistic suppliers (£153). On 15 February 1952, Anderson wrote to Bacon, shortly and perhaps a trifle sarcastically: 'I have paid Miss Belcher, Mr Turpin and the tailor. I hope the effect on your work will be electrifying.'

The letters which Anderson retained from Bacon do contain snippets of interest beyond the financial. Thus, in the first (undated) letter, which Anderson has tentatively dated to 1945, Bacon invited Anderson to his studio in his absence, to look at work in progress and to help himself to a drink (at this point the studio was at 7 Cromwell Place, SW7). Bacon mentioned that there would be things to look at, although some of them were in an unfinished state. 'An orange one is one of a group of three which I have just sold and I am afraid the other two have been dispatched to the buyer and this one was left to make an alteration to.' 'The large dark one is a central one of three which are unfinished.'

In the first of the begging letters in 1947, Bacon says: 'I am working on a large crucifixion group and I am so anxious to finish them in this light.' As a tentative repayment proposition, Bacon promised that he would return to London later in the year and sell the 'quite valuable pieces of furniture' in the flat in order to generate some cash. He goes on to say that there are three pictures, 'possibly a little larger than the one you bought for the Contemporary Art Society.[25] They are in a kind of blue violet colour and I like them very much at the moment.' (That 'at the moment' was ominous because Bacon destroyed many finished pictures which he took a dislike to.) When this letter was written, Sutherland had recently left the area to return home. It had been his first visit to the South of France and quite a lot of socialising had taken place with Bacon. In the letter, Bacon commented on the pictures referred to above that 'I had not done them at all when Graham was here a few weeks' ago so do not know if he would have cared for them or not'.

In the next letter (3 July), Anderson had obviously made a comment about Sutherland because Bacon said, 'I am so glad to hear about Graham's work. He seemed to like the light and colour here and find it very stimulating. He talked of coming back in the autumn.' By the time of the next letter (9 October), Sutherland was indeed back in the area. Bacon wrote to Anderson twice that day, firstly to say that he had put Cromwell Place on the market for £1,500 and to say how excited he was that the work had taken a 'new turn'. He was also pleased to be able to paint much smaller pictures. By the evening of the same day he had remembered that he needed another £300 loan. The response to this loan was to offer Anderson a picture, 'a study of a figure by a window'. He also said that 'Being on this coast with this light one always seems to be on the edge of the real mystery.' In February 1948 Bacon again promised a picture (of Monte Carlo) and said that he was coming over for a show at the Redfern. The pictures were 'much the best I have done and get nearer the reality I long to do'. He also said that he wanted to go to America to work for a while. By 5 February 1952, writing from 30 Sumner Place, SW7, Bacon asked for £400 and said that 'the work is going really well and I feel at last I have got through the nonsense and will really be able to paint – I am starting on the autobiographical pictures which I want to do and believe with them I can really get on to the nerve'. In an undated letter tentatively ascribed by Anderson to 1954, Bacon tells him that he is working on a study (2ft

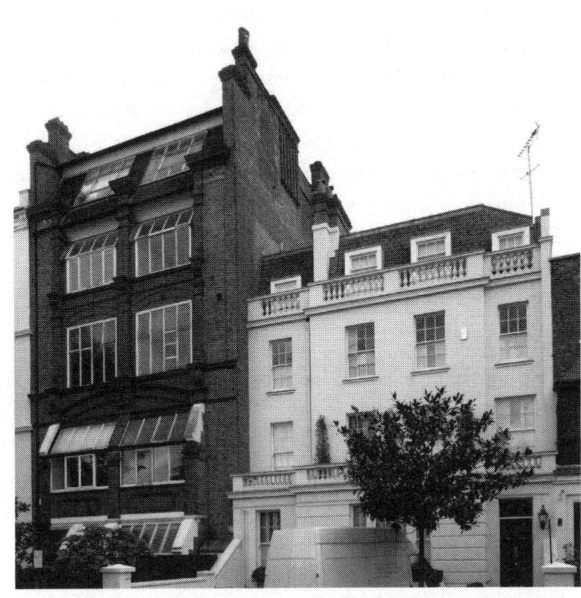

Nos. 77 and 81 Bedford Gardens, W8. The left-hand building (No. 77) was a purpose-built block of studios where 'the Roberts', Colquhoun and MacBryde, arrived in 1941, next door to the Anderson family home at No. 81

6in x 3ft 4in) for a much larger picture to be called *Christ shown to the people*.

In 1949 Freud asked for and got £110. 'I do hope you will forgive my asking you, but I find I suddenly need it very badly. I think I would be able to repay you within three years.' There is nothing to show that the money was ever repaid. Then in 1952,[26] in his curious handwriting and spelling, Freud wrote that 'with wolves at the front and back doors… PLEASE could you lend me two hundred pounds… I don't want you to think that I am imposing on you as a friend so could you consider it as a business arrangement as if I was a firm or company.' Anderson wrote back an exceptionally interesting letter, on 30 January 1952, which is worth setting out in full, as it tries to explain something of the mental process which Anderson went through in deciding how to respond to Freud's requests.

My dear Lucian,

How rash of you – how unwise – to ask me 'to think of you as a firm or company'. As such you would be turned down flat, as being unable to provide any security for such a loan. Luckily for you I know so much more of those extraordinary creatures, firms and companies, than you ever will, that I cannot even begin to think of you in terms of them.

So I must think of you, as you forbid me to do so in terms of friendship, as Lucian Freud, just a person of that name, with certain talents and habits and commitments and potentialities.

Looked at in that cold way the commitments seem rather large. Is Lucian Freud living with proper frugality? Is he flesh potting, like some bloated shipowner? How and where have these £200 gone – and how much more do the wolves really need? I'm sure you don't lightly ask your acquaintance for such sums. And similarly I don't think your acquaintance should lightly cough them up. It isn't good to do these things without a bit of introspection.

Or am I just being too smug in expecting everyone to be balanced neatly? I dare say I am. You must forgive me, but remember I live in two worlds and carry into each some of the habits of the other. Among the business men I appear to be remarkably aesthetic and strange in my likes, my opinions and my friends. Among the other artists I appear to be business-like, prudent, powerful and, alas, sometimes smug. I suppose that is happening now.

I enclose a cheque for £200. I promise you it gives me no kick as a pleasant exercise in power-patronage. Rather the reverse, I feel somewhat ashamed of being able to afford it and yet, at the same time, not giving it sweetly without all this lecturing.

I hope your show is a success and that you will look back at it (when, in 10 years time, the Royal Navy commissions you to paint the whole Royal Family) as having been a most superior brew of wolf-poison.

With love to all three of you,

Yours, Colin.

Whether there was any connection between the artists' requests for money is not known. What is known is that Bacon, Freud, Colquhoun and MacBryde were all friends and it is no doubt at least possible that they told each other about Anderson's generosity and begged accordingly.[27]

In addition, he helped them in other ways. In the case of the Roberts, he at one time paid the rent of their flat; he provided them with an account at their suppliers which they could draw upon in order to get materials for painting; and he even equipped them with other essentials such as blankets when their flat was broken into and badly damaged in 1955. All in all, he tried his hardest to help them, eventually writing to the Artists' General Benevolent Institution in early 1956 and requesting it to help the Roberts financially. He drew the line at helping them to buy a house in Suffolk. This, of course, was all on top of buying their pictures. At the 17 Collectors Exhibition, which he organised and for which he wrote the foreword, he included amongst his own pictures *Two Widows* by MacBryde and two oils by Colquhoun, as well as two monotypes. By the time of the 1958 Colquhoun exhibition at the Whitechapel, he was shown as lending *The Two Sisters*, *Fortune Teller*, *The Conjuror* and *Masked Figure*, as well as a number of drawings and monotypes, many of which had been given to him by Colquhoun as a way of repaying some of the money so freely given to them by Anderson.

In the case of Bacon, Anderson caused the CAS to buy *Figure Study II* in 1946. At the same time, he himself bought *Study for a Crucifix* (1933) from the Redfern Gallery and much later, in 1957, Bacon gave him a picture called *Owls*. Anderson acquired two drawings by Freud in 1948 and 1952 and a third in 1969. Some idea of the widespread nature of Anderson's more traditional support for modern British art – that is by simply buying pictures – can be gleaned from the list of painters whose works he lent to the 1950 and 1952 CAS shows at the Tate mentioned earlier. For the earlier exhibition, he lent works by Ardizzone, Colquhoun, Craxton, Freud, Jones, Wyndham Lewis, Moore, Ben Nicholson, Richards, Smith and Sutherland. In 1952 he was showing works by Denis Matthews, Piper, Moore, Sutherland, Hepworth, Hill, Sickert, Grant, Ceri and Frances Richards, MacBryde, Colquhoun and Nolan.

Anderson was knighted in 1950. From 1952-56 he was Chairman of the Royal College of Art, and from 1956-60 he was Chairman of the CAS. Before then he had been made a member of the Executive Committee, attending his first meeting on 1 November 1945 and his last in 1965. He was promptly appointed the buyer in his first full year on the Committee, 1946, with £500 to spend, and a measure of his perceptive taste was the fact that the first two pictures which he presented to the other members of the committee on 7 March 1946 for their approval were *Figure Study II* by Bacon and *Woman with Birdcage* by Colquhoun. His next offerings were pictures by Weight, John Barrow and Le Brocquy, which were approved on 2 April 1946.

From 1952 to 1967 he was a Trustee of the Tate (from 1953-59 as Vice Chairman and from 1960-67 as Chairman of the Trustees) and as such he was heavily involved in the infamous 'Tate Affair', which embroiled Sir John Rothenstein. From 1963-67 he was a Trustee of the National Gallery and from 1967-80 he was Provost of the Royal College of Art. He was one of the Royal Fine Art Commissioners from 1959 and Chairman from 1968-76. In 1974, when he was 70, Anderson published a book of his own poetry, called *Three Score Years and Ten. A backward glance*. At the end of his life Anderson wrote a deeply moving letter to Clark[28] dated 9 October 1980, in which he thanked Clark for his friendship: 'You are the friend to whom I owe more pleasure, instruction and hospitality than any I have had through life.' It was a fitting conclusion to a fine life, from one great man to another.

Peter Watson

Peter Watson (1908-56), whose real name was Victor William Watson, was also educated at Eton and Oxford (St John's College)[29] and in his case his wealth meant that he never had to work.[30] For many years in the 1930s it was not at all clear that Watson was going to lead any life other than that of a rich homosexual dandy. There was a (black and orange) Rolls-Royce and a chauffeur, a flat at 10 Palace Gate in Kensington[31] and an apartment at 44 rue du Bac in Paris.[32] He bought pictures by many of the leading European artists of the time (his first purchase of a Picasso drawing being made after leaving Oxford, while visiting Munich).[33] He was the object of an apparently unrequited passion on the part of Cecil Beaton. Then, for whatever reason, his life seemed to become more serious.[34] He agreed to back *Horizon* with Cyril Connolly when it started in 1939. He remained its financial backer and art editor throughout its life (until it closed in 1950). He helped to found the Institute of Contemporary Arts in 1946, and he went out of his way to help other young artists who were starting out and who needed help.

The reader may not be surprised to find that Colquhoun and MacBryde were amongst the first to tap this alternative source of generosity.[35] When they arrived in London from Scotland in early 1941, they stayed initially with Peter Watson in Palace Gate, a ménage which conjures up a curious image.[36] He wrote to Kenneth Clark in February 1941 with a view to getting Colquhoun taken on by the War Artists' Commission and before too long he had found them a studio in Adam and Eve Mews off Kensington High Street. I do not believe that letters which Peter Watson may have received from them thereafter have survived, but it is probably safe to assume that they at least sought money from him.

Another early beneficiary was Freud, who had joined Cedric Morris and Arthur Lett-Haines at the East Anglian School of Painting and Drawing in Suffolk, shortly after leaving school in 1939. A letter[37] from Watson to Morris, frustratingly only dated 2 November, stated, 'As there has been some question of Lucian's father urging him to discontinue his painting and take some other job, I decided that I would pay his expenses for the time being, to enable him to carry on with his work. I am doing this because I am very fond of him and believe in him.' Next to benefit were Freud and Craxton together. While the bombing of London had rendered properties cheap, they were not necessarily cheap enough for young artists. In 1942 Watson paid (at the rate of about £40 p.a.) for Freud and Craxton to have rooms in the same building at 14 Abercorn Place in St John's Wood. Craxton didn't actually live there (he was at this time still living at home in nearby Abbey Road Mansions, with his parents), but Freud slept there and the rooms were used on a regular basis. Many early works by each artist were done at a time when they were using these rooms. This arrangement lasted until some time in 1944.

Watson clearly helped his protégés in other ways. For example, he had bought at least one work by Graham Sutherland – *Steep Road* – which Craxton had independently admired at the Lefevre in 1939. When he then saw it in Watson's flat in the early 1940s, Watson gave it to him. (Craxton later sold it to help pay for the purchase of a house in Crete.) In 1946 Watson helped Craxton to get an exhibition in Switzerland by recommending him to a Swiss dealer.

Watson's tastes in art were international and highly sophisticated. His astonishingly far-sighted collection of European pictures which he left in the rue du Bac on the outbreak of war in 1939 and which had gone by the time the flat was reoccupied in 1946, had included works by de Chirico, Gris, Klee, Picasso, Dalí, Rouault and Miró. By the time of his death in 1956, he left works by Giacometti, Moore, Renoir, Braque, Gris and Poussin.

A number of people have commented how Watson's London flat acted as a sort of hub, in about 1941, for the group of artists who were at that time close to him. As well as the pictures, the art journals which were available in his flat, particularly *Cahiers d'Art*, along with the possibilities of meeting other artists meant that some were drawn into contact with those they might not have met so easily elsewhere. Craxton, for example, was introduced by Watson to Sutherland and Watson and Craxton subsequently joined the Sutherlands on a trip to Wales. Another example is Keith Vaughan. He was introduced to Watson in Oxford in 1941 and soon visited the flat in Palace Gate, where he was to meet Minton, Craxton and so on.[38] Watson also knew Sutherland, although he was not really part of the Palace Gate milieu.[39] Again, contact with Watson led Vaughan to Sutherland, whose work had an influence on Vaughan as a result. Watson owned two important pictures by Sutherland at this time: *Entrance to a Lane*[40] and *Gorse on a Sea Wall*. The only problem for Vaughan was that he found it impossible to keep up with the extreme cultural sophistication of Watson's life. By contrast, he found the company of the Sutherlands more 'normal' and refreshing.

Watson was friendly with Roland Penrose and, as we have seen, he had been a director of the London Gallery. It was therefore natural that he should be in at the beginning of the formation of the ICA, no doubt helping with occasional funding demands, and certainly helping by bringing into play his vast range of contacts in the international art world. So, for example, it was,[41] through him that the ICA was able to hold the first post-War poetry reading in London of W.H. Auden and it was also due to Watson's friendships that works by composers such as Poulenc and Stravinsky were performed under the auspices of the ICA.[42] When the ICA gave Francis Bacon a show in January 1955, the catalogue had an introduction by the French poet Max Clarac-Sérou, which had been translated by Watson.

As art editor of *Horizon*, Watson did little in the way of written contributions, save for an article on Gris and occasional translations from French, but he gave opportunities to his friends to get their paintings reproduced in *Horizon* (Craxton, Colquhoun, MacBryde, Bacon and Freud) and he encouraged *Horizon* to look beyond British art and particularly to Paris.

He commissioned articles on artists who were barely known in England, such as Balthus, Morandi and Klee; he persuaded Picasso's dealer, Daniel Kahnweiler, to comment on the contemporary art market; and he also got Michel Leiris to write about Giacometti.[43]

Watson's widespread popularity in the wider cultural community of Britain, in particular, in the 1940s, shines out in many unexpected ways. For example, Stephen Spender dedicated his novel *The Backward Son* to him in 1940. Cyril Connolly dedicated *The Unquiet Grave* to him in 1944. Cecil Beaton's *Scrapbook* (1937) is dedicated to him, as are a number of Craxton's pictures.[44] In Roland Penrose's *Scrap Book* there is an illustration of a drawing of Watson by Giacometti, whose portrait of him, dated 1953, was given to the Museum of Modern Art in New York by Pierre Matisse; Pavel Tchelitchew painted a portrait of him in 1934 as a knight in armour[45] and so on.[46]

In 1974, following Connolly's death, there appeared a number of tributes to Connolly and Watson. Alan Pryce-Jones, who had known Watson since 1923, entitled his article 'The Kind, Sad Benefactor'. Roland Penrose quoted what he had written in 1956 on Watson's death: 'By the integrity of his actions and the acumen of his judgment, Peter Watson has created a tradition for the ICA in which devotion to the arts as a life-giving force becomes the antidote to anxieties of a pessimistic age.' Priaulx Rainier described Watson as the most generous of men, 'perhaps the last

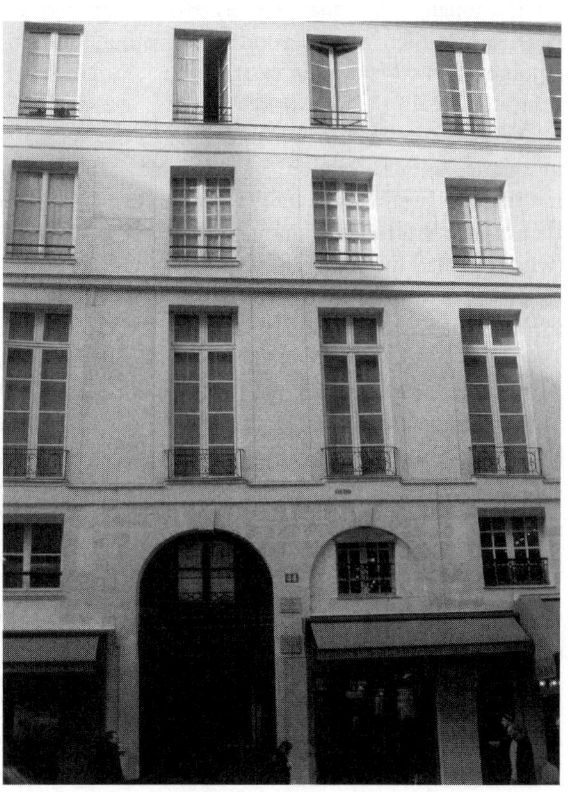

The Paris home of Peter Watson at 44 rue du Bac

true patron of the Arts'.[47] David Mellor noted that there existed no history of patronage in England and America for modern painting of the 1930s and 1940s, but if it existed it would have to include Peter Watson.[48]

Some indication of what a highly sophisticated member of the London art world read at the time can be seen from the 146 lots of books sold at Sotheby's by Watson's executors on 29 October 1956. These lots consisted of a great variety of art books (it is impossible to know whether there were many other books retained or not sold for some reason). Many of them were by or about contemporary artists and, while it is not surprising that the collection included works by his old *Horizon* colleagues, Connolly and Spender, inscribed personally to Watson, there cannot have been many Englishmen with books including the works of Picasso and Dalí also personally inscribed to him.

Kenneth Clark

Kenneth Clark (1903-83) dominated many aspects of the London art world for a considerable period. Immersed by his own precocious characteristics, rather than by any family pressure, in the history of art from an early age, and brought up in considerable wealth, such that his buying tastes could be (and were) indulged throughout his life, he became director of the National Gallery in 1933 at the age of 30, forming his own extensive collection of pictures along the way. He resigned as director in 1945. By then he was familiar in an international, rather than merely British, art world of Duveen, Gulbenkian and Bernard Berenson, which was beyond most others in England at the time. Two volumes of autobiography[49] chart his extraordinary, privileged life, with its plethora of positions and achievements in the art world.

Whether he should fall under the category of patron, in the same way as the others mentioned in this section, is debatable. He almost falls into a category of his own, so multifarious were his activities and interests. His books did not deal with 20th-century British art,[50] although among his seemingly innumerable close friends were Sutherland (whom he had met in 1935), Piper and Moore.

It is possible to follow the relationship between Sutherland and Clark in some detail through the 77 letters held in the Tate Archive.[51] The first of these dates from 3 September 1936 and its tone typifies the whole sequence of this correspondence. In it Sutherland thanks Clark for his letter and for the enclosed cheque. On 28 February 1938 he thanks him for something else Clark has done for him. On 7 September 1938 he says 'as for your general kindness all round, I always count myself the most fortunate painter in history'. He even acknowledges that he values Clark's criticism of his work, which he tries to act on 'where possible'. A year later a letter begins 'you are angelic to us'; it goes on, 'your generosity transcends all that I could ever have believed of one human to others'. And so it goes on. There is something faintly disagreeable in this endless catalogue of thanking, which stretches all through these letters. Gradually they meet less, although the families are close enough for the Sutherlands to spend Christmas with the Clarks in 1945, 1955, 1957 and 1959, for example.

While it is not usually possible to tell what Sutherland is thanking him for, a whole range of small examples can gradually be assembled. Clark gives him books; he lends Sutherland £2,500 for the purchase of The White House at the end of 1945; he helps Sutherland to get the portrait of Somerset Maugham through Customs in April 1951; and in the same letter (of 15 April) Sutherland also thanks him for performing the opening ceremony at Sutherland's big exhibition in London that year. All in all, it would be accurate to say that Clark was Sutherland's patron.

It may be assumed that he exerted extensive influence over the fame of certain artists through the series of small volumes published in paperback under the Penguin imprint called 'The Penguin Modern Painters', for which he acted as general editor.[52] At the time, art books were not produced as small-scale, cheap volumes intended for a wide readership; they were expensive specialist productions aimed at those who were already connoisseurs (Peter Watson comes to mind). Under the influence of Allen Lane, these Penguin books were therefore breaking new ground. Clark's contribution as editor was largely made early in the process: he chose the artists to be included and he suggested who should be asked to write the text. The first four books came out in April 1944 (although some bear the date of 1943). Their production, on comparatively high-quality paper and with carefully created reproductions of the pictures, was astonishing in light of the wartime conditions which affected the printing industry and also because of their cheapness. The earliest issues cost 2/6d and this did not increase (and then only to 3/6d) until 1947. Moreover, the sheer effort involved in the fairly primitive Penguin publishing house getting texts settled, pictures photographed and reproductions adjusted to satisfy some incredibly demanding painters, commands respect. It is significant that the volumes were produced wholly in co-operation with the artists, who were allowed to vet and, in most cases, to adjust the texts. Some artists – Paul Nash and Bawden seem to fall into this category – were very demanding in settling the books so that they met with their satisfaction. When it is considered that the first four volumes each sold in excess of 40,000 copies, it may be imagined that the artists were right to take such care over what must have been a major widening of their reputations.

The British artists chosen by Clark, and their respective authors, were, in order of appearance: Moore (Geoffrey Grigson), Sutherland (Eddie Sackville-West),[53] Grant (Raymond Mortimer), Paul Nash (Herbert Read), Smith (Philip Hendy), Piper (John Betjeman), Burra (John Rothenstein), Pasmore (Clive Bell), Bawden (JM Richards), Stanley Spencer (Eric Newton), Ben Nicholson (John Summerson), William Nicholson (Robert Nichols), Hodgkins (Myfanwy Evans), Jones (Robin Ironside), and Hitchens (Patrick Heron). A book on Ardizzone by V.S. Pritchett was announced but never published. A few foreign artists

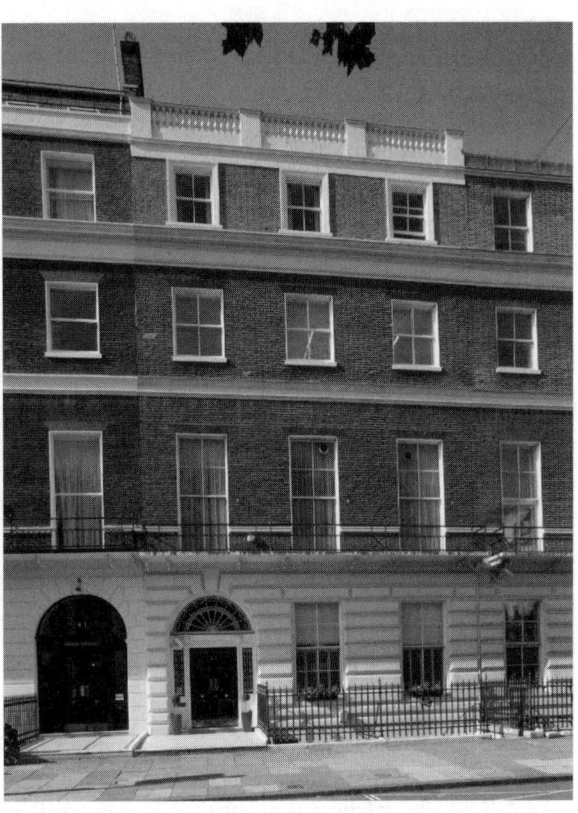

43 Portland Place, London W1, home of Kenneth Clark

were published. Those involved, including Clark, gradually lost interest in pursuing the series, which was really born out of a wartime feeling that more should be done for artists in such dire times. In addition, the market for such books changed after the War as other publishing houses caught up and competed for the cheap art-book market.

Shortly after the beginning of the War Clark had also been largely responsible for establishing the War Artists Advisory Committee, with the intention of saving artists from military service (although even this was not without risk, as the deaths on active service of Ravilious in 1942 and Hennell in 1945 indicate). In this rôle, he had plenty of opportunities to advance the interests of all sorts of artists who were potentially available to participate in the scheme and there is little doubt that he exercised his powers of official patronage with some vigour. There are glimpses of this in the letters retained in the Clark papers in the Tate.

Mervyn Peake, for example, wrote to Clark with increasing frustration, begging him to help get him into a War job which was relevant to his skills.[54]

As another small illustration of Clark's ability to influence the way in which the modern British art world developed, he found himself, following the end of the War, appointed as Chairman of what was called the Allocations Committee[55]. This reported to the Treasury and its task was to arrange the dispersal of the approximately 5,500 pictures which the WAAC had obtained. The Tate was given first choice, then the British Council. The Imperial War Museum got some works of art and priority in what were called 'records'. The distributions proposed by the Allocations Committee were approved by Parliament on 25 March 1947 and the physical distribution of the works began.

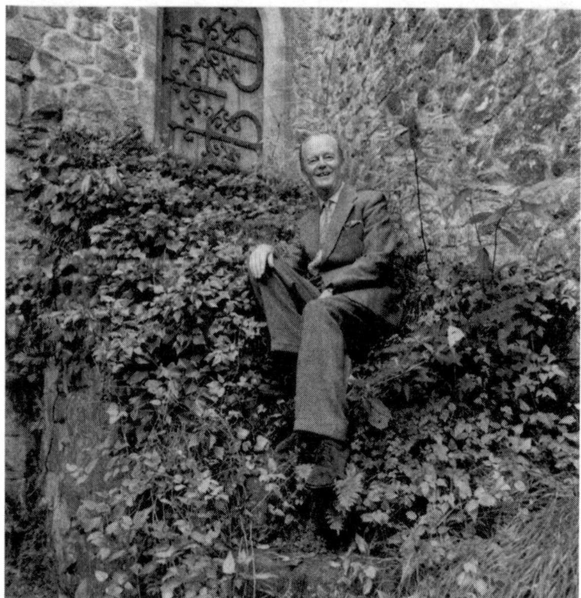
Kenneth Clark at his house in Kent, Saltwood Castle

During the War, Clark was still Director of the National Gallery and, in that rôle, his surreptitious efforts at helping a wide variety of artists are apparent. For example, his papers[56] contain letters from John Betjeman in 1941, when he was working as the Press attaché to the British Ambassador to Ireland. In these letters, Betjeman encourages Clark to help find a London gallery prepared to show the work of Nano Reid and he also asks him if there is any chance of Clark holding a Yeats exhibition at the National Gallery. One feels a bit sorry for Clark coming under this sort of pressure. He duly wrote to Rex Nan Kivell at the Redfern and asked him if he could exhibit Reid's work (she was not at the time very well-known), and he thought about the Yeats proposal (and then wrote back saying he was not so sure about Yeats).[57] Betjeman also badgered Clark into coming over to Dublin and giving a lecture in 1941.

As a complementary scheme, he was also involved in setting up the programme known as 'Recording Britain'.[58] This involved artists being paid to make topographical watercolour drawings of places and buildings of characteristic national interest, particularly those exposed to the danger of destruction by the operations of war.[59] The Pilgrim Trust supported this initiative (as it did the Council for the Encouragement of Music and the Arts) by providing grants amounting to about £6,000. The administration of the fund was handed over to P.H. Jowett, who was principal of the RCA at the time, Clark and the artist, Russell Flint (representing the Royal Academy), although the day-to-day running of the scheme was in the hands of its secretary, Arnold Palmer. They chose the artists (Clark, for example, nominating Piper, Graham Bell and Rowntree) and agreed the subjects they should cover. Exhibitions were held during the War, as the number of pictures flooded in.[60] Eventually 1,549 watercolours were produced by a total of 97 artists and the works were published after the War, by Oxford University Press, in four volumes from 1946-1949.[61] The significance for this study is, of course, that it was yet another opportunity for Clark to influence directly the life of contemporary British artists, no doubt many of whom were grateful for an opportunity to get paid for some sort of national service without joining the forces, especially at a time when the national markets for their work may have been difficult. Particularly satisfying, both now and perhaps at the time to Kenneth Clark, is that the nature of the commissions meant that serious, professional and traditional artists were engaged, many of whose names did not feature at all in shows of modern British artists, either at the time or subsequently. A good example is the exquisite work of Stanley Roy Badmin. Some of the artists were those noted elsewhere in this book – such as Hennell, Michael Rothenstein, Rowntree, Spear and Piper – but most are now little known.[62]

Clark's status as a collector of modern British art is not always noticed. In fact he owned an extensive collection, as can be seen from the amount he was prepared to give away. In 1946 he notified the committee of the CAS that he was proposing to donate a number of pictures which were surplus to his requirements. Some members of the committee were invited round to his house in Hampstead to see them. In all there were over

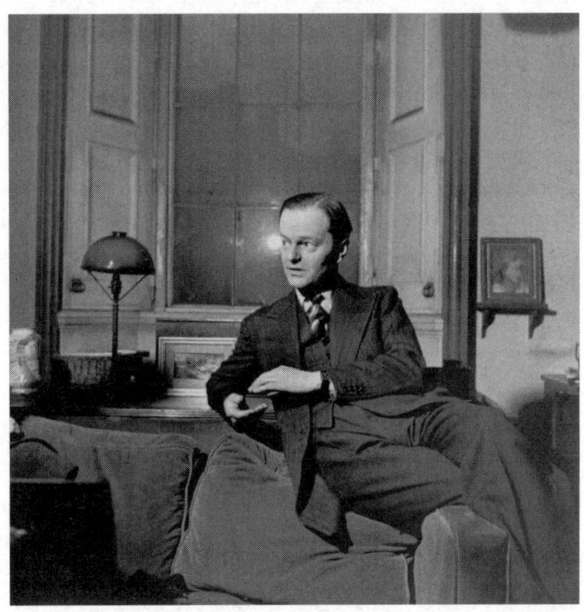

Kenneth Clark as a young director of the National Gallery

70 pictures. This included seven works by Sutherland, four by Piper, eleven by Duncan Grant, three each by Pasmore, Vanessa Bell and Ardizzone, six by Mary Kessell, two by each of Gowing, Roberts, Spear, Suddaby, Tibble and Paul Nash and single items by, among others, Graham Bell, Coldstream, Collins, Colquhoun, Darwin, Freedman, Fry, Hodgkins, Henry Lamb, Lowinsky, Frances Macdonald, Weight and Wilde. The Committee later in the year gleefully reported that all the pictures had been allocated to museums and galleries around the country (and, in some cases, the world: the Colquhoun went to Tasmania). As if this wasn't enough of a clear-out, he started talking about giving more pictures away in late 1947. In April 1948 this second batch was listed as consisting of two by Ardizzone and Graham Bell and one each from a number of others, including Craxton, Dunlop, Freedman, Sutherland, Spear, Grant, Macdonald and Peake.

Clark wrote in 1939, just after the beginning of the War, about the decline of patronage. He thought that a major consequence was that important artists had withdrawn into a closed world, in which they painted to please each other rather than seeking to communicate with an audience. Such artists needed patronage, but it was not widely available. Patronage to him involved the commissioning of art, although in Clark's case this was not a principle widely followed at his own expense-portraits commissioned from Duncan Grant and Pavel

Tchelitchew not amounting to a great deal. On the financial side, he set up a trust fund, which benefited some artists with a monthly payment. As we have seen, he played some part in the financial support of the establishment of the art school later to be known as the Euston Road School. During the War he helped Sutherland and Moore financially and he also helped David Jones financially over a long period, through a fund organised by Jim Ede. In 1953 Clark was to be instrumental in obtaining a Civil List pension for Jones.[63]

Considering that Clark's artistic focus was usually backwards, or at least towards modern painters working in a recognisable style, such as Coldstream, it is not surprising that he could find no place in his heart for abstract work and there can be little doubt that the astonishing – and surely incorrect – praise of Pasmore ('whom I believe to have been one of the two or three most talented English painters of this century'), in the second volume of his autobiography was based on the representational Pasmore, rather than the utterly different, but equally unimportant, abstract Pasmore. It may, indeed, not be a coincidence that those 'modern' British painters favoured by Clark (a Wykehamist) were Pasmore (an old Harrovian), Sutherland (Epsom College) and Piper (ditto). An ability to blend in with the rather grand social life that Clark enjoyed was certainly – for his artist friends – not a bad feature.[64] As Clark said in *Another Part of the Wood*, 'The Sutherlands did not recoil from smart society, and came frequently to our dinner parties, where they were much admired.'

Jimmy Bomford

Jimmy Bomford died in 1979 at the age of 83.[65] Starting out[66] as a gilts jobber on the Stock Exchange with Wedd Jefferson, he had given up the City in 1938 and bought a farm at Aldbourne in Wiltshire. He bought (and eventually sold) various collections, including an extremely impressive collection of modern European art which had been put together with the help of André Derain. This included work by Renoir, Modigliani, Cézanne, Manet, Utrillo, Picasso and Degas. Under the auspices of CEMA, he allowed his French pictures, which included pictures from many centuries and not just contemporary ones, to be toured around England during the War under the title 'Paintings of the French School from a private collection'.[67] As with so many collections assembled at great cost over the years, the possibility that some of Bomford's pictures were fakes was aired publicly by Thomas Bodkin, Director of the Barber Institute of Fine Arts at Birmingham University. He published a letter in the *Times* in November 1943 wondering why CEMA was allowing an exhibition including fakes to be toured. He alleged, in particular, that three Monets were obvious fakes. This led to replies by Bomford and Clark and a series of letters culminating in a *Times* leader.[68] Bodkin was, of course, a notorious letter-writer with a reputation for enjoying controversy when it suited him. (His role in the development of the arts in Ireland is dealt with in the section on Dublin in Chapter 1.) The show eventually reached London after the end of the War, by now under the auspices of the Arts Council rather than CEMA.

The catalogue to the CEMA show had an introduction by Eric Newton and an article by Bomford himself ostensibly on the question why the lady in the Modigliani picture had such a long neck. Bomford used this question as an excuse to attempt a general elucidation of modern art. The catalogue to the Arts Council exhibition began with a curious preface stating that, while the original intention in showing the pictures had not included the idea of showing them in London, it was now felt necessary to do so to enable London viewers to see for themselves the pictures which had been challenged by Bodkin. A total of 46 pictures were shown.

At this point Bomford seems to have started another collection of pictures, this time of contemporary British art. In this phase, with really considerable prescience, he alighted upon Francis Bacon. This was in 1945, when Bacon was little known and even less respected. Bomford was undoubtedly the greatest early Bacon collector, only later to be joined by the better-known Sainsbury family. Bomford ended up with over 20 works by Bacon, but he sold them all when, according to his own account, he took offence at Bacon's Van Gogh pictures, which started to emerge in 1956. Exactly when he sold them is not clear. The catalogue for the retrospective Bacon exhibition at the Tate from 24 May-1 July 1962 notes a number of Bacon's works which had been owned by Bomford, but it doesn't list him as a lender. The fact that he 'recalled' his Bacon pictures from the Swindon collection, the latest in February 1960, suggests that he was perhaps reassembling his complete collection prior to sale. The works from the Tate catalogue which mentioned a Bomford provenance are:

1 *The Crucifixion* of 1932
2 *Study for the Human Figure at the Cross II*, 1945-46
3 *Head IV*, 1959
4 *Pope Shouting*, 1951
5 *Pope with Fan Canopy*, 1951
6 *Landscape*, 1952
7 *Study for Portrait III*, 1953
8 *Three Studies of the Human Head*, 1953
9 *Pope*, 1954
10 *Chimpanzee*, 1955
11 *Man with Head Wound*, 1955
12 *Self-Portrait*, 1956
13 *Lying figure no. 3*, 1959
14 *Lying figure no. 4*, 1959.

All were listed as having been owned by Jimmy Bomford's wife and all are followed in the provenance section by a reference to Marlborough Fine Arts, and so perhaps the collection had been sold to the Marlborough sometime around 1960-1962.[69]

It is not now that easy to piece together whether Bomford should be called a collector or a patron. Pointing towards the latter is the fact that he purchased a cottage in the village where he lived – Aldbourne – for the painter Jankel Adler, in the 1940s and it was there that Adler died in 1949.[70] Furthermore, he gave some of his contemporary British art collection to Swindon Art Gallery, much of it in 1946. The pictures given were by Adler,[71] Bacon, Despiau, Downs, Gowing, Le Brocquy, Lowry, Martin,[72] Mason, Melhuish, Moore, P. Nash, B. Nicholson, Jack Smith, Sutherland[73] and Szobel.[74] At least in the case of Le Brocquy, who had been introduced to Bomford by Adler, Bomford retained some pictures. In the catalogue for the Le Brocquy retrospective held at the Municipal Gallery of Modern Art in Dublin in November 1966, Mrs Bomford was shown as owning *Man Creating Bird* of 1948 and he was listed as owning *Children in a Wood* of 1954. Following his wife's death, Bomford returned these works to the artist as a gift, an act of considerable generosity (bearing in mind that he had paid £300 for the latter picture in 1955).

What became of Bomford's collection of foreign pictures is not known. Le Brocquy records that Bomford lent various pictures to the 'Irish Exhibition of Living Art' in Dublin in 1952, including *Portrait of Madame Eluard* (1937), *Harlequin* (1927) and *La Plage* (1934) by Picasso and *La Révolte du Sage* of 1916 by de Chirico.[75]

COLLECTORS

A thin line exists between patrons and collectors of the period and a reader who disagrees with my categorisation may well be right. What is certainly right is that almost all contemporary pictures were bought by private individuals and not by the State or the supposed new bodies of patrons. It would not be possible to identify clearly what percentage of pictures were initially sold to institutions or State entities, as distinct from private collectors, but we may assume the percentage to be small.[76]

In March 1950 the CAS put on an exhibition at the Tate called 'The Private Collector', which consisted of 339 items from the collections of 88 members of the CAS. Sir Colin Anderson wrote the foreword to the catalogue as the honorary treasurer. The catalogue cover was designed by John Piper. Robin Ironside was heavily involved in the organisation of the exhibition. Those who lent the most pictures were Anderson, Bliss, Clark, Evill, Le Bas, Marsh and Ridley (all of whom will be dealt with in the next section).[77] Two years later the CAS had another go at the same theme, again at the Tate, with an exhibition called 'Seventeen Collectors' and it is interesting to see who these collectors were. In the order in which they appeared in the catalogue (with another foreword by Anderson), the collectors were Sir Philip Hendy, Raymond Mortimer, E.C. Gregory, Kenneth Clark, Mrs Cazalet-Keir, the Queen Mother, Hugo Pitman, the Hon Sir Jasper Ridley, Howard Bliss, Eardley Knollys, Anderson, W.A. Evill, Eric Newton, Lord Methuen, Sir Edward Marsh, Edward Le Bas and Sir John Rothenstein.

This is a useful starting point for analysing in a little more detail the English people with notable collections of modern British art of the period.[78] (Details of non-British art lent will be given, in order to give some idea of how these individuals chose to collect. They mostly owned work by non-British 'modern' artists, as well as British – the main exception being Evill. Many of them would also have owned earlier work. Howard Bliss, for example, owned many works by Gainsborough.)

Sir Philip Hendy

Hendy had worked his way up from a lowly position at the Wallace Collection, where he had worked from 1923-27, to become director of the National Gallery, in succession to Kenneth Clark, in January 1946, a position he held until December 1967. In the meantime he had been appointed curator of paintings for the Boston Museum of Fine Arts in 1930 and, as such, had already been responsible for buying modern European and British paintings, including work by Sickert, Gore, John Nash and Bevan. Having returned from America after a controversy arising from his purchase of a Matisse, he had been appointed director of the Leeds City Art Gallery in 1934 (and was also Slade Professor at Oxford 1936-46). In 1944 he had published a slim Penguin book on Matthew Smith, as one of the well-known series at the time. In 1945, shortly before leaving Leeds to take up his appointment at the National Gallery, Hendy organised a retrospective of the work of Hitchens, held at Temple Newsam House. His presence at Leeds ensured that the Art Gallery there now has one of the most representative collections of British 20th century art outside London.[79] During his period as director, works by Sickert, Gertler, John Nash, Paul Nash, Wadsworth, Smith, Wood, Hodgkins, Spencer, Sutherland, Epstein, Hepworth, Tunnard, Ben Nicholson, Piper and Hitchens were acquired, either by purchase or gift (or through the CAS). He was knighted in 1950.[80] In the 'Seventeen Collectors' show he lent pictures by Adler, Herman and Sutherland, together with two Moore sculptures.

Raymond Mortimer

Mortimer's status as a collector is not in doubt. There are occasional mentions of his various homes over the years being crowded with pictures and on 21 November 2003 Christie's held a sale in London of what must represent at least part of his former collection. This had passed on Mortimer's death from one friend (the architect Paul Hyslop) to another (the historian Jack Lander). The catalogue had a useful note from another friend (the art historian Richard Shone), briefly describing the origin of the collection. The highlights of the lots sold at Christie's were the large Sickerts, Hitchens, Sutherlands, one Scott and the Gores, but there were also works by Hill, Daintrey, Le Bas, Tibble, Banting, V. Bell, Piper, Grant, Gowing and Philpot. Shone also mentions work by Alan Reynolds, but that was not included in the sale.

In fact Mortimer's collection had not been limited to works by English artists.[81] He had had works by Manet, Pissarro and Rodin, for example, and his treasured works by Picasso, Matisse and Braque, which had been sent away to a friend's house in Vermont in America for the War for safety had, ironically, been destroyed by fire while there. He said that he bought pictures 'which excited immediate sensuous desire, like lips or strawberries'. This desire did not, of course, extend to abstract art. For 'Seventeen Collectors' he lent work by Constance Lloyd, Brabazon, Bussy, Matisse, Rodin, Klee, Anrep, Scott, Sutherland, Hitchens, Grant, Sickert, Le Bas, Renoir and V. Bell.

Eric Gregory

Often known as Peter Gregory, he was a printer and publisher and the managing director of the art publishing house Lund Humphries. He endowed the Gregory Fellowships at Leeds University in 1950,[82] was a director of the *Burlington Magazine*, a committee member of the CAS, and governor of Chelsea Polytechnic, St Martin's School of Art and the Bath Academy of Art at Corsham. He was friendly with Herbert Read and Henry Moore and was very supportive of the ICA in its early years, acting as its first treasurer and frequently supporting it financially. A selection of 57 items from his collection was displayed after his death at the ICA.[83] The catalogue had an introduction by Henry Moore whom Gregory had supported early in his career. In this, Moore described their friendship as the closest of his life. Moore set out a good case for describing Gregory as a patron of modern British art: 'If he felt that a young, unknown painter or sculptor was sincere, serious and talented, he would buy – as much to help the young artist as to add to his collection. That will explain why there is a certain unevenness in the works here shown: and an examination of the dates at which many of these works passed into his hands will show that he frequently bought from artists who only later achieved fame and fortune. There is no need to say what an enormous help such generous perspicacity is to young artists.'[84] When his collection was sold at Sotheby's on 4 November 1959, it included about 100 works, with particular emphasis on artists who had worked in St Ives, namely seven Ben Nicholsons, seven Hepworths, five Frosts, an Alfred Wallis and a Barns-Graham. It also included pictures by Ayres, Vanessa Bell, Blow, Coxon, Daintrey, Davie, Fry, Gear, Hennell, Hepworth, Hodgkins, Henry Lamb, Moore, Pasmore, Pitchforth, Scott, Sutherland and Turnbull, together with sculpture by Gabo, Butler, Dobson, Hepworth, Meadows, Clatworthy, Paolozzi, Moore and Turnbull.

It would be interesting to compare this list with the list of works lent to 'Seventeen Collectors', which consisted of pictures by Modigliani, Derain, Hartung, Picasso, Froy, Braque, Richards, Kauffer, Henry Lamb, Smith, Pasmore, Marcoussis, Paolozzi, Ben Nicholson, Gritchenko, Sutherland, Frost, Hepworth, Arp, Giacometti, Moore and Penrose, together with quite a few items of sculpture.

Following his death, two memorial services were held for him, with the addresses subsequently printed together in a booklet. The first was held at Bradford Cathedral on 2 March 1959, where the address was given by Sir Charles Morris, while the second was at St Luke's, Chelsea, on 5 March, the address by Sir Herbert Read. Completing the tributes to him was the 'Gregory Memorial Exhibition' at Leeds City Art Gallery from 9 March to 10 April 1960. The introduction to the catalogue was also by Read, commenting that Gregory 'was an intimate friend of our greatest artists, and supported them long before they were well-known or successful'.

Thelma Cazalet-Keir

Born into great wealth as a Cazalet (sister of the rather better-known Victor), she grew up in a highly privileged way, her parents owning at one stage four houses when she was a child, and she was immersed in the political life of the 1920s to '40s. She knew many political leaders as friends (Lloyd George, Baldwin, Chamberlain and Churchill, as examples) and, having begun her own political career as a member of the London County Council, she became a Conservative MP for Islington East in 1931, a seat she held until the landslide Labour post-War general election victory of 1945 turned her out as well as Churchill. That was the end of her political career, which had culminated in early 1945 with her reaching the level of Parliamentary Secretary to the Board of Education.

Her autobiography, *From the Wings*, is an incredibly boring read, with almost nothing to indicate why her name should feature at all in the British art world. In fact, she must have used some small part of her wealth to buy pictures. She mentions owning works by Augustus John (a family friend), Smith, Sickert, Stanley Spencer, Paul Nash and Sutherland, and she was a member of the CEMA Council from the beginning. She joined the CAS, through the influence of Eddie Marsh and David Balniel (later Earl of Crawford and Balcarres) and was one of their buyers during the War (persuading, according to her own account, Augustus John to sell the CAS his portrait of Dylan Thomas for £150). For the CAS 'Private Collector' exhibition at the Tate in 1950 she lent works by Hitchens, A. John, G. John, Smith and S. Spencer and for the 'Seventeen Collectors' show in 1952 her contribution was work by Sickert, A. John, G. John, Smith, Sutherland, S. Spencer, Richards, P. Nash and Jones.

If she can be discounted as a figure of real substance in the art world, her astuteness as an observer may also be questioned. It was meaninglessly loose of her to write (in 1967) that 'private patrons of the arts have been taxed out of existence', although no doubt that does indicate a contemporary attitude at the time which we should acknowledge.

The Queen Mother[85]

A recent study[86] has reminded us that the Queen Mother was a regular collector of watercolours and drawings of our period and, although not the subject of the study, also of oil paintings. Some of these she bought and some she commissioned; others were gifts, often from artists who had become personal friends. Her buying was guided by friends in the art world, particularly Kenneth Clark and Jasper Ridley, and also by artists such as Augustus John and Edward Seago and friends such as Osbert Sitwell, but it is not suggested that she was incapable of making her own choices and, while her collection was not unduly adventurous, it was by no means as 'safe' as it could have been. Choosing Piper during the War to paint a series of pictures of Windsor Castle, in case it was destroyed by bombing, was not, for example, the safest of choices. We tend to use hindsight when looking now at an artist like Piper, who was certainly not a traditional landscape or architectural draftsman. It is also worth having in mind the huge size of her collection. Susan Owens mentions that, at her

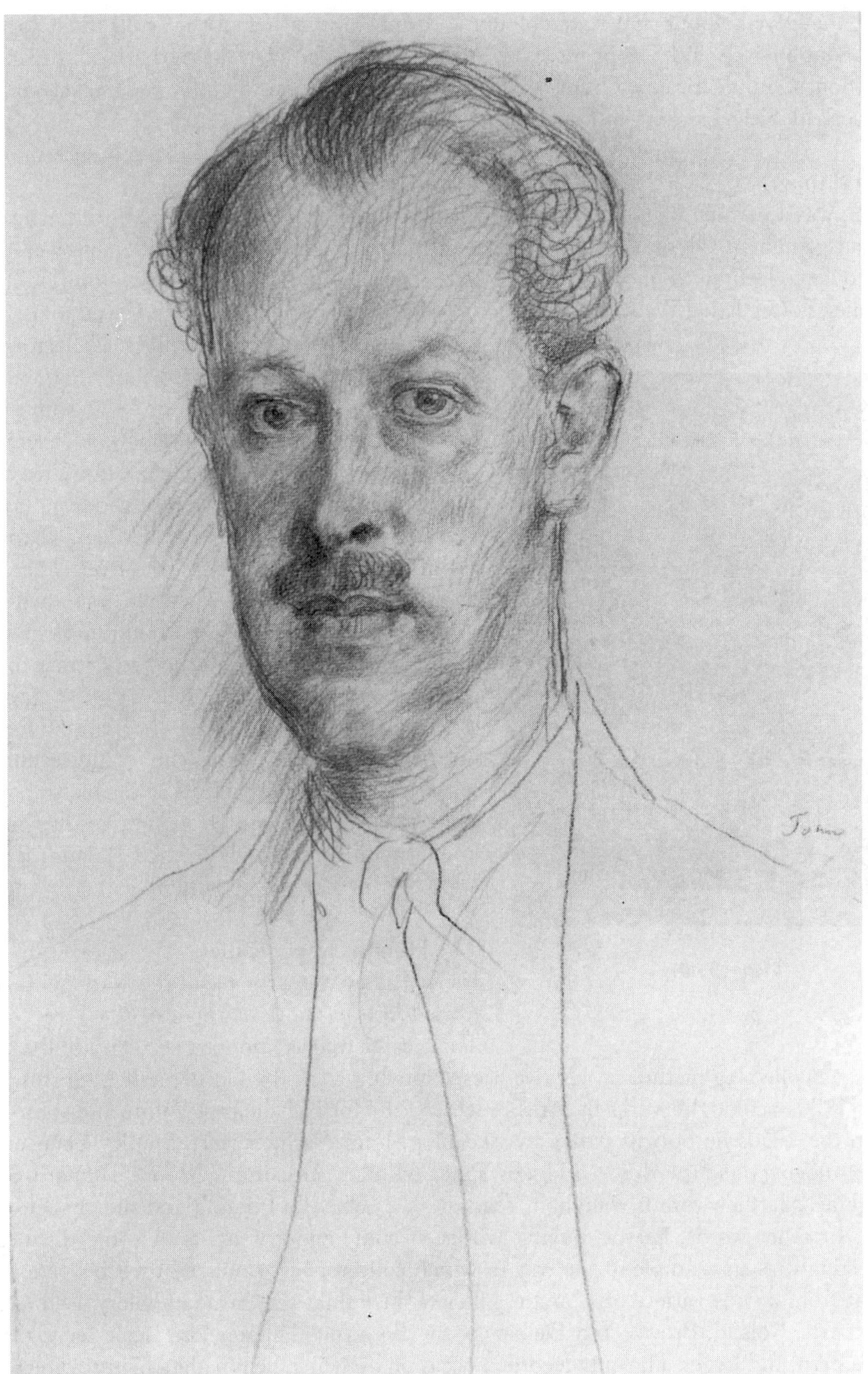

Hugo Pitman by Augustus John. Private collection

death, there were about 550 watercolours and drawings in her private collection, together with about 300 oils and 350 prints. Her collection included work by Sutherland, Piper, Paul Nash, Jones, Smith, Bratby, Grant, William Nicholson, Augustus John and Sickert and she lent work by Sisley, Sickert and Smith to 'Seventeen Collectors'.

Hugo Pitman

Pitman was a partner at stockbrokers Rowe and Pitman from March 1922 until his death.[87] He had gained an Olympic rowing medal in his youth. A man of considerable wealth, he formed a collection of modern British art, lending works by Augustus John, Gilman, Daumier, Potter, Ethel Walker, Winifred Nicholson, Yeats, Innes, Gowing, Gwen John, Steer, Pasmore and Monet to 'Seventeen Collectors'. He was married to a niece of the painter Sargent, and was a friend of Augustus John,[88] at some point becoming his financial adviser,[89] and there is a portrait of Pitman by John. He became a trustee of the Tate. His support for modern art is interestingly revealed in Lillian Browse's autobiography, *Duchess of Cork Street*. There she describes how, in 1944, when she was invited by Roland and Delbanco to join them to form an art dealing partnership, she turned to Pitman before agreeing. Apart from free advice, he also gave her a few thousand pounds as her capital for the business, suggesting that she could eventually repay him in pictures if she was unable to pay the money back. She says that, as a result, he was known within the newly formed Roland, Browse and Delbanco as 'the godfather'.

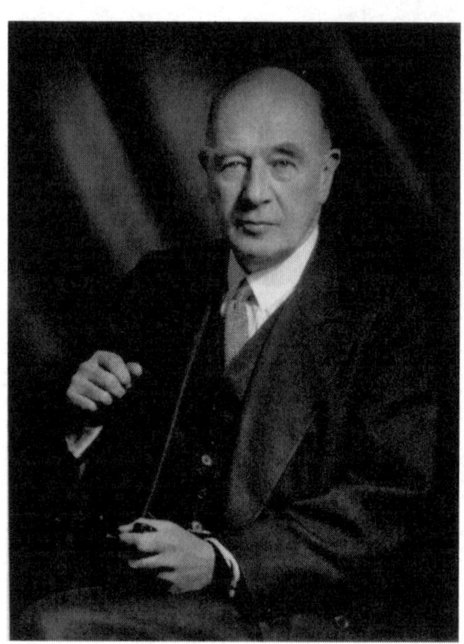

Jasper Ridley

The Hon Sir Jasper Ridley

Jasper Ridley was a trustee of the National Gallery from 1939-46 and Chairman of the Tate Gallery Trustees, as well as honorary secretary of the CAS. He began collecting pictures in his twenties,[90] buying works by Gertler and Augustus John. In the 1920s he bought works by artists such as Pitchforth, Ethelbert White and John Nash and in the 1930s he bought works by Skeaping, John Nash, Sickert, Stanley Spencer and Tibble, moving on in the '40s to Suddaby, Piper, Minton, Armstrong, Moore, Tunnard, Spear, Hodgkins, Matthew Smith, Vaughan, Yeats and Appelbee and Sutherland shortly before his death. In other words, he was buying works of contemporary artists of some distinction. Interestingly, as an example of the way in which collectors accumulated their collections, he bought from a wide variety of London galleries, including the Arcade Gallery, Lefevre, the Beaux Arts, Roland, Browse and Delbanco, the Berkeley Galleries, the Leicester Galleries, the Redfern, and Leger. The only recorded occasion on which he bought a picture direct from the artist was in February 1948, when he bought the Yeats in Dublin for £40. The highest price he ever paid for a picture was the £157 he paid for an oil portrait by Henry Lamb in February 1930. He commissioned Henry Moore to produce a *Madonna* for St Peter's Church at Claydon in Suffolk,[91] which was intended as a war memorial to his son and to three other villagers killed in the War. It was completed in 1949. By the time 'Seventeen Collectors' opened in 1952, he had died, but his executors lent works by Pissarro, Villon and Toulouse-Lautrec, as well as many of the artists mentioned above.

Howard Bliss

The overwhelming emphasis of Bliss's collection of modern British art was on the work of Hitchens. Bliss's father was an American businessman settled in England and his elder brother was the composer Sir Arthur Bliss. Bliss had made contact with Hitchens in 1944 and rapidly began to acquire works by him. He was said to own over 50 works by this artist by the late 1940s. It would be no exaggeration to say that Bliss became obsessive about collecting and promoting Hitchens' work and, in the process, he subjected the artist to a barrage of correspondence until his death in 1976. In 1950 the Arts Council put on an exhibition of Bliss's collection of works by Hitchens and the next year it exhibited Bliss's collection generally, his taste being described by the *Sunday Times* as 'fastidious'. Wyndham Lewis in the *Listener* (on 19 January) was a little more direct. The collection showed a 'pervasive dimness'. Bliss was obviously keen on the 'thin, brown dim amorphous world of Ivon Hitchens'. The pictures were all weightless and soft – there was, Lewis pointed out, no place for Robert Colquhoun in this collection.

It is easy now to forget that Bliss collected works by many other contemporary British artists, including Piper, Vaughan, Scott, Heron, Craxton, Collins and Le Brocquy, but never to the same extent as his collection of Hitchens. A large number of works from the collection were sold at the Leicester Galleries in January 1950 in a show called 'From Gainsborough to Hitchens. A Selection of Paintings and Drawings from the Howard Bliss Collection'. This consisted of 145 works, including 17 by Hitchens, 5 by Tunnard, 21 by Le Brocquy and 5 by Hurry, together with work by Piper, Sickert, Minton, Hodgkins, Vaughan, Collins, Evans, Scott, Spear, Smith, Heron, Gotlib, Adler and Craxton. Without knowing how many works were actually sold by the Leicester Galleries, it indicates the extraordinary extent of his collection to see that, by 1952, he was still able to lend to 'Seventeen Collectors' (presumably without totally denuding the walls of his home), four works by Gear, three by each of Hitchens, Adams and Scott, two by Heron, James Hull, Adler and Murray, together with individual pictures by le Witt, Frost, Hilton, Le Brocquy, Tuckwell, Sickert, Craxton and Fraser.

Eardley Knollys[92]

Knollys took up painting late in life, but before then he had run the Storran Gallery in London and had worked for the National Trust (he features regularly in James Lees-Milne's diaries). During our period he wrote occasional art criticism for the *New Statesman and Nation*. His only loans to 'Seventeen Collectors' were five works, all by foreign artists.

Wilfrid Evill

Evill was a solicitor whose clients included Stanley Spencer and Sutherland.[93] (For example, he acted for Sutherland when he was buying his house in Kent – the White House at Trottiscliffe – towards the end of 1945.) It seems possible that he was not universally popular. There is a letter from Raymond Mortimer to Clark in the Tate Archive dated 23 November 1951, in which Mortimer begs Clark to do something to ensure that Evill does not become chairman of the CAS (following the death of Jasper Ridley). Mortimer says that he would rather support anyone else than see Evill take on the job. A selection of 44 pictures from his

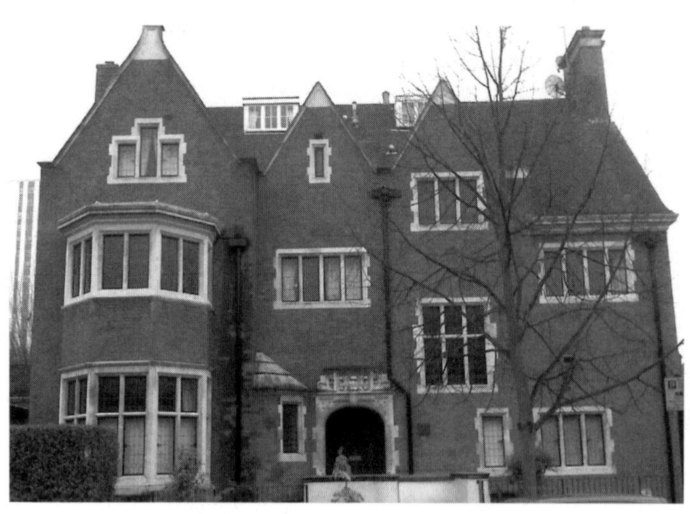
House of the solicitor and collector
Wilfrid Evill at 39 Eton Avenue, London NW3

collection of modern British art was displayed at the Leicester Galleries in 1952[94] and the whole collection[95] was ultimately given to the CAS in 1961 and a catalogue was produced to list the works which were put on display in April and May 1961. The collection had been formed over the period 1927-1961 and its extent is astonishing. Without distinguishing for the purpose of counting between paintings, drawings and prints (although most were paintings), Evill had amassed, for example, 26 works by Sutherland, 21 by Roberts, 16 by Gilbert Spencer[96] and a staggering 47 by Stanley Spencer. That is not to mention four by Burra, five by Alan Reynolds, five by Hitchens, two by Freud, three by Paul Nash and individual works by many others.[97] The other unusual feature is that his collection was entirely British. The Brighton Art Gallery put on a show of the collection in 1965 when 284 items were on display, although by this time some of the pictures had passed out of the collection following Evill's death.[98]

Eric Newton

Newton was a journalist who wrote art criticism for the *Guardian* and for the *Sunday Times* and he clearly had quite a collection of modern art, judging by the fact that he lent to 'Seventeen Collectors' work by Rossetti, Lowry, Freedman, Hodgkins, Wood, Sutherland, Lewis, Tisdall, B. Walker, Fitton, de Chirico, Renoir and de Botton.[99]

Lord Methuen

A landscape and figure painter who had been taught for a while by Sickert, Paul Methuen had held his first one-man show in London in 1928. This was followed by shows at the Leicester Galleries and at Colnaghi's. He was, at various times, President of the Royal Watercolours Academy and a trustee of the National Gallery and the Tate. He was elected RA in 1959. His family home, Corsham Court in Wiltshire, features occasionally in art-world memoirs and so on because after the War he allowed part of it to be used by the Bath Academy of Art and a number of well-known artists subsequently taught there. For 'Seventeen Collectors' he provided work by Augustus John, Sickert, Dobson, Segonzac, Fisher Prout, Devas, Hurry, Gilbert Spencer, Gross, Dunstan, Connard, Ososki and Guthrie.

Sir Edward Marsh

Marsh could have qualified for inclusion in the earlier part of this chapter, in the rôle of a patron of the arts. Support for this comes from the comment made by Jasper Ridley when Marsh's term on the committee of the Tate trustees finished in 1944: 'You are, if I may humbly say so, the ideal 20th century patron of art and we all know it.' He has been included here rather than there simply because his patronage really pre-dated the War. Following his retirement from the Civil Service in 1937 he became a trustee of the Tate (1937-44) and chairman of the CAS (1937-52). He had an extensive art collection,[100] although he claimed, in the introduction to his long list of loans in the 'Seventeen Collectors' catalogue, that, following his retirement from the Civil Service, he had barely bought a dozen pictures. Even so, the fact is that works were lent by Frith, G. Spencer, Dunlop, Morris, Ihlee, Pitchforth, Grant, B. Parker, Etchells, Fairweather, Ethel Walker, N. Newton, P. Nash, Steer, Buhler, Hitchens, Roberts, V. Bell, S. Spencer, Appelbee, Monnington, Wood, Gertler, Methuen, Pride, Ryan, R. Wyndham, Weight, Lady Ramsey, Drury, Currie, Bergen, Gore, Dane, Newton, Heath, Dawnay, H. Lamb, Medley, Smith, Birky, Coldstream, Galt, Grant and Gowing.

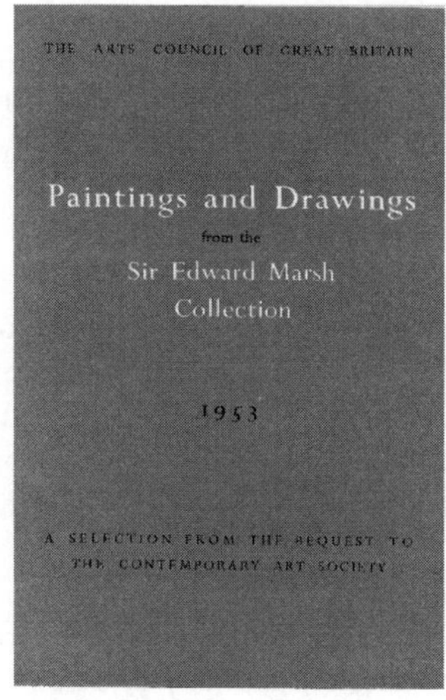

Before the War, he had become personally friendly with a large number of developing artists, such as Stanley Spencer, Mark Gertler, Paul Nash, Eurich, Wolfe, Pitchforth, Armstrong, Rex Whistler, Hillier, Freedman, Appelbee, Ravilious, Peake, Devas, Rothenstein, Coldstream, Buhler and Sutherland. According to his biography, he corresponded with 86 artists between the Wars, about 30 of whom were said to have known him as a regular visitor to their studios. He also kept in touch during this period with his older painter friends, such as the Spencer and Nash brothers, Smith, Roberts and Wadsworth. In October 1929, no fewer than 270 of his pictures had been exhibited at the Whitechapel. When Marsh died, he bequeathed his collection to the CAS and the Arts Council promptly staged an exhibition of a selection from the bequest. Bearing in mind that this was a selection, the whole collection must have been extensive. The Arts Council showed 30 oils (by Appelbee, Coldstream, Gertler, Gore, Gowry, Grant, Hillier, Hitchens, Innes, Morris, J. Nash, P. Nash, W. Nicholson, Roberts, Sickert, Smith, S. Spencer, Steer, Wadsworth, Weight and Wood) and 20 watercolours and drawings of similar quality.

The CAS also promoted the publication of a book.[101] The book, which astonishingly came out only four months after Marsh's death, contained short passages from a wide variety of his friends in the different worlds where his influence had been felt. There are many descriptions of his bachelor rooms in Raymond Buildings in Gray's Inn and the incredible stock of pictures which they contained, and the first section of the book contains contributions from friends in the art world. It begins with a warm piece by Raymond Mortimer, who had just replaced Marsh before his death as Chairman of the CAS: 'In his patronage of contemporary painting Eddie Marsh was nothing less than magnificent.' (What Mortimer seems to have meant by 'patronage' in this context was that Marsh had gone out of his way to choose pictures to buy by young artists who particularly needed sales.) Mortimer also pointed out that Marsh had given over 100 works to the CAS during his life, as well as the approximately 250 bequeathed in 1953. He added that the CAS had, on Marsh's retirement from Chairmanship of the CAS in late 1952, sought to commission Sutherland to paint Marsh's portrait. The artist had accepted, but had indicated that he would be unable to begin until the autumn of 1953, by which time, of course, Marsh was dead. The other contributions from the art world were from John Rothenstein, Brinsley Ford and Graham Sutherland himself.

As a mild corrective to the tone of adulation set by the book, and as an introduction to the next collector, it is interesting to note the comments of J. Wood Palmer in 1963 in the introduction to the catalogue of the exhibition of the collection of Edward Le Bas, held at the Royal Academy.[102] Commenting briefly on the great collections of other British collectors, he says about the Marsh collection viewed at his death: 'Seen by everyone, at his death, to have a tiara of pearls but a rather prolonged tail, since his heart clearly ruled his head and from kindness he bought many indifferent works.'

Edward Le Bas

A minor painter himself, Le Bas had private means which enabled him to collect pictures extensively and, to judge by the introduction to the catalogue referred to above, to assemble one of the great collections of British and other paintings. There were works by such British artists as Agar, Ardizzone, Colquhoun, Craxton, Ginner, Grant, Herman, Heron, Hitchens, Hurry, the Johns, MacBryde, Minton, John Nash, Roberts, Rowntree, Scott, Sickert, Spencer, Weight, Wolfe and Yeats, which is a fair selection of the leading artists in the previous 20-30 years. His particular favourites amongst these were Ginner, Grant and Sickert. Among the smaller number of foreign artists represented, it would be difficult to fault the names of Picasso, Braque, Matisse, Léger, Bonnard, Degas, Delacroix, Klee, Pissarro, Soutine and Utrillo (although of course the quality of the work he owned has not been analysed). Great claims are made in the introduction for the extraordinary perceptiveness of Le Bas' choices of works by artists at the peak of their achievements, but the quality of this claim may be queried when one notes, for example, that the two works he owned by Colquhoun were not from the 'great' period of the second half of the '40s, but were comparatively weak and derivative works from early in the artist's career.[103]

Sir John Rothenstein

Son of the artist Sir William Rothenstein and brother of Michael Rothenstein, Sir John was the longest-serving director of the Tate Gallery (1938-64). He inevitably had a lot of works by members of his family and many of these passed to his daughter, Lucy.[104] He was constrained while director of the Tate by not being able to buy pictures unless they had first been offered to the Tate itself. His collection was, therefore, haphazard rather than planned. It included work by Burra, Lewis, Spencer, Collins, Reynolds, Frink, Houthuesen, Lowry, Smith, Piper, Delacroix and de Maistre.

Zoltan Lewinter Frankl[105]

Frankl, who was Hungarian, arrived in Belfast as a refugee in 1939. He was an early and important collector of modern British and Irish art, such that, by the summer of 1944[106] his collection was shown by CEMA. The 39 pictures included some by English artists[107] and many from Northern and Southern Ireland: Leech, Keating, Yeats, Conor, Iten, Carr, Lamb and Sidney Smith (Frankl was later to join the Art Advisory Committee of CEMA). He was obviously not unknown in English art circles either, for he lent an Epstein bronze to the very

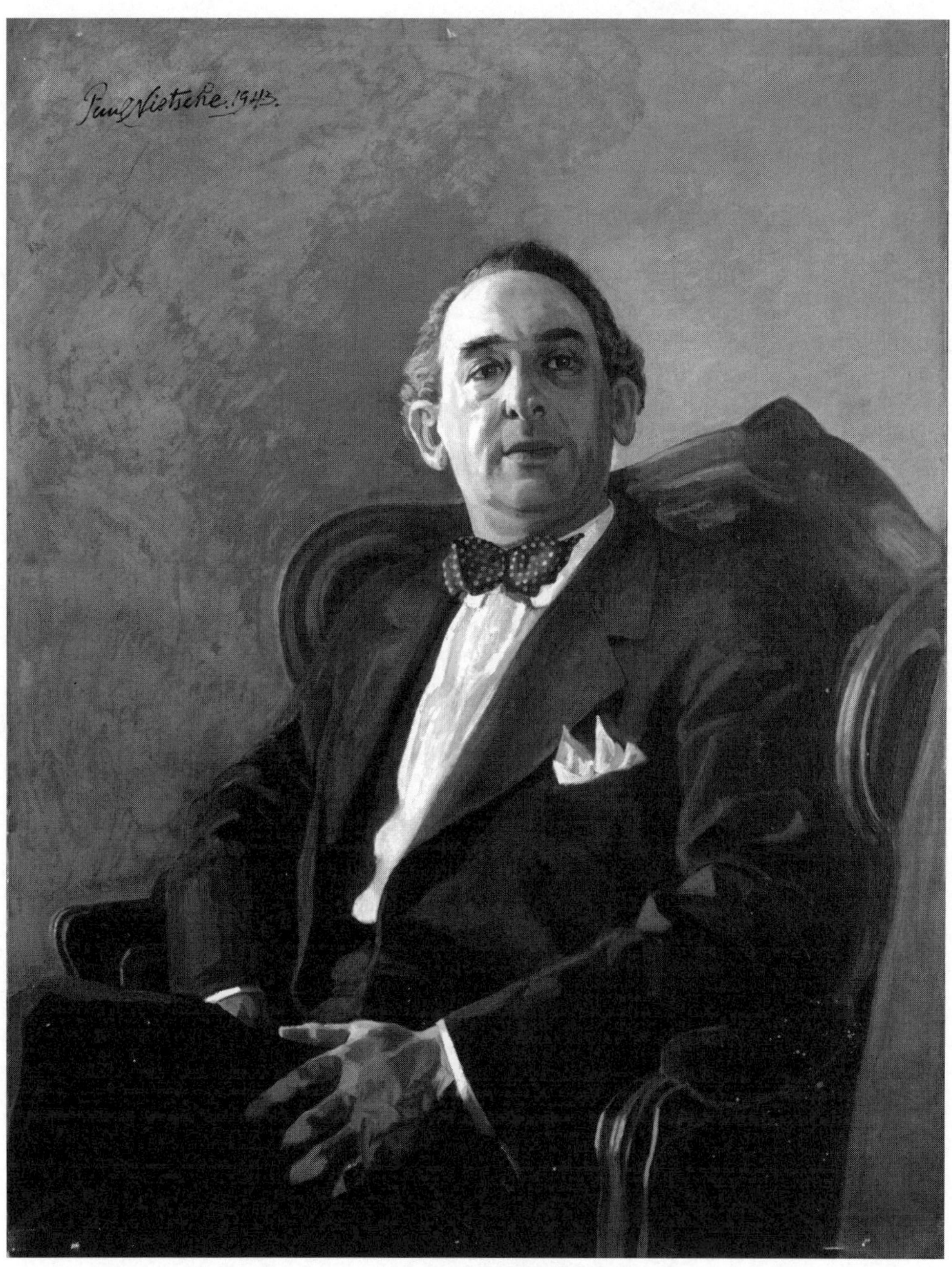

Zoltan Lewinter Frankl by Paul Nietsche, 1943.
Ulster Museum

first show put on by the ICA in February 1948 ('Forty Years of Modern Art 1907-1947'). In 1951 the Scottish Committee of the Arts Council put on a show in Edinburgh with the title 'Contemporary Ulster Paintings' and all but four of the pictures were taken from the Lewinter Frankl collection. By 1958 his Irish collection had grown to include Blackshaw, Campbell, Dillon, Hennessy, MacIntyre, Middleton, O'Neill, Reid and Robinson. According to his obituary in the *Times*,[108] Frankl had a selection from his collection on permanent display in his works canteen. He was undoubtedly the leading patron of the arts in Northern Ireland in the immediate post-War period. Indeed, in the 'Foreword' to the catalogue for the 1958 exhibition of the Lewinter-Frankl Collection at the Belfast Museum and Art Gallery, Frederick Allen said that 'it is certain that Ulster has never before possessed such a patron of art'. The Ulster Museum has a fine 1943 portrait of him painted by the Russian artist Paul Nietsche, who worked in Ireland.

Leicestershire Education Authority

In December 1967 one of the most curious[109] of the many strange exhibitions to be held at the Whitechapel opened: 'British Sculpture and Painting from the collection of the Leicestershire Education Authority'. This contained 60 pieces of sculpture and 91 pictures and the collection had been formed from the end of the War onwards by Stewart Mason, the Leicestershire Director of Education from 1947-71, using money available to the County, rather bizarrely, from royalties received on two religious services books published for schools. He had been helped by Alec Clifton-Taylor as art adviser and particularly by Rex Nan Kivell of the Redfern Gallery. He later got help from Bryan Robertson. The pictures in the exhibition included works by Clough, Colquhoun, Craxton, Hillier, Hitchens, Jones, Lewis, Lowry, MacBryde, Middleditch, Minton, Nolan, Pasmore, Piper, Reynolds, Richards, Roberts, Scott, Stanley Spencer, Sutherland, Trevelyan, Uhlman, Vaughan and Wood. All of the works were exhibited in schools and colleges around Leicestershire and apparently they were given no choice as to which works of art they got from the collection. As if this strange exhibition wasn't enough, the Whitechapel, under the directorship of Nicholas Serota, gave another airing to the County Collection in 1980 with the title 'Growing up with Art'. The pictures and sculptures were then toured round the country by the Arts Council. This time the artists who got a showing included Ayrton, Bellany, Bratby, Clough, Colquhoun, Craxton, Heron, Hitchens, John, Moore, John Nash, Nolan, Pasmore, Piper, Richards, Roberts, Scott and Trevelyan.

Other collectors

It should not be forgotten that many of the collectors mentioned above were focused on buying pictures by artists selling in London, whatever their national origin. Collectors of modern Irish, Welsh or Scottish painters are less easy to identify. We know about Dr Robert Lillie, an Edinburgh collector who acquired over 500 works by Gillies, bequeathing at his death over 300 pictures to the Scottish nation, most of them by Gillies. This gift now forms the bulk of the Gillies collection held by the Scottish National Gallery of Modern Art.[110] We also know about another Scottish doctor, Harold Fletcher, who seems to have built up a large collection of works by John Maxwell. For example, the catalogue of the Maxwell retrospective held after his death at the Scottish National Gallery of Modern Art contains a list of 208 works, which is said to be a complete list of Maxwell's oeuvre. Of these, Fletcher was the owner of the largest number of pictures (23). As regards Wales, a prominent supporter of Welsh artists from the early years of the century, particularly of John Elwyn, but also of other Welsh artists such as Evan Walters,

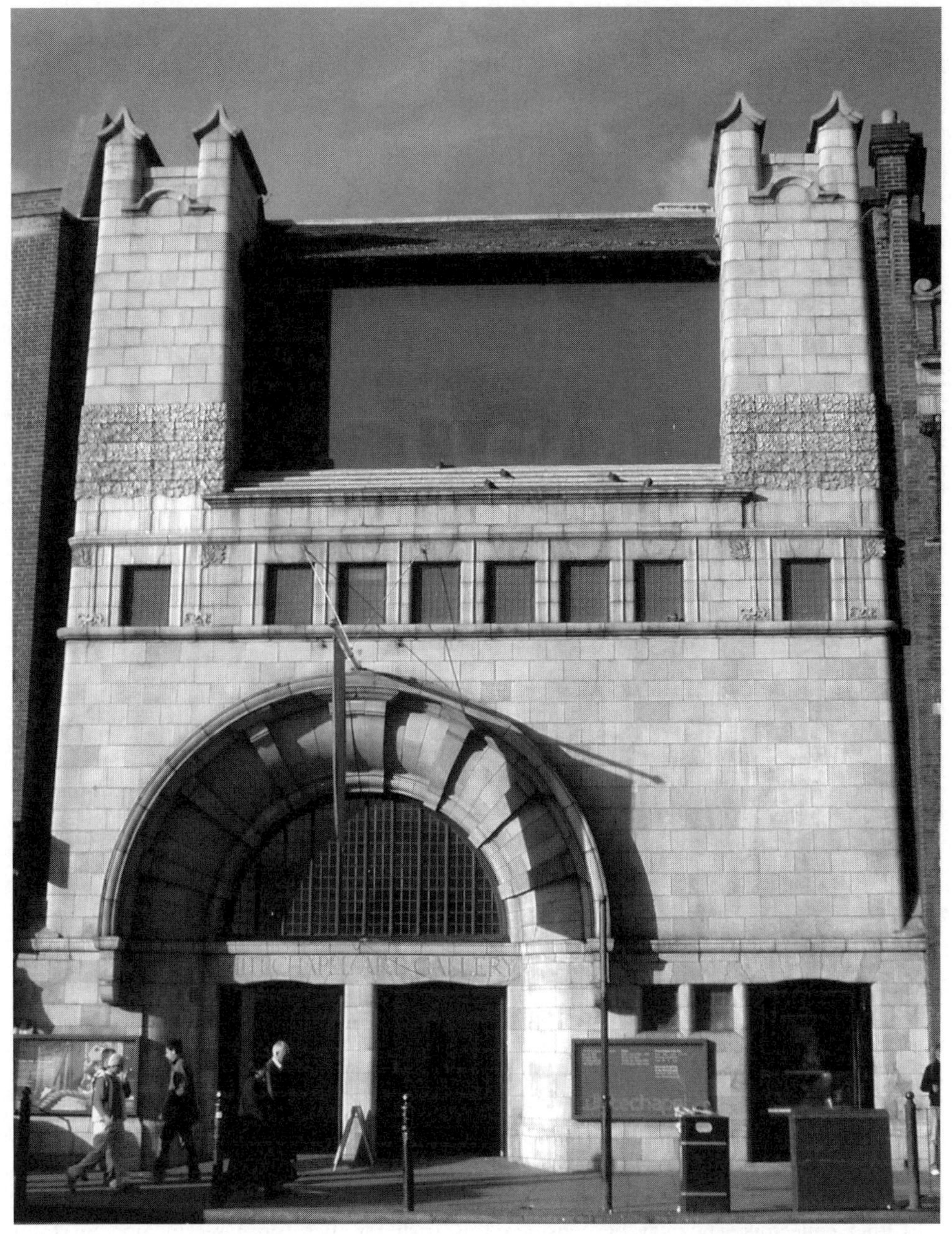

The Whitechapel Art Gallery, London, venue of two exhibitions
of works of art collected from 1947 onwards by the Leicestershire Education Authority

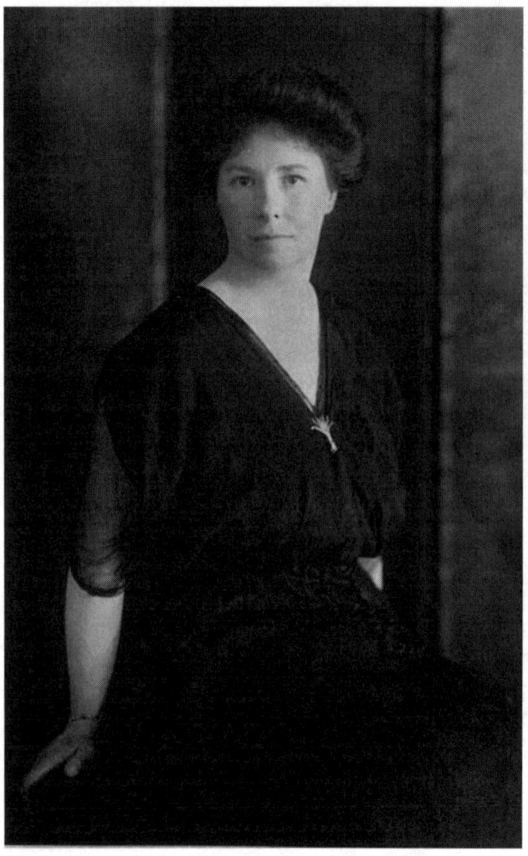

Winifred Coombe Tennant (1874-1956)

was Winifred Coombe Tennant (1874-1956).[111] Another important figure, this time in Northern Ireland, was Neville MacGeough Bond[112] of the Argory in County Armagh. From the 1930s onwards he collected the works of many Irish and English artists. At an exhibition of his collection held at the Ulster Museum in 1966 (curated by Anne Crookshank), work by Campbell, Dillon, Middleton, Blackshaw, T.P. Flanagan and F.E. McWilliam was included alongside pictures by Sickert, Freedman, John Nash, Piper, Nolan, Grant and Brangwyn. During his life his house passed to the National Trust, but his modern art collection seems to have been dispersed after his death in 1986.

Other collectors who may be considered as Irish for these purposes include Sir John Heygate[113] who lived at one stage at Bellarena in County Londonderry and had a collection of modern art, as of course did the English artist, Derek Hill, who came to live at Church Hill in County Donegal. The well-known writer John Hewitt collected pictures from the 1930s, being particularly supportive towards Luke and Middleton, and his collection (including works by Campbell, Luke, Middleton and O'Neill), was eventually left to the Ulster Museum.[114]

Chapter 4

Artists' lives

Money

From 1945 to 1951, living solely by producing and selling pictures was difficult, particularly if the artist was concerned to paint in a 'modern' way. For most of the painters covered in this book, the economics simply could not be made to add up. A helpful starting point for the consideration of the financial lot of the British artist as our period began is provided by the Arts Enquiry book called *The Visual Arts*, which was a report sponsored by the Dartington Hall Trustees and first published in March 1946.

The Arts Enquiry had been established in the autumn of 1941, staffed by the Arts Department at Dartington Hall and financed by the Trustees. The Report was designed to give an account of the place of the visual arts in England's national life, their economic and administrative background, their social importance and their value in education. The authors of the Report were unnamed, but were described as 'a group of fourteen experts, among them artists, designers, gallery directors, art critics, art school principals, teachers of art and secretaries of art societies.' The initial draft of the text was then submitted for further criticism and revision at a conference to which were invited some 70 specialists in the various aspects of the visual arts examined by the Report. The text was thereby finalised during 1945.

The Report was wide-ranging.[1] Its seven chapters covered:

(1) Painter, Sculptor and Patron;

(2) The Commercial Artist and the Illustrator;

(3) Design in Industry and the Artist-Designer;

(4) Schools of Art;

(5) Public Art Galleries;

(6) Art in General Education; and

(7) Prints, Reproductions and Art Publications.

The work began with a long section called 'Argument and Conclusions' and another called 'Proposals'.[2]

Almost the first point to leap from the pages of this report is that modern artists, especially younger ones, found it extremely hard to survive financially. To do so, most had to teach. Patronage was too sporadic and selling through London dealers was unreliable and on too small a scale. The dealers had to sell Old Masters and 19th-century French pictures to meet their own commercial objectives. State patronage tended to focus on buying the work of the past rather than the present. It was particularly notable that the practice in the 19th century of patrons and collectors paying large sums for the work of fashionable artists had largely disappeared. Young artists, particularly those working in a modern style, now got hardly anything for an oil painting.

Interesting statistics emerge from the Report. It is said that, in the 1931 census, some 10,000 people had described themselves as artists, but most were either amateurs with private means or had other sources of livelihood. It considered that no more than 700 painters and

30 sculptors in England were actually earning their living through art. Those prepared to paint what the buying public was prepared to pay for – especially portraits – were still able to make serious money. It estimated that Sargent and Orpen had had an enormous income and that a dozen or more portrait-painters before the War had been earning the considerable amount of over £10,000 per annum. But purely creative artists were, by contrast, 'faced with poverty'. Very few artists indeed were thought to be making even as much as £500 per annum.

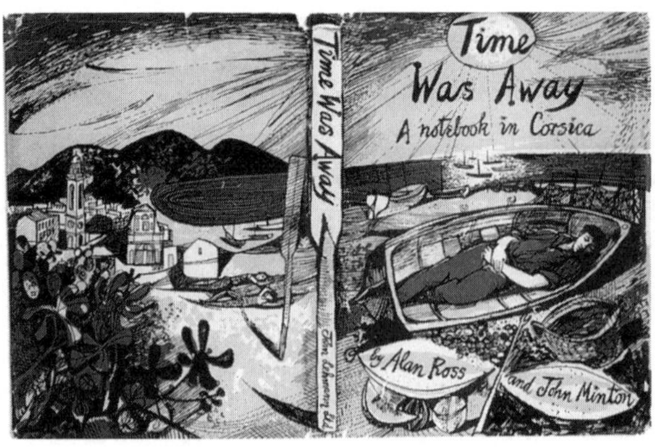

Artists' problems were not made any easier by the fact that they were self-employed and, in most cases, not business-like in their approach to their financial affairs. Their position was often made even worse by the need to retain money to pay income tax,[3] which requires a complex financial calculation made difficult by not being able to afford accountants. Dealers often had to play the rôle of financial minders for their artists. Many artists in fact had other sources of income; in particular, some form of private income or financial support provided at least a cushion for some, such as Morris,[4] Smith,[5] Ryan[6], Minton, Wadsworth, Burra, Craxton, Vaughan, Agar and Clough, and teaching art in one or other of the art schools underpinned the economic health of others (Sutherland, Piper, Vaughan, Pasmore, Rowntree, Weight, Gross, Collins and so on).

Others sought to alleviate their problem by engaging more openly with the commercial world. So, for example, we have seen how many artists of the period were helped by being commissioned by Sir Colin Anderson to produce works for the ships of the Orient Line[7]. John Minton was commissioned by a variety of companies to produce designs for marketing materials and so on.[8] He was also one of the quite large number of contemporary British artists[9] who were commissioned to illustrate books – in his case this later included the famous cookery books by Elizabeth David and, within our period, the splendid *Time Was Away* by Alan Ross, recording a trip they made together in 1947 to Corsica, with illustrations by Minton.[10] His design work also reached an extremely wide audience after the War, when he was commissioned by the editor of Penguin New Writing, John Lehmann, to design the cover. He produced four variants based on the changing seasons and one of the pages of a book fluttering between buildings. The journal had a large print run (even during the War, when paper was severely rationed, this was 75,000), and Minton's covers appeared from 1946 until it closed in 1950.[11]

Kenneth Rowntree designed a number of dust-jackets for books during our period: for *Passengers of Destiny* by Louis Aragon in 1947; *Wennon* by Cledwyn Hughes in 1948; and *Master Mariner* by Leo Walmsley also in 1948. His most famous cover, in the same year, was for the King Penguin, *A Prospect of Wales*, for which he also supplied many watercolour illustrations.[12] The following year he was commissioned to produce a large mural for the Barclay School in Stevenage.

Another possibility was to be commissioned to design posters advertising films. Bawden was helped by this when, in 1947, he produced a poster for a film called *Hue and Cry* for the Ealing Studios. He was, apparently, seriously hampered by not having seen the film and simply had to invent a scene for the poster based on the title. Even Colquhoun seems to have tried his hand at producing a film poster – in his case for the film *Frieda*, which came out in 1947 starring Mai Zetterling. It is not thought that his design was used.[13]

For those artists prepared to engage with the world of illustration, commissioning opportunities could come from unexpected directions. After the War, for example, J Lyons & Co began to commission a whole series of British artists to produce lithographs for their teashops.[14] Advice on appropriate artists was taken from Jack Beddington and he was supported in this by Barnett Freedman, who was a leading authority on autolithography. Sixteen artists were initially commissioned to produce posters and they received a fee of between £50 and £150. The artists also benefited from royalties on copies sold. The products were revealed to the press at the Trocadero Restaurant by Sir Stafford Cripps, President of the Board of Trade, on 21 October 1947. The

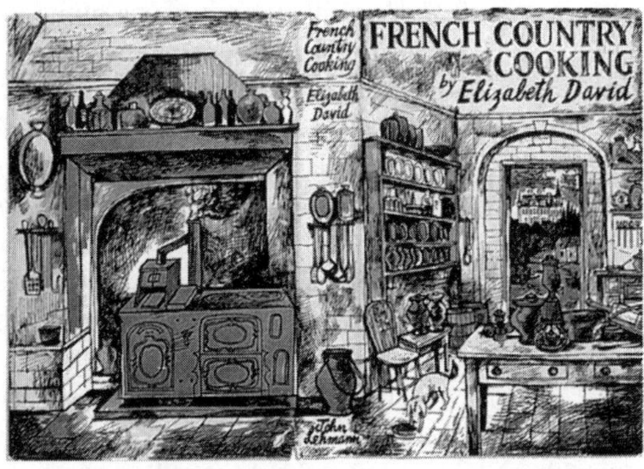

artists in this first phase of commissioning included Ardizzone, Bawden, Freedman, Grant, Gross, Kessell, Lowry, John Nash, Scott, Spear and Weight. In 1951 twelve more appeared. There was some overlap with the previous series (Freedman and Gross for example), but also many new artists were included for the first time, including Ayrton, Minton and Uhlman. (A final series of twelve was to appear in 1955, the only notable new inclusion at that stage being Piper). Interestingly, such artists as MacBryde, Moore and Sutherland were said to have been considered but rejected.

A similar commissioning opportunity arose for some artists through the School Prints series. Brenda Rawnsley ran a scheme for producing prints for schools and, after the War, she took on Herbert Read to advise her on which artists to commission. The first series of 12 lithographs was advertised to schools in 1946 for £3.10, for an annual subscription. The artists were Skeaping, Barbara Jones, Rowntree, John Nash,[15] Rothenstein, La Dell, Phyllis Ginger, Thomas Carr, Trevelyan, Charles Mozley, Tom Gentleman and Gerald Cooper. The second series was advertised in 1947 for £4. (The prints were also by now being offered for sale to the general public.) This time the 12 artists were Clarke Hutton, Tisdall, Felix Kelly, Feibusch, Russell Reeve, Tunnard, Topolski, John Nash, Lowry, Buk Ulreich, Adolf Delin and Gabriel Couderc. Artists invited but who for whatever reason did not participate in the scheme included Ben Nicholson, Lynton Lamb, Weight, Spear, Sutherland and Freedman. The letter to Freedman asking him if he would like to participate in the second series, specified a payment of £5 for a rejected picture and a standard fee of £85, plus a royalty of £5 per 1,000 copies sold to Education Authorities (after the initial run-off of 2,000) and £10 per 1,000 copies sold to the general public.

A particularly unusual commission was the 500 guineas paid to Laura Knight in 1946 for a painting and drawings of the Nuremberg trials in Germany. Maintenance and (modest) travelling allowances were on top.[16]

Sometimes artists produced books on art. John Piper had published *British Romantic Artists* in 1942. An extremely interesting and sensitive analysis of roughly contemporary

British art was prepared by Michael Rothenstein in 1947, in a book called *Looking at Paintings*. Rothenstein covered the work of Paul Nash, Moor, Piper, Ravilious, Hodgkins, John Nash, Tunnard, Bawden, Grant, Jones, Sutherland, Spencer, Smith, Lewis, Wood, Ben Nicholson, Hitchens, Minton and himself. Presumably one purpose of such a book was to make a bit of money. A work of rather a different kind was Fred Uhman's *Captivity*, a series of 24 drawings published in a book in 1946, with an introduction by Raymond Mortimer. As a German living in England when the War began, Uhlman was interned and these drawings were one result.[17] We will also see how a number of artists got themselves commissions for scenery and costume design, either at the Opera House or for leading theatres, and how some were commissioned to design textiles or to paint or draw portraits. Some used their talents for journalism to good effect – Lewis, Heron, Ayrton and Piper, for example – although this is unlikely to have been particularly lucrative.

Nevertheless however much money they started with, many of them chose to live well beyond their means. In particular, the social exploits of Bacon, Freud, Colquhoun, MacBryde, Wilde and Minton have become legendary and, in at least the cases of Colquhoun, MacBryde and Wilde, their expenditure rapidly reduced them to penury and a degree of artistic decline or even collapse.

If we take it that in 1945 the average annual wage in London was approximately £305 (perhaps the equivalent of between £9-10,000 today) and in 1950 about £419 (equal to £9,000), we get some feel for the small sums of money which needed to be earned to eke out a living. But these figures would not have enabled their owners to drink champagne in the way that, say, Minton and Bacon did, nor to live anywhere comfortable anywhere near central London. They would have enabled an extremely modest lifestyle.

If we consider the costs which painters had to incur, and the possible means at their disposal to meet these costs, the position is as follows. To begin with, unless painters could live with their parents – like Craxton or Burra – or their families, like Dillon staying with his sister in Abbey Road, or Gillies in Scotland, they would have needed to rent or buy property, with sufficient room to accommodate a studio. Those choosing to do this in London gave themselves the advantage of being near the galleries from where they might hope to sell their work, but they also exposed themselves to the greater costs and distractions of living in London. The better-off artists were able to afford a studio separate from wherever they lived.[18]

Some artists during our period were, of course, well-established and settled in their careers (William Nicholson and Augustus John spring to mind) and to them the cost of living was perhaps a challenge which they had, by the post-War period, resolved for themselves. When considering the position of the artists covered in this study, we need therefore to bear in mind the great range of ages involved and also the geographical disparities between central London and elsewhere in the British Isles – which was invariably cheaper than London, whether another city or somewhere in the country or a smaller town. Artists who were developing their careers must always have been balancing any wish they may have had to gravitate towards the selling possibilities of London against the comparatively high cost of living and working there.

In fact, few of our artists spent the whole time living and working in London and the tendency to move away after a while (even if they came back later) must have had something to do with economic exhaustion as well as a wish to get artistic and indeed personal inspiration elsewhere. We will come on to see, later in this study, how many artists chose to travel abroad, once this became more feasible after the War, sometimes for quite long periods, such as Bacon and Sutherland in the South of France, and sometimes, as with artists like Craxton, who was to buy a house in Crete, on a semi-permanent basis.

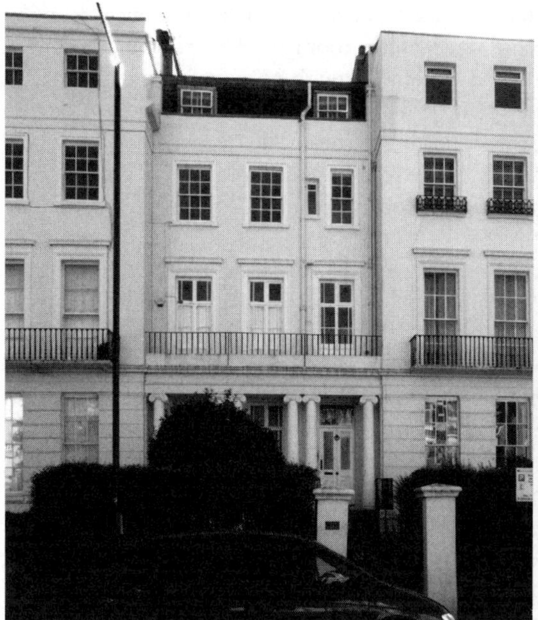

14a Abercorn Place, London NW8, where Freud and Craxton had studios at a time when it was still bomb damaged, the rent paid by Peter Watson

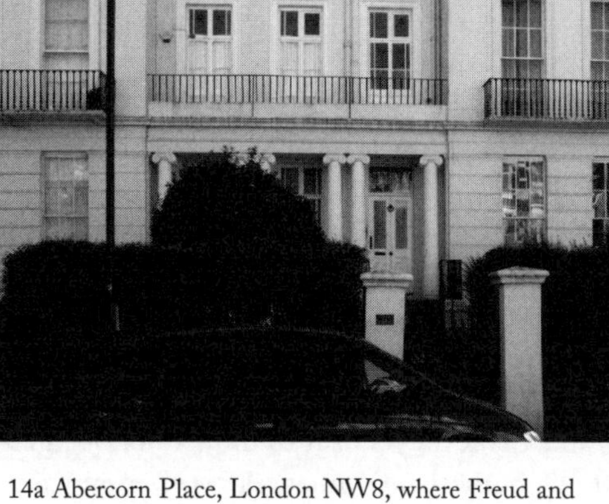

14 St Mark's Crescent, London NW1. William Roberts, with his wife and son, rented a room here and later bought the freehold

Those who largely stayed and worked in London during our period were either those with some family support behind them, such as Freud, Minton and Clough; or those who lived more quietly and were industrious (and perhaps had the support of wives as well), such as Richards, Roberts, Lewis, Uhlman, Coldstream, Pasmore, Weight, Trevelyan and Moynihan. Others were in the London orbit of dealers and buyers, but set themselves up outside London, no doubt partly for financial reasons: Sutherland, Piper, Hitchens, Burra, Herman and so on. (Many of course, were always based well away from London and kept away for understandable, non-financial, reasons.) The actual cost of artists renting modest accommodation in London at this period can be seen occasionally, although it cannot be reconstructed in any great detail, even if it were possible or sensible to try to compare and contrast different sizes and location of properties and their cost (the subtleties of the London property market then being complicated, as they are now, particularly by the widespread effect of bomb-damage in large parts of London). Some examples will give an indication of the sort of money involved, without providing definitive guidance for every situation. So, for example, slightly before our period, during the War itself, when perhaps a different economy prevailed because of bomb damage in parts of central London, we know that Peter Watson paid rent at the rate of about £40 p.a. for Freud and Craxton to rent rooms in a bomb-damaged house in Abercorn Place in St John's Wood. It should be noted that these rooms were taken for use as studios and their facilities were inconsiderable, although Freud chose to sleep there from time to time. Another example from outside our period (in 1956) is when MacBryde wrote to Anderson about the possibility of getting a studio in Cheyne Walk for 30 shillings a week (£78 p.a.), which he described as a bargain. (Because of the way they lived, this would have been intended as a base where Colquhoun and MacBryde could both live and work.)

Occasionally we have evidence of what it took to enable an artist to buy a London freehold. William Roberts and his wife[19] and son rented a room at 14 St Mark's Crescent in Primrose Hill in 1946.[20] It was, apparently, an extremely rough property at this time, with many unsavoury tenants occupying the rest of it.[21] These tenants gradually moved out, so that by 1949 the artist and his wife had the opportunity to buy the freehold of the whole house at £1,200. Even so, they were only able to do so because an old friend literally gave them the entire purchase price in exchange for a few Roberts' pictures. They were to live there for the rest of their lives.

Sometimes we get an indication of what long leaseholds cost in central London. Bacon wrote to Colin Anderson on 9 October 1947[22] from Monte Carlo to say that he had put his studio in Cromwell Place, SW7 on the market at £1,500 for the remaining two-and-a-half-year lease (its annual rent was £100). This property consisted of the studio, a large room, a bedroom, bathroom and 'kitchenette'. Bacon seemed to think this was very cheap (it included the contents). He described himself as being 'in desperate straits as usual for money'.

Outside London, examples of prices can be found, although they are more likely to be examples of purchase prices rather than rents. So when John Nash bought the farmhouse in Essex – 'Bottengoms' – which he was to have for the rest of his life, in 1943, he paid £750.[23] When Sutherland sought to buy the house in Kent which he and his wife had rented for some years (latterly at a rent of £75 p.a.) towards the end of 1945, he could not raise the £2,500 required.[24] Watson refused to give it to him and Clark duly lent it to him, at 4½% interest, and also guaranteed Sutherland's overdraft.[25] Sutherland's finances were eventually to improve sufficiently to enable him to pay off the loan. At the wealthier end of the scale was the Surrealist artist and collector, Roland Penrose (presumably on the basis of inherited wealth rather than his earnings as an artist), who bought Farley Farm in Sussex at auction on 16 February 1949. For £22,500 he bought the farm, the farm buildings, some cottages and 200 acres.[26]

A little outside our period we find MacBryde writing to Anderson on 11 August 1953 asking him to help him and Colquhoun to rent a cottage in Suffolk for £60 per annum. Even that small sum was beyond them. Instead they stayed on at Tilty Mill, commenting in 1954 that this was costing them £1 per week in rent.

Mervyn Peake[27] was often chronically short of money, despite being extremely prolific in writing novels, poetry and plays and illustrating books, as well as painting and drawing. After the War he found himself in London with a wife and two young children and little money. His answer was to remove himself to Sark, where he was able to rent a comparatively large house for £80 p.a. for a 99-year lease. Unfortunately, although life there was cheap, it was culturally limiting, and Peake ended up spending time and money travelling backwards and forwards to London (a laborious journey even now), so as to seek work or keep in touch with his contacts there. Eventually, in September 1949, the family moved back to London, to a council flat in Embankment Gardens.[28] As if to illustrate the point made earlier about how some artists needed to live in or be near London, but simply could not afford to, the Peake family were soon on the move again, this time buying a house in Kent for £6,000 in 1950, borrowing almost all the money. The cost of servicing this debt was about £300 per month, which was well beyond what Peake found it easy to earn, and it soon had to be sold again, with Peake's brother bailing them out by paying off the outstanding £1,000 of the debt, since the house had been sold at a loss.

An artist whose finances were even more chaotic than Peake's was Stanley Spencer.[29] The combination of supporting his former wife as an invalid and paying an allowance to his second wife meant that, however many pictures he painted, and however many he sold, at whatever price (bearing in mind that he was a very well-known artist by this time), his finances were always in a mess. His only respite was when he effectively put all his finances into the hands of his dealer, Dudley Tooth, who managed to balance the books, but only at the cost of paying less and less to Spencer for him to live on (he was down to an allowance of £2 per week by 1943). Spencer's problems were not particularly caused by property expenses, because for the most part he lived cheaply in Cookham. He remained dependent on the Tooth allowance for the rest of his life (he died in 1959).

We should not forget to mention prices, where available, for artists outside England. We find the English-born artist Joan Eardley (regarded now as Scottish because most of her working life was spent in Scotland) fretting in 1951 because she was at risk of losing her modest Glasgow studio, which was conveniently near the slums which she liked to paint, because it was for sale for £100 and she did not have that amount of free capital.[30] By contrast, the reasonably affluent Scottish painter MacTaggart bought a house at 4 Drummond Place in Edinburgh's New Town in 1938, when he was thirty-five. Slightly more modest was the house which John Maxwell inherited from his parents in Dalbeattie and which he returned to occupy in 1946. He retained an interest in a family business and this, together with sales of his work, made him financially secure. Gillies also lived in the country, in his case in the village of Temple in Midlothian, in a small house shared with his mother and sister. Another English-born artist, Nevill Johnson, records in his autobiography[31] that, following the War, he and his family rented a house near the University in Belfast for £60 p.a.

Materials and other costs

A significant cost for artists, after they had found somewhere to live and made enough money to eat and drink, was the cost of buying their materials. The artists' correspondence retained by the Anderson family gives a sufficiently clear idea of the sort of cost involved, although both examples we will look at come from outside our period. In February 1952, Anderson agreed to settle Bacon's bill with The Chelsea Art Stores of King's Road. He paid £153, of which £145 was from an unspecified outstanding bill. Of the itemised balance, 14/6d was the cost of cutting a stretcher and £3.1.6d of covering it with canvas; paints and quantities used were listed at the following prices:

Amount	Colour	Cost each
3	titanium white	3/9d
2	black	2/-
4	flake white	3/9d
2	raw umber	2/-
2	cadmium red	8/-
2	cadmium yellow	8/-
2	alizarin crimson	3/6d
1	viridian	5/9d

By 1956, Sir Colin must have been becoming familiar with the cost of artists' materials, as he was by that time trying to help the Roberts by paying their bills with Messrs Cornellissen directly. So, on 30 June that year he was presented with an unitemised record of what the Roberts had been spending from his account with Cornellissen, as follows:

Date	Amount
16 March	£12.9.11
20 April	£15.12
1May	£4.9.
14 May	£21.2.6
25 June	£10.10

By the standards of time, that must have been a huge sum of money to be spending on artists' materials. In addition, those artists who liked to work from live models had to pay them if they were professionals (such as the models used by Coldstream). Framing had to be paid for and, if relevant, photographs of the work had to be paid for. In theory, insurance should have been maintained, but the artist who did this has not been identified (by me). Only when the works were exhibited were they insured and then at the cost of the galleries. (Exhibition files which survive from public exhibitions of the period often contain enormous quantities of correspondence between the organisers of the exhibition and the owners of the pictures and the insurers regarding appropriate insurance valuations. They also sometimes contain a debate about damaged pictures and how they might be mended and what recompense would be appropriate.)

Selling pictures
A vast amount of original material survives, in gallery records and in printed gallery catalogues, as well as in newspaper reviews of exhibitions, to enable a certain amount of reconstruction of the amount of money which pictures cost to buy in the period 1945-51. We know in some cases what the gallery paid for pictures and what they sold them for and in other cases we only know the latter figure. What we tend not to know is how much the painters themselves received from the sales of their pictures, because the details of the financial arrangements between the galleries and the artists are less easy to find. (The commissions charged by galleries will be mentioned in the next section.)[32]

The prices charged for pictures varied depending upon a number of factors. First of all, the stature of the artist was important. Some artists who were very well known and well regarded, at least to the art-buying public at the time, if not necessarily to the critics, sold their work for what must have seemed to other less well-known artists like enormous figures.[33] It is sometimes hard for us now to comprehend this, blessed or cursed as we are by the effects of hindsight. A good example is provided by the catalogues of the London Group for their exhibitions from 1948-52 (although in all cases we do not know if the works were actually sold). In 1948-49, for example, in an exhibition at the New Burlington Galleries, Yeats had two pictures for sale at £400 each. To us now, conditioned as we are to regard Yeats as one of the greatest painters of the century from the British Isles, this seems logical, but what would today's reader make of the fact that the next highest price – and it should be borne in mind that this was an enormous show, with 285 works for sale by many of the most eminent British artists working at the time – was £315 for a work by Gotlib? Today he is little regarded. Next highest came Duncan Grant, again with a limited reputation today, at £250.

By 1951, the highest price went to Bomberg (£300), which again seems fair to us. The next highest was Ceri Richards at £210, exactly double Lowry at £105, and closely followed by the minor figure of Topolski at £200. At a later show in 1951, Matthew Smith was highest at £450, followed by Augustus John at £400, both older artists who were well-established by this time. (For some reason, 1952 saw a marked increase in prices at the London Group generally, with Smith now up to £1,050 and £600, the extraordinary Gotlib at £525 and Bomberg at £500.)

Another useful list of prices is available from the '60 Paintings for '51' exhibition, because all the pictures shown were for sale, although far from all of them were actually sold. The artists themselves set the prices (and presumably would have got the prices without deduction of the usual dealers' commission, although perhaps that depended on their individual arrangements with their dealers). Again confounding all market expectations if today's values are used, the highest priced picture belonged to, of all people, Rodrigo Moynihan, at £1,000. This was followed, more understandably on the basis that his reputation was by this time high, by Ben Nicholson at £850. Then another surprise, with the Australian Roy de Maistre coming in at £750 and Hitchens at £700. Thereafter most of the works were in the £250-£500 range, with Sir William Nicholson for some reason the cheapest at £100, followed by Minton at £105 and Clough surprisingly not last at £120.

According to one writer,[34] in Scotland in the 1950s small oils by such leading names as Gillies, Redpath, Eardley and Philipson sold for as little as £50, and major paintings for under £150. The same writer, in his book on Gillies, notes how in the early '50s some Scottish artists encouraged his dealers, Aitken Dott, to increase his prices, since he was regarded as the market leader in Edinburgh and his prices, which inevitably set the benchmark for everyone else's prices, were extremely low. His small watercolours, for example, were priced at £14 and medium-sized ones at between £20 and £25. At her first exhibition at the Scottish Gallery, which opened in October 1950, Anne Redpath showed 64 pictures, the most expensive of which was priced at £150. Most were under £100.[35]

Prices of pictures in Ireland at this time are not so easy to discover. It is, however, possible to track some of Yeats' prices. In 1945 Waddingtons in Dublin held a Yeats show at which 23 works were for sale. The total amount asked[36] for all the pictures was £2,920 (which means an average of approximately £127 per picture); the three highest priced pictures were for sale at £300 each; and it was said that, within minutes of the gallery opening, £2,000 worth of

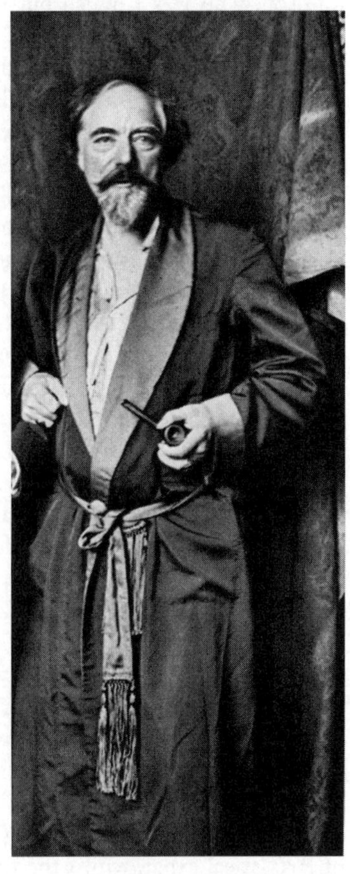

Augustus John

pictures were sold. It can, I think, be said with some certainty that Yeats was the market leader among living Irish artists at this time and other painters were not able to sell for these amounts (or so easily).

This status was maintained by Yeats through the period of this book. In commenting on the annual exhibition at the RHA in 1947, the Irish Times' art critic noted that the top price paid was £300 for a Yeats.[37] By contrast, a picture by James Sleator, who was at the time President of the RHA, was bought from the same show by the Haverty Trust for £70. The *Irish Times* gleefully reported (on 7 October 1947) that £2,970 worth of pictures by Yeats had been sold at Waddington in the first two hours of the private view. In October 1951, at another Waddington show, it was reported in the Irish papers that, of the 21 works on display, 16 were sold almost immediately for a total of approximately £6,000 (which works out at an average price per picture of £375), with 2 temporarily unsold at the very considerable price of £2,500 each. A rather humbling contrast is provided by the exhibition which opened at London gallery, Tooth's, in May 1951 called 'Five Irish Painters'. Even selling in London and having already established himself to some extent (at least in Ireland), Gerard Dillon's 6 oils were for sale at prices between £25 and £45. The other artists represented were Thurloe Connolly, whose pictures were priced from £45-£75, Nevill Johnson, who was English but who had worked in Ireland for some time, whose pictures ranged from £25-£55, Colin Middleton, whose range of £45-£180 indicates that his reputation had already developed to some extent outside Ireland, and Daniel O'Neill, whose work commanded from £35-£65. Further comparison with Yeats comes from Le Brocquy's prices at Waddingtons in December 1951. He showed a total of 40 works (12 oils, 3 tapestries, 16 watercolours, 6 pastels and 3 lithographs). The prices ranged from £4 for an unframed litho to £400 for an oil of *The Family*.

Another leading Irish painter at this time was William Leech,[38] who was living in London. Late in the War, he was taken on by the Dawson Gallery in Dublin, which held a one-man show for him in June 1945. The prices of the thirty-five pictures on show ranged from £10 for a watercolour to £145 for a large oil.[39] This was for an artist who already had a well-developed reputation. Some artists had a small output of tapestries. The Edinburgh Tapestry Weavers, under the patronage of the Marquess of Bute, commissioned tapestries from Le Brocquy, Sutherland, Adler and Stanley Spencer; and Le Brocquy soon went on to work with the Tabard workshop at Aubusson in France.[40] One of Le Brocquy's was noted by the *Irish Press* on 8 December 1951 as being for sale at Waddington's for 150 guineas. Another minority production was stained glass. In an Irish context, the work of Evie Hone is often mentioned. Her most famous English commission was to replace the great East window of the chapel at Eton, which had been destroyed by bomb blast in 1940. Her replacement, on which she worked for a number of years (it measured 33 x 45 feet), was finally completed in June 1952.

It was an even worse story for young painters trying to sell pictures in Belfast in this period. James MacIntyre[41] describes how, in January 1948 an exhibition was held in Belfast called 'Art in Ulster. An exhibition by nine painters'. O'Neill was pleased to sell an oil for £25; and MacIntyre sold an oil for £12 (to the well-known buyer of modern art in Belfast, Frankl). The *Belfast Telegraph* for 11 November 1948 presented a sorry picture of the state of the Belfast art market. Commenting on sales from the annual exhibition of the Ulster Academy of Arts, it said that, whilst the total value of the 259 works on display was £2,600 (in other words, at an average cost of only £10 each), only 9 had actually sold (with an aggregate value of less than £50). This was despite the fact that the show had had a record attendance, and that the average price of oils was only £19. It was also in marked contrast to previous years. In 1947, for example, approximately £300 worth of pictures had been sold and in 1946 the comparable figure had been £442. Portraits were, in Northern Ireland as elsewhere, a potentially more lucrative source of income. The *Belfast Telegraph* reported[42] that Belfast artist, R. Taylor Carson, was asking £150 for a picture of a local winner of the VC.

A source of serious money, although not necessarily of artistic satisfaction, was for an artist prepared (and able) to paint a good likeness to take portrait commissions. Moynihan at some point in the late 1940s/early 1950s was commissioned by the printing firm Gestetners to paint its chairman, and the fee was an incredible £9,000. Quite a number of artists did take commissions in this way, although there is a sharp difference, at least of interest and probably of painterly quality, between some of the exquisite portraits done by Stanley Spencer and the stultifying official portraits of obscure businessmen and military people done by Coldstream, for example. Sutherland's later and very famous commissioned portraits fall somewhere in between.[43] For those artists whose techniques could bear it, it was also possible to get mural commissions. Pasmore did a certain amount of this after he went abstract and we know from the *Times* that Hitchens was paid £1,500 for the huge mural he was commissioned to paint for Cecil Sharp House in London in January 1951.

Where stature became sharply relevant was in the case of younger artists whose reputations were, at least potentially, developing. At Vaughan's first exhibition in 1946, his gouaches cost £21 each; in 1947 one sold for £85; and in 1950 one sold for as much as £200. His top price for an oil in 1947 was £150; in 1950 it was £200; and his large Festival of Britain picture was priced at £350. Colquhoun, whose gallery was the highly prestigious Lefevre, had oils for sale at his first show in 1944 at prices from £8 to £45. By late 1947, when his reputation was about at its peak, the prices ranged from £26 to £210. By the time of his last Lefevre show, which opened in December 1950, his reputation had come off the boil and his prices reflected that. While there was one picture at £150, the gallery priced the rest at between £25 and £85 (and very few sold). His large picture at the Festival, although comparatively modestly priced at £250, failed to sell and he collected it at the end of the show and later painted over it so as not to waste the canvas. (By comparison, MacBryde apparently didn't even bother to collect his unsold picture which had been optimistically offered at £500.) Kenneth Rowntree took part in a large mixed show in Leicester in February 1946 under the title '1946 Spring Contemporaries'. His pictures were for sale at prices ranging from 20-30 guineas (compared to a Pasmore oil at 300 guineas). By 1950, at an exhibition in November called 'Exhibition of Paintings by the Visitors and Staff of the Ruskin School of Drawing and Fine Art', two of Rowntree's works were priced at 35 and 45 guineas. (By contrast, pictures by Albert Rutherston and Barnett Freedman were priced at 145 and 150 guineas respectively.) Sutherland took part in a mixed show at the Lefevre just before the War ended – in April 1945 – and we know that three pictures sold for £68, £85 and £105. (It is worth noting that all three went to individual buyers, two of them with a part to play in this book. Colin Anderson bought one and Wilfrid Evill bought another.) We know, from the amount sent by Roland, Browse and Delbanco on 7 December 1949, what Prunella Clough made from her recent show with them. After deducting commission of a third, she was sent £303 for the 17 paintings sold at prices ranging up to 60 guineas.

Another occasional source of information on prices can be gleaned from more recent sales of collections put together at the time. Peter Meyer's collection was sold at Christie's in London on 6 June 2008. He had begun collecting in the 1940s and the catalogue for the sale mentions that, during our period, he paid £55 and £89 for works by Vaughan (in 1950 and 1951 respectively); £126 and £157 for pictures by Sutherland; £15 for a work by Freud (in 1950); £7 and £42 for pictures by Clough (1950 and 1951); £57 for a picture by Scott in 1950; £126 for a Hitchens in 1950; £57 for a Ben Nicholson in 1950; and £157 and £210 for sculptures by Moore in 1951.

Sometimes the pictures taken on tour by the British Council were for sale. For example, in 1951 the show called '21 Modern British Painters', which went to Vancouver, Seattle, San José, San Francisco, Salt Lake City and Portland, contained 37 pictures, all of which were for sale. The prices, in dollars (US or Canadian?) ranged from $2,210, $1,815 and $1,320 for Smith and $2,145 for Stanley Spencer, at the top of the range, down to $990 for a Ben Nicholson (note the huge gulf), $906 for a Hodgkins, $825 for a Bacon and on down through $594 for a Lewis and $577 for a Colquhoun, down to $145 at the bottom for a Vaughan. The Arts Council occasionally allowed artists showing at its exhibitions to offer their pictures for sale. So, for example, a few were for sale at the exhibition held in London in 1946 called 'British Painters 1939 to 1945'. The range of prices of the five artists who had pictures for sale is striking. Appelbee had two oils, one for 35 guineas and the other for 75 guineas, whereas Augustus John's four pictures were priced at £300, £400, £500 and £800 (for a portrait of Vincent Massey).

If stature was the first pricing consideration, size and medium were the other main issues. Oils obviously sold for more than drawings or any form of prints, and large pictures sold for more than small ones. In fact, at least some dealers simply graded their prices for works of the same medium by size. The case which Professor Brian Clarke brought in the London High Court in 2001, as executor of the Francis Bacon estate, against Bacon's former gallery, the Marlborough, revealed some fascinating information on the financial arrangements between Bacon and his gallery (although they related to 1958 onwards). Some of these details will be mentioned later, but the relevant point in this context is that the Marlborough had a written agreement with Bacon that it would pay him according to the size of the pictures delivered. The range was from £165 for a painting of 24 x 20 inches to £420 for one of 78 x 65 inches. The agreement contained no provision for a price increase (bearing in mind that it had to last for at least five years), and it therefore took no account of the possibility that the artist might become commercially very successful during that period. Crucially, it also took no account of the price for which the gallery was able to sell the pictures. One has to say that, as always with the benefit of hindsight, this must have been a very good deal indeed for the gallery; the only justification for it in equitable terms would be if, at the time it was entered into, there was still some reasonable degree of risk that Bacon's work would not be easy to sell.

Other sources of income
Teaching was often the first thought of the penurious artist of the period, unless there was enough family money to avoid it. Sometimes this meant that they became teachers at art schools where they had only recently ceased to be students. Whatever their technical proficiency – and of course those who had been through the art school system in the British Isles by this time would have had the sort of academic training which at least gave them technical skills – it may be doubted whether all these practising artists who were, at least to some extent, working for the money, would have made satisfactory or inspiring teachers. In fact, there is a considerable body of evidence to indicate that the quality of their teaching was not, in the academic sense, high, although a number of them were able to inspire their pupils by example or by enthusiasm or simply by imparting occasional and apparently casual, but significant, advice.[44]

By teaching in this context is meant teaching at an art school and not giving private lessons, although we have seen how Ben Nicholson took on Lanyon as a pupil in Cornwall early in the War.[45] We have also seen the wide variety of art schools which existed at the time, spread around England, though with few in Ireland, Wales or Scotland. What is usually missing, however, is any indication of exactly how much money a teacher could expect to earn[46]. We know that it will have varied between those who taught full-time and those many who were either only prepared to compromise themselves by teaching for a small part of their time or who simply were not needed on a full-time basis. We can also surmise, without being able to prove it, that comparable positions in the central London art schools would have paid more highly than provincial or non-London positions. Yet details are hard to come by.

In an undated letter,[47] which can be dated from its address to the early 1950s, from that indefatigable letter-writer Robert MacBryde, there is a passing reference to Michael Rothenstein's earning £16 for two days' a week teaching. (It has not been possible for me to identify where this could have been.) Rothenstein was living in Essex by this time, but could easily have been travelling in to London, where he taught at both Camberwell and Hornsey at different periods.

Helpfully, the rate of £8 per day is exactly the same as Coldstream was paid by Professor Randolph Schwabe in 1947 for coming in as an occasional 'visitor' at the Slade.[48] Annualised, £8 per day works out at just over £2,000 per annum, which should have been easily enough to live on at this time. By contrast, Minton appears to have been paid at a much lower rate in 1948 when he moved across to the RCA as an assistant in the School of Painting. His annual salary for two days' a week teaching was only £425. At about the same time, Gilbert Spencer's salary at the RCA was raised from £300 p.a. to £500 p.a. after he had been there for 18 years. Shortly afterwards he was fired.[49]

Another useful supplement of an artist's income could be had by being commissioned to do textile designs.[50] Two remarkable refugee families were prominent in this area in London during the 1940s: the Aschers and the Judas. In 1946 the Aschers launched a collection of fashion fabrics and headscarves, the designs of which has been commissioned from leading British and French artists. First to be commissioned were Moore and Topolski in 1944 and Sutherland, Piper and Wilde were also commissioned by various designers. The stature of the Aschers was endorsed by the Lefevre Gallery, which held a show in 1947 dedicated to the designs which they had commissioned. The cover of the catalogue whets the appetite by mentioning Matisse, Moore, Derain, Sutherland, Hitchens, Hodgkins, Laurencin, Cocteau and others. In 1945 Sutherland contracted with Hans Juda[51] to make 20 fabric designs over a 12 month period for a fee of £250 and this contract was renewed in 1947 at the increased fee of £300.[52]

Another form of commissioned design which helped supplement an artist's income, but could not, on its own, be sufficient to live on, was in respect of film, opera, theatre and ballet. Here, costumes and stage-sets needed to be designed. This was elaborate and potentially time-consuming work for the artist, especially as not many of them seem to have been commissioned more than a few times each to produce such designs, with the result that none of them probably became very expert at doing it efficiently. In 1948 Burra, for example, designed sets for a film produced by the Rank Organisation.[53] His papers do not record what he got paid and there seems to have been some difficulty about getting paid, Burra being no more financially astute than most artists. Our old friends, Colquhoun and MacBryde, desperate as always for money, especially if it could be extracted up front before the work had to be done, provide a good case study of how the commissioning system worked with regard to ballet and how difficult it was for an artist to make sufficient profits from it.

Leonid Massine created a ballet called *Donald of the Burthens* which opened at Covent Garden on 12 December 1951, with costumes and sets designed by Colquhoun and MacBryde. The Royal Opera House Archives reveal the sorry tale which lay behind their participation. The first shock is the time which it had taken to get their work from its first inception to the stage – a period which, surprisingly, appears not to have been the fault of the artists. The first letter in the file is dated 30 May 1948.[54] In it, MacBryde asks the

General Administrator of Covent Garden, David Webster, whether they should proceed with executing the first designs and get a contract. If so, needless to say, they would like money in advance. (It isn't clear how the Roberts came to get this commission in the first place. The ballet was intended to be Scottish, in some way, and no doubt this encouraged someone to think of the infamous London-based Scottish duo. I suspect that someone was Colin Anderson, although possibly it was Duncan Macdonald of the Lefevre or even Kenneth Clark.) Webster was clearly a man who was used to dealing politely, but firmly, with impecunious artists and the Roberts were brushed aside. This caused MacBryde, on 21 June 1948, to write direct to Massine himself, asking for clarification as to what was going on. (He could not resist at the same time helpfully making suggestions as to which composers Massine might like to consider for the score, favouring Britten or Tippett.) Although Massine's secretary responded helpfully by writing for them to Webster, he neatly sidestepped the additional purported pressure by pointing out, logically, that since Covent Garden did not at this point even have a contract with Massine himself, they could hardly put themselves in the position of giving the Roberts a contract first.

The Roberts tolerated this for a while, but then wrote again on 22 April (1949?) saying they wanted payment for the six months' work which they had done and threatening action by the Lefevre Gallery's lawyers. The Roberts then went off to Italy with George Barker and seem to have tracked down, or just come across, Massine himself in Positano, where they managed to extract 50,000 *lire* from him in cash on 15 August, causing him to have to write to Webster asking for his own reimbursement! Back in England more nagging followed, until Webster wrote a very firm letter on 5 April 1950 saying there was still no contract with Massine and, even if there were, and the Roberts themselves had a contract, he would not have let them have any more than the 50,000 *lire* which they had already had.

More sporadic niggling followed from MacBryde until at last, on 12 June 1951, six months before the ballet was due to open, Webster's assistant wrote telling them to begin. Now the balance of pressure tipped the other way and Webster may have taken some pleasure in writing to them on 10 August to say that Massine was now waiting for their designs! However, at the same time Webster explained what he proposed to pay them, which would, he said, normally have been £300 for a ballet, but which would, in this case, because there were two of them, be £400, with £100 payable at the time of signing a contract and the balance on the day of the first performance. The contract was then signed and eventually, more than three years after their initial contact, Colquhoun and MacBryde got paid.[55]

THE ART MARKET

The auction houses

As a generalisation, it is possible to dismiss the impact of the great London auction houses quite simply in relation to their trade in contemporary British art in the period 1945-51: there wasn't any. Christie's was at this time traditionally the pre-eminent house for pictures, but the pictures traded at Christie's were not from the contemporary period. Sotheby's was in the same position. This was partly due to the fact that auction houses, generally speaking, have not traditionally tended to deal in contemporary works of art, whether of pictures or anything else. Such things usually pass either direct from the artist or via a gallery to their first owner for a while before they need to take their chance in the art market, and also the art market is not very effective at trading at proper prices works which have had no chance to achieve an objective value. Similarly, unless forced to sell by an unexpected circumstance like death or divorce, the first owner will often resist selling a comparatively recently created artwork if there is no reliable market value for it. Therefore, one way or another, it may take some years before the auction houses can trade pictures at a price which may be acceptable to the vendors.[56] So, if we note when works by those artists who were later to become famous started to appear at auction, the following emerges:

Name	First auction record for oil	Price (£)
Freud	20 July 1966 (Sotheby's)	200
Bacon	27 March 1957 (Sotheby's)	110
Sutherland	14 December 1955 (Sotheby's)	120
Minton	20 February 1959 (Christie's)	130
Vaughan	13 December 1961 (Sotheby's)	100
Le Brocquy	6 July 1960 (Sotheby's)	100

Although it is hard to gauge the value of money from such a distance, these all seem to have been lower prices than the artists would have expected to get when selling their work initially and the pictures were being sold far earlier than they should have been if the vendors were seeking to maximise their returns. Just occasionally one gets a glimpse of the auction scene for contemporary art elsewhere. On 31 March 1950 the *Irish Times* reported that the Criterion Art Auction rooms in Dublin had sold two pictures by Yeats, for £135 and £125 (again, lower prices than Yeats' pictures cost when new), and one by Paul Henry for the low sum of £22.

Relations with Galleries

Galleries choosing to take on and give shows to young artists were taking a risk. If they could catch them young and back them whilst their fame grew, it was no doubt possible to make some money out of them. On the other hand, by choosing to occupy expensive gallery space with shows of young artists, the galleries were perhaps foregoing an opportunity to show more quickly saleable material, such as French Impressionists, for example, by this period, or even earlier pictures falling into the category of Old Masters. The problem was that, once prices had risen or become stable at higher levels, such that there was some sort of established market for the work, the competition among galleries to retain the artists grew and it became harder to retain them (and certainly harder to retain them whilst also paying them badly for their work). So we see artists moving around quite a lot, the most legendary move of all coming outside our period when Bacon abandoned the Hanover Gallery, which had been good to him in his less well-known days, and moved across to the Marlborough, which was then on its way to becoming the leading gallery in London for modern British work.[57] They were, in many cases, able to move freely because they were not party to any contract with the galleries. Again, the galleries (and the artists) had to make a nice decision on the question as to whether it was in their interests to enter into a contract. From the galleries' point of view, the main reason to have a contract covering more than one show would be if the artist was already well known (in which case the artist probably would not feel the need for a contract anyway), or if his work was particularly promising, such that the gallery could foresee that, by committing itself to a number of shows, it might be able to get the benefit of fixed up-front prices between itself and the artist and ever-increasing prices vis-à-vis the public. (This is the sort of contract which the Marlborough was later to have with Bacon. Entered into at a time when his reputation was growing, they managed to persuade him to sign himself up to an arrangement whereby he was paid at a fixed price for the works that he provided to them, based simply on their size and they could then sell them at whatever price they could. This, of course, proved a very favourable deal indeed once his reputation shot up, as the market paid increasingly high prices for work which the gallery was getting at a fixed cost.)

Since neither of these conditions often applied in the case certainly of the young artists at this time, the galleries were quite happy to take on an artist on a show-by-show basis, in which case a contract was often not signed.[58] Unfortunately for the artist, the ambiguity which this state of affairs created in the legal relationship between the gallery and the artist was most likely to work in favour of the gallery. If the only thing that was agreed at the time of the show was the amount of commission which the gallery was entitled to retain from successful sales, that inevitably left many areas of potential disagreement – and potentially unpleasant surprises for the artist – outstanding.

One such area was whether the gallery was authorised to effect a sale by reducing the price. There is an interesting exchange of correspondence in the Tate archive between the rather peculiar artist Cecil Collins and Duncan Macdonald of the Lefevre, in the late 1940s. Collins' letters are very hard to decipher, partly because of the shockingly bad handwriting and spelling, but also because they ramble alarmingly from subject to subject. It is, in fact, a lot easier to ignore his letters and work out what they must have been saying by reading Macdonald's replies. In one instance Macdonald has to defend what must have been a decision to sell a Collins at a lower price than had previously been agreed between him and the gallery. The price was only slightly less than originally intended and, once commission had been removed, it was only a very small difference in what Collins received from the gallery after the show closed.[59]

Another fruitful area of argument (although it was always a one-sided argument in favour of the gallery in the case of the less well-known artists really being considered here, since the galleries had by this time got their hands on the money from sales), was where it was unclear who paid for the catalogue, any framing that had been done and any photographs of the works that had been arranged by the gallery. John Craxton recited a story about how he was in the Redfern one day and witnessed the poignant scene of Alan Reynolds being told by Rex Nan Kivell that, although there had been many sales of his work at a particular show – or indeed all of his work – no money was due to Reynolds from the gallery because of all the extra costs on top of commission which they had deducted. Indeed, the position was in fact, that he owed them money!

Some galleries were, of course, regarded as being fairer than others. Whereas many charged commission of 50% to the artists, the Leicester and Roland, Browse and Delbanco only charged 33%. Indeed, a letter from Burra in 1942[60] recites that he had been offered a show at the Redfern where they would frame the pictures and, if sold, the artist would pay for the frames and the gallery would only charge 25%. Sometimes artists and galleries remained loyal to each other for many years, even across periods when the artist's reputation went up or down, which implies that at least some galleries were honourable. Le Brocquy started in London in 1947 with Gimpel Fils and is still with them today.[61]

FOREIGN TRIPS

By the end of the War, there was a pent-up demand among British artists to visit other countries. One country which had been visited comparatively easily and which remained a favourite destination for trips after the War was Ireland. Time and again one comes across references to British artists visiting Ireland. Without attempting a rigorous analysis of this, the following artists visited at some stage, sometimes on a number of occasions: Freud, Vaughan, Burra, Agar, Hillier,[62] Colquhoun and MacBryde, Weight, Bawden, Uhlman, Piper, Ayrton, Lewis, Hamnett and Craxton.[63] In return, and more for economic reasons than for finding somewhere interesting to paint, Irish artists not only visited London, but in many cases chose to live and work there for at least some part of their lives. This applies to Le Brocquy, Swift, Hennessy, Dillon, Armstrong, Campbell, Middleton, O'Neill, McGuinness and no doubt many others.

Otherwise, tripping abroad to paint was attractive to many British artists once this became possible after the interruption of the War (before which, a number of those covered by this book had been on trips, often scholarship trips from their art schools). The attractions were no doubt various. It is undoubtedly the case that six years of wartime conditions in London, and the inevitable and longer-lasting consequence of physical decrepitude and shortages there after the War, produced a longing on the part of those who thought in these terms to escape such conditions. There was also the painter's natural wish to explore the purer – or simply different – light of Europe, especially France and Italy, but also Spain and parts of the Mediterranean. If this could be done in a place where life seemed to be going on in its pre-War way in terms of absence of bomb damage and food shortages then so much the better, especially if the cost of living was low and the wine cheap.[64] France, in particular, drew the painters, especially Paris. Although it is fashionable to emphasise the Paris-based training and focus of Scottish-trained artists at this period (an image some of them were keen to cultivate), in fact there is no reason to doubt that by the mid-1940s many, if not all, of the artists working in the British Isles had either taken some influence from France or were conscious of the French artistic inheritance from at least the first part of the century. Whereas Italy had, of course, its famous Old Masters, many of these were perhaps exerting less influence on the young artists of the 20th century than the Impressionists, the Cubists and all the other less easily categorised French artists of the past 50 years.[65]

Some artists had lived in France before the War (Smith, Scott and Anthony Gross for example). Others lived there for some time after the War (Sutherland, Bacon, Turnbull and Gear) or visited for long periods.[66] A good example of someone who resumed his pre-War contact with France as soon as he could after the War was Matthew Smith, who went to Paris in the summer of 1946. (He was to return to Paris and the South of France every year between 1946 and his death in 1959, save for 1948 and 1957.)[67] For others, France was insufficiently exotic or simply not different enough from the British Isles. Craxton spent a large part of the period travelling. Apart from trying the limited, but at least available, difference of the Scilly Isles, with Freud in 1945, his 'Biographical Note' from his Whitechapel exhibition catalogue in 1967 records that he went in 1946 to Paris, Switzerland, Zurich, Bern, Athens, Poros, the Cyclades and the Dodecanese islands; to Paris, Marseilles, Piraeus and Poros in 1947; to Paris, Athens, Poros and Crete in 1948; to Istanbul, Athens, Madrid, Toledo, Seville and Granada in 1949; to Paris, Rome, Naples, Poros, Crete and Sphakia in 1950; and to Paris in 1951 (the pattern continued outside the scope of this book). I think this may be a record for a post-War British artist and is probably explained by Craxton's personal characteristics, being a particularly thoughtful and reflective artist. In 1960 he began living in Xania in Crete and his life continued to be split between there and the same house in Hampstead which his parents bought after the War – a curious contrast to all the travelling.

Vaughan was also keen to travel, to Paris in 1949 and La Rochelle and then back a few months later to cycle around Brittany. In 1950 he went to Italy (Pisa, Siena and Naples), returning through France. In 1951 he cycled around Avignon, the Rhône Valley and the Camargue, sketching as he went. Burra, despite his chronic poor health, was able to manage Ireland in 1947, followed by two further trips there and a trip to America in 1948. In 1950 he visited France twice and again in 1951. Minton went on his famous trip to Corsica with Alan Ross in 1947, leading to the travel book published by John Lehmann in 1948, *Time was away*, with text by Ross and splendid pen-and-ink illustrations by Minton. The following year he visited Paris and also Spain (travelling to Barcelona, Granada, Alicante and other places). France again in 1950 was followed by another famous trip in September, this time to Jamaica, which led to more pictures, one of which – *Jamaican Landscape* – was his contribution to '60 Paintings for '51'.

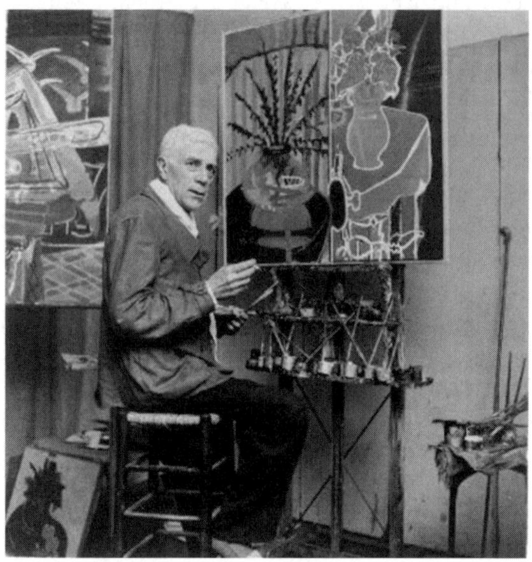

Georges Braque in his Paris studio where he was visited by Graham and Kathleen Sutherland in March 1949

Sutherland set off for the South of France for the first time on 10 April 1947, with Eardley Knollys. The Sutherlands went at least partly in order to see Bacon, who had reached Monte Carlo in the autumn of 1946, perhaps utilising the £200 made from the sale of *Painting 1946* to Erica Brausen. Bacon spent a considerable part of 1947 there, gambling at the Casino. He was to spend some part of each year there until 1950, painting and begging money from Colin Anderson and Brausen's backer Arthur Jeffress as well as, presumably, soaking up Eric Hall's money. Once the Sutherlands met up with Bacon in Monte Carlo they also lost money gambling in the Casino. They also met Somerset Maugham at the Villa Mauresque in Cap Ferrat (Sutherland was, of course, later to paint his portrait). Having returned to England in May, it is clear that the Sutherlands were smitten with the exotic South and they returned as early as September, this time with Freud instead of Knollys. Sutherland on this trip visited both Picasso and Matisse. When the Sutherlands returned to France in 1948, it was to rent a house in Villefranche-sur-mer, next to Cap Ferrat (for less than £2 a week). In March 1949 they went to stay with Maugham and to begin the portrait, calling in on Braque in his studio in Paris on the way. In England for the summer, they were back in the South in November, spending Christmas there. Another destination for the Sutherlands was to be Venice, where they went for the first time in September 1950 and which they were apparently to visit, with the exception of 1951, every year for the rest of Sutherland's life.

Chapter 5

Artistic reputations

There can be no precise definition of an artist's reputation. Different categories of people will look at artists differently and will have different tests as to whether or not they regard an artist as successful. Artists themselves sometimes have strong views on the merits or otherwise of their fellow artists; certain journals and newspapers during our period published regular serious art criticism which helped to form the environment in which artists' work was considered; those public institutions which bought contemporary art, particularly the CAS, must have had some influence on reputations, as of course did those private individuals who bought modern British art, particularly if they were individuals of some importance in the art world. It is also necessary to distinguish between the geographical limitations of artists' reputations. It would, for example, be quite possible for an Irish artist to have a reputation in Dublin alone and/or in London. Only a few British artists went on to break through to a European reputation, let alone an international one. A few may have greater reputations abroad than they do at home. Furthermore, who is to be trusted as a judge of these reputations? English writers about English artists may have the critical equipment to enable them to make reasonable judgments (if they can resist the temptation to find favourites); but can they be trusted to judge fairly even Irish artists, assuming the judging has to contain a subjective element? Which 'judges' are to be trusted when looking at the European scene? English ones? Have any French or German art historians, for example, written synthetically about European art of the mid-century and, if so, have they been equipped with enough knowledge on British artists to do so 'fairly', or fairly in the eyes of British onlookers? Furthermore, can those British critics who knew a bit about, say, French work (one thinks of Patrick Heron), be trusted to use their scraps of knowledge fairly or reasonably when comparing native work with that by the French masters of 20th-century art? Moreover, when adjudging reputations, which comparisons should be used? The work of contemporaries, or near contemporaries, or which other group of artists? These are all difficult questions. Judgments made about artistic work are easily challenged.

Although not a major feature at the time, the auction houses of the British Isles have, with the passing of time, increasingly traded in work from our period. So, of course, have major British, and occasionally international, art dealers. The interaction of market reputations with pure artistic reputations is a different subject. It would be necessary to conduct a long and detailed analysis of many auction records, far beyond the scope of this book, to establish the relationship between developing artistic reputations and changing auction prices. Even then, one would, as always, need to make assumptions before any conclusions could be drawn from the raw data.[1] For in this area the influence of fashion is a dangerous and unstable element. If we let prices govern our estimate of artistic worth, we should have to conclude that Bacon was the greatest painter of the 20th century in the British Isles: a claim which can be argued. But then we would have to allow high status to Freud, which is surely much less arguable; to Le Brocquy and Yeats whose popularity is surely influenced by the recent economic power of Irish businessmen as much as by an objective artistic analysis; and to Hockney. Tables of artistic worth led by market analyses are clearly not infallible. On the other hand, those claiming high artistic importance for artists whose work has not commanded substantial auction prices may also need to worry about their conclusions. If it is assumed that not all paintings are bought at auction by those solely driven by the dictates of fashion, the success or failure at auction of many artists operating below the highest fashionable levels should not be ignored.

Another possible strand to the making of reputations is the treatment of artists in monographs or in more wide-ranging studies of periods or groups or schools or whatever. In practice, the strength of this connection is hard to prove. Sylvester's incessant promotion of Bacon undoubtedly contributed to the creation or to the development of Bacon's reputation,[2] but it probably did this more by journalism than by the books (with the possible exception of the famous interviews). Which artists have had their reputation transformed by a book about them? One conclusion which will emerge is that, although at first glance there appears to be a plethora of writing about art, in fact a comparatively small number of writers was involved. Adding together those who wrote in the serious newspapers and journals, the total number would be small. Some writers appeared all over the place. Sylvester loomed large over the artistic scene. Even during our brief period, a casual survey of his journalism shows him writing for *Art News & Review*, the *Burlington*, the *Listener*, *Tribune*, the *Nation*, *The Studio* and *Britain Today* (in England), together with the American magazine, *The Tiger's Eye* and the French magazine, *Les Temps Modernes*. John Berger's period of regular journalism did not really begin until the early 1950s, but even in our period he pops up in the *New Statesman* and *Art News & Review*. Patrick Heron wrote regularly for the *New English Weekly* and the *New Statesman & Nation*, but his work also appeared in *Time & Tide*, *World Review*, the *Architect's Year Book*, the American *Magazine of Art*, the *Penrose Annual*, *Art News & Review*, the *Listener*, the *St. Ives Times* and *House & Garden*. We may not be able to ascertain how all this journalism affected the reputations of those painters being written about, but it is certainly true to say that any prejudices which the writers possessed would have been capable of being very widely disseminated indeed, whether those prejudices were in favour of, or hostile to, the artists concerned. And so, with those few remarks on this diffuse area, let us see how, in particular, certain journals and newspapers treated the artists of our period and whether they helped to create or break certain reputations.[3]

NEWSPAPERS

Many national newspapers during our period, whether daily or weekly, had regular art columns. Those appearing in the leading newspapers, particularly those which were written about living artists, made some contribution, hard though it may be to measure, to the environment in which artistic reputations were created and tested. For example, by 1950 the circulation of the *Sunday Times* was over 500,000.[4] Making only a modest assumption about how many people read each copy, that means that over a million people were likely to be scanning its eight pages every week. Even if they did not read the arts column every week, it must be the case that quite a large number of people around the British Isles (and perhaps further afield), were getting some insight from Eric Newton's column into what was going on in the art world. Therefore what he chose to write about and the way in which he chose to write it must have had some part in contributing to the public's attitude towards art. That is not a contentious statement. What is more controversial is to identify whether the views of those reading this art journalism had any – and, if so, what – influence on the creation or destruction of the artist's reputation. Add to the *Sunday Times* the other leading newspapers, with their art columns, and allowing for some overlap where the same people read more than one paper, and one can begin to see a large population of potentially influenced readers.

The detailed analysis which follows of the journalism appearing in those papers from mid-1945 to mid-1951 will therefore have, as one of its ambitions, the display of this process as it occurred; the contemporaneous nature of the journalism will be a refreshing feature, in that the usual overlay of later writers' prejudices will be able to be avoided.[5] What also has to be borne in mind is the environment in which a journalist in a newspaper has to operate. For a start, there were obviously severe restrictions on space. For example, the *Observer* and the *Sunday Times* came in one part only, and the total length of each paper was usually only 8 or 10 pages.[6] That had to cover everything, so the room for arts coverage was very limited. Secondly, a newspaper arts journalist cannot simply write about anything: he is responding to the events in the contemporary art world. These events, even in London, were incredibly diverse. This book is not intending to describe, in monumental detail, the art scene as a whole in the British Isles between the given dates. If it were, it would have to give heavy emphasis to what can loosely be termed Old Masters, as well as to French artists of the 19th and 20th centuries, together with those of other nations, and also the occasional focus on African carvings and so on. That is not to mention the sculptors covered with some regularity. Only occasionally did the writers indulge in a piece that could be said to have been contemplative and unrelated to something actually going on. Thirdly, the journalist faced with

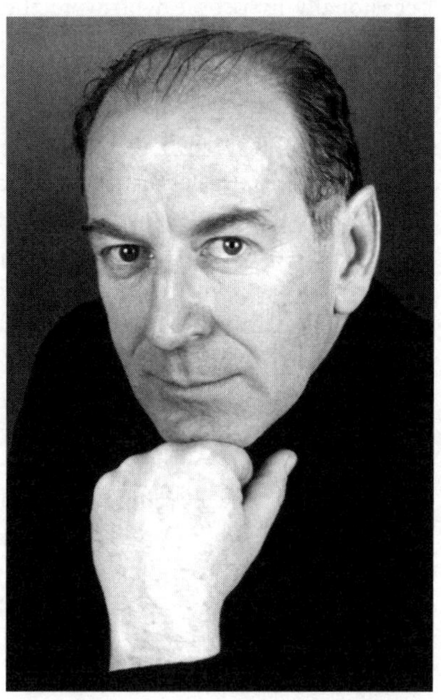

The artist Patrick Heron (1920-99),
art critic of *The New Statesman and Nation*

the constant stream of exhibitions, at galleries both public and private, will make a series of decisions as to what to emphasize and what to ignore. An interesting, detailed study could be made of comparing what the leading journalists chose to cover, partly in order to show where they coincided, but also to point up the differences of treatment between the individual writers. Equally interesting would be to compare how they covered those exhibitions where they did coincide. It may be thought that those shows which they all covered were truly significant in contemporary circumstances. Fourthly, it has to be acknowledged that the journalists in the English papers were normally writing about exhibitions at galleries in London (stretching very occasionally to Edinburgh or Dublin). That may reasonably reflect the balance of where art galleries were in the British Isles at the time, or it may be no more than the usual bias towards London in our national papers which has from time to time been commented upon. The attempt will be made here to redress the balance slightly by including detailed coverage of some relevant Irish and Scottish newspapers, but a full analysis of how journalists in all the different parts of the British Isles were covering the contemporary art scene at this period would be a very large and intricate study in its own right.[7]

The Times
The *Times* was only 8-10 pages during our period, but it provided a rich variety of art coverage of different types.[8] Although all the criticism was unsigned, apart from occasional large, set-piece articles, much of it during this period was written by Alan Clutton-Brock.[9] His style was dry and even-handed. It is possible to break the coverage down into a number of approximate categories. In the first place, the paper clearly tried to cover the major exhibitions going on in London. Some of these, particularly the great Picasso/Matisse exhibition at the V&A at the end of 1945, also attracted letters to the famous letters column, occasionally by people who were themselves famous.[10] Secondly, the paper commented on many shows at the leading galleries, and so it frequently mentioned the Lefevre, the Leicester Galleries,[11] the Redfern, Gimpel Fils and so on. Thirdly, it recorded the shows of the various official, or semi-official, groups, such as the Summer Exhibition at the RA, the NEAC,[12] the RWS, the Royal Society of Portrait Painters, the United Society of Artists and the Royal Society of British Artists, together with groups such as the London Group. Fourthly, it acted as a sort of noticeboard for events happening or planned at the leading galleries, particularly the Tate and the National Gallery, such as re-openings following war damage, new appointments and planned shows and so on. Finally, as mentioned, there were just occasionally much larger articles falling into none of the above categories. John Rothenstein, for example, had a large piece in 1947 reviewing the history of the first 50 years of the Tate and there was a leader article in 1949 when the Chantrey pictures were exhibited.

Despite the great wealth of coverage, however, sometimes coming up in some form or another two or three times in a week, most of the pieces were short, too short for the expression of any developed opinions, and they were generally written in a quiet and balanced style which militated against the expression of strong likes or dislikes. The journalists' character, in keeping with their anonymity, does not, therefore, emerge, especially as there was no room (or inclination?), to publish reflective pieces away from the demands of recording the events of (usually) the London art world. The overwhelming impression is of the many different art events covered. This reflected the rich variety of the London art world of the time and, when considering the contribution made by this body of work to the creation or destruction of artistic reputations, it is as well to bear in mind that, although the journalists no doubt had some choice about what they covered (at least in the second category referred to above, where exhibitions at private galleries were concerned), in many cases the real decision as to which artists should be favoured with some exhibition had been taken by the gallery owners or managers in the first place. Thus, for example, where the journalists picked up on new artists, perhaps having their first shows at important galleries, they only wrote about them because the gallery had chosen to show their work in the first place. What is clearly demonstrated, over and over again, is that a great national newspaper such as the *Times* was not seeking to cater for the avant-garde, or to create or lead taste, but was intent on describing a large range of types of work, no doubt to suit the range of styles appreciated by its widespread readership.

A wider overview of what the *Times* chose to mention in our period illustrates just how much foreign, and particularly French, art was available to London art viewers at this time, including contemporary French art. Without trying to be comprehensive, it is easy to note that shows were held of work by Picasso and Matisse, Rouault, Renoir, Daumier, Lancret, Toulouse-Lautrec, Lurcat, Dufy, Marcoussis, Degas, Cézanne, Corot, Léger, Vuillard, Courbet, Bérard, Bonnard and Camille Pissarro. That is not to mention a number of general shows of French art.

Contemporary British artists got their share as well, often noting what influence they had taken from Picasso, as ever, and also Sickert. For example, the review of the Royal Academy Summer Exhibition in May 1945 remarked that a lot of the artists, such as Ruskin Spear, were influenced by Sickert (who had only recently died). Craxton is described as having borrowed from Picasso (in a review in November 1947), as is Richards. Occasionally the writer regrets that a young artist has allowed perfectly good draughtsmanship to be deliberately distorted by partial abstraction. This comment is made, for example, about Craxton and Le Brocquy, and a similar point (in February 1949) is made when an interesting tension is noted between how the writer thinks Minton wanted to paint (reasonably straightforwardly, in a representational style) and how his work had in fact developed as a result of contact with the style of his contemporaries.

Sometimes a young artist's work is neatly skewered. Trevelyan is said, for instance, to use all the tricks of the 1920s, such as those of Dufy and Christopher Wood: 'The amusingly incorrect perspective, the figures which never stand firmly on the ground, the deliberate flattening of solid objects, the display of arbitrary lighting.' Lucian Freud (in November 1947), still not taken seriously by the art world, makes accurate representations of lots of small objects 'which are no doubt intended to have an esoteric incongruity'. The critic goes on to say that 'the special mode of illustration with which he seems to be preoccupied gives little scope for anything beyond neat craftsmanship'. Clough is said to have a 'strange combination of interests and styles' and he picks up Heron as he passes through one of his many changes of style: 'The general effect is curiously decorative; there is a complete absence of any sign of struggle and many of his designs seem to ask to be transferred to some less exacting branch of art than the easel picture.'[13]

The Sunday Times

When the War finished, the art critic of the *Sunday Times* was Eric Newton. He also wrote at other periods for the *Guardian*, to which he was to return after leaving the *Sunday Times*. His books *European Painting and Sculpture* (1941) and *War Through Artists Eyes* (1945) had been well received and he was an important part of the post- War British art world, becoming quite widely known in the 1950s through his broadcasts for the BBC.[14]

It is clear that during the first few years of our period, the status of Newton's column in the paper gradually increased. By 1947 it was usually appearing on the second page, in a position of some prominence, having previously been likely to appear almost anywhere in the paper and in widely varying lengths. Some themes emerge from his writing. He usually disliked the Royal Academy Summer Show, but liked the mixed summer shows of those commercial galleries which held them, particularly the Leicester Galleries' 'Artists of Fame and Promise'. (He believed, not unreasonably, that the galleries were able to reveal the character of their owners at the summer shows, because they had chosen the blend of artists to show.) French art gets a reasonable showing and he has interesting views on the situation in the British art world at the end of, and as a result of, the end of the War. First (27 May 1945) he notes that the return of the first batch of pictures to the National Gallery throws into stark relief the work of some contemporary painters (he picks, for some reason, on Craxton – 'after the National Gallery it is impossible to take him seriously'). Then, in reviewing the summer shows on 2 September, he remarks that the interest in art which was notable amongst the public during the War seems to have relaxed ('the arts seem to matter a little less than they did six months ago'). A week later he notes that 'British painting is at a turning point. For five years it has been characterised by intense activity on the part of our more mature creative artists, complete isolation from the steadying influence of the old Masters and comparative isolation from the contemporary movements on the Continent'.

Newton was a serious and reflective critic, clearly finding irksome on occasion the limitations of space imposed by the paper. In comments which remind us about the transience of taste and reputation, he remarks on 11 November 1945 on the Tate pictures being shown at the National Gallery (the Tate itself still being incapacitated by its severe War damage), '... late nineteenth and early twentieth century painting is now passing almost unnoticed through that strange sieve known as the judgment of posterity.' While the Impressionists have gone through the process and been vindicated, and contemporary art is too recent, one needs to look particularly critically at those in between. Interestingly to our eyes, while he fully accepts Cézanne, he questions Van Gogh and Gauguin.

Otherwise a huge mixture of art, both foreign and British, is considered. Irish artists get noticed as appropriate (Mackinnon, Yeats, McGuinness); he approves of Sutherland and also notes the occasional appearances of Bacon, with some respect. He is very taken with Hodgkins and gives Paul Nash a glowing tribute following his death. There are sometimes notes which seem to jar to the modern ear. For example he gives considerable praise to Moynihan, describing (on 17 March 1946) his *Model Resting* as one of the best pictures painted in England in the last decade, a claim which most would now query. He likes Leslie Hurry's work and mentions a number of times an artist who would now never feature – Vera Cuningham. Smith is said – towards the end of 1947 – to be 'our only contemporary giant'. Gotlib has many failings, but nevertheless has 'full volume fused with colour'. Topolski is skilful, but basically an illustrator. Newton is also capable of admitting that he may have made an error or may have only gradually come to understand an artist's work, after initially failing to do so. (He says this, on 8 December 1946, about Richards.)

Sometimes (although quite rarely) Newton is rude about an artist. He clearly has little time for Klee, regarding him as lightweight; for Surrealist artists, expressing amazement that the London Gallery should re-open in 1946 and still be showing Surrealist works, which he had assumed to be 'obsolete'; and for Geoffrey Tibble ('fundamental emptiness'). Frequently he points out technical weakness, while still admiring the work overall, or hoping that it will develop through a period of weakness or tentativeness. And so (in 1947) he spends a considerable amount of space on Colquhoun, remarking on his great importance as a contemporary artist, but noting that he was now at a crossroads. The less significant painters, Trevelyan, Vaughan and Minton, were encouraged up to a point, but were clearly not fully developed. Suddaby painted attractive pictures, but the landscapes were crowded with 'badly distributed accents'.

One significant area of Newton's journalism which has to be addressed is his approach to what might be called new or lesser-known young artists. This is dangerous territory, with the quicksand of hindsight all round. All artists at some stage are young, new or unknown; those we recall now from 50 or 60 years ago have managed, in some way, to attain a status which catches our attention, justifiably or otherwise. But as they appear in front of the contemporary viewer, as it were for the first time, the ability to identify at that point whether their particular skills will lead them to a lasting reputation is a rare gift. It may even be a gift which does not really exist, except in respect of the easiest of cases. The critics seem to have been able to sense early in their public careers that artists such as Bacon were going to be significant (were, indeed, already significant), but their attempts to spot other future stars were not so successful.

Newton made many mentions of young artists. He occasionally tried to explain why he found them difficult to judge. On 29 January 1950 he said that 'in a period like our own, when lack of craft-tradition makes an inherited style impossible, and lack of a common faith makes subject-matter unimportant, anything may happen to any artist at any moment in his career'. This led him to the comment that 'the art critic need not be ashamed of refusing to act as a "talent-scout".' All the critic of today can do is note the tendencies amongst artists which are in the ascendant. Having said all that, it was perhaps one degree easier for the critic than for the private gallery owner, because by the time the critic was getting to look at the work of new artists, some process of sifting had usually already occurred, since they had usually already been selected to appear in a gallery show. By implication, other young artists had tried and failed to achieve even this level of recognition (although that is not to say that getting shown at a leading gallery of itself created a reputation, it clearly helped). On the other hand, those whose names Newton picked out from amongst large-scale group shows had not necessarily been so blessed and there he was really making no more than an experienced guess as to whether those mentioned would have any larger future reputation.

One example of the latter point may indicate the problem. On 1 February 1948, he chose to review an exhibition held by the AIA called 'Painters under 30'. He picked on seven to name individually (while noting that none showing were 'geniuses'). They were Eric Thornton, Joseph Deliss, Jane Douglas, Patrick Carpenter, Stella Marsden, Margaret Littleton and Carl Cheek. Using the (single volume first edition of the) most reliable of modern reference works – David Buckman's *The Dictionary of Artists in Britain since 1945* – I have sought to identify whether any of these seven artists achieved reputations in the art world (having personally heard of none of them). The *Dictionary* contains more than 10,500 entries, and so failure to appear in it must indicate an artist who certainly did not reach the first rank and, of the seven, only one appears (Jane Douglas) and she merits four lines.[15] So much for talent-spotting. On other occasions Newton comments on artists who do merit some sort of entry in the *Dictionary*, but whose names are – I suggest – largely invisible in the wider scene of art history. An example would be John Verney (mentioned on 14 September 1947 as part of a show of 'Three Young Artists' at the Léger Gallery). He has quite a long entry, but it doesn't amount to much, apart from the fact that he ended up illustrating (and writing) a number of books. Another example would be Robin Rae, who got a couple of mentions and has a long entry in the *Dictionary*, but whose work is not now widely known.

Otherwise, the varied diet continued throughout our period, with Newton's last column in the *Sunday Times* appearing on 19 November 1950, appropriately enough on Picasso. This followed an interesting communication received from Newton by the CAS and recorded in its minutes for 16 November 1950. He had apparently written to the CAS complaining that, because of the continuing newsprint shortage, the *Sunday Times* had decided that it would have to curtail its art criticism and that therefore the paper was cancelling his contract. The CAS minute recorded the indignation of the committee at this and the Chairman was mandated to approach the proprietor of the paper, Lord Kemsley, to remonstrate with him. Before then, Newton's column was occasionally the beneficiary of an illustration, the first I noted being Craxton's *Homage to Alones* on 12 March 1950. He continued to review the annual exhibits of the Royal Scottish Academy and to prefer it to the RA's Summer Exhibition. Occasionally when he was away for some reason Raymond Mortimer filled in. Towards the end of his period, he commented on 'Art and the Public' by saying that there was a continued interest among the public in looking at and buying pictures. While there could be no evidence for the statement that 'the visual arts are beginning seriously to compete with music and literature as objects of intelligent popular interest', we should not ignore such a comment from someone in his position.

The new year of 1951 began with a new art critic, John Russell, who was also to become a famous critic in his time.[16] In the brief period of his column before the end-date of this book, there is not enough time to identify his likes and dislikes. He regarded Sutherland (on 15 April) as being the only living English painter of an international reputation; he had an eye for the Irish, picking up Le Brocquy on 10 June as well as 'Five Irish Painters' at Tooth's; but he was prepared to make the shocking statement on Pasmore that he believed him to be 'the best painter in England': a sad note on which to leave Mr Russell's reputation.

Observer

As the War finished, the *Observer's* art critic was Maurice Collis.[17] His column normally appeared once a fortnight and his last column was on 27 July 1947.[18] It is clear that he was deeply impressed by Picasso, reviewing him in June 1945 ('what a stature the man still has') and also the exhibition of Picasso and Matisse at the V&A at the end of that year (an exhibition 'of first importance'). But he also paid a lot of attention to exhibitions of modern British artists, whether solo shows or group exhibitions. He was not frightened to criticise and grade the artists: in 1945 he noted that a Roberts self-portrait was 'poor painting'; that a Grant was 'very dull'; and that Gotlib was good but not great.[19] He thought that Peake's drawings 'show a mastery of pure line far beyond the reach of any other English artist'. In view of his Irish background it is not surprising that he took an interest in the Irish art scene. He visited Dublin in December 1945 and wrote about the artistic scene there with some excitement, noting the ascendancy of Yeats[20] and the '2nd rank' of Hone, McGuinness, Le Brocquy and the White Stag Group. By early 1946 he was being equally perspicacious about Sutherland, saying that 'during the last few years [he] has risen to a high place in public esteem, being assisted thereto not only by his talents, but by winds blowing from the Fortunate Isles. A sudden elevation has its dangers. The public hankers for new and frequent proofs that its judgment was right and expects a flow of paintings from the admired artist, each one due to be better than the last. The modern celebrity has to work in a frightening publicity'.

Collis's writing in 1946 followed a similar pattern, with almost all his attention paid to modern British artists, often in group shows, and with only very occasional notes on foreign artists (such as Ensor). It is clear that he was interested in Irish artists, praising Le Brocquy again (at the Leicester Galleries) on 20 October 1946[21] and picking out Hone from a group show a week later. (He was to carry on doing this, picking out the work of Mary Swanzy for praise on 30 March 1947; remarking on a show of British art at Waddington's in Dublin in April and noting Le Brocquy's first one-man show at Gimpel Fils on 25 May 1947. No such attention was paid to Scottish artists.) 1947 saw Collis trying to go well beyond his normal recital of current shows. He clearly decided that change was in the air among some British artists and he first noted this in reviewing a show by the British Surrealist artist Eileen Agar, saying that she had now 'emerged' from her Parisian non-representational style ('which leads at the last to no more than the reshuffling of forms and colours and becomes a decoration without significance'). He thought that he could detect a number of British artists going in the same direction (Ceri Richards was thought to be another), so much so that Collis thought he could identify what he called a 'School of London', to distinguish it from that over-used term 'School of Paris'. A few weeks later (2 February), he was back to the same theme, identifying the work of Tunnard as of the London School, moving away from Cubism 'towards forms more directly connected with nature'. Even Colquhoun, in some of his monotypes, was apparently abandoning 'his former angular apparitions'. On 16 March Collis noted in passing, approvingly, when reviewing Hitchens that 'no French ghost looks over his shoulder', whereas on the same date he swats Uhlman as 'French' and 'nondescript'.

Collis stopped working for the *Observer* in July and his place was taken by Colin MacInnes,[22] who followed a similar pattern, although perhaps picking up more foreign shows, probably reflecting the increase in that sort of work in London as the galleries settled back to London after the War. MacInnes was not averse to sniping at those he thought overpraised. On 26 October he noted that in Matthew Smith 'the colour is there in generous abundance, but distributed over the picture surface without strong mental control' (surely an acute comment, especially if one sees a group of works by Smith en masse, as one can nowadays in the Guildhall Art Gallery in the City of London). Craxton gets tapped to one side on 9 November 1947 ('style largely made up of intelligent borrowings'), as does Freud ('a depressing and restricted world of mildly hallucinating minutiae'). As 1948 begins he covers Rouault and then Chagall, glances at Paolozzi ('lightweight') and moves onto Paul Nash's memorial exhibition at the Tate. Here he sees Nash heavily influenced by French artists, but not able to continue their experiments in any way, his handling of paint 'often hard and frigid'.

After Macinnes's last column on 9 May, there is rather a hiatus, with occasional columns by James Laver[23] and a glowing article on Yeats at the Tate by 'a correspondent' and before the launch of one of the most well-known of all contemporary art journalists of the time, Nevile Wallis, on 10 October. Wallis generally got weekly columns and was able to range far and wide across the London art world, taking an early opportunity, as did others, to despair of Pasmore's move to abstraction (on 5 December). Wallis still covered all sorts of art from all sorts of periods and places, only occasionally having the space or inclination either to praise or criticise the British artists covered by this book. He praises Hitchens, is not convinced by Eurich, notes the new artist Edward Middleditch, and so on, but no themes emerge and there is a general absence of strong comment until the piece headed 'Nightmare', on 20 November 1947, which, needless to say, is about Bacon. He thinks Bacon 'technically superb' and impossible to ignore, although 'in certain cases it is impossible to apply the normal canons of art criticism'.

1950 sees Wallis despairing of the huge variety of unpruned work at the London Group show (interestingly, one of the very few artists he picks out for praise is Le Brocquy). Then he moves on to Minton, whose pictures of Spain were on show, remarking that 'Minton's paintings have never yet communicated to me any emotion whatsoever',[24] although he sees the Spanish pictures showing 'greater freedom and assurance'. Wallis pays quite a lot of attention to Leslie Hurry and, as usual, he picks up Le Brocquy's latest exploits, this time in his tapestry work for the Edinburgh Tapestry Company. Trevelyan is not approved of, his work 'often marred either by a discordant note of colour, or the artificiality of some stylisation which the colour fails to redeem'; Burra seems always to be praised; Smith, as ever, is criticised for his obsession with colour; and Spencer's large work at the Royal Academy Summer Exhibition is obviously striking, but more at home in a 'Revivalist meeting-house'. Richards gets faint praise ('near abstract designs are organised purely as flat patterns'); Derek Hill is, rather curiously, said to be 'an extremely interesting painter'. Vaughan is treated seriously – 'the impression remains of a singular artist, of undisputed integrity, faithful to an austere concept and style'.

There is subsequently, on 24 September 1950, another large interaction with Bacon, with Wallis noting that his work is 'easier to discuss than to criticize'. He mentions the widespread commentary which Bacon's work attracts, but asserts that because of its extreme subjectivity it is not easy to apply normal principles of criticism to it. He ends ambiguously, with a comment which may or may not indicate approval: 'And who can say that, but for an urge to give expression to the pictorially inexpressible, Francis Bacon might not be numbered among the few outstanding painters of this century.' Next comes (on 1 October) a good piece on Daniel O'Neill, in which he praises his work highly. Then the usual comment on Pasmore's bizarre decision to paint abstracts ('one can only regret that such a sensitive and individual artist should have so far submerged his identity and impoverished his art'), and a super piece of swatting at Ben Nicholson: 'A glance at his drawings is sufficient to assure one that abstraction is not for him a temporary refuge, but the only possible expression of a talent which could scarcely otherwise merit serious attention.' 1951 goes in much the same way, although Wallis was ill for the first three weeks of January and Nigel Gosling[25] took his place: Wadsworth, not great, but 'independent and gifted'; Scott (praised); Spear (ditto). (The comments on the Festival exhibitions will be dealt with later.)

Belfast Telegraph

This consisted of only six pages and carried only occasional pieces on art.[26] When art is mentioned, the key seems to be that the artists have a connection with Ulster. There is a brief reference on 2 January 1946 to the fact that a locally born artist, Boyd Morrison (although he was living in England at the time), had had a picture in a show at the Royal Academy. That was followed, on 17 April, by a note picking out for comment the works by Northern artists at the RHA annual show in Dublin. Only seldom do local shows get mentioned, either because they were quite rare, which seems quite likely, or because the paper was not commenting on them. A good example was on 19 June 1946, when an exhibition of five contemporary artists (Olive Henry, Nevill Johnson, Aaron McAfee and Gladys and Max MacCabe), was held at the MacGaffin Gallery. This was treated as a rare opportunity to see contemporary local work. In the meantime, the influence of John Hewitt at the Belfast Museum and Art Gallery was beginning to be felt. There were certain local artists whom he was keen to promote, one being John Luke. On 4 September 1946 the paper noted that there was a solo show at the Art Gallery of Luke's work. This was his first one-man show and attracted some attention from outside Ulster, with James White commenting very favourably on it from Dublin.

Each year the annual exhibition of the Ulster Academy of Arts, held in October, got a mention, and that was often the largest article on art of the year. That is not to say that there was any real attempt at criticism; the coverage was more in the nature of reportage, simply noting the work of artists who had caught the eye.[27] The gradual emergence of George Campbell as a leading local artist is striking. He even had the status to open an exhibition for his fellow artists, James McIntyre, Arthur Armstrong and McCreanor in April 1947.[28] His one-man show at Waddington's in June 1949 was commented on, with almost all the 33 works reported as being sold. By 24 October of the same year he was back in Belfast, with a show at Donegall Place.

The Imperial War Museum in London presented relevant War pictures to the Belfast Museum and Art Gallery and on 4 October 1948 the paper recorded the arrival of works by local artists, together with work by English artists who had recorded some aspect of Northern Ireland in the War (such as Ardizzone and Pitchforth). The straightforward portraiture of W.

Taylor Carson was picked up from time to time and appearances by Northern artists either in Dublin or in London were occasionally spotted. O'Neill, Dillon, Johnson and Campbell had 42 works on show at Heal's Mansard Gallery in London in May 1948, and that was noted, as was an exhibition of Northern Artists at the Grafton Gallery in Dublin in the same month (comprising Jack Cowan, Friers, McEndoo, the MacCabes and Maurice Wilks). An exhibition of Irish artists in Holland was even picked up (on 2 February 1949). The paper carefully counted the number of works by Northern artists (18 out of 57 in total, being Conor, Henry, McGuinness, McKelvey, Middleton, Campbell, Hunter, Johnson and O'Neill). In 1949 the arts coverage concluded (on 16 December) with a large and affectionate portrayal of the life of Morris Harding. Generally, in our period, the paper was prepared to comment on art, but really only on local artists and only in passing. There appears to have been no dedicated art critic at this time.

Irish Times

The *Irish Times* in 1945 was an extraordinary newspaper. Its flavour, although gradually changing, was still under the ownership of the Protestant and Unionist Arnott family.[29] It accordingly reported the social comings and goings of the Anglo-Irish on a daily basis and was particularly interested in the famous episode shortly after the end of the War when the students of that Anglo-Irish bastion, Trinity College, hoisted the Union Jack over the college and caused a large and hostile demonstration by the people of Dublin in front of the college. Its editor (from 1934-54) was the eccentric, and of course Protestant, R.M. Smyllie;[30] it carried a daily piece which has passed into literary history, called 'Cruiskeen Lawn' by Brian O'Nolan, aka Flann O'Brien, aka Myles na Gopaleen. The later to be famous star of British television's 'Call My Bluff', the Hon Patrick Campbell,[31] wrote various pieces for it;[32] and Samuel Beckett wrote occasional pieces and reviews. All this was contained in six or eight pages.

Art criticism under the initials 'A.P.' (Arthur Power) appeared with some regularity from the beginning of our period until some time in late

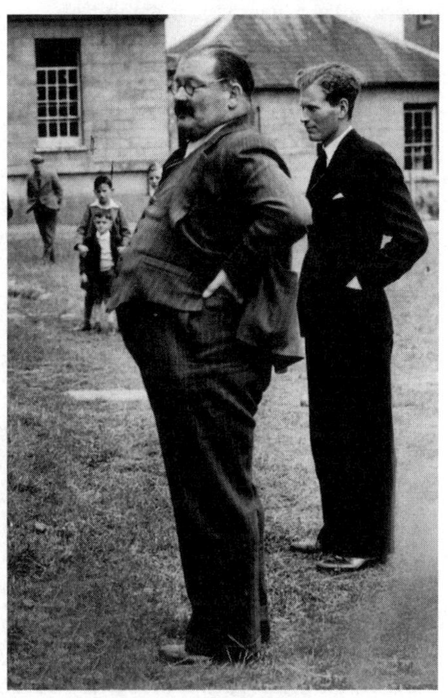

R.M. Smyllie,
editor of the *Irish Times*

1948. There were also reasonably regular mentions of what was happening to Irish and other artists in the London art world in the column headed 'London Letter'. For example, it was reported (on 6 May 1946) that Colin Anderson had recently bought a picture by Le Brocquy for the CAS. On 5 March 1947 the column commented on a show of Jack Hanlon's at Wildenstein in London and on 21 May of the same year it picked up Le Brocquy's first solo show at Gimpel. As an example of the column commenting for the benefit of its Irish readers on what was happening generally in the London art world, the big 1948 memorial exhibition for Paul Nash at the Tate was reviewed on 31 March, as was the introduction by

J Lyons & Co of its series of lithographs (on 4 May). The column even found time to comment on some of the artists covered at one of the annual 'Artists of Fame and Promise' at the Leicester Galleries, noting George Campbell on 15 July 1948. While some of those covered were either already famous (Yeats and Leech, for example), or were to become well-known Irish artists (such as Colin Middleton), others were and have remained little known. Sometimes these were severely dealt with. On 28 June, 1945 Stephen Gilbert[33] had a one-man show which received a savage mauling: 'Such efforts have no relation to art as such; and, even as illustrations, have no value.' Even well-known names were occasionally slated. The treatment of Le Brocquy and Hennessy will be mentioned later but even Yeats was sometimes met with less than enthusiasm. Power's review on 3 October 1947 of an exhibition at Waddington's was quite critical. Norah McGuinness was described on 29 October 1949 as 'not an important painter' and there was a strongly critical review of Nano Reid's work on 11 March 1950. The oil section of the RHA show was that year (on 1 May) described as a 'very vulgar exhibition'.

Dublin received occasional cultural visits from the London art world. On 8 December 1945 it was noted that John Rothenstein had been to Dublin to lecture at the Royal College of Surgeons on 'Recent Developments in English Painting'. On this trip he selected a Yeats, *Two Travellers*, which the Tate was to buy in 1946, according to a brief mention in the paper on 3 April. On 28 January 1946 it was reported that Cecil Phillips, a director of the Leicester Galleries in London, had been in Dublin recently, presumably surveying the local market, and had taken back to London with him pictures by Maurice MacGonigal for showing at the Leicester Galleries. On 5 September 1947 the paper reported that Herbert Read was to give a lecture in a week's time on 'The present situation of art in Europe'. It then reviewed the lecture on 13 September. On 12 February 1949 the paper reported that Eric Newton had been lecturing in Dublin. On 9 June 1950 it was noted that Kokoschka had come over to open an exhibition at Waddington's.

While Arthur Power usually covered current exhibitions in short reviews, on 14 January 1946 he published a large piece under the heading 'The Work of Irish Painters in 1945' in which he reflected widely on the shows held in Ireland during the previous year. Another larger piece than usual appeared on 16 April 1946 when he thoroughly reviewed the work on display at the annual RHA exhibition. Occasionally, Power strayed away from Dublin. He noted (on 20 July 1946) the 4th annual exhibition of the Galway Art Club and he announced the opening of what he described as the first gallery in Ireland to be devoted to Irish Art, in Limerick (on 4 September 1946).[34] He reviewed the Ulster Academy and Ulster Arts Club shows in Belfast on 26 October and he was quick to mention that the Leicester Galleries were to hold on exhibition in London to be called 'Living Irish Art'.[35] Later in the year he picked out the 24th Annual Exhibition at Cork School of Art of the Munster Fine Art Club, and on 30 January 1947 he noted the first ever art exhibition held in Bangor in County Down.

One particularly notable feature of the paper's coverage of the arts in Ireland was the frequency of reviews of solo shows by female painters, many of whom were to have no prominence at all even in the small Irish art world. It is not known whether this reflected the taste of Mr Power or if, in fact, there really were a lot of worthy female artists at work in contemporary Ireland.[36] The following list of reviews for the seven months beginning in November 1946 will give an impression of the point being made here, although it may not be representative of all periods:

1946

Grace Henry[37]	(7 November)
Mabel Young[38]	(8 November)
Margaret Stokes[39]	(21 November)
Kay Casson[40]	(23 November)
Dawn Steele	(12 December)

1947

Evelyn Ruffer	(12 February)
Evie Hone[41]	(12 March)
Lilah O'Brien[42]	(10 April)
Sylvia Cooke-Collis[43]	(17 May).

Patrick Hennessy got support from Power as a result of his 'first-rate ability'.[44] He thought him 'one of the outstanding painters of this country'.[45] When, however, Power was replaced by a journalist under the initials 'GHG' (a writer whose identity has not been traced), the tone changed. On 19 November 1948, reviewing a Hennessy show at Waddington's, the reviewer noted that the work was disappointing, with a tendency to repetition. He was also irritated by what he called the 'preposterous titles' attributed to many of the works. The following November (there seems to have been an annual show by Hennessy at this time, always in November), GHG agreed that the artist was technically good, but not to everybody's taste. (Another reviewer, under the initials 'MN', had, in reviewing a show by the Dublin Painters' Group on 23 March 1949, described Hennessy's work as 'vaguely irritating'.)

There were three main opportunities for the *Irish Times* to review contemporary Irish work en masse: the Annual Exhibitions of the RHA and the IELA and the Oireachtas Annual Show. As always with these large shows, it was difficult to do justice to all the work on display (English writers had the same problem with the RA's Summer Exhibition). Even in the long reviews that were sometimes possible, it was difficult for the reviewers to do anything other than list names and to try to give a general overview of their impression of the shows as a whole. These impressions varied. The RHA show in 1946 was praised.[46] The 'Oireachtas Exhibition', opened by the Earl of Longford[47] in the Municipal Gallery, and only open to Irish artists, contained 150 pictures. The long review[48] said that 'we may not be having an actual renaissance, but, at least, the younger generations have realised that they were on the wrong road in following the conventional line and the Orpen manner'. By 1947 the RHA show was still generally well-thought of[49] and it was noted, 'Some Irish artists are asking higher prices than well-known English artists!' By the end of this particular show, Power thought it worth recording[50] that, during the last five weeks, 4,000 people had attended, a figure which was higher than the previous year, as were sales. Almost 50 pictures had been sold, the top price, not surprisingly, being for a Yeats (£300).

The IELA show that year (1947) was reviewed[51] by an author with the initials 'BI', who was presumably another journalist later to achieve considerable fame as a TV personality, Brian Inglis. The review was generally tame, and not particularly critical. Power, however, was less pleased[52] with the 'Oireachtas' show, finding the Irish artists technically acceptable, but lacking inspiration. They were painting Irish subjects, but still using English or French techniques. There was no sign, in his view, of any Irish school of painting developing.

The 1948 RHA show was thought[53] to be good, but not brilliant. The best, of course, was Yeats. Le Brocquy, interestingly, may have been punished because of his removal to London by this time. His large (and now well-known) work *Tinker breaks whitethorn* struck 'a strange and ultra-modish note': 'This artist's taste does not seem to have improved with transportation.' This attack was repeated when Power reviewed the IELA show.[54] Another well-known picture by Le Brocquy, *The Fearful World*, 'makes truly a fearful picture, too': 'In his present phase, this young artist seems to have lost his distinctive personality, which made his early work so important.' This 1948 IELA show also included pictures from the Bomford Collection, which were given a mixed review by Power. The 'Oireachtas' show, of 111 exhibits was also[55] criticised for its lack of works of genuine Irish character. The following year the same show was described[56] as falling somewhere between the RHA and the IELA, and it was generally not impressive. The writer commented particularly on the selection committee, which this year consisted of James Sleator, Sean O'Sullivan[57] and Fergus O'Ryan.[58]

Other Irish newspapers

A number of other Irish papers contained occasional art criticism at the time. In order to do full justice to the contemporary Irish art scene, one would have to review the *Irish Independent*[59] and its sister paper the *Sunday Independent*, together with the paper controlled by the de Valera family, called *The Irish Press*. One would also have to work through the two Dublin evening papers, the *Evening Mail* (which closed in 1962) and the *Evening Herald*,[60] not to mention papers such as the *Cork Examiner* and those published in the North. While this review would result in a satisfying completeness (unless one also felt the need to cover other regional Irish papers), one feels that the resulting picture would not be substantially different from the one which has been built up here from the Irish journals and from a detailed review of the *Irish Times*. The reality of the Irish artistic situation was that the number of noteworthy practising modern artists was small and well identified; and, although one hesitates to say it, their identification is reasonably uncontroversial.

Scotsman

The *Scotsman*, based in Edinburgh, had a reasonable amount of art commentary, including fairly regular reports from its London correspondent, Douglas Percy Bliss (after the War). So, for example, at the end of the War Bliss was commenting on the RA's Summer Exhibition (on 5 and 12 May) and the paper was also running a detailed examination in three parts of the annual show of the Royal Scottish Academy.[61] The RSA show was treated quite favourably, although the point was made that, as so often with these large shows, a reduction in number to the 50 best works would have produced an effect which 'would astonish the adverse critics of Scottish art'. There were, in fact, various annual events which caught the attention of the *Scotsman*'s unnamed art correspondent. In October he picked up the 84th annual exhibition of the Royal Glasgow Institute of Fine Arts and in the same month there were two detailed review pieces (on 10 and 18 October) of the 51st annual exhibition of the Society of Scottish Artists. In the following month he also picked up the 21st annual show of the Scottish Society of Women Artists, whose president was Anne Redpath, and in January it was the turn of the Royal Scottish Society of Painters in Watercolours. At certain periods the London correspondent seemed to be working overtime. On 13 October 1945 he commented on the 'War Artists' show at the RA; a week later he picked out various shows at the Leicester Galleries, the Lefevre and the Fine Art Society; the following week he drew the attention of his readers to work at the Beaux Arts Gallery and the New English Art Club; then it was the turn of the St George's Gallery and Redfern. There was, of course, extensive coverage of the Picasso and Matisse show when it reached Glasgow in January 1946.[62] In

April 1946 the paper's London correspondent was appointed Director of the Glasgow Art School, although he certainly carried on writing for the paper from time to time.[63]

Each year the annual shows were covered, often in considerable detail, but there were few reviews of shows of individual artists in Scotland.[64] When attempts were made to pick out artists for praise from the larger shows, the results were inevitably mixed, with the benefit of hindsight. History would have little hesitation in approving of the focus on Gillies and Maxwell from the RSA show reviewed on 26 April 1946, or the selection of MacTaggart at the annual show of the Royal Glasgow Institute of Fine Arts on 5 October of the same year. But one struggles to accommodate the choice of two lady artists by the names of Dorothy Peach and Joyce Peters at the Society of Scottish Artists show reviewed on 9 October.[65]

Glasgow Herald

This paper also covered the arts reasonably regularly, on a similar basis to the *Scotsman* in that it picked up the big Scottish annual exhibitions and also noted a number of individual contemporary shows. For example, in 1945 Crosbie was reviewed; as he was in 1946, 1947, 1948 and 1950. In 1946 the elderly George Houston was noted; in 1947 Cowie, Gillies and MacTaggart got a mention, as well as Colquhoun. English artists were also picked up from time to time (Paul Nash, Sutherland and Vaughan in 1948; Eardley, Lewis, Paul Nash and Smith in 1949; and the Spencer brothers in 1950, for example). Northern Ireland got some attention in 1951, with a review on 9 April of a show by the MacCabes and a review of an exhibition called 'Ulster Contemporary Paintings'.

JOURNALS

Journals tended not to have large circulations compared to newspapers, but their format did enable them to permit journalists the opportunity to write at greater length about their subjects and also, in some if not all cases, to write without feeling it necessary to try to cover the main exhibitions which happened to be passing through the leading galleries. This freedom was certainly available to the writer in *Horizon*, which appeared monthly, if not to the regular columns appearing in places like the *Listener*, which was weekly. There were, of course, some traditional art journals, such as *Apollo*, which were focused on a wide variety of fine arts, not just painting or sculpture. *Apollo* had little room for articles on modern British art (although, for example, an article on Moore appeared in November 1946), but it did have a piece every month on the London art scene, under the by-line 'Perspex'. This picked up some modern British art, generally approving of Sutherland and Paul Nash, but not of Bacon and certainly not of Picasso.[66]

It is neither possible nor necessary to review every journal in which serious reviews of modern British art could appear. Even a magazine such as *Harper's Bazaar*[67] had a review called 'Mr le Brocquy's Water-Colours' in its May 1947 edition. In Ireland, the obvious journals are covered here, but relevant articles also appeared in things such as *Irish Monthly* (for example, an article by D. Shields on Yeats in December 1949), and in *Social and Personal*, where there was an article by Edward Sheehy on Yeats in August 1949. In Northern Ireland the quarterly poetry magazine *Rann*, which began in the summer of 1948, contained nothing on art, but did at least give an opportunity to local artists to provide a design for the cover. Rowel Friers, Catherine Wilson, H.E. Broderick, Anne Yeats and Paul Nietsche were to benefit from this policy.

Burlington Magazine

When the War finished, this grand monthly heavyweight art magazine was under the editorship of Tancred Borenius.[68] But he was described as 'acting editor'. Ellis Waterhouse was apparently briefly editor in 1946, but a more permanent replacement was found with the appearance as editor of Benedict Nicolson[69] in the May 1947 issue. The magazine listed the names of its 'Consultative Committee', who played relatively little rôle in its life, but whose names added prestige. Some of our old friends appear on this committee: Clark (of course), Campbell Dodgson, Read, Ridley, Maclagan, Rothenstein and John Witt. Apart from the editor, the other regular contributor and later assistant editor was Edith Hoffman. While the *Burlington* had no principal articles at all about contemporary British artists – apart from two on Henry Moore by Sylvester in June and July 1948 – it did occasionally notice what was going on in the contemporary British art world. There were sometimes reviews of books on modern artists. Hoffman reviewed Betjeman's book on Piper in January 1946 and also the

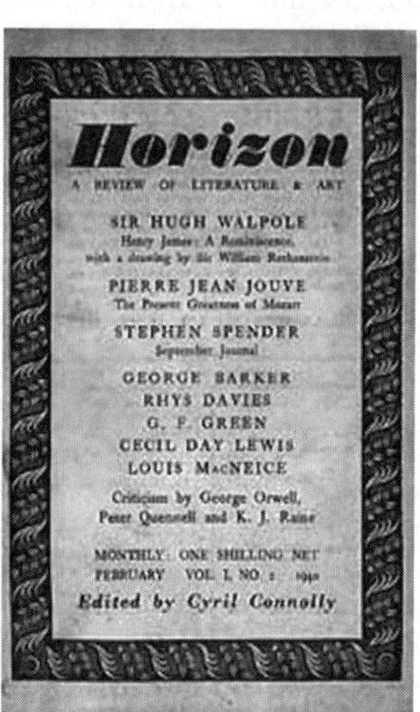

Penguin Modern Painters book by Hendy on Matthew Smith the following month. There were also obituaries of people such as Paul Nash, Hodgkins and Campbell Dodgson and, just occasionally, short reviews of shows of contemporary art. The irascible Douglas Cooper seemed to appear quite frequently in one guise or another. In December 1946 he duly criticized 'Select Acquisitions of the Contemporary Art Society' at the Tate, saying that the CAS lacked discrimination in its purchases (citing recent purchases of works by Ironside, Lowinsky and a 'singularly inept' Bacon). The ICA's early exhibitions were also noticed and there was an extremely careful and balanced review of the Chantrey exhibition in the issue for March 1949. Generally speaking, however, although Nicolson had stated at the beginning of 1948, when introducing a new format to the magazine, that he would occasionally publish articles on modern art, this did not really occur during our period.

Horizon

The first issue of *Horizon* came out in 1939, the last in 1950. Cyril Connolly was its public face as editor, but financially it owed a great deal to the support of Peter Watson (who was also its art editor). There is a debate to be had about the wider cultural significance of *Horizon*, as indeed there is about all small-circulation literary or more widely cultural journals. In the context of the population of the UK, one would be tempted to dismiss the possible influence of a journal whose monthly circulation was between 8,000 and 10,000. However, this would be to overlook the comparatively small number of 'taste-formers', in the 1940s, just as today. It is not possible to say how many individuals in the UK were in the habit of buying new pictures by British artists, but it is perhaps the case that a number of those who did were readers of *Horizon*. (It is certainly difficult to imagine that the number was ever more than a few hundred.) In just over 10 years, 121 issues were published. In 1945, Connolly instigated a heavy focus on France, in all its cultural aspects. On the painting side, there was an article on Braque (translated by Watson) and an article by Kahnweiler on 'The State of Painting in Paris'. Then came an appreciation of the work of Klee by Ironside.

Two months after the end of the War, Connolly and Watson were in Paris and generally it has been observed that Watson's post-War artistic interests, so far as contributions to *Horizon* were concerned, were more focused on Continental than British artists. He nevertheless included reproductions of work by his friends Freud and Craxton; by Paolozzi in 1947; and by Bacon in 1949. The work of Le Brocquy had been discovered on a trip to Ireland in April 1946 and an article about his work by Earnan O'Malley duly appeared in the summer of 1946.

Britain Today

The main art writer during our period in the monthly *Britain Today* was Philip Hendy. He regularly contributed a two or more page piece, usually commenting on a current exhibition or an issue which interested him. Consequently a number of the articles were not about contemporary art, although many were and Hendy's sympathies can be identified over the six-year period covered. Since he was writing while Director of the National Gallery, although not in that capacity, his interests and concerns take on an added importance in this area. In other words, he was not just another art journalist. As such, it is interesting to see how concerned he was about the economics of the young artist in Britain in this period. His concerns were triggered by the publication in early 1946 of the report *The Visual Arts* prepared by The Arts Enquiry sponsored by the Dartingon Hall Trustees. In the March 1946 edition of *Britain Today*, under the heading 'Art, its present condition', Hendy picked up the concerns of the report about the fact that it was incredibly difficult for young artists to make ends meet. Compared with the situation in the 19th century, when a number of British artists had been able to earn very considerable incomes from their work, it was now very difficult indeed for artists to do that. Many, if not most, had to supplement whatever they could earn by selling pictures by taking other jobs. Only Picasso's income might be thought to be on the scale of a number of Victorian artists and the only British artists making enough money to live comfortably off painting alone were a handful of fashionable portrait painters, who were, by definition, hardly at the cutting edge of contemporary artistic developments.[70] He came back to this theme in April 1947, with an article headed 'The Germ of State Patronage', in which he commented on the helpful fact that the Arts Council paid a 'hiring fee' to artists whose work it needed to borrow for its exhibitions and that the Arts Council was also now buying its own collection of contemporary British art, so as to reduce the need for extensive borrowing.[71]

He was similarly pleased to note (in the issue for April 1948) the establishment of the ICA, partly because it would be good for encouraging the work of young artists who were otherwise dependent on getting shows through the dealers, whose galleries were inevitably small and who had to show work which they had some confidence in selling. He also approved (January 1950) of the adoption of the large New Burlington Galleries at the back of the RA by the Arts Council, because large exhibitions would be able to be held there. Otherwise London had few extensive premises for large temporary exhibitions which did not involve the temporary removal of permanent collections. (He was particularly thinking of the National Gallery here and, perhaps, overlooking places like the Whitechapel.) When it came to the work of individual British painters Hendy's tastes were definitely contemporary. He particularly liked Sutherland, reviewing solo shows in August 1948 and then again in June 1951, querying why at the time 'our leading painter' had not been given an official solo show as part of the Festival. He clearly respected, if not liked, Colquhoun's work, picking it out for comment on at least three occasions during our period. Bacon got his attention in January 1950. Hendy balanced admiration for Bacon's remarkable sense of form against aspects of his technique of which he was less sure.

Hendy was also interested in sculpture, picking up the big sculpture exhibition in Battersea Park in 1948; Reg Butler and Ayrton in September 1949; Paolozzi and Turnbull in May 1950; and the Battersea Park show which was part of the Festival in 1951. Occasionally, Hendy did not write the monthly column. His place was taken a few times by David Sylvester, and also by Colin MacInnes. Sylvester, for example, contributed articles on Moore's drawings (in November 1949), on Spencer and Freud (in July 1950) and on Pasmore (in December 1950).

Spectator

As the War ended, the *Spectator*'s art critic was Michael Ayrton. Most weeks (less so in the summer), he had a short art column in which he either focused on a particular exhibition or attempted to cover what was going on at a number of the leading galleries. He was, needless to say, fairly opinionated (although perhaps not quite so irritating as Heron). For example, his reaction to the Picasso and Matisse show at the V&A in December 1945 was to be rude about the Picassos: not, as with many members of the general public, because he could not understand them, but because he thought they just were not very good. Contemporaries were not always well treated in his reviews. Craxton was said to be in too much of a hurry in trying to create a reputation (8 June 1945); the older painter Adler was a 'chef in paint... A good decorative painter without being a very interesting artist'. One of his last regular columns, on 10 May 1946, made the usual comments on the RA Summer Exhibition: 'The same qualities of meaningless vulgarity, decadence, incompetence and juvenile sentimentality are displayed in the vast majority of the exhibits.'

On 24 May 1946, Ayrton's place was taken by M.H. Middleton.[72] He continued the same pattern of general reviewing of the contemporary art scene. He noted a Bacon at the Redfern ('the big, impressive Francis Bacon'); saw the Irish pictures at the Leicester Galleries in October 1946 (he liked Le Brocquy in particular); recognised the worth of the Scottish painter Crosbie at the Lefevre in April 1947; picked up Le Brocquy again in his May 1947 solo show at Gimpel Fils; and, needless to say, particularly admired Colquhoun in October of the same year ('at least two of the big pictures are mature masterpieces'). Although he was clearly following the appearance of Irish artists in the London galleries, Middleton was not necessarily always positive about them, and was quite capable of both changing his view on an artist he had previously liked, if he thought their work had changed, or disliking an artist who was generally widely acclaimed. In June 1948, he was not impressed by Le Brocquy at the Leicester Galleries and, in writing about Yeats at the Tate, in August of that year, he went against what was becoming the received attitude towards Yeats amongst contemporary art critics (at least in Ireland) by saying that he was not convinced of Yeats's stature. Was Yeats anything more than an illustrator? He could 'seize a moment of importance', but he was no match for the likes of Soutine or Kokoschka for form, tone or colour.

On 17 December 1948, Douglas Cooper made an appearance, reviewing an exhibition of David. 1949 saw Middleton contributing again, but there were also appearances by Derek Hudson and long periods where no art column at all appeared. In 1950 this trend was even more exaggerated and it would be fair to say that the *Spectator*'s art coverage in 1950 was sadly diminished. When it came to the Festival, Middleton was a little disappointed by the sculpture at Battersea (seeing some pieces as being out of scale for their setting), and had the usual approach to '*Sixty Painters*' of 'seeing which artists had managed convincingly to cope with the demands of the large canvas'. Evans, Bellingham-Smith, Moynihan, Gowing, Nicholson, Pasmore and Freud got particularly favourable mentions. When mentioning the Festival, he still found time to note the Irish show at Tooth's and another Le Brocquy solo show at Gimpel.

New Statesman and Nation

One of the journalists whose work ought to be dealt with is Patrick Heron. Although he wrote for a number of journals, he will be covered under this heading, as he wrote widely for the *New Statesman* during our period. Heron merits serious consideration as a writer on other artists and is a good example of a writer some of whose assumptions are easy to identify and expose. Rather neatly in terms of chronology for our purposes, his first published art criticism appeared on 18 October 1945 in The *New English Weekly* (on the subject of Ben Nicholson), and between then and the end of 1951 he was to write many articles, principally in that journal and in the *New Statesman and Nation*, but also occasional pieces in other places, such as *Art News and Review*.[73] In order to give some context to Heron's art criticism, it is worth noting that, at the time his first piece was published, he was twenty-five. He had been to various schools as a child, but had emerged without academic qualifications at the age of 17 and had then gone on to attend the Slade for two days a week for a period of two years. He had spent some years of the War as an agricultural labourer and was gradually developing his own painting and drawing skills, not through training but through self-education. As his biographer Mel Gooding says: 'Heron had not read widely (and never has) but he had read deeply.'[74] His qualifications to write serious criticism of the work of other artists have to be assessed in the light of this non-academic background.

Heron wrote a very great deal of art criticism in the period 1945-51, covering contemporary art, both foreign and British, and also pottery. Certain themes emerge. His criticism was dominated by a reverence for the work of Cézanne, Picasso, Braque and Bonnard. He also admired aspects of Matisse, Léger and Gris. British artists, by contrast, found it a lot harder to get Heron's blessing. Ben Nicholson managed it, as did Hitchens and artists somehow associated with St Ives; others were damned with faint praise. Heron was often opinionated and dismissive about British artists; they never live up to their Parisian counterparts, to his mind, and their techniques are always faulty. On the other hand, when he is writing about one of his favourites, his journalism can be fascinating and full of insight. Here, his status as a working painter helps him to disentangle the intentions and achievements of complex artists whose work cannot have been easy for an English readership. Unfortunately, when he allows himself to pass judgment on his British contemporaries, it is difficult to forget that his own painting was, in its interesting phase, very much derived from Braque, and thereafter of little significance in the wider scheme of things. It is hard to imagine Heron's work as a painter surviving any sensible grading of British artists of the 20th century and the arrogant young man's sneering at the work of others is unlikely to reflect (or create) the judgment of history.

When the War ended, the art critic of the *New Statesman and Nation* was Roger Marvell. He did the usual job of covering the big set-piece exhibitions (he liked Picasso and Matisse at the end of 1945 and also Klee), whilst also picking out dealers' exhibitions that happened to catch his attention. He was quite amusing about the hubbub which followed Picasso and Matisse. On 5 January 1946 he commented that 'the commotion about Picasso has been great fun, a harlequinade to enliven our Christmas'. Noting the flood of letters that had appeared in the *Times* letters columns, he said that 'so many of the letter-writers evidently felt in 1945 just as much at sea as their parents had felt at the first Post-Impressionist exhibition in 1910'. He also thought that 'the chief moral to be drawn is that the world is very full of things that are very difficult to understand and that, if we do not understand something, it is sensible either to try to learn or to keep quiet'.

As 1946 went on, others started to appear. Eric Newton had a piece (on Braque and Rouault) on 13 April; Benedict Nicolson on 27 April; Henry Crabbe on 11 May; and Topolski had a big piece, including a very rare reproduction, on the Nuremberg trials on 31 August. By 1947 Heron had appeared, his first piece being on 11 October. He covered a lot of contemporary British painters, generally slighting in one way or another. (Eardley Knollys also appeared from time to time.) Heron particularly liked to judge whether or not young painters had learnt the lessons of Cubism: Colquhoun and MacBryde had not; Craxton had; Gear had not; and so on. What also aroused his anger was to read any praise of an artist in the catalogue of an exhibition he chose to review, and so Yeats got a particularly vicious savaging because MacGreevy had had the temerity to say in the catalogue that Yeats was an important artist.[75]

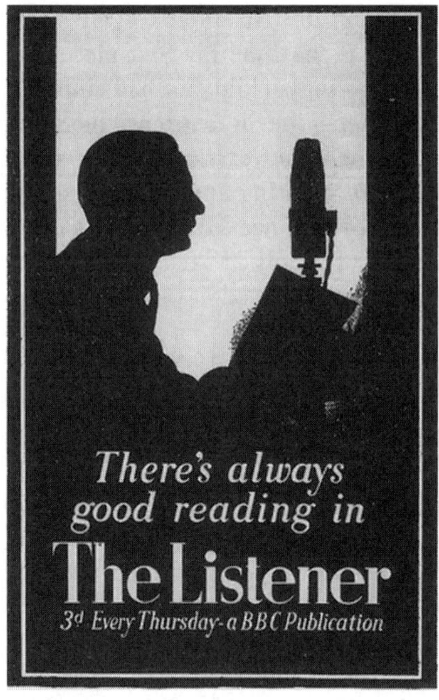

Raymond Mortimer, who had been the literary editor until 1947, contributed a dryly amusing article on the Chantrey problem at the beginning of 1949 and on 22 January David Sylvester appeared for the first time.[76] Continuing the general trend for the *New Statesman* to attract high-level writers, John Richardson had a column on 9 July in which he swatted poor Craxton.[77] By early 1950 Heron seems to have moved on. There was a brief period when Basil Taylor[78] wrote a few columns, together with Benedict Nicolson, but for many weeks there was no art criticism at all. 1951 opened with a rare piece by Anthony Blunt, followed for the first time by John Berger (on 10 February) on Wadsworth. Berger was then to cover the events around the Festival (which will be dealt with elsewhere).

The Listener

A number of things are striking about the *Listener*'s art coverage in our period. In the first place, a large amount of writing about art was included, some of it being the text of talks which had been given on the wireless (whether the Third Programme or the Home Service). Secondly, one is immediately struck by the great variety of writers who appeared. During the eight months of 1945 following the end of the War, one could have read pieces by John Russell, Nikolaus Pevsner, Newton, Jean Helion, Read, Ayrton, Leonard Greaves, John Pope-Hennessy, Ian Finlay, Piper and Philip James. In 1946, Read, Newton, Rothenstein, Clark, Cooper, Grigson, Hendy, Mortimer, Wyndham Lewis and Myfanwy Piper appeared, among others. This is an incredibly high level of art writers and it is hard to think of any comparable journal matching contributions from this type and range of author.[79] Indeed, the overall attention paid by the *Listener* to contemporary art is striking. Covers were sometimes specially designed for it by young British artists (presumably on a paid basis), for example, Wadsworth (9 October 1947), Rowntree (13 November 1947), Farleigh (1 January 1948), Minton (9 December 1948) and Rothenstein (13 October 1949), just to take a random selection. There were, in addition, often reproductions of pictures, either accompanying the text of an article (for example,

Colquhoun's *Dancer* accompanied Lewis's review on 23 October 1947) or appearing as a selection of works from different current shows, by way of pictorial rather than verbal coverage of what was going on in the London galleries.

It is not easy to identify who, if anyone, could be said to have been the art correspondent during our period. Gallery coverage, in the form of a general round-up of what was going on, rather than a feature on a particular event or artist, seems to have been done by Russell, Newton, Mortimer and Lewis, although the piece did not appear regularly. When it did appear, the reader will not be surprised to find that the most trenchantly written pieces were those by that great natural polemicist, Lewis, by this time gradually reaching the end of his eyesight through the later 1940s. He had no hesitation administering such chastisements – or, to be fair, encouragements – as he saw fit. Tunnard's pictures were set aside with the phrase 'extremely monotonous', whilst Colquhoun was highly, although not uncritically, praised. Sutherland, however high his then reputation, was treated on his merits as Lewis saw them and a show at the Marlborough was, on 10 June 1948, said to have a general effect which was 'somewhat garish and raw'. Ceri Richards (on 14 October) was thought to be so good that he could be placed 'beside Robert Colquhoun' as the very best of the younger painters. Interestingly Lewis approved of Le Brocquy and had no hesitation at all in supporting Bacon, saying that no young painter painted so beautifully as him and that his pictures were amazing. 'Bacon is one of the most powerful artists in Europe today and he is perfectly in tune with his time.' Collectors were not immune from disparagement. The exhibition of the Howard Bliss collection at the Leicester Galleries, heavily focused on Hitchens whose work Lewis clearly did not like, caught his attention for its 'pervasive dimness', the pictures all tending towards the 'weightless and soft'.

Art News and Review

This self-styled art 'newspaper' was founded by Richard Gainsborough[80] and the first edition came out on 12 February 1949, with Bernard Denvir as the editor. It cost 6d and was to appear fortnightly. Distinctively, it had on its front cover a portrait or self-portrait of an artist, usually, although not always, living and often, but again not always, British. The portraits were accompanied by brief descriptive pieces on the sitters. From the living British artists covered from the first issue to the end of 1951,[81] we get another opportunity to see which artists were regarded as significant or interesting enough to be covered in this way (and also another opportunity to reflect on the vagaries of historical evidence, in that the list was an individual choice, no doubt with its own bias built in, and also it was a list of those prepared to participate. I am not aware, for example, how many artists refused when approached). Apart from the portraits, *Art News and Review* is interesting for us because it tried to record all the exhibitions going on (at least in London) and also because of the exhibitions it chose to review. So, for example, in the first issue reference was made to the Lefevre showing Minton; the irrepressible Leicester Galleries showing Appelbee, Grant, Hitchens, John, Lewis, Moynihan, W. Nicholson, Piper, Pryde, Scott, Sickert and Spear; the Redfern showing Spender and Rothenstein; the Marlborough, Colin Hayes; the Mayor Gallery, Smith; and Thomas Lowinsky at Wildenstein. The first issue also contained favourable reviews of Colquhoun, MacBryde, Craxton and Minton. In the next issue a review of Minton placed him 'among the half-dozen British painters of his generation', whereas by 17 June 1950 Sylvester was writing on Freud as having 'succeeded Dylan Thomas as the legendary figure of the younger generation' (an odd comparison).

New English Weekly

This journal was owned by the Orage family, having been established by Alfred Orage[82] in 1932.[83] Its editor was Philip Mairet.[84] Its antecedents may have meant that modern British art was not its principal focus, but it had the great honour of sheltering our old friend Patrick Heron as art critic for a while. In fact, it seems to have had the pleasure of publishing Heron's first piece of art criticism, on 18 October 1945. This was a flattering review of Ben Nicholson. Most of Heron's work for the journal was concentrated in 1946 and 1947, his last piece coming out on 26 February 1948. During that period, he used the journal to praise some of his heroes (Picasso, Klee, Cézanne, Bernard Leach and Braque) and to vilify Paul Nash in two long pieces following the artist's death. Heron dismissed Nash – 'we must conclude pretty quickly that he is a minor figure' – despising his use of colour ('by far his weakest point') and laughing at his technique ('another defect of Nash's lay in his actual handling of the brush'). Eventually he finds a few small redeeming features in Nash and regrets that he was not a bit cleverer with colour. Heron got his comeuppance on 19 September 1946, when the poet R.F.C. Hull[85] spent some time analysing Heron's earlier review of a Braque exhibition. He found the writing full of jargon and either meaningless or appallingly trite. (Needless to say, Heron was stung into defending himself in a later edition.) Otherwise, there were very occasional pieces of art criticism before the journal expired in September 1949. Alex Comfort wrote approvingly of Cecil Collins and there was a brief flurry towards the end of 1947 when the paper tried to instigate a review of current exhibitions, but after three attempts that stopped.

Image

This beautifully produced magazine lasted for only 8 issues, 1949-52. Its editor was Robert Harling and it focused on graphic work, with a large number of high-quality illustrations. The graphic side of a number of contemporary British artists was covered, such as John O'Connor, Minton, Piper, Gross and Ardizzone. In addition there was an article on the drawings of Leonard Rosoman. Although it charged the large sum of 5 shillings per issue, it closed because of losing too much money.

The Studio

The monthly *Studio* had been founded in 1893. When the War ended, its editor was Geoffrey Holme. Its format was to have a series of articles on particular subjects, which could be paintings, but of any period or area, or which could relate to applied arts from anywhere in the world. There was sometimes an article on an institution (such as the Tate, the National Gallery of Scotland, the Society of Scottish Artists and so on). The articles were usually followed by a detailed review of the London art scene, called 'London Commentary', at this time by Cora Gordon. Sometimes there were 'Commentaries' from other places. Book reviews completed the edition, although these were generally short.

An attractive feature of *The Studio* was that it seemed to be trying to get well away from an English bias. Other areas of the British Isles were covered regularly in the articles. In June 1945 the article mentioned above on the Society of Scottish Artists, by C. Pilkington Jackson, was included and the same edition had an article on Mainie Jellett by James White. Stanley Cursiter wrote on the National Gallery of Scotland in October 1945; Tom Honeyman did a Scottish 'Commentary' in July 1946; John Hewitt introduced the Belfast Art Gallery in January 1947; David Baxandall did the Manchester City Art Galleries in July 1947; G.V. Barnard did the Norwich Castle Museum and Art Gallery in the following month; George

Furlong covered the National Gallery of Ireland in August 1949 and in the same month John Hewitt wrote on 'The Landscapes of John Luke'. James White was back in March 1950 to explain 'Irish Painters of Today'.

Another feature was the fact that artists themselves sometimes contributed articles. Ayrton did a series of four artists under the general heading 'The Heritage of British Painting', starting in August 1946. Charles Ginner wrote on 'The Camden Town Group' in November 1945 and the same edition contained an article by John Farleigh on 'The Arts and Craft Exhibition Society'. Significant articles drew together the threads of the contemporary scene. The article on 'Irish Painters of Today' by James White has already been mentioned. This was an important attempt to analyse and group the key artists practising in Ireland, with illustrations of works by Cecil Salkeld[86], Hanlon, Frances Kelly, McGuinness, Luke, Reid, O'Neill, Middleton, Dillon and Le Brocquy. Similarly important had been Bryan Robertson's review of 'The Younger British Artists' in March 1946. The profuse illustrations to this article caught many old favourites (Craxton, Ayrton, Vaughan, Colquhoun, MacBryde, Minton, Appelbee and Scott), but also some very surprising and today rather obscure names – Geoffrey Rhoades,[87] Alicia Boyle,[88] Walter Poole,[89] Maurice de Sausmarez,[90] Clifford Frith,[91] Hilda Scott,[92] Helen Grunwald,[93] Keith Henderson,[94] Leonard Greaves,[95] Fred Adams[96] and so on.

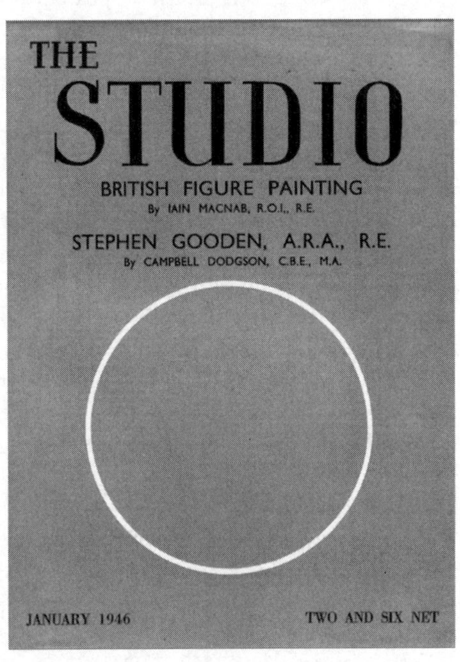

Bernard Denvir contributed an interesting series of articles on individual artists: Peake in September 1946, Ayrton in March 1947, Minton in July 1947, Colquhoun in August 1947 and Adler in January 1950. He also wrote articles on particular collectors: Eddie Marsh in November 1947 and Wilfrid Evill in February 1949, for example. *Studio* seemed to like to have articles running in series. In 1951, Whittet embarked upon a series on the individual galleries, starting with Agnews in April, the Redfern in May, the Lefevre in June, Wildenstein in July, the Fine Art Society in August and Colnaghi's in October.

Scottish Art Review

This began in 1946, under the encouragement of Tom Honeyman, as the journal for the Glasgow Art Gallery and Museums Association, under the name of *The Art Review* (becoming the *Scottish Art Review* in 1948). It had little or nothing on contemporary art, although occasionally featuring photographs of modern art acquired by one of the art galleries. At last, in volume III, number 1 (1950), Harvey Wood wrote an article entitled 'Contemporary Scottish Art'. This was extensively illustrated, with works appearing by W.Y. Macgregor, Robert Sivell, Maxwell, A.A. McGlashan, Leslie Hunter, Donald Bain, Crosbie, Henderson Blyth, Gillies and David Sutherland. The slightly backhanded compliment was paid: 'Painting in Scotland is in a healthy and lively condition – a condition of infinite promise, if not of massive achievement.' Inevitably, Maxwell and Gillies received a lot of attention. The position in Aberdeen was noted, as the School of Art there had David Sutherland and Robert Sivell as its teachers. Furthermore, the author, who was the Scottish representative of the British Council, was pleased to point out that the Council had just sent an exhibition of about 60 works representing modern Scottish art on tour to America and Canada.

Scottish Art and Letters

Only five issues of this journal appeared, at irregular intervals between 1944 and 1950. It was edited by R. Crombie Saunders and the art editor was the artist J.D. Fergusson. A certain amount of art material was included, but it was fairly heavily biased towards short stories and poetry. The first issue had an article by Robert Melville on Rousseau and de Chirico, as well as a number of illustrations by local artists such as Donald Bain. The most significant article for our purposes appeared in the second issue, in spring 1946. This was by the artist T. Elder Dickson[97] on 'The East Coast Painters'. This slightly contrived category was used to cover a number of artists, all of whom had at one time or another studied at Edinburgh College of Art. Needless to say, they were all described as having at some stage studied abroad and as having been influenced by French Impressionism. The artists covered included names familiar to this study (Maxwell, MacTaggart and Gillies), but also some names which are now less well-known: Thomson, D. Sutherland, W. Wilson, Hislop and Westwater. The third issue (1947) contained an article by William Crosbie on 'Oriental and Occidental Art' and the fourth issue had a review by John Tongue of a Fergusson exhibition and by Bain of the Bonnard and Vuillard show at the Edinburgh Festival in 1948.

Dublin Magazine

This quarterly, founded in 1923, had a two-page section headed 'Art Notes' by Edward Sheehy. This tried to cover exhibitions of note, but it also took an opportunity to discuss more general art topics. Its structure reflected the key events of the comparatively small and overlapping Dublin art world: the annual exhibitions of the RHA, the IELA, the Dublin Painters and, occasionally, the Watercolour Society of Ireland; together with the key shows at the leading commercial galleries (Waddington and the Dawson Gallery, in particular). The same artists come up over and over again and the same list of those approved by Sheehy gets regular prominence. The leading name was always Yeats, who was regularly and thoroughly reviewed during the period under consideration. Interestingly, the next most 'approved' artist was Le Brocquy, whose developments were followed closely, with much appreciation. Middleton was a great favourite of Sheehy and, to begin with, so was the ultra-realist work of Patrick Hennessy. However, as time passed and Hennessy's style failed to change or develop (in sharp contrast to Middleton, who was proficient in a bewildering variety of styles), Sheehy's view of him changed and he became quite critical, although still admiring the impeccable technique. The work of Cecil Salkeld was usually on the approved list, as was that of Thurloe Connolly. Campbell and Dillon started to get noticed towards the end of our period, with some reservations, and O'Neill was sometimes acclaimed as a great Romantic and sometimes chastised for weakness of technique.

Overall, although he clearly had favourites, Sheehy's criticism was balanced and fair. He was quite prepared to pick up failings even on the part of his favourites when necessary – Le Brocquy for example, being criticised for getting too much like Picasso at one point. Where he did not like or respect the work of a painter, he made that clear. So, in the April-June 1945 issue, he said this about Kenneth Hall, who was one of the co-founders of the White Stag

Group: '[He] seems content with a kind of animated geometry as the vehicle for a childish symbolism, and which, moreover, involves a technique so over-simplified as to be practically non-existent.' Undoubtedly his harshest words were reserved for much of the work shown at the RHA's annual exhibition. In 1945 he noted: 'This year's Academy exhibition fulfilled expectations in producing the usual few competent portraits, a large body of meaningless mediocrity, and a very few genuine attempts at original painting.' By 1948 he felt that the Academy was giving 'the impression of a catastrophic decline in the art of painting in Ireland'. By contrast, the annual show of the IELA was always better, although the whole scene was confused by the fact that many of the same artists showed in both exhibitions. He liked the fact that, in 1945, the IELA included work by contemporary French and English artists, while noting that the best of the Irish work was just as good. (By this he was usually referring to Yeats, Le Brocquy and Middleton as the best Irish work.) In 1950 an interesting development occurred in respect of the IELA: its organising committee actually rejected a work because of concerns about its religious subject matter being insensitive in that most Catholic of countries. That the committee should do this – and to an artist of the stature of Middleton – was a very worrying development for Sheehy. It appeared to show the IELA taking itself seriously as an alternative Academy, which he felt should not be its rôle at all.

The Bell

The *Bell* had been founded in 1940, its initial editor being Sean O'Faolain. Although of some significance in Irish cultural history of the 20th century, its attention to the visual arts during our period was spasmodic. Occasionally a big art event in Dublin would attract its attention. For example, the Yeats Loan Exhibition in 1945 elicited a long and praising article from Elizabeth Curran, in the June issue of that year. In October 1945, a group of four distinctively different writers gave their short thoughts on the IELA for that year. Oliver St John Gogarty wrote intemperately: 'The abominations I behold at the ELA were not Reality. They were attempts to exploit the already debauched taste of ignorant and dealer-directed public.' Curiously he thought that some of the pictures were 'illustrations for the dermatology of a leper colony', which perhaps says something for his familiarity with modern art. The other writers generally approved of the exhibition.

From April 1946 the new editor was Peadar O'Donnell, who generated occasional art pieces. The English artist Derek Hill,[98] for example, wrote on 'New French Painting' in February 1947; Earnan O'Malley contributed a detailed review of the 'School of London' exhibition at Waddington in June 1947 and, for some reason, two articles on Mexican art in the same year. Cecil Salkeld contributed an article on 'The Progress of a Painter', describing generically how a painter develops. Herbert Read was a big-name contributor in March 1948, with 'The present situation of art in Europe' and in April the magazine ground to a halt allegedly because the British Government had imposed trade restrictions on the importation of Irish books, thereby killing off a large part of *The Bell*'s circulation. It was not to reappear until November 1950 and the only further article of note, right at the end of our period, was by the young artist Patrick Swift, who reviewed the RHA exhibition in rather savage terms, noting that it was, to a large extent, only really worth considering the contribution of the invited English artists, such as Bacon (with the exception of Yeats and Le Brocquy from amongst the Irish). As for the rest of the Irish contributions: 'We reach a level of badness at which the ordinary terminology of criticism ceases to apply, and in any case it is obviously quite futile to attack pictures so invincibly mediocre and patently dull as these.'

Envoy

The monthly literary journal *Envoy* was the creation of John Ryan,[99] and appeared for the first time in December 1949 (just as *Horizon* in England was coming to an end), carrying on for 20 issues, until July 1951. It set out with clear intentions to cover contemporary art (presumably reflecting Ryan's own interests, as a painter himself) and there was a series of long articles about particular artists: Salkeld on O'Neill in December 1949; Patrick Collins on Campbell (January 1950); Noelle Brissac on Thurloe Conolly (February 1950); Patrick Swift on Nano Reid (March 1950); Edward Sheehy on Middleton (April 1950); W.J. White on Le Brocquy (May 1950); Edward de Courcy on the sculptress, Hilary Heron (June 1950); and finally Ryan himself on Swift (who was Ryan's brother-in-law) in the last issue (July 1951). In between came articles by Sheehy on 'Recent Irish Painting' (September 1950). He cantered through the obvious names: Le Brocquy, Middleton, Conolly, Johnson, Reid, O'Neill, Anne Yeats, Dillon, Campbell and Swift (and an artist less well-known to us now called Doreen Vanston).[100] In February 1951 five artists were given the chance to publish a piece of their own writing under the general heading 'The Artist Speaks. Irish painters join in a symposium of artistic opinion'. The artists involved were Le Brocquy, Dillon, Reid, Campbell and Swift.[101] Lionel Miskin[102] wrote a long and surprisingly wide-ranging article on 'Modern English Painting' in March 1951, covering a huge range of artists working in England at the time.

Commentary

The Irish monthly magazine *Commentary* (the name changing to *Irish Commentary* at some point) was edited by Sean Dorman.[103] It covered a wide range of fashion and film items and was always full of pictures of pretty girls. But it usually had quite a serious page of art criticism by Theodore Goodman. He pursued the usual line of contemporary Irish criticism: Yeats together with Paul Henry and perhaps Leech were always treated as the best of the older generation; followed by some permutation of Le Brocquy, Dillon, O'Neill, Middleton, Campbell, Conolly, Salkeld, Jellett, Hone and Hennessy from amongst the younger artists. On that basis, he liked the IELA, but he was honest enough to acknowledge that Irish artists had to avoid complacency when faced with the many excellent artists working in England. He welcomed, on this basis, the visit to Dublin of John Rothenstein (who had delivered a lecture there) and the fact that Kenneth Clark had lent pictures from his collection to the 1945 IELA. Boldly for an Irish critic, he was even prepared to acknowledge that Yeats himself would perhaps be no more than a footnote looked at from a European standpoint – and all other practising Irish artists would be unable to stand up to their English contemporaries.[104] Occasionally articles appeared on individual Irish artists, such as Campbell, Salkeld, O'Neill and, of course, Yeats. He was particularly appreciative of the impact made by Waddington since they were quite prepared to show young non-Irish artists, this being almost the only way to see this sort of work in Dublin.

CHAPTER 6

CHANGING FASHIONS

ANALYSING REPUTATIONS

Some artists' work enjoys periods in and out of fashion. This may be because their specific work moves in or out of favour, or it may be, for example, because the style or origin of their work is, for some reason, fashionable. Evidence for these related but different points can be adduced. Bomberg's work has returned to fashion, or popularity, after a long period in which it was largely ignored by the critical establishment. Vaughan has become very fashionable (although it is quite difficult to see why in any objective sense), whereas Minton, for example, has not. In terms of groups, the most astonishing rise has been seen in Irish art, with a number of Irish artists of the mid-century moving into positions of serious status in the market. Abstract art has gone in and out of fashion in the years since the 1940s. Work from St Ives remains fashionable; that from Great Bardfield not (with the exception of Ravilious). While these changes can be tentatively identified, they cannot so readily be explained. The work of the mid-century is now regularly exposed to the vagaries of the auction market and perhaps it is enough to say that fashion displays itself through the appetite of those buying and dealing in art.

An explanation of how reputations were formed and have shifted was begun in the last chapter. An artist's reputation can decline. It can be evanescent, quickly vanishing after years of apparent growth or stability, or it may steadily increase and remain high. As Eric Newton said in the *Sunday Times* on 22 July 1945, reviewing an exhibition at the Leicester Galleries, 'Reputations are easily made, but they are also rather easily forgotten.' It is sometimes said that a particularly testing time for an artist's reputation is in the years following his death, when opportunities for self-promotion vanish.[1] An attempt will be made here to track selected reputations in some detail, with a view to displaying at least some aspects of the mechanism whereby this strange growth – and decay – has occurred. General lessons may emerge about the way in which reputations were or are formed, but the intention is not to teach lessons of that nature. The intention will be to explain what had to happen in an artist's life for his reputation to develop; how much it was to do with the artist himself, beyond the production of the raw data (the paintings); and what influence, and on whom, had to be exercised in order to alter that reputation.[2] The choice of those covered in this chapter has not been easy, and an inevitable degree of subjectivity has had to be applied but, by admitting this now, the hope is that the reader will feel more tolerant of the selection. What can be said clearly is that the artists chosen had particularly high reputations at one time or another over the years from 1945 to date: Robert Colquhoun, Gerard Dillon, Louis le Brocquy, Graham Sutherland, Paul Nash and Francis Bacon.[3]

Robert Colquhoun[4]

Robert Colquhoun died in 1962 aged forty-seven. His reputation as an artist had begun to develop nationally in 1942, with the publication in May of an article in *Horizon* by John Tongue reviewing an exhibition at the Lefevre Gallery called 'Six Scottish Painters'. Thereafter he attracted widespread critical attention. His exhibitions were regularly reviewed in the leading newspapers and art journals of the time and in the serious weeklies, such as the *Spectator*, *New Statesman* and the *Listener*, and in 1958 he had a large solo retrospective at the Whitechapel. In 1959 he appeared on the BBC television arts programme *Monitor*, the fame of which has grown because of the subsequent success of its director, Ken Russell. Colquhoun's works are in many public collections in England and Scotland and the Museum of Modern Art in New York has one of his pictures.[5] At first glance, therefore, his was a career which was far from ignored but, as the details come into focus, the picture changes. A fast rise to a reasonable degree of artistic fame occurred from 1942 to about 1947; then Colquhoun's reputation wobbled; then it fell. Since his death, his reputation has been at the mercy of others and the result has been a sad, lurching progress down the artistic cul-de-sacs of Neo-Romanticism and Scottish art, where, rather forlornly, it now rests.

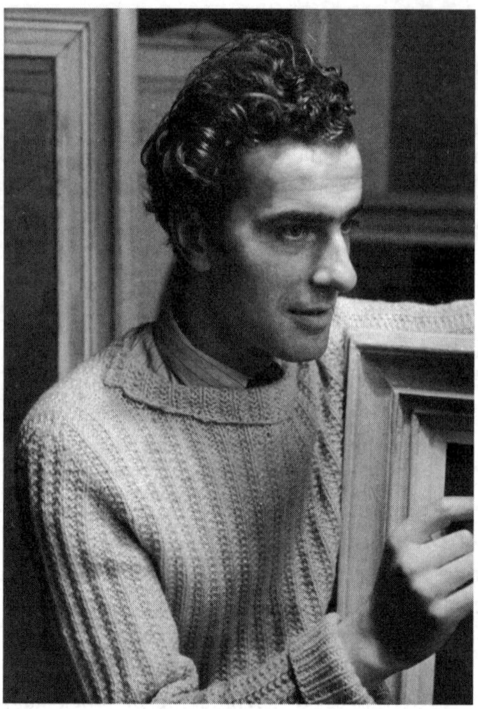

Robert Colquhoun

Until very recently, no book had ever been published about Colquhoun.[6] The most serious attempts to describe his career appeared in *Modern English Painters* by Rothenstein[7] and in *The Spirit of Place* by Malcolm Yorke.[8] There was also a reasonably substantial, albeit brief, review of his career by Bryan Robertson in the introduction to the Whitechapel catalogue in 1958 and an interesting attempt by John Griffiths to analyse Colquhoun's work in the introduction to the catalogue of a 1990 exhibition in Glasgow.[9] Otherwise, there are brief mentions in catalogues and articles and in general reviews of the period, in books on Scottish art and Neo-Romanticism and in literary and social records of life in London in the 1940s and 1950s. The broad outline of Colquhoun's artistic career is clear and uncontroversial. He showed promise at art at school in Kilmarnock in the 1930s;[10] and went to Glasgow Art School, where he met MacBryde. He was therefore trained in a fairly academic way, and he was obviously a skilled draughtsman. After a brief skirmish with the War, he arrived in London in early 1941 and moved into the orbit of Peter Watson. Watson wrote to Kenneth Clark on 20 February 1941[11] sending drawings and asking for Colquhoun to be considered by the War Artists Advisory Committee. Another result was the *Horizon* article in May 1942. Colquhoun was also introduced to Duncan Macdonald at the Lefevre Gallery. Solo shows followed in 1943, 1947, 1950, 1957, 1958 and 1962.[12] He participated in a joint show with MacBryde in 1959,[13] and his pictures appeared during his life in various different types of group shows in England and abroad (often under the auspices of The British Council) in 1942 and 1944 and then each year until 1957.[14] An Italian trip in 1949[15] produced pictures that the critics did not like and some years of increasing wretchedness, punctuated by the Whitechapel exhibition and the television show, with scattered exhibitions culminating in one at the Museum Street Gallery in 1962. It opened shortly after his death while he was at work preparing a monotype for the exhibition.

Art history faces the same problem of objectivity as other types of history when it tries to summarise reputations: facts get simplified and crude caricatures settle in the collective mind. Writers on artists have both to know and to reveal their prejudices before their readers can assess their objectivity. They also have to know and to take account of the prejudices of the age in which they are writing (which may not be possible except in retrospect). Not many commentators on Colquhoun have been able to resist certain themes. They like to mention, first of all, Picasso. They sometimes assume that Colquhoun approached Picasso's work directly; sometimes through the mediation of Jankel Adler. Gauging an artist's reaction to Picasso was a critical tool that art critics of the mid-20th century found difficult to resist. As time has moved on and the task of painting something without it being judged by comparison with the still-developing work of Picasso has passed, it has become easier to treat the influence of Picasso as merely one of a number of possible influences and tests. It has to be accepted, however, that it was a lot easier for the erudite John Griffiths, writing in 1990, to analyse Colquhoun's pictures by reference, in equal measure, to Picasso, German Expressionist, Celtic and Assyrian influences, and so on, than it was for Heron in 1947. Some critics have also found the theme and malign influence of drink and physical decline irresistible. From a certain chosen perspective, Colquhoun's life can be presented as tragic, and there is a well-populated room ready for artists able to be labelled as having caused their own personal and artistic demise: Dylan Thomas is an example from Colquhoun's milieu. As I said earlier, since Colquhoun's death, many critics have tended to hide him among the Neo-Romantics and made him a hero of Scottish art.

A number of things would seem in fact to have influenced Colquhoun's painting. His Scottishness came into it, at least initially (although not necessarily in any deliberate sense), as may have the fact that Kilmarnock in the 1930s was a poor place, with real poverty visible during Colquhoun's early life. The War may also have scarred him, along with so many others. While the generally received version of events is that Colquhoun was invalided out of the army because of physical collapse due to strain, there is an old typewritten note in the Colquhoun file in the Imperial War Museum, of uncertain provenance, which states that he was invalided out owing to mental illness, precipitated by the conditions he suffered and by not being able to devote time to his painting.

The subjects of a number of his pictures grieve; they suffer in some way; they are patently inadequate. Another influence which helped to attract some of that initial critical interest arose from the fact that Colquhoun was not English, had not been trained at an English art school and, indeed, had travelled before the war to France and Italy. His trips abroad set him apart from other painters. Although there were a few Neo-Romantic pictures at the beginning of his London career, tentatively ascribed to the passing influence of Sutherland[16] (pictures such as *Marrowfield* and *Church Lench*), the first really clear Colquhoun style, developing in his well-known pictures of *The Whistle Seller, Woman with a Birdcage, Woman with Leaping Cat* and *The Fortune Teller*, was not like other British work of the time. The pictures appeared to be an original synthesis of Picasso and other influences.

In *Apollo* in 1943[17] an unnamed commentator described the earlier work, presumably approvingly, as having a manner 'reminiscent of Gauguin's later work – i.e. conceived as a pattern in two dimensions, with the third dimension suggested but not stressed'. In the same year, John Piper described Colquhoun in the *Spectator*[18] as 'one of the best of the younger painters who have a rhetorical bias. "Rhetorical" because his paintings are constructed on common foundations as to subject, out of largely irrelevant forms and colours'. He concluded by saying, 'Already his work is more than promising.' Jan Gordon in *The Studio*[19] also commented on his gifts as a colourist and, interestingly, was already comparing his work with that of Adler, whose own solo exhibition was being reviewed in the same issue. Eric Newton reviewed the 1944 Lefevre show observing that Colquhoun and MacBryde:

> ... use paint with a fine sense of its preciousness. Both are ascetics, but in a special sense. Theirs is not the flimsy asceticism that makes a smug virtue of self-denial, but the strong asceticism that knows the value of working within self-imposed limitations. Both, for example, can take a patch of colour and give it the maximum of sonority by dovetailing it into a chord of surrounding colours, chosen with meticulous care. And the same combination of sensitiveness and deliberation is characteristic of their closely knit design.[20]

In February 1946 Colquhoun took part in a group show at the Lefevre, alongside Ben Nicholson, Bacon, Sutherland, Craxton, Freud, Trevelyan and MacBryde. He showed seven oils. Clutton-Brock in the *Times* on 19 February thought that Trevelyan was most concerned with painting: 'With most of the others the emphasis is on the invention of recondite symbols.' His short review laid particular emphasis on Colquhoun. He saw him as using 'an idiom based on Picasso's later works, but as an illustrator he has something of his own to say; his schematic figures have a definite character of their own and suggest witches living in shabby, modern rooms, with their familiar's cat or canary'. Maurice Collis in the *Observer* thought that Colquhoun had successfully 'digested' Picasso; Newton in the *Sunday Times* noted Colquhoun and MacBryde pursuing 'their earnest, painterly austerities. I find their draughtsmanship exciting, but their favourite chords of colour quite unpalatable'.

In 1946 both Colquhoun and MacBryde had work on display in Paris at the British Council sponsored 'Exposition internationale de peintures modernes'. The catalogue was written by Herbert Read and contained illustrations of work by both artists. He bracketed the two artists together and said that their work was:

> ... beginning to occupy a very definite position in the contemporary scene, [and] may owe something to the general tradition of cubism, but perhaps as much to the Celtic love of abstract linear design. Like some of the younger painters in Paris, Colquhoun and MacBryde seem to be attempting a new synthesis, based on the technical discoveries of the past fifty years: but essentially their attitude towards the human figure corresponds exactly to Sutherland's attitude towards landscape – that is to say, they take the intellectual and emotional essence of the subject and paraphrase it into an expressive design.

A show at the Lefevre in early 1947 received strong support from Lewis in the *Listener* (on 13 February): 'Robert Colquhoun is generally recognised as one of the best – perhaps the best – of the young artists. That opinion I cordially endorse.'[21] Then, between 25 October 1947 and 20 August 1949, Colquhoun's work caught the attention of Patrick Heron, writing in the *New Statesman*, on four separate occasions. This body of criticism constitutes the most sustained attempt by any contemporary critic to review the work as it developed and it will, therefore, be given some weight here.

Characteristically, Heron was not easily impressed, although he was prepared to admire some aspects of Colquhoun's work. In 1947 he described Colquhoun as a 'conceptual' painter, but by comparison with, for example, Sutherland, Heron thought that the concept or image derived more from the images of other modern artists than from Colquhoun's own contemplative researches. Heron saw Adler and Picasso as being more responsible for Colquhoun's style than any sitter: 'There is nothing wrong with this, but the more oblique the impact of the natural scene is in an artist's work, the more inward or poetic the source of

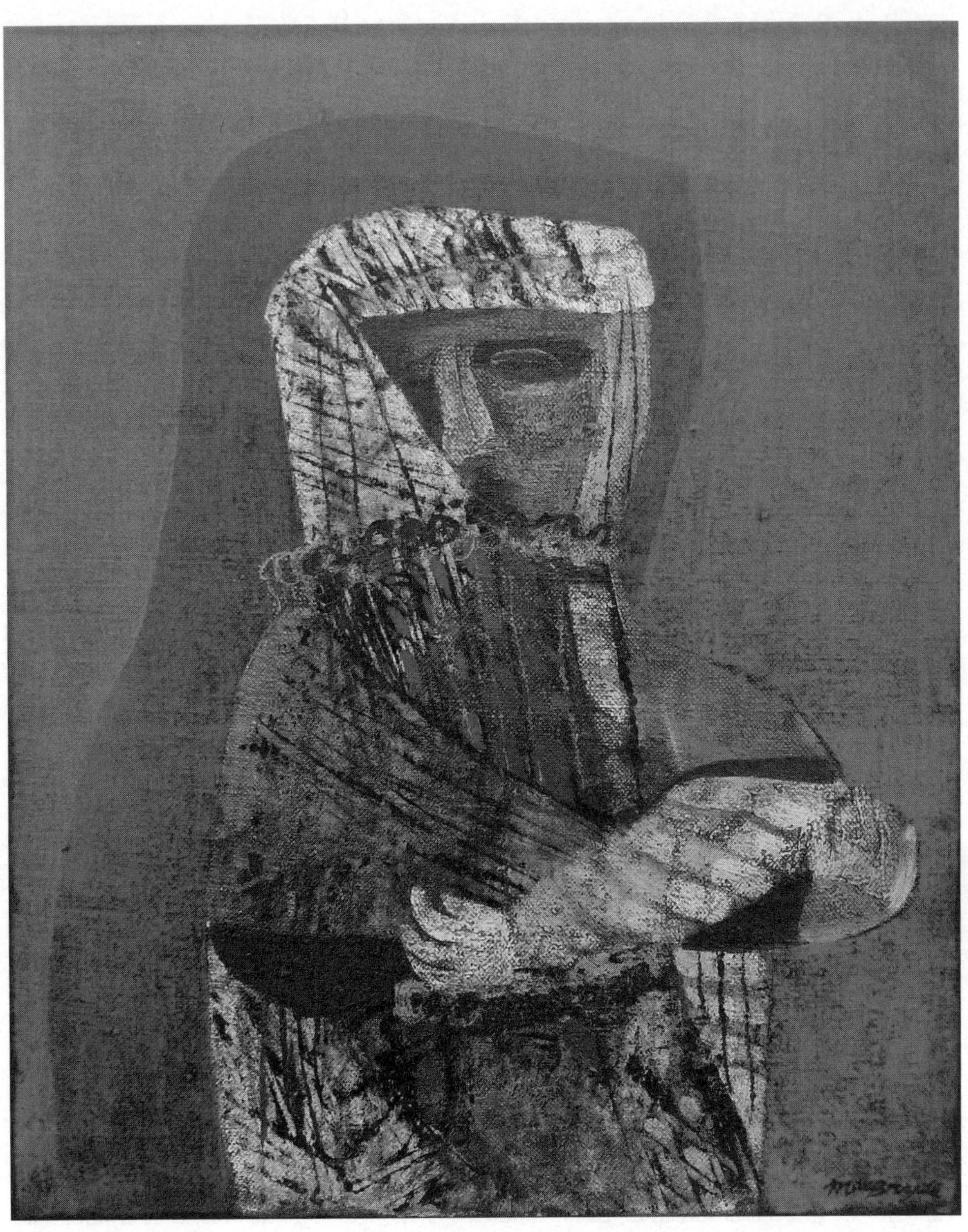

The Irish Actor by Robert MacBryde who with his lover Robert Colquhoun
formed the notorious 'Roberts'.
Private collection

vitality must be.' (It is interesting to note that although Wyndham Lewis was more of a supporter than Heron, his review[22] of the Lefevre show of October 1947 was quite critical. He lamented the fact that Colquhoun appeared to have formed images in his head as oil-paintings before he started painting, rather than studying his subject and then transmuting it into a picture. Lewis thought Colquhoun needed to work more directly from nature, not necessarily to put nature into his pictures, 'but to enrich, with memories of carefully studied form, the pictorial intelligence within'.) Meanwhile, Colin MacInnes in the *Observer* on 26 October praised Colquhoun's sense of style, but also noted that the pictures did not always work: 'So often Colquhoun masks the absence of real feeling by gifted pastiches of his own work.' Newton in the *Sunday Times* of the same date also devoted considerable space to Colquhoun, starting by remarking that 'his work would have to be included in any seriously representative collection of paintings by the dozen most truly creative contemporary British artists', but then going on to say that he was puzzled, rather than convinced, by the latest pictures in the Lefevre. He saw Colquhoun as having arrived at a crossroads:

> All the queer bitterness and some of the pathos of his earlier painting have disappeared. In their place is a clearer, brighter but emptier set of colour-harmonies, a harsher, less mysterious system of design, figures that have lost their hieratic dignity and begin to gesticulate feverishly – but in obedience to what inner compulsion? Certainly they are not paintings to be ignored, but equally certainly they are transitional.

Heron had clearly been following Colquhoun before he first came to write about him in the *New Statesman* and what is missing is a direct record of Heron's reaction to the Lefevre show of 1946 which, by general agreement, appears to have contained the best of Colquhoun's work. In 1947, commenting on the subsequent Lefevre show, there was already scope for Heron to compare the developing work, unfavourably:

> Robert Colquhoun's first success was due to his discovery of a highly distortional, highly formalised equivalent for the human figure, which somehow gave off strong whiffs of forlorn personality. Co-existing with the formal elements was a flavour which might be called the 'poetry' of the works. This poetry was newer and more interesting than the configuration of the formal elements which tended to be derivative; and it is this poetry which seems less strong in the present works.

While Heron liked a picture called *The Fishwife*, he only liked it because a small part of the sleeve of the right arm met with his approval: 'The quality of the colour and tone... is such that light and space are really generated.' As in so much of his art criticism, Heron was writing here as the professional artist and there is something more than a little pretentious in this isolation of a small patch of one picture out of a whole exhibition as being worthy of note. Heron was, however, capable of real insight, despite the burden of using Picasso as a testing apparatus. He noted that Colquhoun had a 'head full of ideas for pictorial exploitation, but he can't get them over as forcefully as he should'. He thought, for example, that Colquhoun's colour did not 'operate, it merely is'. He also thought that the design was 'falsely complex in an effort to supply the impact the colour denies, and the result is that the original sensation or conviction is half-drowned in secondary abstractions'. Perhaps Adler was to blame? He described Adler's paintings as static, referring to little more than themselves. Heron's conclusion on this occasion was that Colquhoun was 'an important painter: it would be a pity if success prevented him overcoming the tendency to repeat himself which is now discernible'.

There have been enough references to Adler now to require some attention to be paid to his influence over Colquhoun. He was originally from Poland, and arrived as a refugee in Glasgow in 1940 where he may well have met Colquhoun. In any event, in 1943 he moved into 77 Bedford Gardens in a separate studio. In his formative years he had worked in Germany alongside Klee and both of them had taken in the overwhelming influence of Picasso, as well as, in Adler's case, the German Expressionists. Adler certainly seems to have influenced Colquhoun in his turn and Colquhoun's painting in the mid-1940s, marking a development from the previous flirtation with Neo-Romanticism, perhaps represents an example of Adler's influence. (Interestingly, John Minton, who was also living in Bedford Gardens at this time, went through a similar phase, in paintings such as *Children of the Gorbals* in 1945. It would seem that Le Brocquy was also influenced to some extent by Adler.) The benefit or otherwise of the Adler influence is not easy to ascertain, although it is necessary to remember the chronology here. On the basis of his oils of 1942-44, Colquhoun would be an even smaller footnote in British art history than he already is. The 'great' pictures date from 1946-47, some time after Adler's influence must have been felt.[23]

Adler's work itself went through different phases, sometimes containing monumental hierarchical figures, often flat, with strong outlines and highly abstracted forms. The main book about Adler was published in 1985 to coincide with a major exhibition in Düsseldorf.[24] On the cover is a picture from 1923 called *Angelika*, showing a woman with two cats. It is fair to say that a number of the pictures from the 1920s (although probably never seen by Colquhoun) bear similarities to Colquhoun's work. For example, *Orphan Girls* of 1927 shows three women, with ovoid faces and blank, grieving expressions. One woman holds another. Similarly, pictures entitled *Three Women* (1926) and *Mother and Daughter* (1927) are strikingly similar to Colquhoun's work, at least in subject-matter. Cats occur frequently, as do humans with animals of various sorts. By the 1940s Adler's pictures had become far more abstract and directly Cubist than Colquhoun's work, but it is not difficult to see how the allegation of influence can be made. Apart from the possible influencing of Colquhoun's subject-matter, the style of the people suggests that Adler may also have influenced Colquhoun. Adler seems to have been seeking to represent a world – in his case, Jewish – that he had lost and that was itself literally to be lost during the War. Many of his human pictures are not portraits, but are 'incorporations of his memories', which have been robbed of their characteristics and reduced to types. This strikes a chord when considering many of Colquhoun's unidentifiable female Celtic peasant 'types'. The problem for Colquhoun was in developing beyond that influence as he had managed to develop beyond the original influence of Wyndham Lewis.[25] Adler has not been treated as a great painter by English critics and the line that he took from Picasso has not been treated as a particularly productive one. If one were simplifying what may be a more complicated pattern of achievement, it could be said that Adler was one of Picasso's many victims. Worryingly for Colquhoun, this was soon to be said of him as well.

Heron returned to the subject of Colquhoun in an article in the *New Statesman* on 4 September 1948, reviewing the next Lefevre exhibition. On this occasion Colquhoun comes in for the full Heron treatment. Here I think we can identify the point in Colquhoun's development where he ran headlong into a critical reaction which could only assess those using Cubist characteristics by testing them against the principles established by Picasso and Braque. Nothing is clearer from Heron's general reviewing career than his near-worship at this time of Picasso, Braque and Matisse. All other modern artists fail by comparison, at least until Heron started to engage with the American Abstract Expressionists (although Heron of course always left room for St Ives). In the late 1940s, however, Abstract Expressionism was some years away and Heron was going through a period of savageness towards attempts to emulate the great modern masters in ways that indicated, to his eyes, a failure to grasp the underlying precepts of Cubism. Heron was therefore very strongly critical of Colquhoun at this time and did not address the possibility that Colquhoun was endeavouring to do something different from pure Cubism. The review takes this line of attack:

> If a painted shape is flat in conception and drawing, an additional devotion to its exact quality as a painted surface does nothing to redeem it. Both painters [he was reviewing Colquhoun and MacBryde] construct a picture out of flat and sometimes flapping shapes which resemble the pieces of a jigsaw, in that their edges are unpredictable. These facets, or pieces, tend not to be rectilinear, as in Cubist pieces. The Cubist facets had a plastic derivation: they were 'planes' and so they invariably invoked a solid form. The edges of Cubist planes were always taut, consisting of straight lines and rigid arcs. Not so the flat pieces here, which are both more and less naturalistic than Cubism. They are more naturalistic in that things will be drawn with flat similitude; less in that these 'correct' fragments are then embodied in surrounding purely fanciful shapes. In Colquhoun these shapes are elaborated with all manner of arbitrary stripes and textures: they suggest a certain desperation.

Here we have the clearest example of Colquhoun's reputation being damaged by a perceived failure to comply with the dictates of pure Cubism. It is clear that an attack from that angle cannot be defeated. An artist in 1948 who simply used original Cubist techniques to produce some sort of 'pure' Cubist pastiche of Picasso would surely not have met with Heron's approval either. Heron may be right: Colquhoun may have been trying to emulate Picasso without grasping the intellectual underpinning that created Cubism in the first place. On the other hand, it is at least as likely that Heron was wrong and that Colquhoun was trying to use aspects of Picasso's achievements and to mix them with other influences and thereby take them in another direction.[26] Certainly, as later critics have found it easy to identify, Colquhoun was influenced by many things beyond Cubism. We will nevertheless see later how the Cubist dilemma carried on hurting Colquhoun's reputation.

On 21 May 1949 Heron reviewed the next Colquhoun/MacBryde (and Winifred Nicholson) Lefevre show. This time he was magnanimity itself in comparison with his crusading defence of Cubism in the previous review. But now he damned with faint praise. Colquhoun's contribution consisted only of monotypes and drawings of people, and Heron approved. It was as if the naughty schoolboy had been chastised for attempting something too ambitious and was now to be praised for limiting his ambitions and keeping away from the big boys' playground. Therefore, while his 'inventiveness is greater than ever', this is contrasted with the unsuccessful paintings. 'The spontaneity of his inventive hand is naturally and swiftly recorded, whereas in the oils he has to "think up" a complicated system of awkward, unwieldy units to communicate a similar vision.' Heron finds the monotype of *Fishwife at Table* to be 'magnificent' and, in a very generous accolade for Heron, he describes it as 'as elegant as Braque'. He ends up by saying that 'too often in the past the formal complexity was excessive; but now he arrives at something enduring at last'.

The last mention in the *New Statesman* came on 20 August 1949 when Heron reviewed an exhibition at Roland, Browse and Delbanco of English and French paintings. This included Colquhoun's *The Whistle Seller* (dating from 1946) and Heron generously described that as the most interesting English picture featured. He was prepared to say that it was a very good picture, 'full of excellent colour and delightful texture'. He could not resist saying, however, that it made all Colquhoun's work of the last two years look 'hasty, crude and forced'.

Wyndham Lewis kept up his relentless support for Colquhoun whenever he got the opportunity. When a single picture appeared at a mixed show at Roland, Browse and Delbanco in September 1950, Lewis spotted it and pushed it in his *Listener* column (on 21

September): 'About the Colquhoun at Roland, Browse and Delbanco, and an almost equally fine one hanging a month ago at the Lefevre Gallery, it is difficult to speak with patience. Why on earth do they remain unsold?' By the time of Colquhoun's last solo Lefevre show in December 1950, his reputation was very depressed.[27] Lewis was still trying his hardest to support the rapidly declining reputation, but his was a forlorn struggle. In the *Listener* for 30 November, he included yet another illustration of a Colquhoun picture – this time *Masked Figures*. He mentioned that he had spoken to the artist about his Italian trip and how impressed Colquhoun had been by the spectacle of the Palio at Siena. Lewis noted, however, that the pictures were not in fact much different from usual. 'The stylistic instrument which is Colquhoun the artist has a very powerfully developed psychological function, and it has a very limited range. His Scottish female figures are essentially x-ray character shots.' He also said 'when a Colquhoun show opens, something, for me, is happening: it is as if I read that a rocket had been fired at Mars or the Moon. In the past Colquhoun's rockets have reached farther than most of those leaving British soil'.

This show attracted the attention of David Sylvester for the first time, and he wrote a long review[28] in which he sensitively analysed the whole of Colquhoun's career to date. Lacking Heron's tendentiousness, the review has a degree of fairness to Colquhoun which repays attention. Sylvester began by noting that 'there were few, if any, young painters in this country, during and just after the War, more poetic or more painterly than Robert Colquhoun. Keeping equally clear of formal exercises without meaning and of the tendency to illustration of the neo-romantic movement, he made his forms achieve a perfect fusion of pictorial and expressive functions'. His figures were husks in that all emotion had been drained out of them 'by a despair which had come to be their motive power'. In 1947, however, the husks lost this 'vestige of life' and became puppets: 'Their gestures no longer came from within; invisible wires jerked their limbs into place. Colquhoun had gone stale.' By 1950, the figures have lost the woodenness of the previous few years, but now they are gratuitously expressive. Sylvester felt that Colquhoun's 'language' was basically that of Gauguin – 'in its use of colour to serve expressive and decorative, not plastic or atmospheric, purposes [and] in the sort of gauche monumentality which it lends the human figure'. Other influences exist, but the 'hotch-potch' disintegrates when not bound together by perception. Colquhoun had become (compare Heron and Lewis's earlier similar criticism) conceptual and for that to work, constant reference back to real sensations is needed. This is where Colquhoun had failed.[29]

Dipping into the biographical side of Colquhoun for a moment, he left 77 Bedford Gardens in 1947 (at least temporarily) and spent a couple of years in Lewes. He came back to Bedford Gardens in the later 1940s and then moved to a house called Tilty Mill near Great Dunmow in Essex until 1954. (This was a fairly remote house rented by the poet Ruthven Todd and sub-let to the Canadian writer Elizabeth Smart.) Complete rootlessness appears to have followed for the rest of his life as he and MacBryde, at times virtually destitute, staggered from one drink to the next in various parts of London or Suffolk. There were occasional exhibitions in the 1950s, but no serious critical attention was being paid to him. Having been criticised for not being sufficiently Cubist, he was seen as even less relevant in the context of the Abstract Expressionists and, in any event, his output of oils, upon which his reputation would have to rest, virtually stopped between 1951 and 1958. (A rare exception was *Figures in Farmyard* of 1953, now in the Scottish National Gallery of Modern Art.) Bryan Robertson appeared out of this gloom as something of a saint. He appears single-handedly to have taken upon himself the task of trying to resurrect

Colquhoun's status and spent a long time gestating a full retrospective exhibition at the Whitechapel, which opened in April 1958. While the critical reaction was not uniformly good, it did serve to remind people that there was an unusual talent struggling along outside the mainstream of international painting which was worthy of some note. However, the worst sort of 'he's not a good Cubist' criticism was still alive. For example, in the *Architectural Review*[30] an unnamed writer came up with the following:

> Robert Colquhoun's figurative system was one of the last contributions to the cubo-expressionist synthesis and has lasted no better than any of the others. All the unnatural-looking formal devices for the figure which stemmed from Cubism and Vorticism have been expressions for the loss of respect for the idea of mankind's redeemability; but with very few exceptions they have proved to be inadequate vehicles for generalisations about the human condition.

This is not so much saying that Colquhoun was a failed Cubist, as that Cubism itself was a failure and that Colquhoun was tainted for being too close to it. Colquhoun was clearly by this time in Morton's fork. Sir John Rothenstein, on the other hand, in his book describes how moving the exhibition was and how profoundly impressed he was by the stature of the body of work. He was also depressed by the lack of appreciation which Colquhoun had had over the years. (The Tate had bought *Woman with Leaping Cat* in 1954 and it was to buy *Woman with Still Life* from the Whitechapel. In 1976 it was given *The Fortune Teller*.)

In his introduction to the Whitechapel catalogue, Robertson wrote sympathetically and encouragingly about Colquhoun's painterly achievements. He really willed him to pick up from the achievements of the 1940s and, indeed, Colquhoun had worked hard to produce eleven large new oils for the Whitechapel show, although not all of these were well regarded, either at the time or since. There were exceptions: *Bitch and Pup* was prepared for the show and was clearly successful. On the other hand, there was a general feeling that a number of the pictures had been put together too quickly and illustrated how Colquhoun's style had formalised and become static in something approaching self-parody. (Sir John Rothenstein quotes Bacon as saying that he deplored Colquhoun's 'destruction of his art by his gradual enslavement to a constrictive style'.)

There followed in 1959 that documentary about Colquhoun and MacBryde on the BBC television show *Monitor*. After his death in 1962, which merited a reasonably full obituary in the *Times*,[31] the art world went silent on Colquhoun until 1977.[32] A small exhibition at the Mayor Gallery in London, with catalogue introduction by Richard Shone, galvanised a surprising amount of critical attention, as if the art world had simply forgotten about him in the past 15 years. Shone wrote enthusiastically, as befits the introduction to a catalogue, but even he could not maintain his enthusiasm for the entire period of Colquhoun's production. He had no difficulty in praising the Lefevre show of 1946: there seems little controversy that, whether those pictures are liked or not, they represent Colquhoun's best efforts. In Shone's view, they contained 'images notable for a taut grandeur of design, restrained yet resonant colour, a steady fluctuation of texture'. On the later pictures of 1958, prepared for the Whitechapel, Shone comments that 'his colour had become brighter, applied more flatly in an almost heraldic disposition of planes (nuances of drawing and texture being virtually removed). His later subjects introduced a forced rhetorical note into already stiffly constructed and unyielding figures. An empty mannerism characterises the least good paintings of his later years'.

Shone has an attempt at estimating why the brief flourish in Colquhoun's reputation after the 1946 show should have been. His view was that the painting was well received 'because of its emphatic imagery, direct emotional appeal and legible modernity. It struck a blow for a celticism which was undecorative and unliterary, a lyrical humanism which was unassailably compassionate'. He ends his piece with the following: 'As the period clutter and aesthetic prejudice recede, Robert Colquhoun emerges a gaunt and impressive figure of maturity and rooted force.'

What did the critics make of it all? James Burr in *Apollo*[33] noted the Cubist influences, but by this time it was no longer necessary to attack or defend the degree to which Colquhoun was treated as having complied with Cubist principles. He thought he detected that Colquhoun's Cubism came via Gris[34] and he saw 'deliberately bold formations, distilled from observation' which 'show an insistence on shape and structure only occasionally weakened by the romanticism they [Colquhoun and MacBryde] were fighting'. Similarly, in the *Burlington Magazine*,[35] the critical generosity which felt no need to criticise the degree to which artists had 'achieved' Cubism manifested itself. The anonymous author noted that Colquhoun had faced 'the usual problem, of course: not of absorbing, but of surviving the influences – above all Picasso and Sutherland'. He went on to say that the 'example of Picasso's 1930s style was particularly dangerous, if accepted, so to say, at its own tempo. The only way out of the Picasso trap was towards either greater abstraction (William Scott) or a more overtly expressionistic idiom (Francis Bacon)'.

By this time the Scottish art establishment had taken up Colquhoun and there was an important exhibition in Edinburgh and other places in Scotland in 1981.[36] This attracted a serious and, in my view, perhaps the best analysis of Colquhoun's work, by John Griffiths, writing in the *Burlington Magazine*.[37] He thought that Colquhoun's 'best achievement was the assertion of energies forceful but uncommunicated and unused – a tension between potentiality and actuality' and that 'the best of his works are set on a stage in the small, close theatre of impulse, which is almost bare of scenery, between the acts. They are often, in a complex way, concerned with the modalities of his emotional and sexual involvement with Robert MacBryde'. Griffiths went on to say:

> Robert Colquhoun's major influences were from central traditions of European art and from stylised conventions of human and animal representations as far apart as the Assyrian and the Hiberno-Saxon, with the eventual constrictions that such styles impose.
> Robert Colquhoun's animals provide extraordinary tension. They recall the *Book of Kells*. These creatures are the elemental forces lost to or quiescent in their human partners. In *The Whistle Seller* the cat, vibrant and youthful, savagely masked, its eyes green glowing, is contrasted with the crippled street vendor. In *Woman with Leaping Cat*, the many-coloured cat forces itself free of the grasp of its life-weary owner. In order to catch the ball she is poised to throw, its frenzied diagonal movement disturbs the solemn vertical structure. In the best of these works the figures – like the painter – are tragic in that they are looking for an aim they cannot discover.

Since 1981 there has been critical silence outside Scotland, save for passing mentions in the exhibitions on Neo-Romanticism at the National Museum of Wales in 1983[38] and at the Barbican in 1987;[39] in Malcolm Yorke's book in 1988; and in the exhibition at the Barbican in 2002 called 'Transition. The London Art Scene in the Fifties'.

The terms of reference employed by the critics who had to assess Colquhoun's work in the second half of the 1940s really came from Cubism. At that time that was the closest parallel they could identify. Whereas at first they seemed to have given him the benefit of the doubt, in appearing to recognise developments in the 1946 Lefevre show that took him out of the orbit of Picasso and into the nihilistic vision which coincided with the views of others in post-war Britain, such as Bacon, it soon became apparent to the critics, as show followed show, that Colquhoun's achievement in oils was to be seriously limited and was not developing, but turning in upon itself and stultifying. Once the artistic world in Britain began to settle, and as the 1940s moved on, with such events as the Picasso and Matisse show at the Victoria and Albert Museum in late 1945, and the increasingly interesting work coming out of Cornwall and from painters such as Sutherland and Bacon, critical patience for Colquhoun's strange and limited, but apparently static, vision evaporated. Alternatively, perhaps the vision evaporated before the patience.

Gerard Dillon

Dillon, who was born in Belfast in 1916 and died in Dublin in 1971, spent many years in between living and working in London, and he is a figure of some significance in the British art world of the 20th century. His reputation in Ireland is now, and has been for a very long time, considerable, although he is rarely mentioned by English writers. His Irish successes started quite early in his career and have continued with little interruption. This brief study will record that, together with his London career, as an illustration of the difficulty of a 'provincial' artist reaching a 'national' reputation, despite strong and consistent local support.[40]

Dillon grew up in a working-class Belfast environment. He left school early and became a house-painter before moving to London as soon as he could, when he was 18, in 1934. It is not known when he started to paint, but he appears to have shown an increasing interest in art in London. His first real exposure to the Irish countryside, which was to have such a profound influence on his mature work, came with a bicycling trip back in Ireland in 1939. This led to his getting stuck in Ireland when the War broke out, as he was refused permission to return to London. Unfortunately, wartime Belfast was not an easy place for a young, homosexual would-be painter who had begun to enjoy the freedom and opportunities of pre-War London, and in 1941 he moved instead to the comparative affluence and variety of Dublin, where Irish neutrality meant that the effect of the War was considerably muted. Once in Dublin he met and was helped by Mainie Jellett and she encouraged him to have his first one-man exhibition, which opened on 23 February 1942 at a gallery called the 'Country Shop' in St Stephen's Green. From that moment his Irish career never looked back, even though he returned to London at the first possible moment, when the War ended in 1945 and largely remained there until returning to Dublin in 1968. There were one-man shows at regular intervals throughout the rest of his life, but rarely outside Dublin or Belfast. For example, he had solo shows in Belfast, organised by CEMA, in 1946 and 1950; two solo shows at Waddington in 1950 and 1953; and 10 shows at the Dawson Gallery in Dublin between 1957 and 1971. The Arts Council of Northern Ireland held a large exhibition of his work in Belfast in 1966. (The only London exception was not to arrive until 1967, only four years before his death, when he had a solo show at the Mercury Gallery.)

Dillon's status as a participant in group shows did grow more widely. Apart from regular appearances at the IELA and the RHA from 1943 through to his death, and in most of the Oireachtas exhibitions between 1949 and 1970, he was included in large shows in Belfast and Dublin, but also outside Ireland. So, for example, he had four pictures at the exhibition entitled 'Living Irish Art' at the Leicester Galleries as early as October 1946. The following year his work was shown in a group show in New York and on 20 September 1947 a review appeared in the *Irish Times* of a show at Waddington called 'Group exhibition by 4 Northern Artists'. This covered the work of Campbell (who was regarded by the reviewer as the best of the four), Dillon, O'Neill and Johnson.[41] The brief comment on Dillon was not flattering, the reviewer finding the work difficult to appreciate. In 1948 he was included, showing eight pictures, in 'Four Ulster Painters' at Heal's in London. He was picked out in the review which appeared in the October-December 1950 edition of the *Dublin Magazine* of the annual IELA show. Sheehy thought him 'our only primitive'.[42] He followed this up in the January-March 1951 edition by praising a Dillon show at Waddington.

In February 1951 Dillon was, significantly, one of the first Irish artists who were given space in *Envoy* to record their thoughts, alongside Le Brocquy, Nano Reid, Campbell and Swift, in what was rather grandly termed a 'symposium of artistic opinion'. Anther Irish journal, *Commentary*, picked up Dillon very early, with a reference to him by Theodore Goodman in the July 1945 edition, in a large piece headed 'Irish Art in the War Years'. A well-known exhibition of Irish art in London was held at Tooth's in May 1951 ('Five Irish Painters'), where he had six pictures. In fact, he continued to appear in group shows in London of different sorts from time to time – in 1955 (three different shows), 1961 and 1962 (two shows), as well as in America and occasionally in other European cities. He was given two quite large profiles in the *Belfast Telegraph*, one on 27 October 1956, the other on 11 November 1960. In both he chose to emphasise how hostile Belfast had been as an environment for young artists. In 1956 he was described as becoming well known; by 1960 he was said to be successful enough to concentrate wholly on his work as an artist, without having to worry about taking the sort of casual building work he had previously done for financial reasons.

It is also important to point out the extent of the exposure which Dillon's work got outside the British Isles. He was far from being a provincial Northern Irish artist.[43] He had an exhibition at the Maxwell Galleries in San Francisco in 1954; and in 1958 he was one of the artists chosen to represent Britain in the Pittsburgh International Exhibition of Contemporary Art. In 1958 and in 1960 he was represented in the Guggenheim International exhibition in the States; in 1960 he had an exhibition at the Raymond Duncan Gallery in Paris. In 1961 and 1963 he exhibited at the Marzotto International in Rome and in 1962 at the Festival of Modern Art in Boston and at the Obelisk Gallery in Washington. In October 1963 he travelled to the USA with an Irish Trade and Culture delegation, contributing to an exhibition of 12 Irish artists at the New School Gallery in New York. In 1966 his work was included in an Irish Cultural Relations exhibition, which toured Wales, Holland, Sweden, Germany and the USA. His work was not, however, widely acquired by English art galleries and the Tate still has no example of his work. The Irish galleries bought or acquired his work and held exhibitions of it – for example, the large retrospective at the Ulster Museum in Belfast in 1972 following his death, which moved on to the Municipal Gallery of Modern Art in Dublin at the beginning of 1973, its catalogue containing an introduction by White. This exhibition, of 104 works, was drawn entirely from Irish collections. The Ulster Museum has eight works by Dillon,[44] including some major works. It is interesting to see the pattern in which they were acquired. Their first two pictures were donated to the Museum by the Haverty Trust, in 1951 and 1956 respectively and in 1957 a further work was purchased. Apart from a donation in 1973, the remaining four pictures were either donated (three in 1992) or purchased (one in 1993).

In terms of his reputation in print, Dillon was regularly covered among other Irish painters from 1943 onwards and when James White wrote about the Irish scene he often mentioned Dillon (for example in the occasional piece he wrote in March 1949 for *Art News and Review* called 'Letter from Dublin'). An example of the Irish press covering a later exhibition was the review in the *Sunday Independent* on 23 June 1968 by Bruce Arnold of a show at the Dawson Gallery. Although favourable, the review made no mention of Dillon's status. Brian Fallon[45] wrote of him in the early 1990s (interestingly, before his market reputation had taken off) in favourable terms. He thought his strongest period of work had been during and just after the War, when he had painted in a 'sophisticated, folksy, pseudo-naïve manner with a crisp personal calligraphy, great humour and charm, and lyrical colour'. As Irish art began to receive more attention from art critics and historians (at least, Irish ones), Dillon's name was rightly accorded a prominent place. What was and is still missing was a recognition on the part of English art writers that here was an artist whose status merited more than just local acknowledgment.

Louis le Brocquy

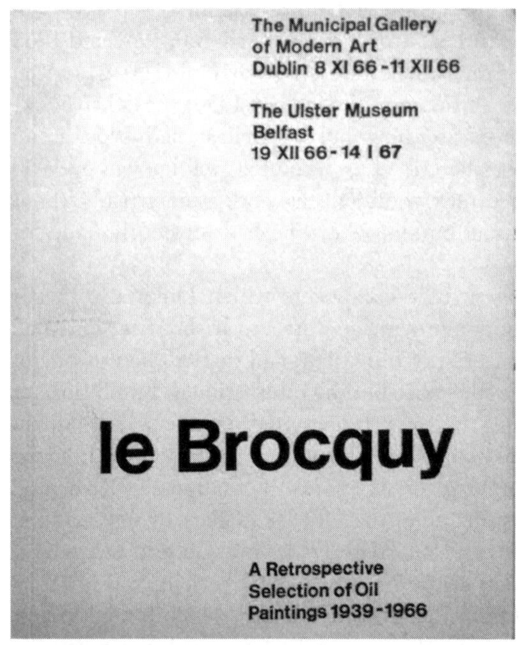

On 18 May 2000 a picture by Le Brocquy called *Travelling Woman with Newspaper*, which had been painted in 1947 in Marylebone in London, sold at Sotheby's for £1,158,500. The only other living British artists whose works sell for over £1 million are Freud, Auerbach and Hockney. Otherwise Bacon sells for more and Yeats and Orpen can, but the 20th-century artists' million-pound club has a very small British contingent indeed. How did Le Brocquy come to be a member?

Le Brocquy was born in Dublin in 1916. His activities in the small art world of Dublin in the early 1940s have been mentioned earlier. Like so many others, he moved to London, in his case in November 1946, where he was to stay until 1958, after which he moved to France, only returning to live in Dublin in 2000. Having lunched with Charles Gimpel in September 1945, he was signed up by Gimpel Fils when it opened in London in 1947 and has remained with the gallery ever since. Like so many 20th-century British artists, it is extraordinarily hard to characterise or categorise his work, particularly as it has gone through a number of transformations of style during a long working life. What is certain, however, is that his work, at least once he arrived in London, has always commanded critical attention, both in London and in Dublin. It is possible, for example, to track his career through the art columns of the *Times*, with reviews of his solo shows at Gimpel and frequent passing mentions in reviews of group shows, but it is also possible to track it through the *Irish Times* and the other Irish newspapers. In fact he quickly became part of the established group of serious young artists in London whose work seemed to appear everywhere and his presence was also emphasised by his taking a teaching position at the Central School in 1947.

Maurice Collis, who was Anglo-Irish, picked up on him quite early in the *Observer*. Having visited Dublin, he reported on 16 December 1945 on the art scene there, noting the heavy emphasis on Yeats, but already putting Le Brocquy in the second rank, with Hone and McGuinness. The *Times* took a little longer to register him than the Irish writers, but they captured him on 11 October 1946 when reviewing 'Modern Irish Painters' at the Leicester

Galleries.[46] Unsurprisingly, Arthur Power in the *Irish Times* also spotted him early, noting him in his large review 'The Work of Irish Painters in 1945' on 14 January 1946. On 6 May the paper's 'London Letter' was pleased to note that Colin Anderson had bought a Le Brocquy for the CAS.

The changes in Le Brocquy's work that followed his move to London in 1946 did not necessarily meet with approval back home. His pictures were still likely to appear at the RHA and the IELA and, on 19 April 1948 the *Irish Times* noted that *Tinker breaks whitethorn*, seen at the RHA, struck 'a strange and ultra-modish note', and also commented, a little sourly, that 'this artist's taste does not seem to have improved with transportation'. This was followed up by *The Fearful World* at the IELA, which elicited the comment that it made 'truly a fearful picture, too... In his present phase, this young artist seems to have lost his distinctive personality, which made his earlier work so important'.

Le Broquy's early Gimpel solo shows in May 1947 and in 1949 received good reviews in the *Times*[47] and there is no doubt that by 1947 his career was taking off. In March that year he had been included in an exhibition of Irish painting in New York and this was followed by the sale of many of his pictures from the first Gimpel show. The more conservative parts of the Irish press were not (at least until his success at Venice in 1956) always convinced that Le Brocquy's departure from Ireland was a great loss. On 11 December 1951, reviewing a show at Waddington, a writer with the initials 'AHR' in the *Evening Herald* said he could not understand what had happened to the artist's work: 'I don't know on what Mr Le Brocquy will lay his claim to fame. Certainly not on excellence of draughtsmanship, and scarcely on genius of composition or colour.' Rather echoing the sort of reviews that Le Brocquy's friend Bacon was apt to get, the writer went on to say, 'Mr Le Brocquy's art is an expression of the restless, sensation-loving and chaotic world in which we live.'[48] His 1955 show at Gimpel was commented on both in the *Guardian*[49] by Stephen Bone, who was generally favourable and supportive, and in the *Irish Times*,[50] where the anonymous reviewer found the pictures hard to like.

1956 saw a major breakthrough in the artist's status as he appeared to move on to an international stage that took his reputation beyond the British Isles. At the Venice Biennale he was as an Irish representative awarded the second highest category of prize (worth about £400). As the *Sunday Press* proudly reported (from Dublin),[51] the membership of the jury that had chosen Le Brocquy in this way represented 34 different nations and they were choosing from about 10,000 works produced by approximately 800 artists. There was no doubt that Le Brocquy had done extremely well to win the prize. The international status which this public success gave him was then increased in 1958 when he exhibited at the exhibition '50 Ans d'Art Moderne' at the World Fair in Brussels. In the same year he left London to live in France.[52]

In 1957, under the heading 'A Strange Painter', he was, for the first time in the *Times*, compared to Francis Bacon. The biographical similarities between the two – born in Protestant Dublin, but moving, irrevocably in Bacon's case, and almost irrevocably in Le Brocquy's, abroad, to London and beyond – do not seem to have been the basis for the reviewer's comment, or at least they were not mentioned. The basis seems to have been a comparison between the sort of pictures that Le Brocquy was by this time starting to produce, of refined and sometimes barely perceptible studies of the human body, with the far more outrageous and aggressive works which typify Bacon. (The reviewer could also have mentioned, although he did not, that Le Brocquy and Bacon were friends.) The next Gimpel show, in 1959, caught the attention of Nevile Wallis in the *Observer*.[53] Having noted the 'international attention' that the artist had been receiving, he expressed a cautionary note: 'The time seems due for a fresh stimulus from nature if so fragile and elusive an art is not to become enervated.' On the other hand, 'JW' (James White?) in the *Irish Times*[54] was pleased that the artist's place in the 'international art sphere' was now secure and the review was very favourable. As time, and solo exhibitions, passed, the *Times* stuck to the idea of mentioning Bacon when reviewing Le Brocquy (was it the same reviewer?). On 14 September 1961, under the heading 'Mr Le Brocquy's Sensuous Paintings', the same comparison was made.[55]

The English coverage at this time could still be a little cautious. Eric Newton in the *Guardian*[56] thought that it was worrying that the artist seemed only able to paint what he called 'whispering ghosts'. The Irish press on the other hand never really looked back following the accolade its artist had received at Venice. The *Irish Times* and the *Irish Press*[57] both approved of the work shown at the Dawson Gallery; there was a large and flattering profile of the artist in the *Irish Press* on 8 April 1965; and then a big retrospective opened at the Municipal Gallery of Modern Art in Dublin in November 1966, before moving on to the Ulster Museum in Belfast. For this, as if to confirm his closeness to Bacon, the catalogue opened with a quotation from Bacon. Then, as if to emphasise Le Brocquy's international status, there was an essay by Jacques Dupin of Paris (in French, with an English translation). The *Irish Times*[58] loved the show. It noted that Le Brocquy had always been more cosmopolitan in outlook than other Irish artists of the 1940s and it picked out the strong influence that the work had picked up from Adler following Le Brocquy's move to London; and it set him firmly in a group consisting of Bacon, Sutherland and Freud. This theme was repeated in the *Irish Times* by Brian Fallon in 1971,[59] when reviewing another show at the Dawson Gallery. He saw the clear influence of Bacon, the temperamental link to Beckett and again the similarity to Bacon, Sutherland and Freud. Nevertheless, and this is worth noting, he also saw 'a faint sense of contrivance and emotional coldness, which somehow prevents one putting the distinguished painter in the very highest class'.

Two later mentions of Le Brocquy in the pages of the *Times* are instructive and both arose in the context of book reviews. In 1981 Dorothy Walker published a book on the artist, which received a short mention by Philip Howard in the *Times* in July 1982. In it he described Le Brocquy, significantly, as 'Ireland's most eminent living painter', an opinion that by that date was surely unarguable, with all other candidates such as Yeats, Dillon, O'Neill and Luke dead, and Middleton shortly to follow. But the word 'Irish' was interesting in the context of a man who had never been to Irish art school and who had not worked there since 1946. The other mention cropped up in June 1983, in a review of 'Contemporary Irish Art', edited by R. Knowles. Here the reviewer noted something which we need to recall when considering how Le Brocquy's reputation has grown so great: he said that few Irish painters, with the exception of Le Brocquy, regularly exhibited abroad. (The Irish word will also be noted again.)

So far as the magazines covering Irish art were concerned, the *Dublin Magazine*'s Edward Sheehy noted Le Brocquy's work in the July-September 1945 issue, reviewing works being shown at 13 Merrion Row: 'An artist with a sensitive perception of life, an expressive and delicate line and a growing control of an individual architecture in composition.' By the January-March 1947 issue, the same writer thought that the artist's development had been 'astonishingly consistent'. But, while he was 'still developing' in October-December of the same year, he was said, in the final issue of 1948, to be too like Picasso. The *Bell* gave Le Brocquy a favourable notice in October 1945, but did not say much else about him during our period. *Envoy*, which only began to be published at the end of 1949, had an article about him in May 1950 and he was referred to from time to time. *Commentary* was one of the earliest, spotting him in May 1945 and remarking on what they saw as his Chinese influence.

In the case of the English magazines, the *Listener* seems not to have commented upon him to any extent until Wyndham Lewis spotted him on 20 October 1949; Middleton in the *Spectator* had noted Le Brocquy at the Irish show at the Leicester Galleries on 18 October 1946 and the magazine's reviewer thought that the oils at the first Gimpel show were good, but that the watercolours were less successful.[60] Indeed, the *Spectator* was not always flattering. There was, for example, an unenthusiastic review of pictures at the Leicester Galleries on 25 June 1948. The *New Statesman* was positive (on 19 October 1946): 'Mr Le Brocquy is highly sophisticated and accomplished, a romantic who invites comparison alike with Colquhoun and Piper.' On 26 June 1948 Le Brocquy almost got away with it in a review by Heron: 'This artist's handling is extremely spirited and his power of spontaneous statement of form in terms of triangular facets is certainly exciting. But [the key word in any Heron review] as yet these triangular planes of his are too indiscriminately alike; too little influenced by the particular forms they describe.' By 29 October 1949 the great sage was taking a different line: in noting that the artist was better in watercolour than in oil, he described 'a sharp dainty line overlaid by featherlight touches, which descend on the white paper like coloured snow-crystals, [and it] seems a more natural medium for the expression of images which invariably lack density and weight'. On 16 June 1951 we find John Berger seeing Le Brocquy as 'one of the most interesting British painters of his generation' (Note the use of 'British' rather than 'Irish'). Four years later he repeated this sentiment (on 12 February 1955).

However many reviews one reads of Le Brocquy, whose work is intelligent, subtle and often incredibly delicate and nuanced, nothing prepares one for his current market status. Being a big man in the Irish art world has not traditionally been to occupy a major status in the British, let alone the international, art world, with the obvious exception of Yeats. Yet a Le Brocquy picture can sell for a million pounds. The answer lies with that word 'Irish'. Since the second half of the 1990s, the great English auction houses, following their Dublin counterparts, have been holding specifically Irish art auctions. This has reflected the extraordinary surge in consumer wealth in Ireland over the same period. Irish art, furniture and houses have all increased significantly in value and this may help to explain Le Brocquy's current market status. He is the beneficiary of his Irishness. Although he was born at a time when Ireland was simply another part of the United Kingdom and educated at that bastion of Protestant Anglo-Ireland, Trinity College Dublin, and although he developed as an artist in post-war London and later in France for over 40 years, Le Brocquy is another example of the tricky notion of characterising artists by nationality. His early pictures – and the million-pound picture was one of these – have some Irishness about them, despite usually having been painted in Marylebone, because they show tinkers and gypsies from the Irish countryside. But the fractured pseudo-Cubist distortional style of these pictures has nothing Irish about it at all: it is the same style that was picked up in one form or another by Colquhoun and MacBryde; by Vaughan; by Minton; and by Craxton. All were influenced by artists they could access in London at the time, such as Adler (who was friendly with all of them).[61] If Le Brocquy was not able to be labelled Irish by modern Irish art buyers, it might be fair to guess that his pictures could no more sell for a million pounds than those of John Minton.

Graham Sutherland

There have been so many books, exhibition catalogues and articles about Sutherland that a full analysis of what has been said about him in print would be a major historiographical task. Even once accomplished, the result would, like all historiography, only reveal a history of what had been written about him, not a history of his reputation. One needs to get away from the bias of the apologist to achieve that, and this leads one to the contemporary reviews of the exhibitions and, perhaps, to the attempts made over the years to see his work in the context of that of other painters.

Sutherland went to Goldsmith's College School of Art in London in 1921 at the age of 18, and in October 1924 he held his first exhibition (of engravings and drawings) at a gallery in London. This was well received by the reviewers and in January 1925 he was elected an associate member of the Royal Society of Painter-Etchers and Engravers, producing at this stage many etchings, partly under the influence of Samuel Palmer. He was remarkably successful as an etcher at this stage in his life, estimating that he was earning the very considerable sum of £700 p.a., including sales to American buyers. However, as the recession of the later 1920s affected his market, he took up teaching, first at Kingston and then for two days a week at Chelsea (for £250 p.a.). He married at the end of 1927. Towards the end of the decade his etchings took on, for the first time, features that would later be particularly associated with Sutherland's mature work – twisting anthropomorphic branches and roots. At this time he also took up design work, but the etchings market was apparently very badly affected by the Wall Street Crash of 1929 and Sutherland had to try to sell watercolours and drawings instead, during what was a period of great financial stress for him.

By this time the impact on his work of Palmer had to some extent been replaced by the influence of Paul Nash, and 1934 was a year of some significance in the development of Sutherland's career, partly because he visited Pembrokeshire for the first time, but also because he met Clark and Anderson. By November 1935 Sutherland had received the (written) support of Paul Nash in the first issue of a magazine called *Signature*. By 1936 Sutherland's pictures were available at the Mayor Gallery for between eight and 12 guineas. His work was shown occasionally in group exhibitions and by 1937 he was starting to produce the sort of work that was to make his name. His first one-man show as a painter came in 1938, arranged for him by Clark, who also wrote the catalogue introduction (anonymously). There was a good reaction in the press and seven works (out of 25) sold. The identity of the buyers is highly significant, both as an illustration of the sort of people buying what could be described as highly experimental art for 1938, but also as a pointer towards the relevance of a number of the people covered in this book, whose names come up in different contexts over and over again. Anderson, Watson and Peter Gregory bought one each, as did Oliver Simon of the Curwen Press, Lord Sandwich, the Redfern and the Tate.

In 1939 Sutherland took part in an exhibition in New York representing Britain, alongside other artists, at the World Fair. The British pictures were, significantly, chosen by Clark. Further help from Clark followed, as he encouraged the Sutherlands to come and live with him when the War started. A second one-man exhibition followed in May 1940, this time at the Leicester Galleries when 22 of the 30 works were sold; to the usual buyers of Clark, Anderson and Watson were added Raymond Mortimer, the CAS and, again, the Tate. Prices ranged from 10 to 50 guineas. The reviews were again widespread and favourable. More Clark help then followed as the commissions from the War Artists Advisory Committee began. On 1 January 1941 Sutherland began an initial six-month contract that paid £325 in three instalments. By this time Sutherland had become an important figure to a number of young artists in London, especially Craxton and Freud, but also Bacon and, to a lesser extent, Vaughan, Minton and Ayrton. In retrospect, fellow professionals seem to have been closest to Sutherland's influence during the War. Eddie Sackville-West produced the first book on Sutherland in 1943 as his contribution to the Penguin Modern Painters series. (Needless to say, Clark had chosen the artists to be included in this series.) In 1944 he started down the path of religious work when he was recommended to Walter Hussey by Henry Moore.

As the War ended, so did Sutherland's busy rôle as a war artist and in April 1945 he took part in a mixed show at the Lefevre, where works were purchased, as usual, by Anderson and by Wilfrid Evill (who was Sutherland's solicitor). By this stage in his career, all his work was selling at the private view, which graphically indicates the level his reputation had then reached. Interestingly, it was at this show that Bacon's seminal work, *Three Studies of Figures at the Base of a Crucifixion*, also appeared, showing the strong influence of Picasso on his work, at a time when Sutherland was also admitting to Picasso having had a great influence on his work. Yet there was not a huge amount of money around, even for someone of Sutherland's stature, and he made a number of agreements to design textiles (and, for example, to design carpets for the Dorchester). His first solo show in New York came in 1946, to mixed reviews, and in 1947 he started his regular visits to France, and he also began his new career as a portrait-painter in 1949. Appointed a trustee of the Tate in 1948, his status was assured. John Russell, writing in the *Sunday Times* on 15 April 1951, said that Sutherland was England's only living painter with an international reputation. Reviewing his show at the ICA in the June edition of *Britain Today*, Philip Hendy described Sutherland as 'our leading painter'.

In 1948 there were a number of shows in which Sutherland participated, some organised by the British Council, two group shows in Paris and Brussels, and one- man shows in London (at the new Hanover Gallery) and New York. At the Hanover show, Sutherland's Mediterranean influences were readily apparent. The *Times* critic (on 24 June) was not entirely flattering, noting that the artist had at least introduced some changes into his work, but adding: 'If the rules of composition are to be ignored in this way, the resulting stiffness requires to be broken by more subtleties of rhythm, by a greater elaboration of minor movements than Mr Sutherland is accustomed to introduce into his work.' Similarly, the *Sunday Times* said this (on 4 July): 'I gather that my colleagues are divided between discomfort and disapproval at the change… The new spirit, as I see it, has only begun to work.' The *Listener* felt that 'the general effect is somewhat garish and raw' (10 June). *Britain Today* (August issue) was more positive, commenting that the colour evolution of Sutherland's work over the last 10 years had been bolder than any other English painter except Smith. Heron in the *New Statesman* (on 12 June) was his usual mixture of criticism and advice for Sutherland. Increasingly, Sutherland's career moved at a fast pace, with exhibitions all round the world, another book about him and endless commissions of different types, including one for an enormous canvas, which became *Origins of the Land*, for the Festival of Britain.

Sutherland was taken up by the Beaverbrook Press after his portrait of Lord Beaverbrook and his doings became the stuff of the popular press. In 1952 he was the main British painter at the Venice Biennale and this increased his international reputation yet further (he soon became the first living British painter to be shown at the Musée d'art moderne in Paris). In 1953 came the first television programme about him and his work and a large retrospective at the Tate (the long support of Clark continued with his statement in the catalogue that he saw Sutherland as 'the outstanding painter of his generation'). The review of this exhibition that appeared in the *Times* was, however, far from sycophantic. It began by noting that Sutherland sometimes got surprisingly close to Bacon 'both in style and sentiment'. It then focused in some detail on the thought that Sutherland seemed to spend his time looking for bits and pieces of stone and wood which might serve as curiosities for painting, in other words, which might become typical Sutherland pictures. In the larger pictures he then seemed to have painted these objects without thinking how to turn them into a proper composition, in some instances simply lining them up and painting them. The reaction of the British press was not, in fact, uniformly favourable.[62] Interestingly, the dealers (Tooth's, the Redfern and Roland, Browse and Delbanco, for example) had no hesitation in buying his work and no difficulty in selling it. The attitudes of the British critics did not seem to affect either them or their clients.

Sutherland's life during the 1950s became occasionally highly controversial, for example, over the Coventry Cathedral tapestry; the dreadful Tate Affair, which involved his rather absurd and over-dramatic resignation as a Tate trustee in 1954; and the notorious portrait of Churchill. By the mid-1950s, his public profile was very high indeed, but not necessarily because of his work. By the end of the decade, he had moved to the fashionable Marlborough Gallery[63] and Douglas Cooper's book about him had appeared, praising him lavishly as 'the most distinguished and the most original English artist of the mid-twentieth century'. Many critics disagreed[64] and they also reacted in a variety of ways to his first large show at the Marlborough in June 1962.[65] By then there must have been some critical agreement that his work was no longer so widely successful as it had been previously regarded, however famous he had become as a person. The *Times*, reviewing on 8 June 1962 a show at the New London Gallery, was prepared to praise, but the context in which the praise was given is worth setting out as it indicates what appears to be the recent critical treatment of his work:

> For years he had been told that he had lost that visionary spark which first put his tortured but poetic imagery among the international currency of our time; that his gifts as a painter did not match the quality of his imagination and had been unable to sustain the demands made on them by his own efforts to widen his range and live up to his fame. There was truth in this and criticism will not be entirely silenced by this exhibition. But he has come back fighting.

Paul Nash

Like other artists covered in this chapter, Paul Nash has had his champions,[66] who have sought to boost (and, where necessary, to bolster), his reputation. There has certainly been a huge number of books about him and his work,[67] despite the fact that he died more than 60 years ago. But in his case the fact is that the books are not dealing with an unchallenged reputation. Above that of many others, his reputation slips and slides and seems often to be in danger of losing its position at or near the top of the 20th-century charts. There are reasons for this. Nash's work was quite different at different stages of his comparatively short life (and here I am just trying to cover his reputation in watercolour and oil and not, for example, as a graphic artist or still less as a photographer). His war work was one thing in the First World War and a different thing in the Second; his romantic Surrealist phase was distinctive from the soft watercolours of English landscapes which appear so regularly now in the saleroom, their delicate faintness of touch so typical and recognisable. In other words, for the setters of fashion – or reputation – to say they like Nash's work, or regard it as important as a whole, sits uneasily with a body of work which has different guises. Moreover, the 'weak' appearance of a basic Nash watercolour has a delicacy which may no longer appeal so strongly or so immediately to a modern audience whose tastes have been coarsened by various common, and bold, styles from the 1950s onwards. Bacon's work can hold its own against anything put against it from America or from Pop Art or even from Damien Hirst, but at least on the surface the same could not be said for that of Nash.

Reading the contemporary criticism of his work as it developed, one is struck by the caution that greeted his work at certain times, mixed with great praise at many of the different stages. For example, the *Times* critic on 4 November 1932 was happy to acknowledge that he was 'one of our more interesting artists' but 'when comparative slightness in the means of execution appears to favour an artistic conception one begins to doubt if that kind of conception is really 'central' in the tradition of painting'. On the other hand, 'this is only to say that Mr Nash is important enough to prompt and justify the most searching inquiry into his aesthetic credentials'. Of his last works, produced during the War, the critic noted (on 18 June 1942) that 'when he succeeds there are few contemporary painters in watercolour who can give greater pleasure or achieve more distinction', but again he is frequently rather confusing in his forms and sometimes 'appears to be aiming at some quite trivial intellectual point'. After his death the coverage started to vary more noticeably. In the obituaries, praise was often fulsome. In the *Listener* on 25 July 1946, for example, Eric Newton thought that his achievement 'was on a big scale' and he had no hesitation in making the bold, indeed rather hopeless, claim that Nash's stature, relative to his contemporaries, would increase as time passed. He said something very similar in the *Sunday Times*. E.H. Ramsden in the *Burlington Magazine* for September said that Nash had been 'endowed with an imaginative genius which belongs to the same order as that possessed by Turner'. But then the generosity often shown by the obituarist moved on at the first opportunity to review the whole work critically, on the occasion of the large Tate 'Memorial Exhibition' in March 1948. Geoffrey Grigson in the *Listener* on 1 April got two whole pages on Nash (reproduced from a talk on the Third Programme). There was quite a lot of critical comment, noting that in some ways Nash was a weak artist. He was disturbed by the weakness of the material through which the immaterial was sought to be conveyed. On the other hand, he noted that the handful of important pictures was enough for most artists and should ensure that Nash was remembered. The *Times* critic was impressed that Nash's inspiration had not weakened – in fact it had continued to strengthen and develop in his last pictures. Newton, who had written the glowing introduction to the catalogue, was in the *Sunday Times* predictably flattering ('a superb painter'), whereas the *Observer*'s critic noted that his 'handling of paint is often hard and frigid'. The critic thought that Nash had adopted Continental idioms, but did not continue their formal experiments: 'Nash is not a great formal artist, like the Frenchmen who influenced him; but one who made use of their pictorial devices in order to express his own eerie vision of an uninhabited Nature.'

By the time of his appearance in a solo show at the Redfern in April 1961, there had been a long gap since a major show and the reaction in the *Times* was, perhaps, typical of what has tended to happen to the reputation of British artists after their death.[68] The critic said that things in the art world had moved so fast since his death that 'it needs a conscious, backward-looking effort of sympathy to savour again the subtle, distinctive mood of so poetic, so insular, and, within his severe limits, so perfected an artist'. Nash had been a minor master of a poetic mood, his 'much-vaunted surrealism' simply a chosen mood of romantic strangeness. In 1971, commenting on an exhibition at the Northern Arts Gallery in Newcastle, organised by Nash's great latter-day Sylvester figure, Andrew Causey, the *Times* reviewer said (on 4 October) that it was now impossible not to mention Nash's virtues and his failings in the same breath. By 1980 (25 June), reviewing Causey's monograph on Nash, John Russell Taylor in the *Times* thought that opinion was still divided as to how good he was. 'He has retained the air of a neglected or underestimated artist throughout the 34 years since his death, despite being more continuously exhibited and having far more written about him than any of his generation.'[69]

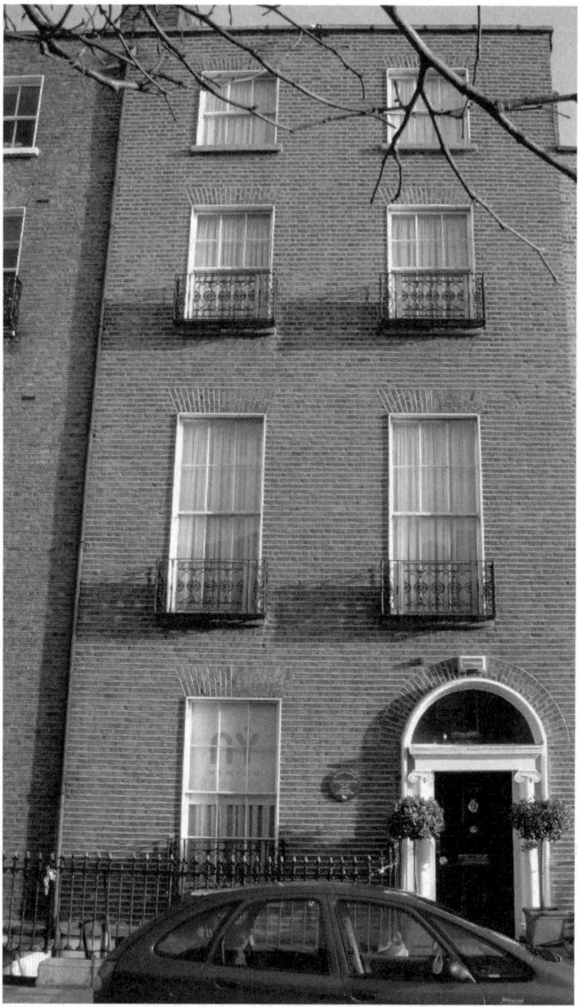

Francis Bacon was born here at
29 Lower Baggott Street, Dublin, in 1909

Francis Bacon

Some features of the development of Bacon's reputation are easy to describe, while others exhibit a complexity which may conceal answers to some of the questions which this book has sought to explore. Thankfully, there can be no need here to sketch out even an outline of Bacon's long life, so well known is it. Nor, indeed, is it even necessary to follow the travel of his reputation through this working life, for it started quite abruptly in 1945, when he was already in his mid-30s and probably reached its destination and current resting place, some time in, say, the early 1960s. The simple fact is that it is now uncontroversial to state that Bacon's reputation is, and has been for quite a long time, at the top of the heap; at least the heap that is made up of British artists from the second half of the 20th century and, quite possibly the whole 20th century. An analysis of whether it deserves to be there is distinctly not the purpose of this study, which is, rather, to describe how it got there.

Although he made attempts to destroy and suppress many of his paintings which pre-dated *Three Studies*, there is enough surviving evidence to show that Bacon had, in fact, been painting for some time before that fateful showing at the Lefevre in April 1945. No matter, he had no substantial reputation as a painter before then.[70] But from the moment that picture appeared and started to receive critical attention, Bacon's reputation was set on its course, and it was never deflected. Reading some of the early reviews now causes an ironic smirk in the light of hindsight.[71] The anonymous commentator on current shows who wrote in *Apollo* under the name 'Perspex' was typical of a type of reaction which Bacon's work was to receive for many years. He wrote in the May 1945 edition, 'I was so shocked and disturbed by the Surrealism of Francis Bacon that I was glad to escape from this exhibition.' In the *Times* it is clear that their regular art critic, Alan Clutton-Brock, was revolted by the pictures. About the mixed show at the Lefevre in February 1946, which the Lefevre had advertised[72] as 'Recent Paintings by Ben Nicholson and Graham Sutherland', with the names of other artists in smaller print underneath, he noted that Bacon was an even more 'sinister illustrator' than Colquhoun, with the pictures suggesting that one had 'got into a room where a murderer has hastily tried to conceal a corpse'. Similarly, in the *Spectator* on 22 February 1946, Michael Ayrton said, 'I must confess that I cannot make out what Bacon is driving at.' Roger Marvell in the *New Statesman and Nation* wrote, on 16 February, 'There is nobody in England who can paint better, and only two or three who can paint anything like as well... I don't cotton on to his symbolism and – far more serious – I find his compositions hard to grasp. But what excitement to find in a young English painter such staggering virtuosity.' Ayrton's replacement as art critic of the *Spectator*, M.H. Middleton (who took over on 24 May 1946), wrote of Bacon's picture at the Redfern (on 26 July) that it was 'big' and 'impressive'. In December of the same year, Bacon again appeared in a mixed show, this time at the Anglo-French Art Centre in St John's Wood. Clutton-Brock said, 'Bacon shows three really alarming but undoubtedly well-designed studies of what appear to be fragments from a dissecting-room.' Middleton in the *Spectator* said (on 29 November), 'The three studies by Francis Bacon seemed to me as

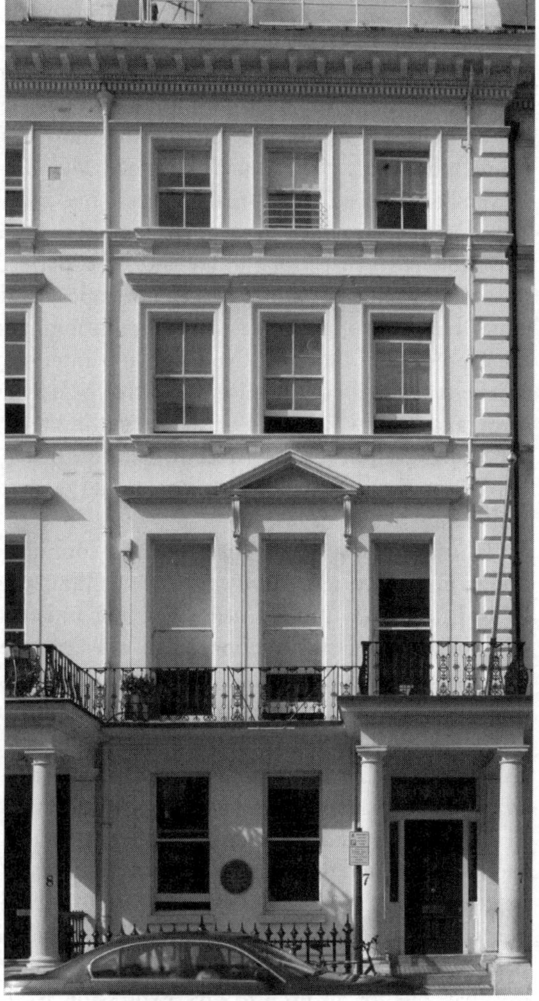

Francis Bacon lived and worked at
7 Cromwell Place, London SW7

peculiarly beastly as they were doubtless meant to.' By November 1949 the *Times* critic had to acknowledge that Bacon appeared to be a capable artist, but with subject-matter so repellent that it was scarcely possible to consider anything else. His themes were as vivid and meaningless as a nightmare. The same exhibition got a long review in the *Observer*, on 20 November, under the heading 'Nightmare':

> Bacon's work is the most profoundly disquieting manifestation I have yet seen of that malaise which, since the last war, has inspired the philosophy of Sartre and the drama of frustration of Tennessee Williams.

> Nevertheless, if all 12 works had been conceived in the manner of three studies of reptilian creatures painted in 1945, I should have ignored the exhibition on the ground that these were pathological documents – authentic as such revelations are, but too sickening to dwell on and (in my view) outside the scope of rational art criticism.

The reviewer nevertheless went on to acknowledge that the works were technically superb and could not be ignored. The *Sunday Times* critic (on 13 November) said, 'I do find them horrifying and "nightmare" is the precise word for the kind of horror they induce in me… Nothing would induce me to buy one of his paintings, but a representative collection that did not contain one would lack one of the most definite and articulate statements made by contemporary art.' The much-maligned Wyndham Lewis, writing in the *Listener* on 17 November, showed how broad-minded he could be. He thought that the pictures were 'amazing' and that no young painter painted so beautifully as Bacon: 'Bacon is one of the most powerful artists in Europe today and he is perfectly in tune with his time.' Philip Hendy's piece on Bacon in *Britain Today* did not appear in the monthly journal until the January 1950 issue: 'He is a prophet of despair, his painting hailed by those who have abandoned hope as the expression of the age… No English painter of his generation has a stronger sense of form or a better capacity to organise it; but the form by which he expresses despair is disintegrating form, and form which goes on disintegrating tends to disappear.' Rather damningly, Hendy concluded that, in his most recent pictures, Bacon was 'not essentially different from James Pryde', by which he meant that Bacon had taken to using mechanical tricks of composition and texture to get his effect.

It will come as no surprise that the contrary view was – of course – taken by Patrick Heron in the *New Statesman and Nation.* Trading, as always, on his own great skill as an artist, he had this to say (on 3 December): 'Bacon is an artist who employs a not insensitive but nonetheless slapdash imitation of an old-fashioned technique to portray figures conceived according to an exhausted and discredited modern surrealist formula… With Bacon the thing just doesn't come off: the creative intensity is missing.' In September 1950, reviewing Bacon at the Hanover, the review in the *Times* was longer and more developed, but the same themes recurred. 'For the most part they [Bacon's pictures] represent atrocities and torments, but with a certain vagueness and lack of definition which makes it just possible, though only just, to contemplate them without the extreme physical revulsion that a more exact delineation of such scenes would provoke.' Where, said the writer, could such pictures possibly hang, except in a museum? The *Observer* was again attentive: 'Baconian theorists abound, for his subjective painting with its sensationalist overtones obviously invites speculation. Indeed this young painter has become accepted as a symbol of the unquiet mood of our time… And who can say that, but for an urge to give expression to the pictorially inexpressible, Francis Bacon might not be numbered among the few outstanding painters of this century.' The *Sunday Times* found the work 'neither easy to forget nor comforting to remember' and, like others, found it 'repellent'.

By the 1950s, the *Times* was commenting fully and carefully on all Bacon's solo shows (and even picking his work out from group shows). On 7 January 1952, in commenting on his show which had opened at the Hanover Gallery in December, the *Times* reviewer said that his 'private mythology, which has always been sufficiently mysterious, has become a distorted and scarcely interpretable dream'. Nevile Wallis in the *Observer* on 23 December 1951 had been more generous: 'One cannot name a British painter today with a greater technical command.' John Berger in the *New Statesman* (on 5 January) thought that Bacon was 'a very remarkable but not finally important painter'. He saw him as 'a brilliant stage manager, rather than an original visual artist'. He thought that there was 'no evidence in his work of any visual discovery, but only of imaginative and skilful arrangement'. Later the same year (on 16 December), in reviewing pictures, some of which had been influenced by Bacon's stay in Africa, the *Times* reviewer said that 'in view of what his appalling imagination has previously made of the European scene there is reason to be thankful that what he has discovered in the dark continent is no worse than it is'. Yet, 'his methods of painting seem so bizarre and his conceptions of design so idiosyncratic that it is difficult to apply any normal standard even to these milder works'. Interestingly, in view of what we now know to have been Bacon's interest in photography (and film),73 the reviewer notes that his image was sometimes that of a film-producer. Again, Nevile Wallis (on 14 December) was more open to noting Bacon's importance. Whilst observing how much Sutherland owed to Bacon, Wallis remarked that 'every exhibition of Mr Bacon's disquieting, curiously momentous paintings causes something of a stir'. Sylvester had taken to the Third Programme to proclaim Bacon's importance:74 'For me he is today the most important living painter – by which I do not mean the greatest – because no other has expressed as he has our particular attitude to human suffering.' Sylvester's view of the Hanover Gallery show in late 195275 was that Bacon was a 'superlative painter'.

By 13 November 1953, the *Times* reviewer felt able to say that Bacon was obviously dependent on photography. Picking up his own – assuming it was the same reviewer – reference to films in the 1952 review, he noted that the effect of some of Bacon's more dramatic pictures was as of a still from a film: as if the film had been stopped at the moment of highest dramatic tension. The influence of photography did not necessarily improve the reviewer's liking for the pictures, for he noted that the artist sought to give his pictures 'the horrible look, and even the disagreeable colour and texture, of a photographic enlargement'. In so doing, 'the effect becomes almost unbearably unpleasant'. This was after the critic had commented that Bacon's admirers 'remain fascinated by the wilfulness of his imagination, the cryptic unpleasantness of his iconography, and his seemingly inexhaustible capacity for discovering yet more perverse and unpromising themes for large and monumental compositions'. The next major review in the *Times*, on 14 June 1954, helpfully titled 'Apparitions of Evil', felt that the pictures at the Hanover Gallery were less alarming than usual and one wonders whether the reviewer was beginning to accept that Bacon's strength might be genuine and not simply shocking: 'There may be a fine dividing line between wilful mystification [the reviewer is implying that this has been his position on Bacon thus far] and the workings of an imagination which should not be subject to prosaic questioning.'

One can well imagine the reviewer feeling that he had to think the unthinkable at this point and start accepting that Bacon was on his way to becoming not only a major British artist, but even an important figure on the international artistic scene, a thing rarely accomplished by a British artist, Henry Moore being the most obvious contemporary example. For example, Bacon participated, together with Freud and Nicholson, as one of the British artists shown at the Venice Biennale. This was the first occasion when a wider European audience would have had the opportunity to see the work. It is significant that the catalogue had an introduction by Sylvester. It is, of course, significant for the growth of Bacon's reputation that he should have been chosen for this rôle in the first place. That this was an indication of Bacon's clear change of status is re-enforced by Wallis in the *Observer* (on 13 June): 'Bacon who, far more than Sutherland, now excites the attention of student painters and the curiosity of a cultured elite, is about to be represented at the Venice Biennale.' Berger, on the other hand, was quick to dismiss Bacon in the *New Statesman* (of 26 June): 'Francis Bacon's new series of paintings at the Hanover are even emptier in design and shallower in content than his last.'

The *Times* was still cautious about accepting his stature. On 24 January 1955, under their usual sort of heading for him (on this occasion 'A prophet of doom'), the *Times* reviewed his 14 pictures being shown at the ICA. By now the critic was prepared to acknowledge that

Bacon's reputation was international, but he still felt misgivings: the pictures were almost too exciting; they failed to generate a sense of wonder. One can already sense descending on these pictures 'the kindly and cloying aroma of a period charm'. Even Sylvester, writing in the *Listener* on 27 January, had to express a cautious note. His worry was that because Bacon was so in tune with the concerns of the contemporary European world (summed up so often by commentators by the word *Angst*), that 'many of the things that make him exciting today may render him laughable for future generations'. He thought Bacon the painterly equivalent of Malraux, Camus and Sartre.

I presume that all of the above reviews in the *Times* were written by Alan Clutton-Brock, as he remained with the *Times* until 1955. Clutton-Brock moved in 1955 to the *Listener* where, by a nice irony, he seems to have replaced Sylvester in reviewing Bacon's next foray at the Hanover Gallery, in rather a different style.[76] Instead of Sylvester's usual gushing enthusiasm, Clutton-Brock amused himself with the following comment on Bacon's William Blake death-mask pictures: 'If he should continue in this vein he might end by becoming an admirable portrait painter or a quietly sensitive observer of still life, a development that would certainly disappoint many of his admirers, but might reveal the true nature of his talent in the end.' Readers of the *Listener* must have wondered whom to believe. Later reviews in the *Times* were markedly more positive. On 26 March 1957, under the heading 'Mr Francis Bacon's Virtuosity. Van Gogh translated', the *Times* reviewer of the latest Hanover show noted that Bacon was topical in his interest in Van Gogh, who had recently been the subject of a well-known film biography. This topicality was a theme of Bacon's work, as his earlier, post-war, pictures had been more infused with the prevailing mood of post-war Angst. Wallis was still following Bacon in the *Observer*. His comment on this show, on 24 March, was, 'Why a fresh exhibition of Mr Francis Bacon's arouses such interest in London is easier to explain than the enigma of his painting.' Wallis repeated his theme throughout the '50s, which was that Bacon was more influential than Sutherland and he now noted that he was even being regarded as important in Paris, which was not easy for a British artist. (He nevertheless did still use language which Clutton-Brock would have appreciated, in saying that Bacon's 'essential quality remains as elusive as a nightmare'.)

John Russell in the *Sunday Times* was also clearly taken with Bacon's significance, noting his success in Paris (on 24 February 1957) and commenting on 24 March of the same year that Bacon was 'the only living English painter to have built up in his work the kind of mythology, at once private and universal, which we recognise at once as urgently related to the world we live in'. In a long and carefully constructed review of the same show, Denys Sutton in the *Financial Times* said, on 16 April, 'He is one of those artists who has the power of influencing their contemporaries, among others Mr Sutherland and Mr Louis le Brocquy.' Clutton-Brock himself, in the *Listener* on 28 March, was relatively non-judgmental. He saw that to some people Bacon was a highly gifted painter who misused his gifts on grotesque subject-matter, whereas to others he was interesting in the same way as Kafka was interesting. Making a comparison with some of the earlier work, the reviewer almost liked the 'Van Gogh' pictures. On 17 June 1959, some of the pictures at the Hanover Gallery were said by the *Times* to be 'superlative'; Clutton-Brock, by contrast, in the *Listener* on 25 June, thought that 'one must try to believe that he is not actuated by pure caprice'. On 28 March 1960, reviewing the show at the Marlborough Gallery, the brilliance of Bacon's portraits was noted by the *Times* critic, as was his ability to engender debate and controversy about the human condition. Basil Taylor in the *Sunday Times* was a little more cautious, saying that he was an 'English eccentric' like Stanley Spencer, and directly in line with Fuseli (a comparison often made at this time). He even went so far as to say that 'there is every sign of a forced over-production which has magnified his weaknesses'. Eric Newton in the *Guardian* was impressed by the painting, but depressed by the mental state of its creator: 'Only a great painter could invent images of such power: but surely only an unhappy creature could isolate such images in an attempt to persuade us that the world we live in is also the world he inhabits.' Terence Mullaly in the *Daily Telegraph* used the word 'considerable' on this occasion (in the context of a 'considerable artist'), as he did on so many occasions when commenting on Bacon. He also thought Bacon a modern Bosch. Clutton-Brock (in the *Listener* on 31 March) was still unconvinced and wrote his most profound piece of criticism on Bacon. This represented the culmination of his views of Bacon ever since he had first commented on his work in the *Times* in 1946. He began by recognising that there could be no doubt that Bacon had 'artistic gifts of a high order', but the use he made of those gifts was 'equivocal and capricious'. There were, indeed, grounds for suspecting frivolity. Clutton-Brock then turned his attention to why Bacon should have achieved the international reputation which he clearly had. He thought that the 'obscurity' of Bacon's work had 'no doubt helped Bacon towards the reputation he is now beginning to gain': 'Bacon's talent is of a kind that might enable him to create a humane and rational art, but fortunately for his reputation there is a great cloud of morbidity and mystification hanging about his work.'

The culmination of Bacon's early reputation really came with the Tate retrospective in 1962 (24 May-1 July). The identity of the contributors to the catalogue was significant, for Colin Anderson (writing as Chairman of the Board of Trustees) wrote the Foreword and John Rothenstein (writing as Director) the Introduction: the mark of approval from two of the key creators of an artist's reputation in mid-20th century British art. Furthermore, in what he wrote, Rothenstein showed that, for him, there was no doubt at all that Bacon was a major talent, perhaps pointing the way forwards to a new way for painting to go (that is, although not said in so many words, to rescue painting from the shortcomings of abstraction). Rothenstein also noted Bacon's obsession with photography.[77]

The *Times*, although reverting to its old type of heading for a Bacon review – 'The horrific vision of Mr Francis Bacon' – was hugely favourable. There was no experience like this available to the art viewer, except perhaps encountering Goya's late pictures at the Prado: 'The emotional shock is extraordinary, because it is instantaneous and at the same time complex and contradictory.' The following passage shows how far Bacon's reputation had travelled: 'No other painter of our day – and for once the phrase can be left as it stands, without worrying about the word "British" – could make these five large galleries look so nearly like an exhibition by an old master, yet leave one in no doubt that here… is the cry of agony of our own age, an age which has lost its faith.' The review closed by saying that this was 'the most stunning exhibition by a living British painter there has been since the war'. Mullaly in the *Daily Telegraph* used his favourite term: 'One of the most considerable of living artists.' Newton in the *Guardian* called him 'a masterly painter'. John Russell in the *Sunday Times* thought it one of the most extraordinary exhibitions ever held at the Tate and thought, in a clumsy phrase, that the pictures had 'a timeless, Old Masterly look'.

On the other hand, Denys Sutton in the *Financial Times* followed the careful analysis of Bacon's work which he had been building up over recent years. While noting that Bacon was 'one of the most fascinating, original and extraordinary members of the British school', he went on to say that 'in a way he is a most traditional artist. He is a typical exponent of the Gothic Horrific, which held sway in this country at the close of the 18th century'. Bacon was Fuseli's heir, 'his message… a trifle banal': 'Mr Bacon may be saluted for his drive, for his dexterity, for his courage. But his painting, once seen, does not live in the mind; it is too temporary, too dependent on external circumstances, too hampered by the hate of passion. In short, his protest is too shrill to hold us for long.'

It is revealing to turn to Edward Lucie-Smith, writing in the *Listener* on 7 June, because he had not previously written extensively about Bacon's work and was not one of the critics who had 'grown up' with Bacon's development. He began a long piece by agreeing that Bacon was often said to be 'the most impressive and original British painter alive', but then he immediately countered by saying that this was a less impressive achievement than it sounded. The competition amongst living British artists was not necessarily a high test. While Bacon's work was 'difficult', it was not as 'hermetic' or unique as had been made out. He was, in fact, just a Romantic, 'the last heir to the great rhetorical painters of the early 19th Century'. He shared the qualities of those Romantic painters, but unfortunately he more than shared their defects and his work was sometimes 'ludicrous'.[78] In particular, Bacon's work shared something with late Turner, and of course Fuseli, but it was the comparison with Géricault which particularly hurt him. Géricault 'mirrors, interprets and transcends his own age', but could that possibly be said of Bacon? Bacon 'touches reality' at certain points, but is not part of it. He 'uses his imagery of cruelty partly as a means of making guilt into art. But the guilt is always somebody else's; it does not become one's own'.

In the 23 years which followed this retrospective before the Tate held a second retrospective in 1985, the *Times* missed no opportunity to comment on, and praise, Bacon's work. By 1985, under the heading 'A master of deep disquiet', the *Times* could say: 'We are in the presence of a very great painter indeed.'

It is not our purpose here to arbitrate on the differing views on the status of Francis Bacon. The analysis of prominent contemporary commentary has been intended to show that Bacon's work attracted serious, if not always complimentary, critical attention from 1945 onwards. A critical momentum quickly built up, no doubt fuelled by the constant support of Sylvester, but also in different ways by such key figures as Anderson and Rothenstein. What is interesting is that despite fairly consistent denials of his ultimate worth from the *Times'* critic, Alan Clutton-Brock, and from John Berger and Patrick Heron, later from the likes of Edward Lucie-Smith and Peter Fuller, Bacon's reputation rolled forwards and, crucially, upwards. A study could be made of the development of his reputation outside England. Using the extensive bibliography at the back of the book on the artist published to coincide with the 1985 Tate retrospective,[79] we find the well-known article by American Sam Hunter appearing in the *Magazine of Art* (an American magazine) in January 1952. Other American references follow occasionally and then, in April 1957, comes the first article in a French journal (*Jardin des Arts*). Another follows (in *XXe siècle*) at Christmas 1958, and the first German references are in 1962 in *Aktuell* and in *Der Spiegel*. That year many foreign articles appeared, including in many different German newspapers and journals. Italian articles also start to appear from September 1962 onwards, with many following throughout the last quarter of 1962.

Whichever way one tests it, Francis Bacon's reputation was, following his 1962 retrospective at the Tate, of national and increasingly international significance. At that date such stature could be compared only with that of Sutherland and Moore and possibly Ben Nicholson. Whether, in ultimate terms, the stature was 'merited' or not there can be no doubt that it existed.

CHAPTER 7

THE JUDGMENTS OF 1951

PLANNING THE FESTIVAL OF BRITAIN

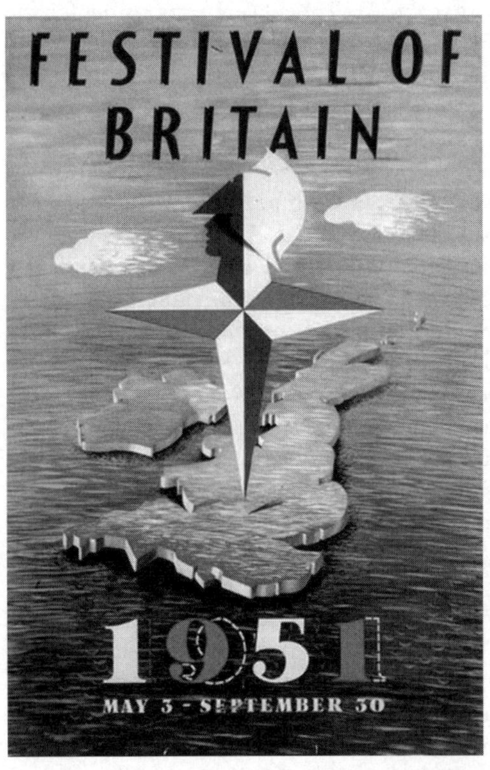

The idea for a festival of some kind arose as early as 1943, when the Royal Society of Arts proposed a commemoration of the 1851 Great Exhibition.[1] This was followed by a letter in the *News Chronicle* of 14 September 1945 to Sir Stafford Cripps, President of the Board of Trade, after which public debate in the newspapers followed. There was, for example, a large article in the *Times* on 20 November 1945 by Viscount Samuel on the possibility of having a 1951 'Great Exhibition'. The initial idea was for some sort of international exhibition, but this was scaled back for cost reasons to a national one. After some debate about using Crystal Palace as the site for the Festival, a large site on the South Bank was finally chosen and, in the years leading up to 1951, the newspapers regularly contained updates as to the progress in preparing the site, with pictures of how it was planned to look and, eventually, photographs of work in progress. Cripps passed the project on to Herbert Morrison, Lord President of the Council, and he presented the plans for a 1951 festival to the House of Commons on 7 December 1947. Morrison created a Festival Council to progress matters and it is notable for our purposes that, when this was announced on 1 May 1948, one of its members was Kenneth Clark.[2]

The official purpose of the Festival was to celebrate the British contribution to civilisation since 1851, in the arts, science, technology and industrial design. Whilst it was a great success with the public, with over 8 million people attending the event on the South Bank before it closed at the end of September 1951, it was, on closer inspection, a rather curious event, reflecting many strands of ambition and intention. Becky Conekin, in her book *Autobiography of a Nation*, has sought to analyse just how the Festival came about and exactly what those who promoted it thought it was about. 'The Festival planners imagined "New Britain" as a consensual, unified society in need of edifying entertainment. The Festival of Britain was simultaneously a public celebration, an educational undertaking, and a constructed vision of a new, democratic national community... The Festival embodied the post-War British ideal of universal, popular access to and understanding of "culture".' Other celebrations of the Festival were held at many places throughout the UK.3

The role of the Arts Council

The Arts Council was responsible for the artistic contributions to the Festival. The first time the Art Panel of the Arts Council recorded mention of the Festival in its minutes was on 19 April 1948.4 At the next meeting, on 19 July, the Chairman (for that meeting) was Sir Ernest Pooley. He informed the meeting that the Art Panel 'were responsible for the kind of exhibition to be held during the Festival and for the acquisition of suitable gallery space for showing the exhibitions'. A special meeting of the Panel to consider these potentially rather onerous duties was held shortly afterwards, on 20 August. At this meeting all sorts of ideas were considered, some of considerable obscurity. Amongst the more normal suggestions was one for a show of 'Contemporary British Art'. This was eventually to become 'British Painting 1925-1950'. At the next meeting (on 9 December), the Contemporary British Art exhibition was approved in principle, as was the involvement of the Manchester City Art Gallery, which had already independently suggested a similar topic. Sculpture then seized the Panel's imagination and some time at subsequent meetings was spent on developing the concept of commissioning new works from living sculptors. £6,000 was earmarked for the purpose at the meeting on 12 April 1949 and, by the time of the next meeting, on 19 July, it was confirmed that the commissions had gone to Moore, Epstein and Hepworth.

The first time that the Panel formally started to consider what was later to become '60 Paintings for '51' was at the meeting on 24 October 1949. The idea, following the sculpture precedent, was to use £5,000 for commissioning pictures. Half the money was to be given to five painters to produce big paintings. The members were all asked to send in their ideas for who should be commissioned in this way and they were asked to submit no more than eight names. The letters which ensued survive and make interesting reading. Anderson's five were Pasmore, Smith, Sutherland, Piper and Colquhoun. Henry Moore (in a letter of 7 November 1949) came up with Pasmore, Smith, Sutherland, Piper, Jones, Ben Nicholson, Hitchens and, interestingly, Bacon. Edward Le Bas went for Pasmore, Smith, Roberts, Grant, Weight, Minton, Spear and Colquhoun. Lilian Somerville suggested Smith, Sutherland, Piper, Stanley Spencer and Ben Nicholson. Gordon Russell suggested Lowry, Jones, Spear, Hitchens, Trevelyan and Minton. Eric Newton thought Piper, Minton, Hitchens, Lewis, Craxton and Pasmore. Percy Jowett was for Smith, Spencer, Sutherland, Pasmore and Ben Nicholson. Hendy volunteered Sutherland, Hitchens, Freud, Ayrton and Bacon. Oliver Brown came up with an unusual list, perhaps reflecting his position as a leading dealer in contemporary British art: Hitchens, Piper, Rogers, Le Brocquy, Evans, Weight, Mason and Roberts. Rothenstein suggested Sutherland, Lowry, Smith, Spencer, Burra, Jones, Ben Nicholson and Piper. Miss Barnard from the Norwich Museum denied her credentials for choosing and then chose Sutherland, Piper, Hitchens, Tibble, Appelbee and Henry Lamb (indeed, a curious group). Leigh Ashton, by contrast, was entirely predictable: Smith, Sutherland, Pasmore, Piper and Ben Nicholson. Ernest Musgrave put his in order of preference as Spear, Gowing, Smith, Le Bas, Coldstream, Appelbee, Vaughan and Sutherland. Interestingly he strongly doubted Sutherland's ability to do such a big picture, particularly if no-one told him what to paint. Finally, Herbert Read tried to be more analytical, instead of coming up with his favourite artists or the artists he thought he was supposed to recommend. In a thoughtful, short letter (of 9 November) he said that he thought the selection should try to be representative of the different styles that were current. He thought it would be possible to have a group of five artists covering the different areas and he therefore suggested two alternative groups of five. Either Augustus John, Lewis, Spencer, Freud and Sutherland or Smith, Spear, Roberts, Ben Nicholson and Colquhoun.

The key meeting of the Panel which determined the shape of the exhibition which was to become '60 Paintings for '51' was held on 1 December 1949. It was pointed out that the Festival Council had already commissioned Sutherland and Herman to produce pictures for the Festival site and they were likely to go on to commission Bawden and Piper and either Hillier or Eric Fraser.[5] Needless to say, it was Anderson who came up with the key structural change which responded to the fact that the Panel did not want to find that they were commissioning any of the same artists as the Festival Council. He suggested awarding prizes rather than commissions and this idea was immediately adopted. It meant that lots of artists could be asked to participate and the five sums of £500 each which had been earmarked for commissions could in fact be awarded as prizes. The outline of the exhibition was then mapped out: five prizes; 50 painters to be invited. 33 names had already been settled on by aggregating the initial suggestions of members of the Panel and Clark, Anderson, Le Bas, Read and Philip James were asked to take soundings and then select the final 50; the artists were to be given free canvas and stretchers; each picture had to cover at least $18^1/2$ square feet;[6] and all pictures would be exhibited and those not winning prizes were to be for sale.

Immediately following this meeting the members of the Panel were asked to come up with some more names, so as to make the numbers up from 33 to 50. Colin Anderson split up a long list of the artists he thought worth considering (bearing in mind that 33 others had already been chosen) into three categories: two stars, one star and 'makeweight'. In the former went MacBryde, Kessell, Richards, Kokoschka, Scott, Bawden and Freedman; then V. Bell, Tunnard, Wilde, Hepworth, Hill, Hillier, Rothenstein, Moynihan, Clough, Ryan, L. Lamb, Potter and Topolski; and finally, and rather ignominiously, Rowntree, Lanyon, Banting, Ironside and, not surprisingly, Ithell Colquhoun.

The Arts Council files contain long lists of names of artists with handwritten comments and it is impossible to work out the sequence in which the lists were produced or the identity of those commenting. Suffice it to say that, by the time of the next Art Panel meeting, on 28 February 1950, the decision had been taken to increase the number of invitees from 50 to 60; 61 invitations had already been sent out and 52 had accepted, five had refused and one – Meninsky – had committed suicide. To plug the gaps, Jones, Augustus John, Gilbert Spencer, Mahoney and Bloch were invited. In addition, with all these invitations going out, it was felt that the separate Contemporary British Art exhibition should now effectively be handed back to Manchester, which would be asked to organise the selection.

And so it went on. By the next meeting – 9 May – more invitees were needed and some fairly obscure names were added (Bellingham-Smith, Hubert, Baynes and du Plessis). A few reserves were identified, in the form of Winifred Nicholson, Rosoman and Collins and, while Smith had orally refused in conversation with Le Bas, it was felt that he should nevertheless still be invited formally, in writing. (They could hardly miss him out, since he had polled more votes than anyone else in the initial sweep of members' views.) Pulling together all the names of artists who appear at one time or another to have been considered produces the following 145 names:

Aldridge	de Sausmarez	Jones (D)	Richards*
Appelbee*	Devas	Jonzen	Roberts
Ardizzone	Dunlop*	Kessell	Rogers*
Armstrong*	du Plessis*	Kokoschka	Rose
Ayrton*	Eardley	La Dell	Rosoman
Bacon*	Ellis (C)	Lamb (H)*	Rothenstein
Banting	Ellis (R)	Lamb (L)*	Rowntree
Bawden	Evans*	Lanyon*	Ryan
Baynes*	Feibusch*	Le Brocquy*	Scarfe
Bell*	Fitton	Lewis (K)	Scott*
Bellingham Smith*	Fleming	Lewis (W)	Seabrooke
Benois	Freedman	Lowry*	Searle
Bloch*	Freud*	MacBryde*	Sinclair
Bray	Gear*	Macdonald*	Sivell
Buhler	Gillies*	Mahoney*	Smith*
Burn	Giner	Martin	Sorrell
Burra*	Gotlib	Maxwell*	Spear*
Carr (H)	Gowing*	McGuinness	Spencer (G)*
Carr (T)	Grant*	Medley*	Spencer (S)
Clough*	Gwynne Jones	Meninsky	Spender
Clutton-Brock	Hayter	Methuen	Sutherland
Coldstream	Hepworth	Minton*	Thomas
Cole	Herman*	Moore	Tibble*
Collins	Heron*	Morris	Tisdall
Colquhoun (I)	Hill	Moynihan*	Topolski
Colquhoun (R)*	Hillier	Napper	Trevelyan*
Connard	Hilton	Nash*	Tunnard*
Copley	Hitchens*	Newton (A)	Vaughan*
Cowie	Horton	Newton (J)	Watson
Coxon*	Horward	Nicholson (B)*	Weight*
Craxton	Hubbard	Nicholson (W)*	Wells
Crosbie	Hubert	Pasmore*	White
Daintrey	Hurry	Peake	Wilde
Darwin	Ironside	Piper	Wolfe
de Grey*	John	Pitchforth	Woods
de Maistre*	Jones (B)	Potter	Wynter*

Those marked with an asterisk were the 54 whose pictures were eventually shown. The following refused: Coldstream, Connard, Freedman, Wyndham Lewis, Stanley Spencer and Sutherland. Gotlib and Meninsky's names were withdrawn (the latter dying in 1950). Bawden and Kokoschka initially agreed, but subsequently withdrew. Buhler, Craxton, Hillier, Kessell, Piper and Roberts were chosen and agreed to produce pictures, but each failed to do so for a variety of reasons.7 Although not chosen for the exhibition, Gerald Wilde was asked to design the cover of the catalogue for the exhibition, which was reproduced in colour.

Manchester popped up at the next meeting on 19 September, with some suggestions for artists for the 'Contemporary British Art' show and the fundamental suggestion that the dates chosen be 1925-1950 and not, as originally planned, 1900-1950. The name ultimately chosen for the title of the big show – '60 Paintings for '51' – appears in the minutes for the first time on 23 January 1951. It was noted in passing that Hillier had said that he would not be able to finish his picture by the deadline and that judges were to be appointed to make the selection of the final winners.

Other events

Quite separately, painters were commissioned to do murals for the South Bank, including Minton, Ben Nicholson, Vaughan, Topolski and Herman. Piper, Sutherland, Tunnard and Pasmore also contributed to the decoration of the South Bank, outside the 60 Paintings exhibition. Otherwise there were two major shows of 'British Painting 1925-1950' and a show organised by the ICA by arrangement with the Arts Council. An open air exhibition of sculpture organised by the London County Council in association with the Arts Council was held in Battersea Park and Wales saw an exhibition of contemporary Welsh painting. Northern Ireland had an exhibition arranged by CEMA called 'Contemporary Ulster Art' at the Belfast Museum and Art Gallery, showing the work of eleven artists. The same gallery also had a loan exhibition of paintings by Lavery and the Arts Council Collection of Contemporary Scottish Paintings.

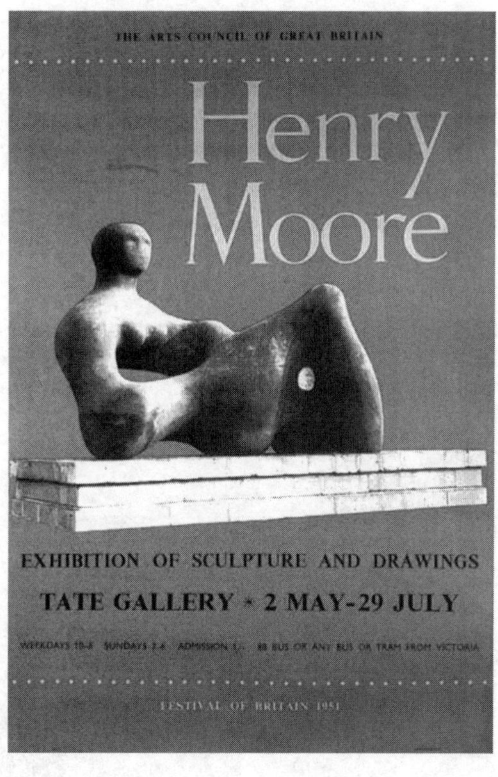

As an example of just how much modern art was on show during this period, both in the capital and elsewhere, it is worth noting that the usual Summer Exhibition at the Royal Academy opened on 5 May, just two days after the Festival began. It ran until 26 August. Of the artists whose names have appeared frequently in these pages, it is interesting to note that none of them were amongst the thirteen Senior Academicians at the time. From the 38 Academicians, readers of this book would recognise only a couple of names: Augustus John and Stanley Spencer. Among the 27 Associates, a few more familiar names arise: Bawden, Buhler, Eurich, Moynihan, John Nash, Spear and Gilbert Spencer.[8] Of the pictures illustrated in the catalogue, familiar names included Aldridge, Eurich, John, Le Bas, Minton, Moynihan, John Nash, Roberts, Spear, Gilbert Spencer, Stanley Spencer and Wadsworth. Although this does not represent an enormous overlap with the art at the Festival, there is overlap and any idea that the 'official' art which found approval at the RA was inevitably different from 'modern' art favoured by the more forward-looking parts of the art establishment should be resisted as being a simplistic interpretation.

There was also a large show by the Royal Society of British Artists at their Suffolk Street galleries. Artists showing at that also included such Festival artists as Minton and Weight. There was also a big Moore retrospective at the Tate and a Sutherland retrospective put on by the ICA, for which Raymond Mortimer wrote an introduction to the catalogue.[9]

British Painting 1925-50: the 'Anthologies'[10]

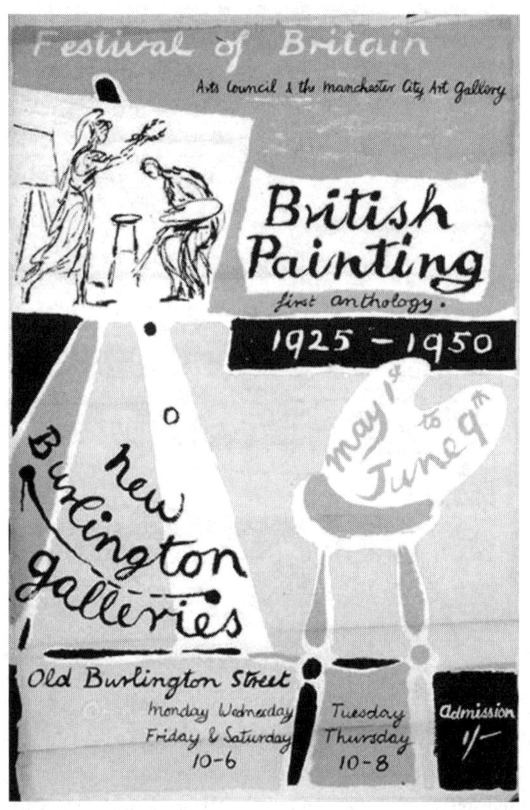

The show whose long period of gestation has been tracked through the minutes of the Art Panel under the loose title of 'Contemporary British Art' turned into two exhibitions organised jointly by the Arts Council and the Manchester City Art Gallery, called 'British Painting 1925-1950'. These exhibitions both had the same overall title, but they were split by the curious title of the 'First Anthology' and the 'Second Anthology'. There was a purported conceptual distinction between the artists put in the two different 'anthologies': the First was intended to represent more experimental art, while in the Second, according to the foreword to the small catalogue, there was 'unfolded the main stream of development largely representing the more traditional achievement in the various versions of realism deriving from and following the English impressionism of Steer and Sickert'.

The 'First Anthology' was selected by David Baxandall, the Director of the Manchester City Art Gallery. Baxandall had been director since 1945 and in 1952 was to move on to being Director of the National Gallery of Scotland, until his retirement in 1970. He eventually chose work by Bacon, Burra, Clough, Colquhoun, Craxton, Freud, Hitchens, Hodgkins, Jones, Lewis, Lowry, MacBryde, Minton, Paul Nash, Ben Nicholson, Pasmore, Piper, Richards, Roberts, Smith, Spencer, Sutherland, Wadsworth and Wood. There were 114 works in total from 56 different lenders (all helpfully named in the catalogue).[11] Fourteen of the lenders were institutional, the rest private. Colin Anderson lent works by Bacon, Colquhoun, Piper, Smith and Sutherland. Clark contributed Hodgkins, Jones, Piper and Sutherland. Of the institutions, the Lefevre lent works by Burra, MacBryde and Minton and the Manchester City Art Gallery itself lent Hodgkins, Lowry, MacBryde, Nash, Nicholson, Roberts, Smith and Spencer. It may be that these latter loans were pragmatic choices rather than the best works available by the artists. To suggest that some of the artists may have been included because the organiser's municipal collection owned examples of their works would simply be to hint at the difficulty of establishing in any meaningfully objective way the way in which decisions were made (and no doubt still are made) in selecting those artists whose careers may be furthered by having their work chosen for large public exhibition.

The Arts Council papers which remain do, however, contain some important glimpses of some elements of the decision-taking about which artists to include. Baxandall produced the original list and that included Ayrton and Vaughan, but not Bacon, Freud, Craxton or Clough. His list was submitted to the Arts Council and they passed it on to a similar sub-committee to the one that had been constituted to sort out the names of the artists to be included in '60 Paintings for '51': Kenneth Clark, Colin Anderson, Herbert Read, Edward le Bas and William Coldstream. They obviously communicated their views to Philip James, because he or Gabriel White reverted to Baxandall with the suggestion that Ayrton and Vaughan should come out and Bacon, Freud, Craxton and Clough should go in. Baxandall clearly was not entirely happy about this. On 13 February 1951 he wrote to Gabriel White, 'I am still unconvinced that when one looks at the quarter-century as a whole Freud and Bacon merit inclusion among the couple of dozen painters who have made the most important contributions, however fashionable they are at the present moment.'[12]

The 'Second Anthology' was selected by Hugh Scrutton, Director of the Whitechapel Art Gallery.[13] To the modern eye, his was very much a second XI, but that is to use hindsight. He chose Bell, Buhler,[14] Coldstream, Coxon, Dodgson, Gertler, Gillies, Ginner, Gowing, Grant, Hunter, Augustus John, Gwen John, Henry Lamb, Le Bas, Edward Lewis, Moynihan, Napper, Sir William Nicholson, Pasmore, Potter, Rogers, Sickert, Spear, Townsend, Walker and Weight.[15] This time there were 132 works from 68 lenders, of which only eight were institutional. The markedly lower percentage of institutional lenders in the 'safer' 'Second Anthology' may, perhaps, be explained by the comparative ease with which representational works found homes with private owners. It may also, of course, indicate that the artists in the 'First Anthology' were more 'modern' and therefore of much greater interest to institutional owners than to the more cautious private buyers of modern art.[16] By contrast, for the 'First Anthology', the only artists called upon to lend their own work had been Nicholson, Pasmore (there being little or no appetite for buying his abstract work) and Richards, together with the executrix of Wadsworth.

It is unnecessary to list the private owners who lent works, since their names are of less relevance in this context: they were, by definition, private buyers (or inheritors) of modern British art, but art of a comparatively 'safe' nature, such that a decision to purchase was not necessarily a bold decision. The lack of overlap between the private owners is interesting. Only J.L. Behrend, Sir Kenneth Clark, Mrs Cazalet-Keir and Edward Le Bas featured in both lists. In the end, the 'Anthology' exhibitions were seen by about 22,000 people, although far more in Manchester than in London, where presumably the public had other opportunities to see the work of these artists.

'Ten Decades, a Review of British Taste 1851-1951'

The cover of the catalogue to this exhibition purports to give it a degree of official approval, in describing it as 'A Festival of Britain Exhibition organised by the Institute of Contemporary Arts by arrangement with the Arts Council of Great Britain'. It had in fact been given a grant of £1,500 by the Arts Council.[17] The organising committee was

Geoffrey Grigson, Robin Ironside, Benedict Nicolson, Roland Penrose and Ewan Phillips. Grigson was responsible for the period 1851-1880; Ironside for 1881-1910; and Nicolson for the rest. The introduction to the catalogue was written by Grigson and he explained that the point of the exhibition was not 'to poke fun at the past, or to be immoderately cocksure about our own judgments of 1951'. Instead, the 'aim is to indicate the waverings and interweavings of taste through a hundred years'. However, while Grigson purported to be even-handed, the last paragraph of his introduction revealed his prejudices. He started by saying that 'the bulk of widely praised art in any period is always without merit. At all times we are most of us deluded by much that has no value'. But, having sought to create the image of even-handedness, he finished by saying that, when it is eventually possible to review properly all the works of 1851-1901, 'the intermittent honesties even of such men, their few sparks of talent, may emerge'.

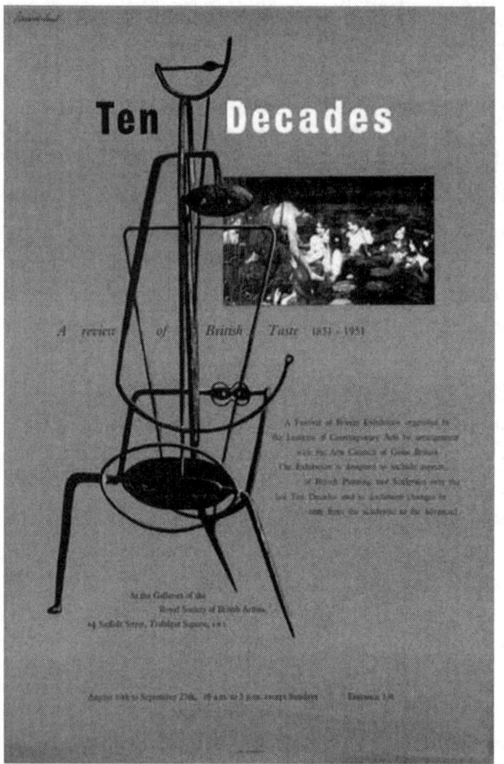

The form of the catalogue itself was divided into decades, with each section given its own brief introduction and many of the individual artists given a little footnote. Unfortunately, as we have noted earlier, arbitrary periods of time are meaningless when applied to history and particularly to the history of art. Artists were, as a result, placed incongruously in decades when they were working, but where they could just as easily have been placed in a number of other decades. Burra, Jones and Ben Nicholson thus appeared in 1921-30 and Hitchens, Piper, Sutherland and Trevelyan in 1931-40. These are not meaningful choices. In the first decade came all the old favourites: Bacon, Colquhoun, Craxton, Freud, Gear, Nicholson, Pasmore, Piper, Spencer, Sutherland and Vaughan, but then some extraordinary choices which can only have been made out of perversity: Jack Bilbo,[18] Devas, W.O. Grey,[19] Algernon Newton (born 1880), Peter Scott,[20] the incredibly old-fashioned Charles Spencelayh (born 1865), Topolski, Scottie Wilson and, of all people, Doris Zinkeisen.[21] The choice of these names is a hint that mischief was at work here. In any event, the reviewers took little or no notice of this exhibition. John Berger noted it in the *New Statesman & Nation* of 1 September 1951, saying rather revealingly that 'many of the pictures of the first 5 decades might have been conceived by Cecil B de Mille'. The *Times* said 'the exhibition resembles nothing so much as a large provincial art gallery the successive directors of which have not been allowed to relegate any of their predecessors' purchases to the cellars'.

Sculpture in Battersea Park

The outdoor sculpture exhibition held in Battersea Park had an interesting genesis, not directly related to the Festival itself. It was described as the 'Second International Exhibition of Sculpture', the first having been held in Battersea in 1948. Accordingly, unlike the British painters who benefited from the encouragement of the Festival, this show was consciously international. The foreword to the catalogue stated that the exhibition was confined to artists of the last 50 years, but the method used to define that period stretches the sculptors chosen well back into the 19th century, since the date of death seems to have needed to fall within the deadline rather than the date of the work. So, the earliest sculptor was the Belgian Constantin Meunier, who had been born 120 years earlier and who had died just within the deadline, in 1905. His work dated from 1884. Rodin, whom one thinks of as an artist of the 19th century (he had been born in 1840), was also squeezed in, with a work from 1892. No doubt the justification was to enable a proper context to be given for the more recent works.

Forty-four sculptors were involved, showing one work each. The Advisory Panel contained a number of familiar names, suggesting that the small number of people who counted for guiding 'official' decisions in the British art world of the time included sculpture in their sphere of influence. So one finds Eric Gregory on the Panel (and his firm, Lund Humphries, producing the catalogue); also the ubiquitous Philip James from the Arts Council, Rothenstein from the Tate and Maclagan from the British Council, together with sculptors McWilliam, Hepworth and Epstein. The catalogue contained an introduction from someone whose name is now so familiar in a different context, Nikolaus Pevsner, writing in the guise of Slade Professor of Fine Art at Cambridge. As for the British sculptors chosen, the usual problem of national definition arises, since a number of those represented were of foreign birth, but practising in London, sometimes no doubt as refugees from Central Europe. Into this category fell Siegfried Charoux (Vienna); Georg Ehrlich (Austria); Heinz Henghes (Hamburg); Maurice Lambert (Paris); Uli Nimptsch (Germany); Willi Soukop (Vienna); and Karel Vogel (Bohemia). The home-grown names were Butler, Chadwick, Dobson, Gill, Hardiman, Hepworth, Jonzen, Ledward, McWilliam, Meadows, Moore, Skeaping, Thomas and Wheeler.

'60 paintings for '51'

In December 1949 the Arts Council published a formal notice whose terms they probably came to regret. For it was called 'Painting Competition'. As a result, innumerable people wrote in, their letters still in the Arts Council files,[22] asking if they could participate in the competition. A standard letter was developed to deal with these people, patiently explaining that it was not that sort of competition. Occasionally quite embarrassing letters were received, such as the one in the file from well-known artist Elliott Seabrooke. He half-jokingly wrote in saying that perhaps his invitation was in the post, but hoping that he had indeed been asked to participate. He wasn't.[23] More importuning came from the Scottish Committee of the Arts Council. They didn't know who was on the list to be invited, but they hoped it included Cowie, Crosbie, Eardley (who was English), Fleming, Gillies, Maxwell and Sivell. Of these, only Gillies and Maxwell were included, undoubtedly on merit rather than simply as Scottish representatives. It is slightly curious to a later eye that the Scottish Committee had not requested MacTaggart or Redpath. It is also interesting to note that they did not mention the most eminent Scottish artists alive at the time – Colquhoun and MacBryde. At this

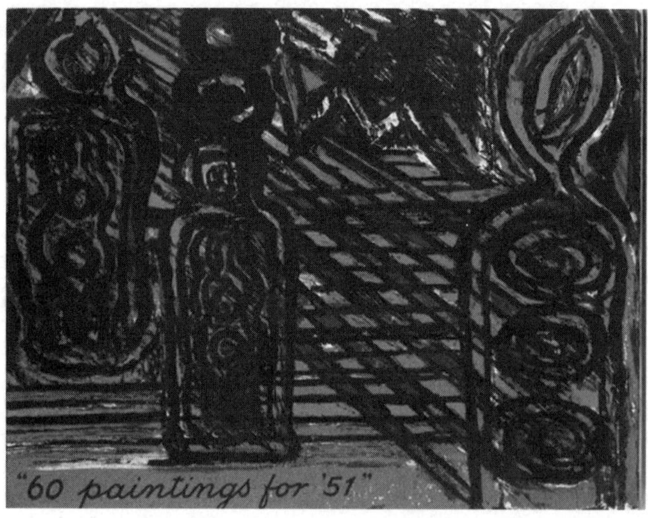

point the Scottish arts establishment was not so keen to claim them.

The identity of the successful 60 artists chosen to participate was announced in the *Times* on 20 July 1950. The files relating to the preparation of the exhibition present an interesting picture of the difficulties of preparing for such a large show with so many different artists. Philip James and Gabriel White seem to have written most of the letters to the artists and they had to put up with a wide range of grumbling about all sorts of issues. Gillies, Heron and Henry Lamb, for example, complained that their birth dates were wrong in the catalogue (Gillies noting that his was out by as much as 20 years, the catalogue rather unkindly referring to him being born in 1878 instead of 1898); Heron also added that the photo of his work in the catalogue had cut off a bit of the picture.[24] John Nash said he was 'heartily sick' of his picture, having struggled to cope with the unfamiliar huge size of his canvas.[25] Having been given deadlines for producing their work, many artists were annoyed to find that the time needed for preparing photos of the pictures for the catalogue meant that even earlier deadlines had to be imposed upon them, on little notice. The most aggressive tone was taken by Ben Nicholson. He was 'quite at a loss to understand the Arts Council's approach to these very significant awards'. He had been assuming that the judges would be what he called 'sensible' people, but he was unable to believe that Clutton-Brock could have been chosen and, if there were to be any foreign judges, why not from Paris? And why would one of them be from Australia? 'It seems to an outsider like myself a most haphazard selection.' Philip James dealt with one point from an earlier letter by noting in a reply to Nicholson (dated 2 February 1951), 'I don't think you would say as a result of these activities of ours 'advanced painting' had been discouraged if you had seen my post-bag during the past fortnight. We have never before received so much abuse for supporting advanced work.'

The judges

The selection of the judges seems to have been done rather casually, and it was left to quite a late moment before the identity of the judges was settled. Philip James wrote to Anderson on 17 March 1951 saying that he had discussed the choice of judges with Kenneth Clark at length. Clark wanted[26] a critic, a collector and a foreigner. For the first rôle he was 'very anxious' to have Alan Clutton-Brock, the art critic of the *Times*, who had accepted. For the collector, Anderson himself being ruled out because he was a member of the Art Panel which had selected the artists to participate, they had asked Robert Sainsbury, but he had declined. The token 'foreigner' asked was the French painter André Lhote, but he had also declined. On 20 March they invited (presumably in the capacity of 'collector') A.J.L. McDonnell, who was the London-based adviser to the extremely well-funded Felton Bequest, of the National Gallery of Victoria, Melbourne, who accepted and on 31 March an invitation went out to Jonkheer Sandberg, who was director of the Stedelijk Museum in Amsterdam, who accepted on 2 April, approximately two weeks before the judging was to be done. Curiously, in view of his very direct involvement in the choice of the judges, Clark was reported as saying, at the 21st meeting of the Art Panel, held just after this, on 10 April, that he thought the Panel should have selected the winners and not the judges. He was saying this at the point when he could not possibly have known what the judges were going to choose. However, at the next meeting (9 July), it would seem that his concerns had been justified, for the minutes recorded the following statement to the meeting, which he chaired: 'The policy of delegating responsibility in the selection of purchases from the '60 Paintings for '51' exhibition to an outside jury had not proved entirely successful.' This statement was not attributed to Clark, and nor was it explained further exactly what it was referring to. The archive material doesn't seem to record how the judges did their work. They went round the exhibition on 16 April and telegrams were sent to the winners on 18 April. Not everyone was to agree with their choices, as will be seen in the following section.

The winners and the reactions

Freud, Gear, Hitchens, Medley and Rogers were selected as the winners by the judges and their names were announced in the *Times* on 21 April. They each received a cheque for £500. The exhibition opened initially at the Manchester City Art Gallery, where it was to be seen by 30,889 people, on 2 May 1951. It stayed in Manchester until 10 June. Its London showing (22 June–31 July) was held in the RBA Galleries in Suffolk Street, SW1, and it was subsequently toured round the art galleries in Leicester, Liverpool, Bristol, Norwich, Plymouth, Leeds, Newcastle, Brighton, York and Preston, ending in June 1952.

It is instructive to consider the comments of Colin Anderson on the show. In 1978, he allowed to be published his own contemporary comments on the pictures in the exhibition. It has to be remembered that the Art Panel had chosen the artists and not the pictures and the members had their first sight of the pictures once they were hung ready for the public. Anderson went round the show and annotated his copy of the catalogue. In May 1978 the Mappin Art Gallery in Sheffield held an exhibition called '25 from '51', in which they brought together almost half of the original works from the Festival of Britain show. In an Appendix to the very interesting catalogue, Anderson rather reluctantly allowed his comments to be reprinted.[27] One understands his reluctance when one reads the comments. Of Armstrong's work he wrote, '[it] bears no relation to contemporary art or thought'; of Bacon, 'not a good example'; Vanessa Bell was 'pathetic'; du Plessis, 'one of the poorest and least competent things in the show'; Freud, 'very good indeed – vision, design and craftsmanship'; Gear, 'good'; Grant, 'more pathetic even than V. Bells'; Lanyon 'very impressive'; Macdonald, 'horrid'; Minton 'flop'; and so on.

The critics in the main newspapers reacted in a muted fashion to the various displays of modern British art represented at the Festival. To them there was nothing shocking or unusual about the works shown or about the artists involved for, as we have seen throughout this book, they were the artists who were, in many cases, steadily rising (or had already risen) to the top of the critical pile. They were the same artists whose shows were likely to have been reviewed at the Lefevre, the Leicester Galleries and the Redfern; they were, indeed, the favourites of the modern British art establishment: Kenneth Clark, Colin Anderson, Philip James, John Rothenstein and so on. We should not therefore be surprised at the responses in the *Times*, the *Sunday Times*, the *Manchester Guardian* or the *Observer*, whether to the Anthologies or to the commissioned large-scale works in '60 paintings'. Regarding the former, there was some feeling in some papers that the 'Euston Road' pictures in the 'Second Anthology' showed up well, but it is easy to generalise misleadingly. The *Manchester Guardian* critic, writing on 25 June, noted that a lot of the Euston Road work was 'sad and lifeless', especially when compared to such a great artist as Sir William Nicholson,[28] and there was a pleasing comment from the *Times* reviewer on the nice opportunity for London to see the work of the eminent Scottish artist, William Gillies, whose work was not often seen south of the border.[29] The extreme mixture of work and styles in the 'First Anthology' made it difficult to review coherently in the small amount of space available to these journalists in the newspapers, the *Times'* comment that it was 'a lively and interesting, if rather uneven, exhibition' being perhaps inevitable. Where more space was available, as in the *Listener*, there was more opportunity to analyse the conceptual basis for the two shows. On 5 July, in a piece taken from a broadcast on the Third Programme, the oddly named and later infamous[30] Le Roux Smith Le Roux had a large piece headed '25 Years of British Painting'. He was very unhappy about the arbitrary time limits chosen; about the fact that some artists had up to nine works on show, where others had three; about the fact that some suitable works had not been available for the exhibition; about the artificial split between the two anthologies; and generally about the timidity of the selections made. Some things he liked. Paul Nash, Ben Nicholson and Matthew Smith were notable and he approved of Richards, Sutherland, Burra and Hitchens. Perceptively for the time, he picked out Freud as being likely to become an important artist, whereas it was not clear to him – again perceptively – where Colquhoun, MacBryde, Minton, Clough and Craxton would be in 25 years' time.

When it came to the big commissioned pictures, the reviewers in the leading papers couldn't resist commenting on whether or not the artists had managed to cope with the demands of size successfully, since many of them had probably never had the opportunity (or even the wish in some cases), to work with canvases of this scale. The commentators varied a bit as to who they thought had brought it off most successfully. The *Observer* thought that Lowry, Ayrton, Minton and Heron had coped, whereas others such as Grant and Evans had struggled. Works by de Maistre and Moynihan were of 'real distinction'. The *Sunday Times*, on the other hand, praised Bellingham-Smith, Freud, Vaughan, Richards, Ben Nicholson and de Grey for their success with the size problem, only agreeing with the *Observer* in respect of Heron and Moynihan.[31]

The *Times* had another shot at the size issue, but chose yet another group as successful – Clough, Herman and Smith, as well as Bellingham-Smith.[32] The *Listener* (on 17 May), interestingly, got David Baxandall, the selector of one of the 'Anthologies', to do its review. He liked the concept of the large paintings and the whole show generally. His preferred list was Moynihan, Herman, Lowry, Lanyon, Pasmore, Richards and Ben Nicholson. The *Manchester Guardian* was the first to review the show (on 4 May), because it opened in Manchester. In fact, the paper had two goes at reviewing it, in Manchester and then again, through their 'London art critic', when it moved south. Interestingly, the reviews were quite different. The Manchester reviewer (only identified by his initials, 'JW'), was very taken with the sheer size of the pictures, thinking that they together made a great impact on the visitor through their unfamiliarly large size alone. He found a lot to praise: Moynihan, Hitchens, Heron, Richards, Medley, Ben Nicholson, Vaughan, Lanyon, Trevelyan, Lowry, Rogers, Spear, de Grey, Smith and Clough, whilst only mildly criticising Colquhoun, MacBryde and Weight. On the other hand, the London critic approved of Moynihan, Evans, Gillies, Lanyon, Spear, Minton, Lamb, Ben Nicholson and Clough. He then provided some rather dry comments on the work of the five winners. Freud's picture (described as being of a dwarf and a potted plant) was minutely realistic; Gear's was dull; Hitchens' piece was sarcastically described as being in a different style in its four yards on the left as compared to its two yards on the right; and the pictures by Medley and Rogers were approved.

The treatment of the exhibition in the *Daily Telegraph* got off to a very rocky start. On 19 April a small black-and-white reproduction of Gear's abstract picture was published, above a short piece recording the winners. In view of what then followed in the paper in the coming days, one wonders whether the paper was being deliberately mischievous in choosing to reproduce the only wholly abstract picture amongst the winners. Whether deliberately or not, many *Telegraph* readers were obviously seriously antagonised (although again, as with reactions in the *Times* to the Picasso exhibition at the end of 1945, one never knows how many letters came in and whether those printed reflected a fair balance of the opinions expressed). In any event, the letters published were, usually, not in favour of the Gear picture. The first two letters appeared on 21 April ('grotesque doodling'); two more the next day; and four more the next day, including one from Sir Alfred Munnings as former President of the Royal Academy and notorious baiter of modern artists. Gear himself then made sure the excitement continued by getting his own response published on 26 April, pointing out, not unreasonably, that it was a bit unfair for all these adverse comments to be made when none of the commentators could possibly have actually seen the picture as the exhibition had not opened. He also at this point wrote a rather charming letter dated 28 April to Philip James, saying, 'In a way I have rather enjoyed the letters to the editor though I felt bitter at some of them making their silly little digs at the Arts Council for petty political ends.' (The Arts Council itself has in its archives[33] a sad little collection of about ten letters, labelled 'abusive letters', relating to Gear's picture.)

After this a few supportive letters were published, one from the Secretary-General of the Arts Council, one from Michael Rothenstein and one very spirited letter from Edith Sitwell. But in among these the general tone of the letters was hostile (another exception was Howard Bliss, who established his credentials by saying that he already owned half-a-dozen pictures by the artist). Enjoying the controversy, the paper published another naughty picture in its 'London Day by Day' section, with the Gear picture reproduced alongside a close-up of a piece of linoleum, showing faint similarities. Gear wrote in again after this (on 7 May), possibly provoked by a report in the parliamentary section of the paper on 4 May that a Suffolk Labour MP, E.L. Granville, had asked a question about why the Arts Council was wasting public money on such art – a question which had been answered by Hugh Gaitskell, Chancellor of the Exchequer. The *Telegraph* then took great pleasure in running a story about the Gear's having been printed upside down in the official catalogue and when the paper's art critic, T.W. Earp,[34] reviewed the whole show when it opened in London on 22 June, the only picture singled out for criticism, bizarrely, was the Gear, which was said to be 'a negation of the precious qualities of humanist expression which give a significance to art'. Otherwise he was reasonably happy about the other winners (although not hugely impressed by Hitchens), and generally had a perfectly polite word to say about all the others mentioned. The overall tenor of the art criticism of the *Daily Telegraph* at this time can be easily divined. In its comments about the sculpture at Battersea, it was teasing and sarcastic about most of the works. There was, on the other hand, a large report of the Royal Academy annual dinner on 3 May, including a fulsome report on all the speeches made and, on 5 May, an enormous report on the Summer Exhibition appeared, far more space being devoted to it than to any of the art connected with the Festival.

In the *New Statesman & Nation* of 30 June 1951, John Berger picked out as his most successful large paintings those by Lanyon, Richards, Heron and Medley. In the *Burlington Magazine* for September, Sylvester noted how most of the artists had struggled with the size issue and picked out Freud, Bellingham-Smith, Moynihan, Lanyon and Pasmore as his favourites.[35] Eventually, on 20 October 1952, letters went out from the Arts Council to those artists whose pictures had now been round the country but had still not sold, asking them where they wanted the pictures delivered.

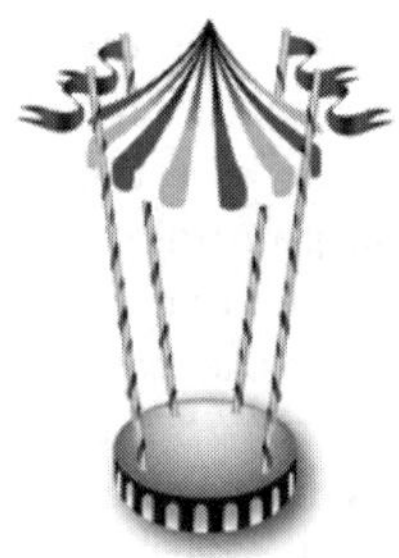

Chapter 8

Conclusion

Gradually, with the passing of time, some views expressed by art historians about artists' reputations may come to have a force which similar views expressed previously could not have had. In this study any number of statements which may seem – to a greater or lesser extent – ludicrous to the modern eye have been noticed. Kenneth Clark commenting on the greatness of Pasmore or Patrick Heron on the weaknesses of many British artists are two examples of this. Claims made by those in a position to have their thoughts read by a wide public will inevitably be tested and challenged over the years. Some claims will thereby fail; others will survive and be consolidated. Those commentators acclaiming Bacon in the mid-1940s were outnumbered by those expressing revulsion or, at least, bewilderment. Now it is the other way round and most would regard Bacon as a serious challenger for the title of the most important artist of 20th-century Britain.

But what is artistic 'importance'? Time rubs away the subtleties and details of artistic reputations; it reduces those which survive to a small and manageable number and, as the context in which reputations are considered gets either longer or wider, the number of survivors continues to diminish. In the longest scheme of things, which British artists of any age compare in significance to the great names of the Italian 16th century? And so the 'importance' of an artist is a relative thing and it only gradually reveals itself. This must mean that artists for whom vigorous statements of support have been made may have thereby developed reputations which will not survive or which will, at least, change. It must also throw into question the motivation of those commentators seeking to claim greatness for certain artists at a time when, logically, that greatness cannot possibly be identified. This does not necessarily mean that all commentators have to be mistrusted or that they will all turn out to have been wrong all of the time. It is perfectly possible, for example, that Sylvester's support for Bacon will turn out to have been right and far-sighted, just as we can already say with some confidence that Clark's high regard for Pasmore and Coldstream was misguided. But it does mean that historians trying to assess in an objective fashion the worth of the opinions of commentators need to tread warily in this area, for it is a minefield. Artists have occasionally painted in what they have regarded as a modern style for no better reason than that it is modern. Their search for modernity may be treated with caution. But so may the approach of the critic or historian or biographer, whose appetite for supporting modernity may be large and must be seen through. In years to come, it may just be that the beautiful, traditional painting skills of Sir William Nicholson will still be more lowly regarded than the abstraction of some of his son's work, but it would be a brave historian or critic who asserted that this was inevitably going to be the case.

That caution in making judgments is, in the last resort, the primary lesson which a study based on facts teaches. As the quotation from John Donne, with which this book begins, says, opinions about qualities can only be opinions. Many good artists worked in the British Isles between 1945 and 1951 and some of their names remain well known;

some names have been lost or nearly lost; some have been simply and crudely categorised. This book has attempted to show that most views on most of the artists concerned are challengeable and need to be challenged as time passes and the focus changes and as our understanding deepens of why certain writers held the views which they expressed. Views based on national pride, personal friendship or even politics may not form the truest basis for that degree of objectivity which we may learn to respect. Furthermore, in the complex interplay of critical and market forces, as they bear upon the work of these artists, views about status which are dogmatic will not withstand analysis. Only time can take those decisions.

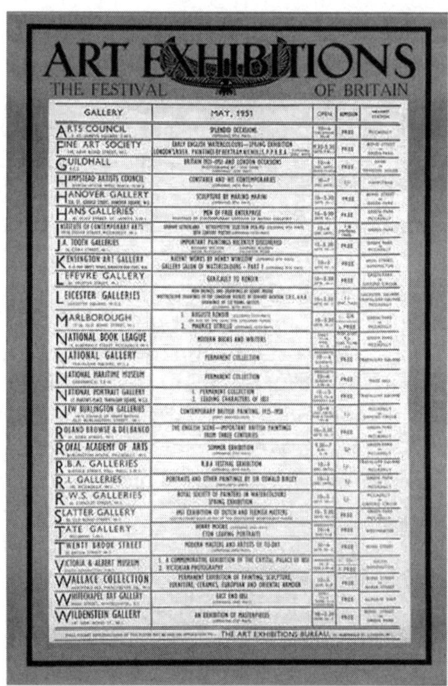

NOTES

INTRODUCTION

1   So, for example, Eric Newton despaired of being able to judge the work of William Gear. On 18 July 1948 he noted in the *Sunday Times* that Gear's work was excellently painted and well composed, but impossible to describe.

2   Other self-glorifying candidates could have presented themselves. On 16 March 1947 Maurice Collis in the *Observer*, commenting on Ayrton, said that 'the difficulty… is to be just to his achievement in the face of his pretensions'. In her biography of Minton, Frances Spalding describes Ayrton at art college as 'odiously conceited' and there are other examples in Ayrton's life of his high regard for his own abilities.

3   Christopher Neve in his book on Leon Underwood makes this point in his first chapter. In describing Underwood's extraordinary versatility as an artist, he says 'all this has left little time for what is called getting one's work across… He has always been where he thinks the artist ought to be, busy with the next idea'.

4   1901-92. Educated at Bedales and Worcester College, Oxford.

5   It is a pity to have to illustrate the work of Rothenstein with such a poor piece of historical writing. He was a perceptive writer on 20th-century British artists. His problem, like most of the other writers whose work on the artists of the period will be mentioned in this book, is that he did not write as an historian, so that when he strayed from the artists to the general scene he was likely to be found wandering in the dangerous world of assertions. The piece quoted bears almost no scrutiny before it falls apart. It simply is not likely that the War would have affected the entire art world, whatever is meant by that. This book will also show that whatever he meant by the 'old Establishment', it must have included himself, Sir Kenneth Clark, Sir Colin Anderson, Peter Watson, Roland Penrose, the Hon Sir Jasper Ridley and so on and we will quickly see that their influence on the art world did not cease to exist for a long time, if ever.

6   Historians have to try to balance a wish to identify and explain change against the need to give appropriate weight to the importance of recognising and describing continuity. A description of the gradual evolution of an institution or even of an 'art world', whatever that is taken to be, may be nearer to the reality of what actually happened with the passage of time, even if the history which it produces is frustratingly cautious to the modern reader.

7   The preface to the first issue of the *English Historical Review* in 1886 stated that 'The object of history is to discover and set forth facts'. That no longer represents the best view of the purpose of historical study but, in the history of 20th century British art writing, an attention to the facts has been a rare attribute.

8   Let the reader who doubts this amuse himself by trying to think in detail about the events of his or her own life. What happened on a day in July, say, 30 years ago? How many pieces of paper does the reader possess about that day in his life?

9   What also needs watching is the inevitable editing which goes on before diaries get published. The historian who really wants to know the thoughts of Keith Vaughan or William Townsend, for example, will have to ignore the printed edition of *Vaughan's Journals*, edited by Alan Ross, or of *Townsend's Journals* edited by Andrew Forge, because both have been drastically reduced for publication. In Forge's case, he notes that the parts published represent 'the merest tip of an iceberg'. In the case of Ross's edition, the selection 'represents less than a quarter of the whole'. In such cases,

whatever the status of the editor, the historian will always be suspicious of how decisions were taken as to what to include and what to omit.

10   *Interviews with Francis Bacon* by David Sylvester. I have used the edition reprinted in 1999.

11   They are certainly used as accurate statements of what Bacon said, as any glance at one of the many books on Bacon will illustrate. For example, on the first page of her introductory essay to the 1985 Tate catalogue, Dawn Ades uses quotations from the interviews on no fewer than four occasions. It is probably accurate to say that all writers on Bacon quote from the interviews at one stage or another apparently in the belief that the words quoted are those of the master himself. My point is not that Bacon's thoughts on art were not interesting and original, it is that Sylvester has interposed himself between Bacon and the reader without necessarily revealing that he has done so.

12   Further analysis of these interviews could be made to reveal a great deal of interesting information about the reliability of historical evidence. For here the interviewer was a close friend of the interviewee. He asked questions which led Bacon's answers, especially after 'editing', to show him in a good light; 'good' in the sense of intellectually developed and thoughtful. Sylvester's many books and articles on Bacon may also suggest that he became obsessed at some stage in his career with promoting Bacon. A natural question may arise, neatly completing a circle, as to how much Sylvester's own reputation as an important critic come to be based upon his promotion of Bacon.

13   The time may be approaching when a critical analysis of Bacon's thoughts needs to be undertaken, by a writer untainted by a wish to prove Bacon's great intellectual acuity. The way in which Sylvester prepared the interviews for publication and, for example, helped to write the famous Bacon preface to the Matthew Smith exhibition at the Tate in 1953, not to mention the long list of written interventions which Sylvester made into the debate about Bacon's status, raises an awkward thought. How many of the supposedly key themes of Bacon's thoughts were his own and how many were supplied to him or developed by him in conversation with Sylvester over many years?

14   Such an admission, while in a sense honest, destroys the status of these interviews as reliable documents. The historically minded reader might care to read chapter 9 of George Kitson Clark's *The Critical Historian* and then imagine what such an eminent historian would have made of this as evidence of anything. ('What is represented as direct speech often has a vividness and immediacy which creates a strong feeling that one is in the presence of the past re-enacting itself without the interference of any human agency. In fact the recording of speech probably presents more problems than any other form of evidence').

15   *Francis Bacon. L'art de l'impossible. Entretiens avec David Sylvester. Préface de Michel Leiris*, 1976.

16   *Francis Bacon in conversation with Michel Archimbaud.*

17   An interesting comparison to the clearly heavily-manipulated Sylvester 'interviews' can be made with the book *Conversations with Painters* by Noël Barber. He omits to explain exactly how he did his 'conversations', but the impression given is that they are transcripts of real conversations. This seems unlikely, in a strict sense, because whilst they do have a feeling of 'real' conversation, there must have been a lot of tidying up of the superfluous words which litter any conversation and which emerge in a genuine transcript. The more one looks at the fluidity of the answers, the more one also questions the apparent quick perspicacity of the artists in answering what were intended to be

fundamental questions on their work. Perhaps Barber submitted questions in advance and then they chatted through the answers which he then edited.

18   As in other areas, the farsightedness of the Leicester Galleries is also apparent in this area. I am unable to ascertain whether they followed a deliberate policy of helping Irish artists in the period covered by this book, but it is notable that Irish artists appeared with some regularity: examples include 'Living Irish Art' in 1946; Norah McGuinness in 1947; Le Brocquy in 1948; and Sine Mackinnon in 1949. The *Irish Times* recorded on 28 January 1946 that Cecil Phillips from the Leicester Galleries had been visiting Dublin and had taken back with him works by Maurice MacGonigal for showing in London.

19   The term 'British' will therefore be used as shorthand throughout this work to describe artists working in the British Isles at the time, wherever they were born or from originally. Irish, Welsh or Scottish readers should take no offence from this usage, in that I am seeking to emphasize the significance of the work of their artists and not to stigmatize it by use of the word 'British'.

20   It is also worth saying that the book focuses on painters. Sculptors will be mentioned in passing, but will not be treated as a separate category.

21   Where it is appropriate to do so, such as in the section about the development of artists' reputations, the limits of the book will stray beyond 1945-51, so as to avoid the artificial limitations which such dates inevitably produce.

CHAPTER 1

1   Attempts by historians to stick as closely as they can to the concept of centuries by writing of the 'long' 18th century or whatever are equally artificial.

2   I am immediately guilty of pre-judging my evidence in selecting this list. There is no reason for the reader at this stage to accept my list, although I should say, in my defence, that the names have not been chosen because their presence 'proves' any of the points which follow. I have, in fact, based it on my understanding of the artists most regularly selected for praise or some sort of attention during the period, but there is undoubtedly scope for sharp-eyed or partisan readers to make a claim for excluding some I include and vice-versa. One useful way for the combative reader to do this would be to start from the slightly later list of 145 names which appears in Chapter 7. These represent a very wide contemporary (in 1950-51) trawl through all the artists who could then possibly be regarded as significant. Another legitimate criticism will be that some of these artists, such as many of the younger ones, were of little significance in 1945, even if their significance had increased by 1951. In order to encourage the challenging reader, I would say that I hesitated before excluding the following: Armstrong, Buhler, Gotlib, Kramer, Medley, Pitchforth, Spear, Suddaby, Tibble, Topolski and Tunnard. Other omissions are some of the great figurative painters who were working through our period, such as Samuel Lamorna Birch, John Anthony Park, Stanley Roy Badmin and Ethelbert White, all of them regularly producing the most exquisite work of a traditional type.

3   The following were born in Scotland: Colquhoun, Davie, Gear, Gillies, Grant, MacBryde, MacTaggart, Scott. The following were born in Ireland, at a time when there was no political separation from England: Bacon, Campbell, Dillon, Hennessy, Henry, Le Brocquy, Luke, McGuinness, Middleton , O'Neill. The following were born in Wales: John, Morris, Richards, Williams. The following were not born in the British Isles: Adler, Ardizzone, Freud,

Herman, Hillier, Hodgkins, Lewis, Meninsky, Uhlman, Wolfe. This means that only the following 40 of the 74 were born in England: Aldridge, Ayrton, Bawden, Bomberg, Burra, Clough, Coldstream, Collins, Craxton, Eurich, Hennell, Hilton, Hitchens, Jones, Lanyon, Lowry, Minton, Moynihan, J. Nash, P. Nash, Nevinson, B. Nicholson, W. Nicholson, Pasmore, Piper, Roberts, Rothenstein, Rowntree, Smith, G. Spencer, S. Spencer, Sutherland, Trevelyan, Underwood, Vaughan, Wadsworth, Weight, Wilde, Wynter, Yeats.

4   An example of an artist whose reputation developed very largely outside London is Theodore Major, 1908-1999, who lived and worked chiefly in Lancashire: see *Vision Splendid. Theodore Major 1908-1999* by Mary Major and June Rose.

5   See *Ivon Hitchens* by Peter Khoroche.

6   For example, the Indian artist F.N. Souza arrived in August 1949.

7   Fuller attention to the way they chose to lead their lives in the second half of the 1940s will be given in Chapter 4.

8   In his case this had involved the horrors of prolonged Japanese imprisonment following capture at the fall of Singapore.

9   Rothenstein has them 'ejected' by their landlord in 1947 and Yorke simply picks this up and repeats it without attempting verification.

10   I am not sure what the connection was, although at some point Caroline Lucas had had a studio in the same block.

11   Unless, of course, history is having the last laugh and the handwritten letters addressed from 77 Bedford Gardens which survived were in fact misaddressed.

12   The scene has been well re-created by Frances Spalding in her biography of Minton, *Dance Till the Stars Come Down*, and what follows depends to some extent on her work.

13   In such pictures as *Church Lench* and *Tomato Plants*.

14   Henryk Gotlib (1890-1966) does not receive full consideration in this book and an argument could have been made for giving him greater prominence. He was a Pole who came to England shortly before the War and remained here and exhibited with some regularity. He was considered for '60 Paintings for '51', but not included.

15   Morris Kestelman (1905-98) could have featured more prominently in this study. He was born in London and studied at the Central School and at the RCA. From 1951-1971 he was Head of Fine Art at the Central.

16   He and Freud had had adjacent studios in a house at 14 Abercorn Place, St John's Wood, 1942-44 thanks to the generosity of Peter Watson in paying the rent.

17   See *Restless Lives. The Bohemian world of Rodrigo and Elinor Moynihan* by John Moynihan.

18   As an example of 'overlap', John Moynihan mentions that when his father socialised with Buhler in his studio, Bacon sometimes joined them. (It was Buhler, of course, who took over Bacon's studio in Cromwell Place in 1951.) It is worth noting that, even if their social lives were usually discrete, many of the artists mentioned in this book would have engaged with each other to some extent whilst teaching at the same art schools. For example, Moynihan's picture of the teaching staff at the RCA in 1949-1950 includes Minton – a real Soho man if ever there was one – as well as people who were socially closer to Moynihan such as Buhler and Spear. John Moynihan also notes that Minton was quite happy to socialise in Hammersmith with Spear and Moynihan when it suited him.

19   See *Bacon and Sutherland* by Martin Hammer.

20   Not as fashionable then as now!

21   He also at some stage met the rest of the gang mentioned

previously, but seems not to have become a regular part of the Soho circuit.

22   As Visiting Instructor, painting and mural design. He was to stay at the Central until 1954.

23   I am very grateful for help with Le Brocquy's chronology to his son Pierre, who has developed a detailed knowledge of his father's life and is also generous in co-operating with arcane enquiries. In addition, the Le Brocquy family maintains a detailed website about him and his work.

24   102 Abbey Road was itself later demolished, which has a certain symmetry. It was at the northerly end of the road, away from the studio and the pedestrian crossing made famous in the later '60s by the Beatles.

25   The financial challenge involved in finding somewhere to live in London will be dealt with in Chapter 4.

26   Readers unfamiliar with Luke might be interested to know that a picture of his sold at Christie's on 20 May 1999 for £441,000.

27   Reviewed in the *Belfast Telegraph* on 4 September 1946.

28   There is a rare reference to a gallery – the MacGaffin Gallery – in the *Belfast Telegraph* for 19 June 1946, showing five contemporary artists.

29   Of which the most significant was Zoltan Lewinter Frankl.

30   An example of how artists based in Belfast travelled South to access the selling opportunities available through Waddingtons can be seen in Nevill Johnson's autobiography, p. 49. Here he describes showing his work to Victor Waddington after the War and some flavour of the relief he felt at being accepted by the gallery comes through: 'On my knees I concluded my first deal. There was light in the tunnel and a chance of freedom.'

31   A good description of this bizarre experience is contained in *That Neutral Island* by Clair Wills.

32   See *Jack Yeats* by Bruce Arnold.

33   Ernie O'Malley was a figure of some notoriety in Irish society. After an early life spent fighting during the tribulations of Ireland in the first part of the century, he developed into a figure of some culture, writing on art and artists in a number of places. Not everyone was convinced of his cultural status and perhaps only in Ireland could O'Malley's characteristics have been combined in one man. He was, in any event, keen on Yeats and owned works by him, Le Brocquy, Evie Hone, Paul Henry and many others, leaving over 600 works of art to the Irish State in the 1970s. See *The Ernie O'Malley Story* by Padraic O'Farrell, 1983.

34   An extremely long review of the exhibition by C.P. Curran appeared in the 1945-46 volume of that most extraordinary of publications, the *Capuchin Annual*, which had been founded in 1930. This cost the high price of 10/6d in 1945-46 and ran to a stunning 512 pages. The rest of it consisted of stories and apparently random works, including rather splendid black-and white photographs. The following year's edition was 590 pages, but contained nothing on modern Irish art.

35   On 4 August 1945. Samuel Beckett as a commentator on modern artists would be an interesting study, if not already done. He was a close friend of Thomas MacGreevy, who became Director of the National Gallery of Ireland. When Bryan Robertson, as director of the Whitechapel, was looking around for someone to write the introduction to the catalogue for the retrospective exhibition of Colquhoun's work in 1958, he wrote to ask Beckett if he would do it. No reply exists in the relevant Whitechapel file and Robertson ended up doing it himself.

36   Although it is important to note that praise for Yeats outside Ireland was far from universal. The art critic of *Apollo*, who wrote under the pseudonym 'Perspex', said of Yeats's work at Wildenstein that he had 'taken to a crude (or should one say "bold"?) impasto of vivid colour applied largely with a palette knife' (March 1946). Reviewing the Tate show of Yeats on 20 August 1948 in the *Spectator*, M.H. Middleton was highly critical of Yeats's stature, comparing him unfavourably with Soutine and Kokoschka. And it is little surprise that Yeats did not meet with Heron's approval in the *New Statesman and Nation*. On 21 August 1948 he gave Yeats a severe mauling: 'Yeats is interesting not because he paints well but because he remains true to a setting which hardly permits painting at all. We must recognise that his colour is toneless and his design almost non-existent. We cannot pretend that he has more than a passing acquaintance with pictorial art.' He went on: 'What design or balance there is exists primarily, I believe, as a flat association of highly coloured smudges: to read into the smudges a subtle or profound spatial meaning is to my mind quite impossible.' It seems that Yeats was not inevitably well received in Scotland either. Commenting on 9 October 1946 on the work of Yeats which had been included in the annual show of the Society of Scottish Artists in Edinburgh, the *Scotsman's* critic said, 'They are not easy to assess, and judgment is not aided by rather facile claims that have been made for their importance.'

37   This is presumably *The Two Travellers*, painted in 1942 and purchased by the Tate in 1946.

38   See Bruce Arnold, op. cit., p. 335.

39   No purpose would be served in this study by attempting to analyse whether those seeking to identify or emphasise the Irishness of Irish art were doing so from 'political' or anti-English motives.

40   See the essay by Sighle Bhreathnach-Lynch called 'The formation of an Irish school of painting. Issues of national identity' in S.B. Kennedy's book on Paul Henry.

41   A prime example would be Paul Henry.

42   In *The Arts of Ulster. A Symposium*, 1951.

43   It is not clear why this was published. The short introduction stated that it was hoped that the book would 'stimulate interest in the development of art in Ireland and encourage artists and members of the public to attain to higher standards of achievement in artistic work and a more widespread appreciation of beauty'. This seems unlikely to have been the effect of the book, which was a dull accumulation of unconnected essays by different people on a wide variety of vaguely artistic subjects. In the area of painting, Mainie Jellett held forth on 'An approach to painting'; Sean Keating had a chapter called 'Reflections'; Rupert Strong wrote on Yeats; and the best contribution, as ever, came from James White on 'Independent Painters': a short review of some contemporary Irish artists. Here he picked up on the fact that many, apart from Yeats, were highly influenced by French painters, especially Cézanne. In Dublin, noting the surprisingly large number of women artists, he picked out Jellett, Kirkwood, Kelly, Reid, Wallace and Hanlon, together with Carr, Conor, McGuinness and Grace Henry from the North.

44   This contained a series of chapters on different subjects by different authors. For our purposes there was a relevant attempt to review the contemporary art scene in Ireland by James White. He focused on Yeats, Keating, Hanlon, Jellett, Connor, Kelly, Reid, Clarke and Grace Henry.

45   It is not worth stressing the point, but the reviewer may have been unaware that three of the five artists were from the North and Nevill Johnson was English. Only one

artist, Thurloe Conolly, was from Southern Ireland (Cork).

46   On 8 April, in an article on Louis le Brocquy.

47   1900-79. Attended the Dublin School of Art.

48   In his *Irish Art 1830-1990*.

49   There were presumably similarities between the attitude of parts of the Irish artistic community of the time towards the RHA and that of parts of the English artistic community towards the Royal Academy. It may be that, in seeking to liberate themselves from the RHA, those Irish artists who promoted the IELA were, consciously or unconsciously, mirroring the reaction of their English counterparts to the RA. Without wishing to suggest that the Irish artistic community was derivative of the English, there is no doubt that many of the Irish artists involved were familiar with artistic events and thinking in London. (So, for example, the creation of the Irish Arts Council no doubt had some background in its English equivalent. Bodkin's Report of 1949, mentioned later, had as one of its conclusions 'the development of an organisation exercising powers similar to those vested in the Arts Council in England'.) It is interesting to note that, whereas those English artists who were particularly hostile to the RA had no need to dabble with it by exhibiting their pictures there or seeking membership, the Irish artistic community was, by contrast, extremely small and many artists exhibited at the RHA and at the IELA. For the establishment of the IELA, see Riann Coulter's article 'A Hibernian Salon des Refusés' in the *Irish Arts Review*, vol. 20, no. 3 (Autumn 2003).

50   *Irish Art* contained a very interesting chapter by A.J. Leventhal on 'The Living Art Exhibition', in which the writer bemoaned the restriction to those of Irish birth: 'It seems a pity that any restriction should have been imposed on the nationality of the exhibitors. There was nothing particularly national among the exhibits; nothing that smacked either of insularity or of narrow regionalism… It is to be hoped that, in future, only merit and space consideration will provide the yardstick for works accepted in an art that, in its healthiest manifestations, has never recognised the boundaries of race or State.'

51   Colquhoun had *Irish Village People* and *The Actors* and MacBryde had *Card Game* and *Mexican Table and an Orange*.

52   I am extremely grateful for this information to Fiona Loughnane of the National College of Art and Design in Dublin.

53   See *A Hibernian Salon des Refusés* by Riann Coulter.

54   I have relied upon S.B. Kennedy's *The White Stag Group*.

55   For example, Stephen Gilbert was one artist whose work appeared from time to time and, as will be mentioned later in the section on the *Irish Times*, Arthur Power was to describe his work as bearing 'no relation to art'.

56   As with O'Malley it is perhaps only in Ireland that the leading cultural journal of the period could be edited by a former member of a terrorist organisation.

57   Cyril Connolly was the editor of *Horizon*, 1903-74. Educated at Eton and Balliol College, Oxford. His mother was from that great Anglo-Irish family, the Vernons, of Clontarf in County Dublin and Connolly, whose middle name was Vernon, may have had some ambivalent feeling towards Ireland as a result.

58   In vol. XIV, no. 79.

59   The well-known Ritchie Hendriks Gallery was not to open until 12 April 1956. Its founder, David Hendriks, born on 2 November 1924 in Jamaica, had first visited Dublin in August 1947, attending TCD in October 1950. Many famous Irish artists were to show with him in the

years following 1956, including Hennessy, Campbell and Armstrong. See G. Lambert and S. McCrum, *David Hendriks: Living with Art*, 1985.

60   My information is from the Hunt Museum's booklet on Jack Yeats for an exhibition held from 16 June-26 September 2004.

61   The account which follows is a necessary simplification of what was, inevitably, a more complicated process than here described. The political process tends not to move in a linear fashion and the attention of the reader who wishes to explore the intricacies of Irish politics in respect of the arts in the 1940s is drawn to chapter 4 of Brian Kennedy's excellent book *Dreams and Responsibilities. The State and the Arts in Independent Ireland*.

62   The appointment was announced by the Taoiseach in the Dáil on 20 July 1949. Bodkin was asked to examine and report upon: (a) the constitution and working of institutions concerned with the arts in Ireland, in particular the National Museum and the National Gallery; (b) facilities available in Ireland for education in the arts both from the historical and from the practical aspects, at elementary to professional levels, with particular reference to the teaching of art and art history in the schools, the universities, the National College of Art and the provincial art schools; (c) existing relations between the arts and industry in Ireland, including such activities as technical training in craftsmanship, the provision of industrial designs and of appropriate advertisements for tourist development, and upon the steps that might be taken to arouse the public interest and the interest of manufacturing industries in the importance of design in industry; (d) advisability of establishing an organisation or organisations for the purpose of encouraging and spreading a knowledge of the arts in Ireland and of Irish culture in foreign countries; (e) advisability of establishing an organisation or organisations concerned with the preservation and acquisition by the State of sites and buildings of national importance and with the maintenance of aesthetic amenities in future building projects; and (f) advisability or otherwise of extending such services as those referred to above and of co-ordinating their administration.

63   Other chapters were not relevant to this study.

64   For instance in the *Irish Press* on 7 December and in the *Leader* on 16 December.

65   When he was sent the draft Bill and offered the position as first Director of the Arts Council, he refused. His objections to the Bill were accommodated by Costello, and Bodkin might have been prepared to accept the job, but unfortunately for him Costello lost his job and with it went Bodkin's chances of being appointed.

66   1884-1963. Educated at University College, Dublin. He had been de Valera's Parlimentary Secretary from 1933-39 and later Minister of Posts and Telegraphs. He was a widely cultured man.

67   Having said that it is probably as well not to be too dogmatic about the relative artistic status of the two cities. As a cautionary note, see the *Sunday Times* for 26 June 1949. In reviewing two shows in Glasgow, the writer states that, in his view, Glasgow was the current centre of contemporary art in Scotland. Similarly, in a review in *Britain Today* in October 1945, Philip Hendy commented in passing that Glasgow was 'the one lively provincial art centre in modern Britain'. In contrast, by the time of the Arts Council show in 1963 called '20th Century Scottish Painting', Douglas Hall, the Keeper of the Scottish National Gallery of Modern Art, stated in the catalogue

that 'the focus in art has shifted from Glasgow to Edinburgh in this century.' One reason he gave for this was the pre-eminence in Scotland of the Edinburgh College of Art.

68 1904-79. A Scottish painter who had studied in Paris.

69 She trained at the Glasgow School of Art until 1943 and worked under James Cowie at Hospitalfield in 1946-47.

70 As with Irish writers on the Irishness of Irish art, it may sometimes be asked why Scottish writers think it necessary to identify Scottishness in their artists. Are their reasons entirely aesthetic?

71 1916-92. Born in Lancashire. Attended Edinburgh College of Art from 1936-40. Became Head of the School of Drawing and Painting in Edinburgh in 1960, until his retirement in 1982.

72 1882-1955. Painter. Studied at Glasgow School of Art.

73 He was to retain this position until 1960 when he became Principal.

74 1917-98. Born in Aberdeen of Italian parents.

75 1886-1956. Painter. Studied at Glasgow School of Art. Prior to Hospitalfield he had been Head of Painting at Aberdeen.

76 The President for at least part of our period was Alfred Borthwick. 1871-1955. He was English, but had studied at Edinburgh College of Art.

77 MacTaggart was appointed in 1948 to represent the Royal Scottish Academy on the Festival Council.

78 Under the section on the Glasgow Art Gallery.

79 He wrote on the RA on 2 May and on the RSA a week later.

80 Although he did allow himself to become President of the South Wales Art Society in 1946.

81 See Peter Lord, *The Visual Culture of Wales. Imaging the Nation*, 2000; Oliver Fairclough, *Things of Beauty: What Two Sisters did for Wales*, 2007; and Peter Lord, *Winifred Coombe Tennant. A Life through Art*, 2007.

82 A keeper at the V&A.

83 This exhibition was selected by Cedric Morris, Ceri Richards and David Baxandall.

84 The Welsh artist Kyffin Williams in *A Wider Sky* illustrates the preference of the art world to compartmentalise artists: 'The attitude of the world of art towards me and my work has been interesting, for art authorities have always looked upon me as the outsider that I am, or as a maverick on whom they have been unable to place a label.'

85 It is often difficult to divine what the user of the terms 'Romantic' or 'neo-Romantic' is comparing them with in the context of British art of the mid-century. Those using the critical apparatus developed with regard to pictures of previous centuries in the British art canon sometimes tried to suggest that an artist's work was 'Romantic' rather than 'Classical'. This does not seem to clarify a great deal in the context of the 1940s, when it might be said to be even harder to identify a 'Classical' artist than a 'Romantic' one.

86 And indeed as the writer of those strange works *In Parenthesis* and *Anathémata*.

87 Not to mention his writings on art and other subject. See Cecil Collins, *The Vision of the Fool and other writings*, edited by Brian Keeble. *The Vision of the Fool* was originally published in 1947.

88 Yorke's book on neo-Romantics, *The Spirit of Place. Nine Neo-Romantics and Their Times*, has chapters on Paul Nash, Piper, Sutherland, Minton, Ayrton, Colquhoun, Vaughan, Clough and Craxton. In my view, Colquhoun, Vaughan and Clough are absurdities in this context, as is a failure to include Jones and Collins. Another possible candidate would have been Leslie Hurry.

89 This exhibition followed one at The National Museum of Wales in 1983, called 'The British Neo-Romantics 1935-1950', with catalogue by Peter Cannon-Brookes.

90 Dealers were not necessarily keen on it either, partly because there was very little market for it. Lilian Browse, one of the founders in 1945 of Roland, Browse and Delbanco, writing in her autobiography on her views on abstract art and the influence of American artists in England during the 1950s: 'For the very first time America took the lead in the development of Western pictorial art whose non-objective form had, many years earlier, already been pioneered by Kandinsky. This esoteric movement, which swept all before it in the country that was the first to accept it widely, shattered the concept of traditional standards, thus opening the flood gates to the stream of indulgence that has informed the succeeding "isms".' On the other hand, the impression should not be given that abstract art was condemned by all commentators. Anthony Bertram in *A Century of British Painting 1851-1951* (1951) went out of his way to say that those seeking to understand contemporary art simply had to make the extra effort required to get to grips with abstract art. He was not thereby saying that abstract art was, in itself, good but that it could not be dismissed as irrelevant simply because it was abstract. There was good and bad abstract art, just as there was with representational art.

91 The chronology of Lewis's knowledge of art has to be remembered. 10 May 1951 was the date of his famous final *Listener* article called 'The Sea-Mists of the Winter'. He recorded how his sight had become poor by 1949, declined steadily through 1950 and had by early 1951 reached the point where, as his article concluded, 'My articles on contemporary art exhibitions necessarily end, for I can no longer see a picture.'

92 *Francis Bacon in conversation with Michel Archimbaud*, taken from p. 145 of the 1999 reprint.

93 Gear's work was extensively teased in the *Daily Telegraph*, as will be seen later in this book.

94 I am heavily indebted here to Alastair Grieve's *Constructed Abstract Art in England*.

95 *Ben Nicholson* by Norbert Lynton.

96 1902-72. Educated at Rugby and Magdalen College, Oxford. Stokes is an interesting figure whose significance is difficult to pin down. He was a painter, but is now better known for his unusual works of art criticism, particularly *Stones of Rimini* of 1934 and *Colour and Form* of 1937. He had studied at the Euston Road School.

97 Barns-Graham had been born and brought up in Scotland and had studied at the Edinburgh College of Art 1931-37. She knew various other Scottish artists of the period, including William Gear and the ubiquitous Roberts.

98 The best way to see works from this area now is to visit the Fry Art Gallery in Saffron Walden in Essex. For an account of the growth of the area's artistic connections, see *The Inward Laugh. Edward Bawden and his circle* by Malcolm Yorke.

99 Younger brother of John Rothenstein.

100 A village in Essex to the north-east of Great Bardfield.

101 Ayrton's grave is in the churchyard at Hadstock in north Essex, near the border with Cambridgeshire. His tombstone, which is to the left of the path leading to the church, bears a representation in bronze of a maze.

102 See Bruce Laughton, *The Euston Road School*.

CHAPTER 2

1   Others showed modern British artists occasionally. For instance, Wildenstein showed Lowinsky in 1949.

2   He completed his memoirs, called *Exhibition*, shortly before his death in 1966. By the time they were published in 1968 they were able to include the address given by Kenneth Clark at Brown's memorial service, which had been held at St Martin-in-the-Fields on 27 January 1967, in which he praised Brown's many gifts, both as regards artists and collectors.

3   For details of shows I have relied upon the website ernestbrownandphillips.ltd.uk.

4   1901-96. A sadly under-studied Irish artist. Born in Newcastle, Co Down, she was a pupil of Tonks at the Slade and lived and worked in France for a long time, many of her works being French landscapes. The fact that she exhibited, as we have seen, at the Leicester and the Lefevre, as well as at Goupil, Tooth's, the Redfern and the Fine Arts Society, indicates that her reputation was once a lot higher than it is now. She has not even been able to benefit from the relentless rise in stature of various Irish artists, because she perhaps falls into a category of deemed non-Irishness, being not only from the North, but also working mostly abroad.

5   1901-80. Painter born in Londonderry. Attended the Dublin Metropolitan School of Art. Later studied in Paris. Founder member of the IELA in 1943 and became its President in 1944. Chosen in 1950 to represent Ireland at the Venice Biennale, with Nano Reid. Exhibited widely and successfully.

6   I have relied here upon Douglas Cooper's book published to celebrate Lefevre's first 50 years, *Alex Reid and Lefevre 1926-1976*. Alex Reid's had been a long-established Glasgow based art dealer. Lefevre had been in King Street since 1871.

7   1910-99. Another artist who may merit more attention. Her work occasionally appears at auction and is always charming. She studied at Brighton Art School, the Royal Academy Schools and at the Slade, but her exhibiting history is not extensive.

8   When a gallery like the Redfern held something like a summer show, it may well have covered a lot of British artists. In 1951, for example, their summer show included Nash, Scott, Bell, Jones, Adler, Ayrton, Gertler, Colquhoun, Vaughan, Wilde, Agar, Wood, Yeats, Grant, Gear, Piper, Spencer, Jones, Minton and Lewis.

9   The Mayor Gallery held a loan exhibition in memory of Freddie Mayor (1903-73) shortly after his death, in late 1973. This included Bacon's *Crucifixion* of 1933 (lent by the trustees of Sir Colin and Lady Anderson) which is the picture which had been reproduced in Herbert Read's book *Art Now* and which had originally been bought by Sir Michael Sadler from the Mayor Gallery.

10   The *Times* reported its opening on 3 December.

11   Born 1928. Educated at Eton. Became 11th Duke of Beaufort in 1984.

12   1926-2007. Educated at Stowe. Worked in the London Gallery. Jazz Musician. In his book *Don't Tell Sybil. An Intimate Memoir of ELT Mesens*.

13   The premises had at one time been those of the Mayor Gallery. The gallery closed in July 1977 and

14   reopened three months later as Browse & Darby. A new gallery was opened in March 1947 and its first show, of the School of London, received a large review in the *Irish Times* on 28 March.

15   See Brian Fallon, *An Age of Innocence. Irish Culture 1930-1960*, p. 242.

16   The only other significant Dublin gallery at this time was the Dawson Gallery, which was founded by Leo Smith in 1944.

17   I have relied for my information on this gallery on a publication called *150 Years of Aitken Dott, the Scottish Gallery*.

18   Duncan Grant seems a slightly curious choice here. It may be relevant that he had been the lover of Lord Keynes, who was to become chairman of CEMA in 1942. On the other hand, it may simply have been yet another example of Clark's great influence, as he was friendly with Grant at this time.

19   1899-1989.

20   In Chapter 3.

21   The minutes do not make it clear whether he was there as a member or as a visitor.

22   She was at this time member for Hendon North. She had been Chairman of the Labour Party in 1939/1940. She was a member of the Arts Council and also a member of the executive committee of the British Council. She was the mother of Michael Ayrton.

23   Reference EL5/1.

24   Reference EL 2/13.

25   His letter offering him the position was dated 15 December 1947.

26   All the details which follow have been taken from the Arts Council illustrated catalogue published in 1979.

27   The minutes of the Committee are available at the National Archive Centre in Kew under references BW 78/1 and BW 78/2.

28   The focus on children's paintings seems to have been something of an obsession of the Committee at this time. Presumably this reflected some current fad.

29   Under reference TGA 8812.1.1.17.

30   The show was at 28 Avenue des Champs Elysées. The introduction to the catalogue was by Hendy and had been translated into French from an article which had previously appeared in *Britain Today*.

31   Bawden, Colquhoun, Hodgkins, Jones, Moore, Paul Nash, Piper, Sutherland and Tunnard.

32   This show was held at the Musée du Jeu de Paume and the catalogue had the appearance of an official Tate Gallery catalogue, with an introduction by the Director John Rothenstein. The artists included were Appelbee, Armstrong, Bawden, Burra, Connard, Dunbar, Gertler, Gilman, Ginner, Gore, Gowing, Grant, Gross, Gwynne-Jones, Hillier, Hitchens, Hodgkins, Innes, A. John, G. John, Jones, Lamb, Lees, Lewis, McEvoy, Moore, Murray, P. Nash, J. Nash, Ben Nicholson, Sir W. Nicholson, Orpen, Pasmore, Piper, Pissarro, Pryde, Ravilious, A. Richards, C. Richards, Roberts, W. Rothenstein, Rutherston, Sickert, Sims, Smith, Spencer, Steer, Sutherland, Tonks, Tunnard, Wadsworth, Walker and Wood.

33   The catalogue explained that the late Lord Wakefield had left £3,000 to the British Council for the purchase of contemporary British watercolours, drawings and prints. 223 items were shown and the

foreword to the catalogue was by James Laver.
Viscount Wakefield, 1859-1941, was educated at the
Liverpool Institute. He was the first and last viscount
and had been the founder of Castrol.

34 In Paris this was held at the Galerie Drouin and
included work by Sutherland, Ben Nicholson, Freud
and Le Brocquy. It was reviewed by Guy Dornand in
Franc Tireur on 25 January under the heading 'La
Jeune Peinture Britannique' and a review appeared in
Rayonnement des Beaux-Arts on 15 February as 'La
jeune peinture Anglaise'.

35 Some support for Philip James's position comes from
Oliver Brown of the Leicester Galleries. In his
memoirs, when commenting on the effect of the War
on the London art scene, he says: 'We noticed,
however, what had surprised us at the beginning of
the 1914 war – the eagerness of the public to look at
works of art in wartime.' This statement, however,
perhaps only supports the notion that the War itself
generated increased interest in art; it doesn't imply
that there was a generally increasing interest in art
amongst the public in any event.

36 It is also, of course, interesting to compare his
statement, which appears to take us back to
1938/1939, with the statement which initially
appears so similar by Sir John Rothenstein, quoted in
the Introduction, which seems to identify something
similar, but dates it quite differently to the end of the
War and to the effect of the War.

37 There were 83 items shown and the introduction to
the catalogue was written by Colin Macinnes.

38 For some reason here given her married name, but
usually referred to as Lilian Somerville, director of
fine art of the British Council.

39 He was a replacement for Hendy, who had originally
been asked.

40 1917-91. Educated at Uppingham and Exeter
College, Oxford. Editor of *Apollo* 1962-87.

41 Minuted on 13 February 1951.

42 According to James King, *The Last Modern. A Life of
Herbert Read*, p. 231, the Coldstream and Gowing
pictures were bought by Bell without consulting
Read.

43 Presumably there was some concern being expressed
as to how many more Pasmores they needed.

44 Another, smaller-scale, activity was the organising of
visits for members to see private collections of
pictures which were not normally open to the public.
The Committee minutes mention a number of these.
There was, for example, a visit in 1948 to see the
extraordinary collection of modern art owned by
Roland Penrose and displayed at 36 Downshire Hill
in Hampstead. There were so many pictures that a
number of them had to be displayed in the garden.
Another relevant example, although outside our
period, was to be the visit to see Colin Anderson's
collection at his house (also in Hampstead) in 1956.
This obviously followed an earlier visit, because
Anderson's name was in a list of the collections
which had been visited which was contained in a
flyer inserted into the catalogue for the Private
Collector exhibition at the Tate in 1950. Other
collections mentioned at that time were those of
Clark, Lord Radcliffe, Mrs Cazalet-Keir, Hugo
Pitman, Miss Ethel Sands and Edward le Bas.

45 The CAS papers for this period are in the Tate
Archive.

46 A letter to him from Robin Ironside, dated 19
February 1940 in the Tate Archive makes it clear
that Clark had also been a buyer. Ironside wrote
saying he wished Clark could have had more money
available to him as buyer.

47 It need hardly be said that Clark's views were
sometimes strongly adverse as well as positive. So, for
example, on 7 May 1946 the Committee had an
opportunity to consider whether or not to accept a
gift of three pictures by John Melville who is even
now regarded as an obscure and not very successful
Birmingham-based artist (1902-86) whose surrealist
style was never widely appreciated. He was the
brother of Robert Melville. The CAS had already had
another picture by this artist, given to them and
accepted previously. Faced with viewing all four at the
same time, the minute-taker could not resist the
opportunity to quote Clark as saying 'that from the 4
pictures they had before them it was clear that the
artist was a bad one in 4 different styles'. The
proposed gifts were then rejected and one can
imagine the chortling around the boardroom table.

48 Born 1912. She was a specialist in collages, although
never particularly successful. Perhaps an odd choice
among some of the other names mentioned, but
hindsight is always easy.

49 1913-1979. To me as obscure as Margaret Kaye, but
in fact his entry in Buckman suggests that his
pedigree was not bad. He studied at Chelsea School
of Art and at the Slade and then went back to teach
at Chelsea from 1936-62. From 1963-78 he headed
the RCA's illustration department.

50 'E. Box' was the pseudonym for a lady artist called
Eden Fleming (1919-88). Having trained at the
Regent Street Polytechnic School of Art, her work is
described as being in a style reminiscent of the
Douanier Rousseau.

51 On 27 September.

52 See Robert Radford, *Art for a purpose*, p. 6.

53 1907-92. Editor of the *Architectural Review* 1947-71.
Author of various books, including *An Introduction to
Modern Architecture*.

54 He resigned in October 1946.

55 1920-2000. Educated at Highgate and Trinity
College, Cambridge. Usually known as the author of
the series of books which began with *The Joy of Sex*,
he also wrote such works as a collection of essays *Art
and Social Responsibility*, 1947.

56 1893-1959. Advertising executive who
commissioned British artists.

57 Consisting of 101 paintings, 25 sculptures and 1
tapestry.

58 1921-96. Stepson of Hoellering. Born in Berlin.

59 Partition in 1921 caused the arrangements to be split,
so that some of the money spent went on pictures for
the South and some for the North.

60 There seems, in this sense, to have been some
similarity of purpose with the CAS in the UK.

61 Another Yeats, *While Grass Grows*, was bought by the
Trust in 1937 and was presented to the Waterford
Municipal Art Gallery.

62 Geoff Hassell in *Camberwell School of Arts & Crafts, its
students and teachers 1943-1960* says that by the end of
the 1940s the School had over 1600 students on its
registers.

63 He had been Principal since 1938.

64 1883-1954. Arrived in England in 1934 and opened

a School of Contemporary Painting with the Australian artist, Roy de Maistre. Held first one-man show in England at the Lefevre Gallery in 1939 and later shared a studio with Herman.

65   Which, of course, did not meet with the approval of Thomas Bodkin. The *Times* published a letter from him on 1 June 1946, just after the committee's report was published, complaining that the members of the committee were all connected with the bodies being reviewed.

66   The joint secretaries were William Gibson and Robin Ironside.

67   Command Paper 6827. Many of its recommendations followed those of the Curzon Committee of 1913.

68   One wonders whether the split between Tate Britain and Tate Modern has belatedly adopted this recommendation.

69   Although the Tate's collection was evacuated from London during the War, that did not mean that pictures were not being acquired, by various means. For example, an exhibition called 'The Tate Gallery's Wartime Acquisitions', was held at the National Gallery from April to May 1942. The catalogue introduction by Jasper Ridley, chairman of the Tate trustees, began by stating, 'The period since the outbreak of war has been, so far as acquisitions are concerned, one of the most active in the history of the Gallery.' The exhibition showed work by various living British artists, including Appelbee, Armstrong, Bawden, Burra, Grant, Hitchens, Hodgkins, A. John, Jones, Le Bas, Mackinnon, J. Nash, P. Nash, B. Nicholson, Pasmore, Piper, Pitchforth, Ravilious, Smith, S. Spencer and Sutherland. Others were listed at the end (not exhibited) in the four different ways in which pictures accrued to the gallery: by gift, bequest, purchase and Chantrey purchase.

70   Particularly, it seems, while Rothenstein was director of the Tate and Munnings was President of the Royal Academy.

71   Until 1922 the Tate had had no involvement in the selection of the pictures. Controversy about this had been investigated by the Curzon Committee, which had reported in 1913 that it found the administration of the bequest unsatisfactory and had described the whole situation as 'absurd and indefensible'.

72   An example of the way the Chantrey money was being used in our period was recorded in the Times on 17 December 1945 when it noted that a work by Millais dating from 1872 had been bought and would be 'handed' to the Tate. Another glimpse of contemporary attitudes to the use of the Chantrey money was seen in the *Listener* on 21 June 1945, when John Russell commented in passing that the Chantrey Bequest had often in the past been 'the sponsor of deplorable monsters'.

73   In a large article in the *Times* on 21 July 1947 on the Tate's first 50 years, Rothenstein took the opportunity to have a little swipe at the way the Chantrey money was being spent.

74   M.H. Middleton in the *Spectator* on 14 January 1949 said that 'out of the entire Chantrey Collection I would say that perhaps 25 paintings, drawings and sculpture… have earned a place in our national collection'.

75   The anonymous writer in the March 1949 issue of

the *Burlington Magazine* wrote a balanced piece in which he took a similar position. While not going so far as to approve of the choices made by the RA, he said that it had to be acknowledged that the RA had tried to honour Chantrey's wishes.

76   It is not the purpose of this book to seek to assess the allegations made against the RA, but some degree of caution may be necessary before accepting the criticism at its face value. It is one purpose of this study to indicate the complex nature of taste and the subtle process of creating and losing reputations in the British art world of the 20th century. Whilst not having any evidence to check whether or not the Chantrey money had been 'wisely' spent, it is essential to remember the widespread hatred of Victorian pictures which gripped parts of the British art world for large stretches of the 20th century and which may or may not turn out to be 'justified' as time passes. Similarly, whatever the Chantrey Bequest had been used on in the first half of the century, it is at least possible that we would view the 'quality' of the pictures bought differently now from when they were viewed in 1949. (We might, of course, find them even less satisfactory.) It is also necessary to note that, even at the time, some reviewers were quite taken with the work on show. Nevile Wallis, who is usually regarded as a serious and sensible newspaper critic, writing in the *Observer* on 9 January, said that the collection was 'a distinguished anthology of modern Academic realism and Impressionism'. There is nothing to indicate that he was being sarcastic. With an eye on 'fairness', it may also be worth comparing pictures bought with the Chantrey Bequest to those later purchased by the Arts Council, for example. Once that strayed away from the recognised artists of the 1940s and 1950s, it got into areas where it will be fascinating to see how history judges its purchases. From the 1979 catalogue of its then entire collection, one finds, for example, a barely credible total of 13 works by Stephen Buckley. To this writer, these are works of little or no importance, a good example being *Untitled Drawing H* of 1972, described rather tantalisingly as being made from paper, graphite, shoe polish, tile polish, staples and thread on paper. Can the Chantrey pictures be worse than that?

77   One reason may have been that the *Times* letter columns were in the middle of a seemingly interminable series of letters about 'ecclesiastical art'.

78   *High Relief.*

79   In vol. 3 of his autobiography *Time's Thievish Progress* Rothenstein makes a point of saying (p. 47) that relations between the Tate and the National Gallery were never 'flawed by the smallest disharmony' while Kenneth Clark was Director of the National Gallery.

80   Henry Moore was already a trustee by this time, having been appointed in 1941. In addition, the trustees included at various times in our period Sir Muirhead Bone, Allan Gwynne-Jones, Henry Lamb and Charles Wheeler, who were all practising artists.

81   It moved on to the Art Gallery in Glasgow in January 1946 and then on to Manchester. It also had a great impact in Scotland and the response to it will be covered later.

82   1889-1956. Educated at Eton and Magdalen College, Oxford. Son of 9th Duke of Marlborough.

83   1884-1964. First baron. Educated at Harrow and

Trinity College, Cambridge.

84 1890-1954. Educated at Winchester and Balliol College Oxford. Youngest son of the former Prime Minister and regarded as a man of considerable intellectual stature. Became a Court of Appeal judge, and was made Lord Asquith of Bishopstone in 1951.

85 Scrutton will appear again in his guise as the selector of one of the 'Anthologies' in 1951. See Chapter 7.

86 Even earlier, it was clear that the gallery was far from averse to showing modern British art. In 1942 it had held an exhibition called 'British Painting Today', with works by Williams, Ben Nicholson, Moynihan, Hitchens, Jones and Medley; in 1939 it had shown pictures from the Artists International Association (including Gill, John, Moore and P. Nash); and in 1937 works bought by the CAS by P. Nash, Bell, Roberts and Meninsky.

87 His extensive art criticism in *Britain Today* will be noted later.

88 It had been hit by a total of 8 bombs and had suffered water damage.

89 Although it would be interesting to know which artists never sent works in.

90 According to his biographer, Jean Goodman, he was particularly sharp on the Arts Council, the Tate and, slightly incongruously, Anthony Blunt.

91 In view of the trouble which John Rothenstein had at the Tate during this period in fighting off the attentions of the National Gallery in London, it is interesting to observe the little spat which developed in 1948 between him and Furlong, when he asked for and got the return of the four works by Turner which had been out on loan to the Irish National Gallery since 1884. Rothenstein complained when he got his hands on them that the pictures were in very bad condition.

92 The curious reader might like to try *Hugh Lane 1875-1915* by Robert O'Byrne. Chapter 18, ominously entitled 'The contested gift', gives a brief overview of the dispute which rumbles on between Dublin and London to this day.

93 It became the Ulster Museum in 1962. The catalogue of its drawings, paintings and sculpture has been published under the editorship of Eileen Black.

94 It certainly has a particularly large collection of works by Luke and Middleton, no doubt reflecting the preferences of John Hewitt.

95 Many works in the catalogue are listed as having been bequeathed to the Ulster Museum by Patricia and John Hewitt in 1987.

96 1872-1955. Since he was 75 by the time of his solo exhibition, he was hardly a young artist. He had been the art teacher at the Royal Belfast Academical Institution for 44 years until his retirement in 1945 and was active in many aspects of Ulster art for many years.

97 1874-1964. Another artist hardly in his first flush of youth by the time of his 1947 solo show, he was a sculptor who had been born in England. The major work of his career, and the original reason for his move to Belfast, had been a commission in 1925 to work on St Anne's Cathedral there. He was one of the 11 artists taking part in the Contemporary Ulster Art exhibition held as part of the Festival in 1951.

98 1867-1953. Even older than the others when he got his solo show (82), he was basically a businessman who painted as a hobby. One may wonder why he got

such attention.

99 1897-1989. A landscape painter born in England and trained at the Dublin School of Art. She was also one of the artists in Contemporary Ulster Art in 1951. She was an early teacher of William Scott.

100 1874-1964. He was a sculptor born in England.

101 1887-1976. He was a painter and printmaker, who had studied at Edinburgh College of Art. His book about the artist S.J. Peploe was published in 1947.

102 One on 5 February, two on 6, four on 8, and one each on 9, 13, 14 and 15 February.

Chapter 3

1 There were, of course, some important British collectors alive at this period, but they were not notably collectors of contemporary art. The most significant was Samuel Courtauld, whose great focus was on Impressionist art. He was at various times a trustee of the Tate and of the National Gallery. His role as collector is described in *Impressionism for England. Samuel Courtauld as Patron and Collector* by John House. There were also collectors who particularly supported one artist, such as J.L. Behrend (1881-1972), whose support for Stanley Spencer was spread over many years and included the commission to decorate the Chapel at Burghclere.

2 An interesting question would be how many collectors in the British Isles during our period focused on contemporary art at all, compared to art from earlier periods. In addition, if they bought contemporary art, was it British? Wilfrid Evill will be noted later as an example of a collector who survived both tests, in that he bought only contemporary British art. Peter Meyer was another collector who certainly bought important examples of contemporary British art during our period and works of this type from his collection by Vaughan, Sutherland, Freud, Clough, Moore, Scott, Ben Nicholson and Hitchens were sold at Christie's, London, on 6 June 2008.

3 The Revd Walter Hussey (1909-85) was another patron, although largely operating as such outside our period. He was the Vicar of St Matthew's, Northampton, 1938-55. While there he commissioned music from Britten and Tippett, sculpture from Moore and a picture by Sutherland. It is thought that this enlightened attitude to church patronage encouraged the creation of the atmosphere which led to the form of the patronage for the interior of Coventry Cathedral in the 1950s. Later, outside the scope of this study, Hussey moved on to become Dean of Chichester Cathedral. There he was to commission a set of copes designed by Ceri Richards, an altar frontal by Cecil Collins, an altar tapestry from Piper, a stained-glass window from Chagall and music by Bernstein and Walton. His archive of personal papers (see *The Dean Hussey Papers – a catalogue*, ed. J. Golden and T. McCann, Chichester 1997), lists 43 letters from Moore to him, during the period 1942-49, and 51 from Sutherland, 1944-78.

4 According to Clare Hopkins, the extremely helpful archivist at Trinity, the staircase was no. 4, in the (Victorian) Jackson Building, in the Front Quadrangle. Clark had moved in there when he arrived in October 1922 and had stayed on there in his second year.

5 Although a letter from Anderson to Clark now in the Tate Archives (Ref. 8812.1.3.51-100), written on 8 January 1980 when both Anderson and Clark were being pressed by Clark's biographer, Meryle Secrest, to answer enquiries about the distant past, states that Anderson did not regard

himself as one of Clark's 'intimates' at Oxford.

6   1905-58. Christ Church, Oxford. Achieved little before committing suicide. Thought by some to have inspired the character of Ambrose Silk in Waugh's *Put Out More Flags*; and some aspects of him were incorporated into Anthony Blanche in *Brideshead Revisited*.

7   1905-74. Magdalen College, Oxford. Became a very distinguished novelist under the name Henry Green, completing his first novel, *Blindness*, while an undergraduate. Later became something of a recluse.

8   Harold Acton. 1904-94. Christ Church, Oxford. Wrote a wide variety of works and perhaps best known for *Memoirs of an Aesthete* and *More Memoirs of an Aesthete*. Also inherited a celebrated villa outside Florence called La Pietra. His younger brother, William, 1906-45 (Christ Church, Oxford), became an artist.

9   1905-41. Merton College, Oxford. Travelled extensively and became an expert on Byzantium. His best-known book was *The Road to Oxiana*, a study of Islamic architecture. Lost at sea during the War.

10   1904-76. King's College, Cambridge. Became an art historian, art critic of the *Times*, trustee of the National Gallery and Slade Professor of Fine Art at Cambridge. He was to be one of the three judges for '60 Paintings for '51'. His father, Arthur Clutton-Brock, had also been art critic of the *Times* and was one of the founders of the Contemporary Art Society.

11   1904-36. Pembroke College, Oxford. Second son of Earl Beauchamp. His main claim to fame was that he became a close friend of Evelyn Waugh at Oxford.

12   1905-2000. Balliol College, Oxford. Became a famous writer (*A Dance to the Music of Time*).

13   He had been reading History, like Clark. Clark got a second.

14   See V. Sekules, 'The ship-owner as art patron: Sir Colin Anderson and the Orient Line 1930-1960', *Journal of the Decorative Arts Society*, 10 (1986), pp. 22-33. Also Colin Anderson's own article on the subject in the *Architectural Review* for June 1967.

15   Works were also sometimes bought for the ships, rather than being commissioned for them. For example, a picture by Craxton was bought for the *Oriana*.

16   Interestingly, it is thought that Sutherland introduced both Anderson and Kenneth Clark to Francis Bacon, in about 1943/1944.

17   In *Graham Sutherland, a Biography* by Roger Berthoud, 1982, the author notes that in a fair copy of this letter, found among Sutherland's papers, the letter opens with 'Dear Peter'. Berthoud surmises that this indicates that the letter was written in fact to Peter Watson, but that Watson distanced himself from it, as art editor of the magazine in which it was to be published, by suggesting the change to 'Dear Colin'.

18   See Mel Gooding, *Ceri Richards*, 2002.

19   Dylan Thomas was at the party.

20   Where they were able to live off the generosity of two sisters, Caroline Lucas (who had at one time had a studio at 77 Bedford Gardens) and Frances Byng Stamper. Their curious story (and their own standing as patrons) is told in *The Ladies of Miller's* by Diana Crook. It has not been possible to track down any letters which the Roberts may have sent to the sisters begging from them, but in Anderson's collection of letters is one from October 1954. Anderson had written to MacBryde complaining about the Roberts' lifestyle and, for some reason, he copied his letter to Mrs Byng Stamper. She replied noting that she had also just had a letter from MacBryde 'on the usual lines'. It doesn't take too much imagination to assume she meant he had asked for money.

21   The full list of gifts which appear from the letters surviving in the Anderson family is as follows:

Date	Amount
July 1948	£125
September 1948	£120
January 1949	£30
April 1949	£20
March 1950	£50
May 1950	£150
February 1954	£100
June 1954	£50
May 1955	£10
August 1955	£25
January 1956	£30
January 1956	£30
July 1957	£10
February 1958	£10
Total	**£770**

22   For the full text of these letters see my article in *The British Art Journal*, VIII, 1 (Summer 2007).

23   Muriel Belcher has gone down in Soho legend as the founder of the Colony Room. She used Bacon as a person who could attract custom to the club and, it has often been said, she gave him free drinks. Clearly, judging by this bill, not everything was free.

24   The reader may be interested to know that in 1952 Francis Bacon was wearing a dark grey worsted bird's eye double breasted jacket and two pairs of trousers, made to measure, at £36 with £9 purchase tax, together with a dark grey worsted flannel double breasted jacket and two pairs of trousers at the same price.

25   This was *Figure Study II*, bought in 1946.

26   I assume 1952 because Anderson's reply is dated January 1952. Freud's letters to Anderson are undated.

27   As is clear from letters from him in the Anderson family archive, Victor Willing also sought help from Colin Anderson, both in the form of loans and asking him to buy his pictures.

28   In the Tate Archive file 8 812.1.3.51-100.

29   According to information kindly supplied by Michael Riordan from St John's, Watson came up in 1927 to read Modern Languages, but only stayed a year.

30   Peter Watson's father, Sir William George Watson, died on 12 July 1930. He had been made a baronet in 1912 and Peter Watson, who was his second son, had been brought up, from 1910, in very considerable luxury at Sulhamstead House in Sulhamstead Abbotts in Berkshire. His brother, Sir Norman Watson, the 2nd baronet, lived until 1983 and the baronetcy became extinct on his death. The exact extent of Peter Watson's wealth is impossible to establish. At his death the grant of probate, dated 13 July 1956, recorded the gross value of his estate as being just over £121,000, and that estate duty of £79,000 had been paid. It is not clear if this figure had been deducted from the total to leave £121,000 or was deducted from it. Interestingly, it is clear from Peter Watson's father's will that something had happened, in financial terms, between father and son before the father's death in 1930. The father's will, made just before his death, contains the following statement in paragraph 12: 'I desire to place it on record that my only reason for not bequeathing any legacy or making any gift of residue to my younger son, Victor William Watson, is because he is already

adequately provided for by me.' The gross value of the father's estate was just over £2 million. Watson's mother died in 1942 and maybe further money came to him then.

31 This was an important modern architectural landmark. The block was designed by Wells Coates and had only been completed in 1939.

32 André Malraux lived at the same address at some point, as did Maurice Couve de Murville, who briefly became French Prime Minister. Another inhabitant was the French poet Olivier Larronde (1927-65), whose book *Les barricades mysterieuses* was published in 1946. The building encloses a courtyard accessed from the street entrance. Watson's flat was at the back on the first floor, according to information supplied by John Craxton to the author on 21 May 2007.

33 This according to Clive Fisher in *Cyril Connolly, a nostalgic life* (1995), p. 185.

34 Although it seems fair to say that he became more serious, it would also be misleading to suggest that the hedonism departed completely. Michael Wishart in his autobiography, *High Diver*, (1977), describes a party given by Watson at the flat in the rue du Bac after the War, which could not be described as puritanical.

35 It is clear that acquaintance with the Roberts brought with it terrible financial dangers. In February 1956, Anderson mentions in a letter that he has just seen John Minton, who had obviously just given them some money which he claimed he could ill afford. In 1955, when the Roberts finally left Tilty Mill, near Dunmow in Essex, a house rented by the author Elizabeth Smart, it was said that she paid their outstanding bill at the local pub and that it ran into four figures.

36 It seems that they met each other in Scotland in 1940 when Connolly and Watson were there on *Horizon* business. The meeting may well have just been with MacBryde at that time, as Colquhoun was away doing military service. It is likely that Watson invited them to London in the first place.

37 In the Tate Archive.

38 Minton and Vaughan later shared a house together in Hamilton Terrace in St John's Wood after Minton, who at the time was sharing the studio in Bedford Gardens with the Roberts, fell out with them.

39 According to John Craxton, Watson declined to advance Sutherland the £2,500 he needed in 1945 to buy The White House at Trottiscliffe in Kent. Instead, the money was lent to Sutherland by Kenneth Clark and, unlike other 'loans' made by people to some artists at this time, was eventually repaid.

40 Watson had bought this in 1940 at Sutherland's second one-man show, at the Leicester Galleries in London.

41 According to Roland Penrose in his *Scrap Book 1900-1981*.

42 After his death, the *Times* reported on 17 October 1956 that the ICA had arranged a concert at the Wigmore Hall at which three of Watson's favourite pieces of music were performed. Indicating his avant-garde taste, the composers were Bartok, Schoenberg and Stravinsky.

43 The way in which Watson supported *Horizon* is apparent from two books, in particular: *Friends of Promise* by Michael Shelden, 1989, and *The Girl from the Fiction Department, a Portrait of Sonia Orwell* by Hilary Spurling, 2002. An article by Michael Shelden about Peter Watson also appeared in *The Independent* magazine on 4 February 1989. Another contribution from Watson was in the special publication produced by *Horizon* in French in 1945, especially for circulation in newly liberated France, called *La Littérature anglaise depuis la guerre*. Despite its title, this contained an article by Watson, 'Note sur deux peintres anglais', in which he wrote about Sutherland and Craxton.

44 For example, the Tate acquired in 1984 a picture by Craxton of 1948 entitled '*Pastoral for P.W.*'.

45 There is a photograph of this picture being painted, taken by Cecil Beaton.

46 Watson's surreptitious help to all sorts of people crops up in many places. For example, in 1943 he gave his financial support to the publication of David Gascoyne's second volume of poetry, *Poems 1937-1942*, which had illustrations by Sutherland. He seems also to have provided some financial support to Dylan Thomas and to the artist Gerald Wilde. His will, which was dated 18 December 1950, made no mention of art or artists, but there were four small pecuniary legacies. David Gascoyne was left £2,000, as were fellow old Etonian Brian Howard and Sonia Brownell (George Orwell's widow). That other, perhaps undeserving, old Etonian, Cyril Connolly, was left £1,000.

47 Watson's glowing obituary in the *Times*, on 5 May 1956, had been headed 'Modern patron of art'.

48 As well as Roland Penrose, Kenneth Clark, Edward James and Peggy Guggenheim. A similar comment was made by James Lord in *A Gift for Admiration* (1998): 'Peter Watson was the only true patron of the arts that I have ever encountered.'

49 *Another Part of the Wood* and *The Other Half*.

50 Although he did write an Introduction to the extended pamphlet published in 1947 on Graham Bell, who had been killed in the War. Bell's work, as a member of the Euston Road School, had similarities with Coldstream's and it met with Clark's approval.

51 8812.1.3.3101-3150 and 3151-3200.

52 *The Penguin Modern Painters* by Carol Peaker.

53 1901-65. Educated at Eton and Christ Church, Oxford. He was particularly known as a music critic. His portrait was painted by Sutherland. Towards the end of his life he became 5th Baron Sackville.

54 Reference 8812.1.3.2401-2450.

55 For this I have relied upon *The War Artists* by Meirion and Susie Harries.

56 Reference 8812.1.3.301-350.

57 Clark's connections with the Irish art establishment should not be overlooked. He corresponded over the years with Thomas Bodkin and also, on at least one occasion, with MacGreevy at the National Gallery of Ireland. MacGreevy had been a colleague of Clark's at the National Gallery in London in the period 1935-41.

58 He also seems to have been involved in encouraging the establishment early in the War of the National Buildings Record, which rapidly built up a huge photographic archive.

59 The stipulation that the work had to be done in watercolour was a significant step in encouraging a medium that was in danger of decline. Russell Flint was President of the Royal Watercolour Society at this time and a number of its members were to be heavily involved in the Scheme.

60 For example in 1942, at the National Gallery, where Clark was still Director.

61 The full set cost five guineas and 8,253 sets had been sold by 1950.

62 There is a book about the scheme called *Recording Britain: A Pictorial Domesday of Pre-War Britain* by David Mellor, Gill Saunders and Patrick Wright.

63 The letters in the Tate Archive, in file 8812.1.3.1501-1550, from Jones to Clark, do not make clear the precise details of Clark's support for the artist, but they do make it clear that Jones very much regarded himself as being grateful to Clark for all the help he had given him. See, for example, a letter dated 11 March 1954.

64 After I had written this, I came across the following passage in an entry for James Lees-Milne's diary for 7 June 1949 (published under the title *Midway on the Waves*), in which he commented on Clark: 'I don't know how unbiased his judgments of modern art are. I suspect he only recommends artists who are among his circle of friends.'

65 I am not aware that anything has been published about him and I have been unable to track down any members of his family. What follows has therefore been pieced together from various sources and may omit substantive issues. If that is the case, I apologise now and would very much welcome reliable additional information or corrections. Some details have been taken from the website of the 'Bomfords of Worcester'.

66 After school at Homefield and Epsom College, the same as Sutherland. Homefield had been owned by Bomford's parents and, in fact, one of his sisters, Connie, was Sutherland's first teacher of drawing there.

67 According to Desmond Morris, in conversation with the author on 14 February 2005, the Modigliani was vandalised on the tour and certainly the modern French pictures had been removed from the exhibition by the time the show reached London. In his autobiography, *Animal Days*, Desmond Morris records that on his first visit to Aldbourne just after the War, he noted pictures around the house by Gauguin, Utrillo, de Chirico, Renoir, Bonnard, Klee, Corot, Cézanne, Manet, Modigliani, Daumier, Dégas, Poussin, Picasso, Sutherland and Moore. Reviewing it at the galleries of the RWS on 15 July 1945 in the *Observer*, Maurice Collis noted its 'astonishing' quality as a collection. By the time it reached London it had a new catalogue which sought to refute some of Bodkin's allegations.

68 There is a letter in the Clark Archive in the Tate, in TGA 8812.1.1.17, dated 2 December 1943, in which Bomford asks Clark if he could come round to see him at the National Gallery.

69 From 9 June-6 July 1959 the Hanover held an exhibition of Bacon pictures from the Bomford collection.

70 Again according to Desmond Morris, the cottage was occupied by Mervyn Levy after Adler's death.

71 Exactly what Bomford retained, or bought later, is unknown, but he certainly had pictures by some of these artists after 1946. For example, when the Arts Council was organising a Memorial Exhibition for Adler in 1951, they wrote to Bomford (on 7 November) and asked for the loan of 8 pictures by Adler.

72 Bomford bought all the works by Martin on show at the Leicester Galleries in 1943.

73 One of the Sutherlands was given later, in 1976.

74 Bomford was not averse to the notion of exchanging pictures when it suited him. So, for example, the catalogue of the Swindon Collection notes, a little wryly, that the work by the little-known Despiau was presented by Bomford on 18 January 1954 in exchange for the drawing for the *Crucifixion* (1931-33) by Bacon, previously given by Bomford in 1946. One feels that Bomford may have got the better of that deal. In view of the incredible rise in value of works by Le Brocquy, the next swap that he engineered was not quite so one-sided, as he presented

two works by Le Brocquy in February 1960, together with works by Smith and Szobel, in exchange for the *Crucifixion* of 1933, which had again previously been given by him in 1946.

75 Invited to Dublin as guests of the IELA as a result of his lending generosity, the Bomfords had the dubious pleasure of having the somewhat eccentric Ralph Cusack as one of their hosts.

76 Of course, many pictures subsequently ended up with official owners because of gifts by individuals.

77 The modern artists whose works were lent included Adler, Aldridge, Appelbee, Ardizzone, Bawden, Bell, Bellingham-Smith, Buhler, Burra, Colquhoun, Craxton, Cundall, du Plessis, Freedman, Freud, Gowing, Grant, Hillier, Hitchens, Hodgkins, John, Jones, Kessell, H. Lamb, Le Brocquy, Lewis, Lowry, MacBryde, Meninsky, Minton, Paul Nash, John Nash, Ben Nicholson, William Nicholson, Winifred Nicholson, Pasmore, Piper, Ravilious, Richards, Roberts, Rowntree, Scott, Shepherd, Smith, S. Spencer, Sutherland, Tibble, Tunnard, Vaughan, Wadsworth, Wood, Wilde and Yeats.

78 It would have been possible to include others, such as Sir Robert Sainsbury (1906-2000). Most of his personal art collection was donated to the University of East Anglia in 1973. The catalogue contains full details of the works, only a small part of which are British paintings and those largely restricted to works on paper by Henry Moore, which he was collecting throughout our period, and works by Bacon, which he only started to acquire later, in the mid-1950s. Otherwise, unless he held back works by British artists from the gift, he cannot be regarded as a significant widescale collector of relevance to this study. Another possibility might have been Ernest Cooper, who ran the London Health Centre and who amassed works by William Roberts, his collection going on display at the Worthing Museum and Art Gallery in 1972. He is described in Roberts's biography (by Andrew Gibbon Williams), as 'the Robertses' financial lifeline', buying many works direct from the artist.

79 See the Arts Council catalogue of a 1980 touring exhibition, *Leeds' Paintings. 20th Century British art from Leeds City Art Gallery*.

80 His obituary was in the *Times* on 8 September 1980.

81 See Michael Yoss, *Raymond Mortimer. A Bloomsbury Voice*, 1998.

82 Artists who subsequently benefited from them included Reg Butler and Kenneth Armitage.

83 From 8 July-9 August 1959.

84 After the publication of his obituary in the *Times* on 11 February 1959, headed 'Benefactor of the Arts', Miss Jane Drew wrote in subsequently to emphasise the support he gave to young artists. She mentioned, in particular, that he supported Moore, Ben Nicholson, Armitage, Chadwick, Butler, Pasmore, Paolozzi and Hepworth.

85 1900-2002.

86 *Watercolours and Drawings from the Collection of Queen Elizabeth the Queen Mother* by Susan Owens, accompanying an exhibition at the Palace of Holyroodhouse in Edinburgh in 2005.

87 My information is largely gleaned from Andrew Lycett's book *From Diamond Sculls to Golden Handcuffs. A history of Rowe and Pitman*.

88 They had met in 1928.

89 There are descriptions of Pitman in Nicolette Devas' autobiography *Two Flamboyant Fathers*.

90 I am indebted to his grandson, Sir Adam Ridley, who went out of his way to make available to me copies of his grandfather's ledgers, which recorded pictures bought and

prices paid in great detail.

91 Since moved to St Mary, Barham when St Peter's became redundant.

92 1902-91. Educated at Winchester and Oxford. He bought in 1945 a house called Long Crichel in Dorset, together with Desmond Shawe-Taylor and Eddie Sackville-West. Raymond Mortimer and Pat Trevor-Roper later acquired an interest.

93 Apparently he also advised Evelyn Waugh.

94 The catalogue for this makes it clear that at least some of the pictures were for sale.

95 There is an article about his collection in *The Studio* of February 1949 by Bernard Denvir.

96 In his autobiography, *Memoirs of a Painter*, Gilbert Spencer mentions that he painted Evill's portrait in the early 1930s.

97 The full list of names with a number of pictures in brackets after each name, was as follows: Lewis (1), Lanyon (1), John Hitchens (1), Roberts (21), MacBryde (1), Rogers (1), Ivon Hitchens (5), Underwood (2), Wilde (3), Gilbert Spencer (16), Ayrton (4), Henry Lamb (2), Kessell (2), Lowry (3), Freud (2), Evans (2), Colquhoun (1), Yeats (1), Paul Nash (3), Pasmore (1), Reynolds (5), William Nicholson (1), Grant (1), Craxton (1), Uhlman (1),Trevelyan (1), Buhler (1), Sutherland (26), John Nash (2), Ben Nicholson (1), Collins (2), Richards (1), Townsend (1), Scott (1), Burra (4), John (3), Hillier (3), Hodgkins (2),Jones (2), Gear (1), Wynter (1), Piper (1), Rothenstein (2), Ardizzone (1), Le Brocquy (1), Vaughan (1), Smith (1), Minton (1), Heron (1) and Spear (1).

98 Although most were owned by this time by Honor Frost.

99 The National Portrait Gallery has a 1943 portrait of him by Barnett Freedman.

100 Formed, it would seem, by using money which he received from his share of the £50,000 which Parliament had given to the family of the only Prime Minister ever to be assassinated, Spencer Perceval (shot in the lobby of the House of Commons on 11 May 1812). Marsh's mother was a descendant of Perceval's. Although Perceval had six sons and six daughters, the fragment which reached Marsh was apparently sufficient to enable him to buy a lot of pictures, which perhaps says something about the cheapness of the pictures. Marsh called it the 'murder money'. There is an article about his collection in *The Studio* in 1947 (vol. 133), by Bernard Denvir.

101 *Eddie Marsh. Sketches for a composite literary portrait of Sir Edward Marsh, KCVO, CB, CMG* compiled by C. Hassall and D. Mathews and published in May 1953.

102 *A Painter's Collection*, Royal Academy 1963.

103 *Portrait in Albion* and *Tomato Plants in Essex*, neither of which shows the artist anywhere near the height of his powers.

104 I should like to record my thanks to her for helping me with my enquiries, in a telephone conversation on 16 May 2006.

105 1894-1961.

106 I am relying here on *Art in Ulster 1557-1957* by John Hewitt.

107 He was, for example, recorded as lending a Paul Nash oil to the Nash Memorial Exhibition in 1948 at the Tate.

108 3 November 1961.

109 Curious not so much in its context as in the concept behind the collection. For further information, see *Stewart Mason: the art of education* by Donald Jones.

110 See *W.G. Gillies. A very still life* by W. Gordon Smith.

111 See *Winifred Coombe Tennant: a life through art* by Peter Lord and also the many references to her in Robert Meyrick's book on John Elwyn.

112 1906-86. Educated at Eton and King's College, Cambridge.

113 1903-76. Educated at Eton and Balliol College, Oxford.

114 Some of my information for this section comes from Martyn Angelsea, Keeper of Fine Art at the Ulster Museum. He was (in May 2006) very generous in providing me with information and copies of catalogues and I am extremely grateful to him. For detail of the pictures bequeathed by Patricia and John Hewitt in 1987 see Eileen Black's *Catalogue of the Drawings, Paintings and Sculptures of the Ulster Museum*.

CHAPTER 4

1 Although not everybody was impressed by it. The editorial of the *Burlington Magazine*, in July 1946, while welcoming the principle of the Report, could not help but comment on what it saw as a large number of factual inaccuracies.

2 A key recommendation was for CEMA to be replaced by an Arts Council, which of course was shortly to happen.

3 Colquhoun wrote to Colin Anderson an undated letter, but dateable to 1948/9, in which he asked for £9-5s to meet a tax demand. 'Two income tax men threatened me with the bailiffs if I didn't pay up.' In his book *A Wider Sky*, Kyffin Williams mentions how, in the 1940s, when he reckoned that his annual income was between £200 and £300, he was amazed to receive tax demands from the Inland Revenue. These he threw away, assuming them to be a mistake, also subsequently throwing away the court summonses which ensued. He eventually got an accountant. In a diary entry for 22 October 1970, Vaughan noted 'Very unpleasant session with Income Tax Inspectors yesterday. Hostile, polite and Kafkaesque. They are after my blood.' In his autobiography, Gilbert Spencer notes how, in the second half of the 1930s, two 'bowler hatted men' arrived unexpectedly at his cottage, resulting in his visiting the local tax collector the following morning. The tax man pointed out to him that, although his position was serious, he didn't want to send him to prison.

4 Cedric Morris came from a family of Welsh baronets and succeeded his father as 9th Baronet in 1947.

5 Matthew Smith never had any financial worries, (according to Malcolm Yorke), following the death of his father in 1914. Some evidence for this is provided by the fact that he left many favourite works unsold at the time of his death (and his popularity was such that one assumes that he could have sold his pictures had he chosen to). A large collection of these is now in the Guildhall Art Collection in the City of London. Similarly, Edward Wadsworth inherited a large sum of money on his father's death and subsequently liked to travel by Rolls-Royce.

6 An Old Etonian, his wealthy background apparently grew less secure with the passage of time. He taught at Goldsmith's College School of Art for a long period beginning in 1948.

7 Bawden's fee for producing 9 large panels for the SS *Orcades* was £600.

8 Bawden, for example, produced press adverts for the Zinc Development Association and William Roberts was in 1951 commissioned by the London Transport Board to design a poster called *Hampstead Fair* to advertise fairs accessible by public transport.

9 According to Malcolm Yorke in his book on Mervyn Peake, p. 142, Peake had been paid £150 in 1943 by

publishers Eyre and Spottiswoode to illustrate *Household Tales* by the Brothers Grimm. For this he was required to produce 70 black-and-white drawings, plus a colour spread.

10   Minton's other book illustrations during our period were for *Contemporary Cookery*, 1947, *Treasure Island*, 1947, *The Snail that climbed the Eiffel Tower*, 1947, *The Wanderer*, 1947, *The Country Heart*, 1949, *Old Herbaceous*, 1950 and *Leaves of Gold*, 1951. At this time Freud illustrated *The Equilibriad* by William Sansom in 1948; Meninsky illustrated Milton's *Poetical Works* in 1947; Bawden illustrated Denis Saurat's *Death and the Dreamer* in 1946 and Noel Carrington's *Life in an English Village* in 1949; Rowntree illustrated *A Prospect of Wales* in 1948; Piper did de la Mare's *The Traveller* in 1946 and Murray's *Berkshire Architectural Guide* in 1949; Henry Moore did lithographs for Gide's translation of Goethe's *Prometheus* in 1950;and Edward Wolfe did John Garratt's *The Dancing Beggars* in 1946. Examples from Ireland would be Nano Reid illustrating Mairtin O Direain's *Selected Poems* in 1949; Charles Lamb illustrating the highly-regarded novel in Irish *Cre Na Cille* by Mairtin O Cadhain, also in 1949; and Harry Kernoff providing drawings for Patricia Lynch's *A Storyteller's Childhood* in 1947 and woodcuts for Devin Garrity's *New Irish Poets* in 1948.

11   John Lehmann's influence on the promotion of the careers of young artists in the 1940s should be noted. See illustrations on page12. He had included reproductions of their work in Penguin New Writing during the War and, once he established his own publishing company in 1946, he used artists such as Vaughan and Minton to help with both design and illustrations. See Adrian Wright's *John Lehmann. A pagan adventure.*

12   The 21 originals were exhibited as 'A Prospect of Wales' by the Arts Council in Cardiff in 1949.

13   It appeared for sale in 2006 at the Goldmark Gallery. Colquhoun also later supplied a design for the cover of the magazine, Nimbus, which first appeared in December 1951, edited by Tristram Hull.

14   My information on this comes from an article by Richard Russell and Peter Bird from the J Lyons and Co website, dated October 2004.

15   Paul Nash had been invited and had agreed to produce something, but had died before completion.

16   See Janet Dunbar's *Laura Knight*, p. 168.

17   Uhlman also illustrated a travel book, in his case on the Scilly Isles, by Geoffrey Grigson, which was published in 1948. During our period, Michael Ayrton produced books called *British Drawings* in 1946 and *Hogarth's Drawings* in 1948.

18   Examples being Clough and Smith.

19   The daughter of the artist Jacob Kramer.

20   Rodrigo Moynihan and his wife Elinor Bellingham-Smith had lived in a top-floor flat at 24 St Mark's Crescent before the War.

21   See Andrew Gibbon Williams, *William Roberts. An English Cubist.*

22   The letter is in the possession of the Anderson family.

23   See John Rothenstein, *John Nash.*

24   In a letter from Sutherland to Clark in the Tate Archive, reference 8812.1.3.3101-3150, of 30 October 1945, the artist credited his solicitor, Wilfrid Evill, with having negotiated the purchase price down from £3,000.

25   See Roger Berthoud, *Graham Sutherland.*

26   See Antony Penrose, *Roland Penrose. The friendly Surrealist*, p. 142.

27   Much of the information which follows on Peake's

finances is taken from *Mervyn Peake* by Malcolm Yorke. Peake's ability to manage his finances is a classic case of an artist who really should not have been left to manage his own affairs.

28   The great legacy of the Sark period was the second volume of the Titus trilogy, *Gormenghast.*

29   See Kenneth Pople, *Stanley Spencer.*

30   See Cordelia Oliver, *Joan Eardley, RSA.*

31   *The Other Side of Six.*

32   An example of financial information which is not easy to interpret is contained in Eileen Agar's autobiography, *A Look at my Life*, p. 166. Here she records that, following a show of small oils and gouaches at the Leger Gallery in January 1947 (when she was 47), she was given a cheque for £100 by the gallery. But we don't know how many pictures she sold or how much the gallery withheld.

33   A sale of pictures by Munnings held at the Leicester Galleries in 1945 apparently yielded the colossal sum of £21,000, including £12,000 on the first day. By comparison, William Roberts had a show at the Leicester Galleries in 1949 at which he sold about 10 watercolours. He claimed that, after deduction of commission of 33.3%, he was due the sum of £181.10, although framing costs still had to be deducted from this figure. He was in his 50s at the time. (This information is taken from William Roberts' *Five Posthumous Essays and Other Writings* of 1990.)

34   W. Gordon Smith writing about Robin Philipson, who was another English-born artist now regarded as Scottish.

35   See Patrick Bourne, *Anne Redpath 1895-1965.*

36   See Bruce Arnold, *Jack Yeats*, p. 321.

37   *Irish Times*, 24 May 1947.

38   1881-1968. Educated at St Columba's College. He rarely visited Ireland after 1910.

39   See Denise Ferran, *William John Leech. An Irish Painter Abroad.*

40   See the Taylor Galleries, Dublin, catalogue of an exhibition of Le Brocquy's tapestries held in November 2000 and the Agnew's catalogue of a similar exhibition held in May 2001.

41   In his delightful book *Making my mark. An artist's early life.*

42   On 25 April 1946.

43   An example of where commissions for portraits could come from, even if only pencil sketches seem to have been required, is in the archives of Trinity College, Cambridge. Many portraits of fellows have been commissioned over the years and from the period 1945-51 come examples by Moynihan, Burn, Spear, Wolfe, H. Lamb, Grant, Horton, Freeth and Weight. I am grateful to Dr Neil Hopkinson for providing me with this information.

44   One problem with teaching was that it restricted the amount of time which the artist had to spend on his own work, especially if the teaching was anything like full-time (which it might have to be if it was to be the artist's principal source of income). So, for example, we see Frances Richards, wife of Ceri, writing to Colin Anderson from Cardiff on 31 May 1944, saying that Ceri 'cannot face starting a fifth year at this teaching as it is very harmful to his work, besides being so exhausting'. Richards was at the time Head of Painting at the Cardiff College of Art.

45   Kyffin Williams undertook a different form of teaching, in that he taught art at Highgate School, a London public school, for many years.

46   Occasionally one gets a glimpse of what a student could

earn. Derrick Greaves won the Royal Scholarship at the RCA in 1948 and, according to James Hyman, this amounted to about £600. See his *Derrick Greaves. From Kitchen-sink to Shangri-la*, p. 20.

47 In the Tate Archive.

48 See Bruce Laughton, *William Coldstream*.

49 See Gilbert Spencer's *Memoirs of a Painter*.

50 In this regard see in particular *Artists' Textiles in Britain 1945-1970* by Geoffrey Rayner, Richard Chamberlain and Annamarie Stapleton.

51 The close relationship between Sutherland and Hans and Elsbeth Juda is illustrated by the number of works by Sutherland which the Judas came to own. In May 1967 the Graves Art Gallery in Sheffield mounted an exhibition of some of the paintings and sculpture owned by the Judas. There were many works by Sutherland and by Piper, together with, for example, Adler, Colquhoun, Moore, Pasmore, Rowntree, Scott, Smith, Vaughan and Wynter, from amongst the British artists covered in this book. The Judas also published a magazine called *The Ambassador*, which was intended to promote higher design standards and efficient export marketing techniques. They commissioned a number of British artists to design the covers, including Wadsworth, Le Brocquy, Piper and Moore.

52 The Roberts, in their endless search for money, contacted Ascher in 1950 seeking a textile commission. Letter to Anderson with the Anderson family.

53 See p. 298 of Jane Stevenson, *Edward Burra*.

54 Interestingly, Burra also worked on a ballet for Covent Garden in 1948. In this case he worked with Frederick Ashton on *Don Juan*.

55 Even this wasn't the end of the matter, as MacBryde had a go at getting more money on the basis of travelling expenses. He claimed an additional £100, saying that they had made 250 drawings, but Webster finally crushed this idea by a letter dated 28 January 1952.

56 I am not aware of any such research, but it would be interesting to know, within a given category such as paintings by 20th-century British artists, how long is the average period between acquisition by their first owner and subsequent sale. I would guess it might be something like 20 years.

57 Even this was to end in tears after Bacon's death, when his executor, Professor Brian Clarke, sued the Marlborough for, among other things, the alleged misappropriation of funds owed to Bacon.

58 Nevill Johnson's autobiography, p. 52, records how in 1946 Victor Waddington gave him a retainer, which enabled the artist to give up his job and take up painting full time.

59 Macdonald was particularly annoyed by the complaint because Collins had been sent a cheque for a large amount, to reflect all the sales in aggregate and also because, as he told Collins, the artist was apparently the only Lefevre artist who never thanked the gallery staff for putting on his shows. Suitably chastened, Collins apologised to Macdonald and the staff.

60 See p. 119 of his letters edited by William Chappell under the title of *Well, dearie. The letters of Edward Burra*.

61 It helps that he is an honourable and decent man and that he acknowledges the debt he owed to Gimpel for their support to him when he was starting out as a professional artist.

62 Whose wife was Irish.

63 Although I am not aware that such likely candidates as Sutherland or Minton ever visited, nor did the Irish-born Bacon ever seem very keen on returning.

64 The cultural environment in which British travel adventures were undertaken by writers between the Wars is described in Paul Fussell's *Abroad. British Literary Travelling Between the Wars*. Some of the points he makes about the reasons lying behind pre-War travel may also be relevant to explain the considerable appetite for travel of post-War artists.

65 The brief period of influence of the Italian Futurists, such as Marinetti and Balla and so on, which had operated on the earlier careers of Lewis, Roberts, Nevinson and Bomberg had, by the post-War period, become an historical footnote rather than an ongoing influence.

66 Leslie Hurry visited Avignon in 1946. William MacTaggart travelled every summer from 1947-53 to Orry-la-Ville, north of Paris.

67 See Malcolm Yorke, *Matthew Smith. His Life and Reputation*, p. 189.

CHAPTER 5

1 Those conclusions would themselves need, in some way, to allow for the changing rôle of the art market, whether tested through auction prices or dealers' sales, in contributing to artistic reputations. The fashionability of some artists whose artistic worth is probably small – one thinks of Hirst and Emin – is a feature of the modern art market which probably did not exist in the same way in the 1940s. On the other hand, there may even then have been a disparity between the worth of the work of those artists whose work was 'fashionable' and the 'worth' of their less favoured contemporaries. An area where this point could probably be made in the context of the mid-century British art world is in portraiture. There were a number of fashionable portrait painters – for example, Moynihan – whose talents as artists are not now regarded as being commensurate with the sometimes extraordinarily high prices which they charged for their work at the time.

2 The symbiotic nature of their relationship may be noted. As Sylvester helped to establish and develop Bacon's reputation, the growth of the latter in turn served to enhance that of Sylvester.

3 No attempt is made here to consider the impact of radio programmes about modern British art. There were programmes which covered this area, particularly on the Third Programme, which began broadcasting in September 1946, but also on the Home Service. Talks were sometimes reproduced in the *Listener*. The potential reach of radio programmes of this type should not be underestimated. For example, the *Irish Times* commented on 5 December 1949 that the work of Belfast artist William Conor had been discussed on the Northern Ireland Home Service of the BBC. There had also been a programme on Radio Eireann on 29 April 1946, under the heading 'Academic versus Modern', comparing the work of Sean Keating with that of Le Brocquy. It can be no surprise to the reader of this book to find Kenneth Clark appearing on the radio from time to time. For example he was on the Sunday Service on 10 June 1946, talking about the return of the pictures to the National Gallery and on 3 May 1947 he talked on the Third Programme about Graham Bell, with Vincent Lines talking about Thomas Hennell, both artists having been killed during or shortly after the War. Also, no attempt has been made to consider the impact of the nascent television service. Occasional glimpses of this new medium are picked up in unlikely places. For example, in her autobiography, *A Look at My Life*, Eileen Agar records how, in August 1948, she appeared on a programme called 'Eye of the Artist'.

This went out live and was apparently intended to explore fantastic art by way of Surrealism. A few months later she appeared again on a different programme, fronted by art critic and costume historian James Laver.

4   At the end of the War, the circulation of the *Daily Telegraph* was about 740,000.

5   Although the prejudices, conscious or otherwise, of some of the journalists will need to be noted as well, where they can be identified.

6   This was partly due to severe restrictions on newsprint, which persisted throughout our period and which seem to have had the effect of artificially restricting the length of the papers.

7   An example of the complexity would be the need to cover the many local newspapers even within London which were capable of covering local art events. The amount of time which one would have to spend in the British Newspaper Library in Colindale does not bear thinking about.

8   The art coverage in the *Times* during this period is extremely difficult to locate, as it comes up quite randomly on many different pages and on many different days.

9   He became art critic in 1945. He also wrote *An Introduction to French Painting*, books on Blake, Italian painting and John Bratby, and a number of catalogue introductions over the years. He was an innocuous painter in his own name. One assumes that the favourable review of an exhibition of his work which appeared in the *Times* on 12 January 1950 was not written by him. He left the *Times* in 1955 to become Slade Professor of Fine Art at Cambridge. He was a trustee of the National Gallery. His obituary appeared in the *Times* on 21 December 1976.

10   See Chapter 1 above.

11   For example, the annual Summer shows entitled 'Artists of Fame and Promise' were covered.

12   The work shown at these 'official' shows was not always well-received. On 31 October 1946 the Times' reviewer said this about an exhibition of the NEAC: 'Impressionism, usually modified to suit a decorative colour scheme and therefore no longer a very exacting discipline of perception, appears to be the approved style.'

13   13 May 1950.

14   The National Portrait Gallery holds a pen and ink and wash sketch of him (from 1943) by Barnett Freedman.

15   I am conscious of the possibility that some of the artists may have become better known under other names.

16   Wrote for the *Sunday Times* for many years and then moved to New York and wrote for the *New York Times*. He also found time to write a large number of books on a wide variety of subjects including Bacon, Ben Nicholson and Henry Moore.

17   Born in 1889 in Dublin and educated at Rugby and Corpus Christi College, Oxford. He wrote extensively about his own life, publishing his *Diaries 1949-1969* and two volumes of autobiography, *The Journey Up* and *The Journey Outward*. He knew well a number of the artists covered in this book, especially Topolski, Peake, Lowry and Scottie Wilson. He had begun to write for the *Observer* in January 1945. He was writing for *Time and Tide* at the time and carried on doing so until 1951. Pieces by him also appeared (in 1947) in *Harper's Bazaar* and in *La France Libre*.

18   He claimed that he parted company from the *Observer* when his views on Munnings became irreconcilable with those of the editor.

19   He clearly had a strong view as to Gotlib's limits. On 16 March 1947 we find him saying that Gotlib's excellence lies 'rather in his paint than in his mind, which hardly transcends the ordinary'.

20   Yeats' exhibition at Wildenstein was also to be highly praised on 24 February 1946; and on 2 March 1947 he picked out Jack Hanlon's work at a mixed show at the same gallery.

21   He claimed that he had introduced Le Brocquy, while he was still in Dublin in 1946, to a director of the Leicester Galleries who was visiting the City and that this led to the show. This is probably a reference to the visit by Cecil Phillips in January.

22   He was to become the well-known novelist who wrote *City of Spades* (1957) and *Absolute Beginners* (1957), as well as many other novels. He was also later to write, jointly with Bryan Robertson and with an introduction by Kenneth Clark, what is still the main book on the Australian artist, Sidney Nolan. What is perhaps less well known is that he was a grandson of Burne-Jones, his mother was the novelist, Angela Thirkell, and he was himself a painter, having attended the Euston Road School. He was on the staff at Camberwell from 1946-1948. His name crops up in various parts of the art world from time to time. For example, he helped to select pictures from the British Council Collection to tour Canada in 1952-1953 under the heading 'Five Contemporary British Painters'. But the picture sketched of his life and character by Daniel Farson in *Soho in the Fifties* does not make for pleasant reading.

23   A prolific author on a wide variety of subjects. He published an autobiography in 1963 called *Museum Piece*. When the War finished he returned to his pre-War job at the V&A as Keeper of Prints and Drawings. (He was an Oxford contemporary of Leigh Ashton, who was by then the Director of the V&A.) A large obituary was published in the *Times* on 4 June 1975.

24   There is a 1952 picture of Wallis by Minton, sitting in a studio in his dark suit, holding his hat in his left hand and his umbrella in his right and peering forwards at a picture on the easel by William Etty. The picture was given to the Brighton Art Gallery by Wallis in 1956.

25   Gosling was to have a long career at the *Observer*, where he started in 1950. He became art critic in 1962 and stayed in that position until 1975. He was also ballet critic 1955-82. He had been at Eton with David Astor, who became the proprietor of the paper in 1948. Gosling's art journalism was later published under the title *Prowling the Pavements: selected art writings 1950-1980*.

26   With this paper it is exceptionally difficult to spot any 'art' items. The paper largely consisted of small news stories, after the main pieces and commentaries, and these are scattered without apparent form. Readers may therefore be able to identify items which I have not.

27   For example, Conor, McKelvey and Middleton on 16 October 1946.

28   At Mol's Gallery, 54 Upper Queen Street.

29   The head of the family at the time was Sir Lauriston Arnott. 1896-1958, 3rd baronet, educated at Wellington. His *Times* obituary on 3 July 1958 could find little to say about him. He was managing director of the *Irish Times* from 1940-54.

30   See Tony Gray's book *Mr Smyllie, Sir*.

31   1913-80. Educated at Rossall and Pembroke College, Oxford. He inherited his father's title, and became 3rd Baron Glenavy in 1963.

32   A good example of Campbell's dry humour appeared on 13 June 1945 when, writing the piece called 'An Irishman's

Diary' under the name 'Quidnunc', he commented on the decision of the Revd Dr Browne, president of University College, Galway, to open the great Yeats retrospective with a speech in Irish, 'a matter of considerable interest to the many members of the Diplomatic Corps present'.

33 Born 1910 in Fife; a member of the White Stag Group and later participated in Cobra. He died in January 2007 and his obituary appeared in the *Guardian* on 14 February.

34 On 24 October he reviewed a Campbell exhibition at the Goodwin Galleries in Limerick.

35 Typical of that gallery's thoroughness, the artists included all the obvious contemporary artists from both North and South.

36 Another possibility is that it reflected the taste of the galleries where these shows appeared, since Power's reviews were necessarily responsive to what was on at the time.

37 1868-1953. Scottish by birth, she was treated as an Irish artist of some importance. Married to Paul Henry.

38 1889-1974. English. She took up with Paul Henry and lived with him whilst he was still married to Grace. Later became Henry's wife after Grace's death. A later review than those we are considering here, also in the *Irish Times*, said 'no critical fireworks could ever be expected to explode over her serene and truthful landscapes'.

39 1915-96. Wood engraver, landscape and figure painter.

40 1915-92. Largely known as a stage designer and what Snoddy describes as a 'landscape fantasy painter'.

41 1894-1955. One of the best known and most significant of Irish artists of the mid-century, she evolved into an important artist in stained glass.

42 1884-1968. Her father was 14th Baron Inchiquin of Dromoland Castle in County Clare. This is one of the great, purely Irish, aristocratic families of Ireland.

43 1900-73. She was based in County Cork and knew the novelist Elizabeth Bowen who wrote the foreword to the catalogue for the exhibition at the Harry Street Galleries in Dublin reviewed in the *Irish Times*.

44 Review of 15 November 1946.

45 10 November 1947.

46 On 16 April.

47 1902-61. Sixth Earl of Longford, educated at Eton and Christ Church, Oxford.

48 On 22 October.

49 On 21 April.

50 On 24 May.

51 On 16 August.

52 On 4 November.

53 On 19 April.

54 On 13 August.

55 On 5 October.

56 On 10 October 1949.

57 1906-1964. Primarily a portrait painter, but also known for his landscapes. From Dublin, attended the Dublin Metropolitan School of Art and the Central in London, before moving on to Paris. A large group of his pictures was sold at Adam's in Dublin on 4 October 2006.

58 1911-1989. Born in Limerick, he was a landscape and townscape painter (according to Snoddy). Studied at the Limerick School of Art and at Dublin.

59 A later writer for this was the leading Irish art historian Bruce Arnold.

60 The *Evening Press*, which was also controlled by the de Valera family, did not arrive until 1954. It closed in 1995. The *Evening Herald* is the sole survivor.

61 We have seen how some of the English newspapers were in the habit of covering both as well.

62 As has been mentioned in reference to the Glasgow Art Gallery in Chapter 1.

63 I have been unable to ascertain whether he carried on as London correspondent. Certainly pieces continued to appear from London.

64 Occasionally shows at the Scottish Gallery were picked up. J. McIntosh Patrick and Nora Paterson were noted there on 23 November 1946, and William Watson and Ian Fleming on 26 April 1947.

65 Neither has an entry in Buckman.

66 Herbert Read also got disparaging notice whenever he was mentioned. I am not aware who wrote the 'Perspex' article. Was it the editor, William Jennings?

67 According to Louis le Brocquy's official website.

68 Professor of History of Art at University College, London in 1922 and editor of the magazine 1940-45.

69 Deputy Surveyor of the King's Pictures 1939-47 and editor of the *Burlington Magazine* thereafter.

70 That this was a particular concern of Hendy's is shown by the fact that he also contributed a long piece on the same subject in the *Listener* for 25 July 1946, headed 'A Square Deal for the Artist'.

71 The detail of Arts Council purchases at this time is set out in Chapter 1.

72 Ayrton made a reappearance on 19 March 1948 to review the Nash retrospective at the Tate.

73 In covering Heron's journalism, I have relied on the 'Checklist of Writings' which appears in *Painter as Critic. Patrick Heron: Selected Writings*, ed. Mel Gooding, 1998.

74 See Mel Gooding's *Patrick Heron*, p. 47.

75 Other writers who appeared in 1948 were Edith Hoffmann and Robert Melville.

76 Heron was still popping up at this time, for example damning Minton on 12 February, Hodgkins on 26 March, Le Brocquy on 29 October and Bacon on 3 December.

77 'Entirely preoccupied with forming a mannerist façade'.

78 Basil Taylor was to write many books on art, including *Impressionists and their Work*, *Painting in England 1700-1850*; *French Painting*; *Cézanne*; *Animal Painting in England*; *Josef Herman Drawings*; *Stubbs*; and *Gainsborough*.

79 Artists also had pieces – often from radio programmes – reproduced in the *Listener*. To Piper, Ayrton and Lewis can be added Trevelyan, Moynihan and Kessell on one occasion (14 November 1946) and an interesting piece by the thoughtful and subtle Michael Rothenstein called 'Notes on the new Romanticism in Art', which was taken from the Third Programme and appeared in print on 9 January 1947.

80 1896-1969. Educated at Magdalen College, Oxford. His second wife was the artist Eileen Mayo. His *Times* obituary was on 17 September 1969.

81 The complete list of living British artists to be pictured in this way during our period is as follows, in the order in which they appeared: Meninsky, Hermes, Moore, Minton, W. Lewis, Ayrton, Dunlop, Woods, Uhlman, Smith, Gotlib, Ryan, Yeats, Roberts, Rosoman, Collins, Jonzen, Suddaby, Hepworth, Epstein, Vaughan, Fraser, Moynihan, S. Spencer, Searle, Freud, A. John, Richards, Bawden, Tisdall, Agar, O'Connor, Hall, Townsend, Hitchens, Boswell, Buhler, Boyle, Rothenstein, Scott, Feibusch, Pemberton, Topolski, Le Brocquy, Rogers, Mayo, Underhill, H. Lamb and Lord Methuen.

82 Follower of Gurdjieff.

83 It incorporated another journal with the more worrying title *The New Age*.

84 1886-1975. Biographer of Orage and keen on something called Christian Sociology.

85 Father of Tristram Hull, who later edited the magazine *Nimbus*.

86 1904-69. A portrait and figure painter, who had been born in India. He was educated partly in England and had attended the Dublin Metropolitan School of Art from the age of 15.

87 1898-1980. Had studied at the Slade. Not exactly young in 1946, he was to go on to teach at the Ruskin School of Drawing in Oxford from 1953-1972.

88 1908-97. Having spent her early years in County Londonderry, she lived and worked in London for some time and then settled in County Cork in 1971 and later Dublin.

89 1916-88.

90 1915-69. Studied at the RCA.

91 Born 1924. Studied at Camberwell and St Martin's. Later taught at Goldsmith's.

92 So obscure that she does not merit a mention in Buckman.

93 1925-88. Born in Vienna.

94 1883-1982. Decidedly not young in 1946. He had been at the Slade.

95 1918-49. He had studied at Chelsea School of Art.

96 Another one not in Buckman.

97 1899-1978. He had studied at Glasgow School of Art and went on to become vice-principal of Edinburgh School of Art.

98 Resident in County Donegal in Ireland for many years.

99 1925-92, educated at Clongowes Wood and the National College of Art. His memoirs of the time are called *Remembering how we stood*.

100 1903-88, born in Dublin, a landscape and figure painter.

101 Swift was the surest writer of that group and, indeed, one of the most impressive writers on art among contemporary practising artists, in my view. This skill was to be used to the full later in the 1950s in London, where he and the deaf South African poet David Wright published the highbrow literary magazine *X – a critical quarterly*. In this he tended to write using the pseudonym 'James Mahon'. A good example of his writing is in vol. 1, no. 4 (October 1960), a long article called 'The Painter in the Press'.

102 Born 1924 and educated at Oxford University, studied at St Martin's School of Art and then print-making at the Central School. Moved to Cornwall in 1949 and exhibited widely.

103 Educated at St Columba's College, Rathfarnham and Worcester College, Oxford. Dorman was an Anglo-Irish Protestant. His autobiographies are called *Limelight over the Liffey* and *Portrait of my youth*.

104 'In painting it still seems that only the work of veteran Jack Yeats would be of the slightest interest to students of modern art outside this country' (February 1946).

Chapter 6

1 In this respect, it will be interesting to see what happens to Freud's reputation after his death. An illustration of a quickly declining reputation is the case of Jankel Adler. He died in 1949, and it is instructive to note how the *Observer* was prepared to describe him in 1961. It started by saying that it was hard to remember that he was influential in the 1940s: 'The irony of it (and what a reflection it is on our artistic provincialism in those years) is that such a rôle should have fallen to so lightweight and eclectic an artist… His essentially confectioner's art was executed with a professional "Parisian" adroitness which in itself made an impression on the British "amateur" tradition' (14 September 1961).

2 Alan Bowness, in his lecture published in 1989 under the title 'The conditions of success. How the modern artist rises to fame', made an interesting attempt to analyse the process. But he did not allow himself any detail to support his arguments, which remained, therefore, at the level of assertions. He deserves credit for trying to reduce this complex area to simple propositions – namely that in his view there were always four stages in a painter's progress to what he called recognition – but the analysis cannot bear the degree of simplification which he subjects it to. At its loosest, categorising the stages as (i) peer recognition; (ii) critical recognition; (iii) patronage by dealers and collectors; and (iv) public acclaim; cannot be challenged. In detail, such crude categories and their token amplification in the context of a lecture cannot assist the reader who has to be persuaded to accept them.

3 In order to make sense of this section, the description of the artists' reputations will be extended beyond 1951; otherwise, the artificial cut-off date would produce needless distortions and lack of clarity.

4 This section is based upon my article 'The reputation and achievement of Robert Colquhoun, a reassessment', *The British Art Journal*, III, 3 (Autumn 2002), pp. 75-83. Subsequent research has enabled certain errors to be corrected and has also revealed a number of new points.

5 *Two Scots Women* (1946).

6 Roger Bristow's book about the Roberts has now been published: *The Last Bohemians*, 2009.

7 *Modern English Painters* by Sir John Rothenstein.

8 *The Spirit of Place. Nine Neo-Romantic Artists and Their Times*, by Malcolm Yorke.

9 'Colquhoun and MacBryde – a Retrospective', Glasgow Print Studio, 1990.

10 The Labour MP for Kilmarnock from 1929-1933 was Craigie Aitchison, father of the painter of the same name.

11 This letter is in Colquhoun's file in the library of the Imperial War Museum in London.

12 1943, 1947 and 1950 at the Lefevre; 1950 at the Redfern; 1957 at the Parton Gallery; 1958 at the Whitechapel and 1962 at the Museum Street Gallery.

13 At the Kaplan Gallery in New York.

14 1942 – 'Six Scottish Painters' at the Lefevre; 1944 – 'British and French Paintings' at the Lefevre; 1944 – 'Robert Colquhoun, Robert MacBryde and John Minton' at the Lefevre; 1945 – 'Quelques contemporains anglais' (Paris); 1946 – 'British Painters' at the Lefevre; 1946 – 'British Painters 1939 to 1945' (Arts Council); 1946 –'British Painters Past and Present' at the Lefevre; 1946 – 'Exposition internationale de peintures modernes', Paris; 1947 –

'British Artists' at the Lefevre; 1947 – 'Contemporary British Paintings and Drawings' (Australia); 1948-1949 – 'Twelve British Painters', Luxembourg, Netherlands, Germany, Belgium; 1948 – 'Modern British Painting' at the Lefevre; 1948 – 'Engelsk Nutidskonst', Stockholm; 1948 – 'Contemporary British Drawings' (Canada); 1949 – 'Contemporary Art from Great Britain, United States and France', Toronto; 1949 – 'Paintings by Contemporary British and French Artists' at the Lefevre; 1949 – 'Robert MacBryde, Winifred Nicholson, Robert Colquhoun' at the Lefevre; 1949 – 'Contemporary British Art from the Collections of the Arts Council and the British Council'; 1949 – 'Contemporary British Painters' at the Lefevre; 1950-1951 – 'Contemporary Paintings', New Zealand; 1951 – 'Sao Paolo Bienal', Brazil; 1951 – 'Sixty Paintings for '51', Arts Council exhibition; 1952 – 'International Exhibition of Painting', Ceylon; 1952 – 'Artistes Anglais Contemporains', Macon; 1953 – 'Figures in Their Setting', Contemporary Arts Society; 1953 – 'Europa Kunst', Copenhagen; 1953 – 'Five Contemporary British Painters', Canada; 1954 – 'French paintings/Robert Colquhoun/Frances Richards' at the Redfern; 1955 – 'Aquarelas e desenhos ingleses do seculo vinte', Lisbon; 1955 – 'Seven Scottish Painters', Edinburgh; 1956 – 'The Seasons Exhibition', Contemporary Arts Society; 1957-1959 – 'Contemporary British Painting' (Africa). (It should be said that not all of the shows contained oils. He sometimes showed only monotypes and drawings.)

15 With the poet George Barker.

16 Sutherland's work was perhaps accessed by Colquhoun through Peter Watson.

17 Vol. 37 (June 1943).

18 25 June 1943.

19 Vol. 126 (August 1943).

20 See Newton's collection of journalism *In my view*, 1949. It is worth noting that, while he had done reviews of Bacon and Freud by that time, he didn't feel they were worth re-publishing.

21 Lewis thought he detected the influence of Rouault in Colquhoun's work.

22 The *Listener*, 23 October 1947. This review occupied the best part of a page, and included a reproduction of Colquhoun's picture *The Dancer*.

23 Maurice Collis in the *Observer* of 24 March 1946 noted that the Roberts had clearly learnt a lot from Adler – who was 'far their superior'.

24 *Jankel Adler*, by various authors, published Köln, 1985.

25 A contemporary view of the relative intellectual strengths of Colquhoun and Lewis is a passing comment by Maurice Collis in the *Observer* on 2 February 1947, when he reviews Tunnard and Colquhoun and then goes on to review Lewis, noting the latter's 'vast intellectual superiority as a man to the two artists above-named'.

26 To be fair to Heron, it is necessary to point out that a few weeks later (on 2 October) he published a curious little piece called 'The criticism of contemporaries'. One wonders if he was feeling guilty about his review of Colquhoun, for he went out of his way to note that, since his visit to Lefevre for the purpose of the original review, the gallery had introduced a very good picture by Colquhoun called *Two Scots Women*. (Presumably the picture that ended up in the Museum of Modern Art in New York.) Heron was keen to give credit to the artist for this work.

27 Nevile Wallis gave it a mention in the *Observer* on 10 December, noting that the pictures had been 'so ruthlessly planned – that all the exuberance of the scene has fled'.

28 *Art News and Review*, December 1950.

29 Bryan Robertson, with characteristic fairness, came up with a similar analysis after Colquhoun's death. Writing in the *Listener* on 6 December 1962, he reviewed the whole career and noted the 'crisis' after 1950 as the work became more mannered and hollow. Mannerism is 'what happens when ideology or feeling departs from a form and leaves the cold, hard empty shell behind'. The nature of Colquhoun's vision helped to precipitate and underline the crisis 'because of the tendency to see human figures as performers, acting out a ritual drama, rather than humans living a life of their own'.

30 Vol. 123 (June 1958), p. 419.

31 21 September 1962.

32 Apart from an exhibition at the Douglas Foulis Gallery in Glasgow in 1963.

33 No. 105 (February 1977).

34 MacBryde certainly seems to have been influenced by Gris.

35 Vol. 119 (March 1977).

36 City of Edinburgh Museums and Art Galleries, 1981.

37 Vol. 123, July 1981.

38 '*The British Neo-Romantics 1935-1950*', National Museum of Wales, Cardiff.

39 '*A Paradise Lost : the Neo-Romantic Imagination in Britain 1935–1955*', Barbican, London.

40 James White's biography of the artist (1994) will be relied upon for factual detail here.

41 The same group of artists exhibited a total of 42 works at Heal's Mansard Gallery in London in May 1948.

42 Sheehy clearly had his eye on Dillon by this time. In the September 1950 edition of *Envoy* he had also mentioned Dillon's work at the same show.

43 I am indebted for what follows to the essential Snoddy in his *Dictionary of Irish Artists, 20th Century*.

44 See Eileen Black's *Catalogue of the Drawings, Paintings and Sculptures*.

45 In *Irish Art 1830-1990*.

46 Collis was pleased to note that the exhibition of Le Brocquy's work which was put on afterwards at the Leicester Galleries led to all his pictures being quickly sold.

47 And in the *Observer* in the case of the 1947 show. Howard Bliss bought a picture at that show.

48 By contrast, the review of the same show in the *Irish Press* on 8 December was perfectly complimentary, noting that it was his first exhibition in Dublin for 8 years and that he had been making a big name for himself in London.

49 On 4 February.

50 On 5 February.

51 On 19 August.

52 As an example of how widely his work was starting to travel by this time, it was shown in 1957 in group exhibitions in Chicago, Buffalo, the National Gallery of Canada and in Moscow.

53 On 15 November.

54 On 13 November.

55 As it was in March 1966 and in October 1968. By the latter date art reviews in the *Times* were being signed, in this case by William Gaunt.

56 On 21 September 1961.

57 On 21 and 23 June 1962 respectively.

58 On 11 November.

59 21 October.

60 30 May 1947.

61   Adler's influence on Le Brocquy would be worth investigating. A picture by Le Brocquy of 1949, called *Child with Doll, hommage à Jankel Adler* appeared for sale at Whyte's in Dublin in 2008, for example.

62   Although one has to sympathise with Sutherland for attracting the inevitable scorn of Patrick Heron, writing in the *New Statesman* on 6 June: 'Without doubt he has little ability for controlling strong colour and even less for creating pictorial sense.'

63   Although the *Guardian*'s Frederick Laws had a large review, with two illustrations, of a show at the Arthur Jeffress gallery at 28 Davies Street, on 14 January 1959. Laws was balanced in his view of the recent pictures (which included pictures of Venetian scenes), but throughout there was a note of caution ('he has seemed recently to be at a standstill').

64   It has to be said that praise by Cooper on this scale was a two-edged sword, in view of his own difficult reputation.

65   The profusely illustrated catalogue for this show had no text at all. There were 37 oils, dating from 1956–1962.

66   Particularly Andrew Causey.

67   The major works on the artist were to include *Paul Nash* by Andrew Causey; *Paul Nash. The Portrait of an Artist* by Anthony Bertram; *Interior Landscapes. A Life of Paul Nash* by James King; *Paul Nash. Master of the Image* by Margot Eates; and *The Landscape Vision of Paul Nash* by Roger Cardinal.

68   Bacon being an exception.

69   The writer was determined to make the point he wanted to make, whatever the facts. My impression is that Nash's work had not been widely exhibited since his 1948 retrospective and certainly not continuously or conspicuously. That doesn't necessarily detract from the general point being made.

70   Other than as a result of the famous white *Crucifixion*, which appeared in Herbert Read's *Art Now* in 1933, passed into the collection of Sir Michael Sadler, and which pops up in memoirs of the period with extraordinary claims being made as to how influential the work had been.

71   Sometimes the absence of comment speaks volumes. When the *Times* reviewed the Lefevre show, which also included one of the few modern British artists whom Bacon claimed to respect, Matthew Smith, together with Hodgkins, Moore and Sutherland, it didn't even bother to mention Bacon, focusing instead on Smith.

72   In, for example, the *Burlington Magazine* for February 1946.

73   For which see the book by Martin Harrison, *In Camera: Francis Bacon. Photography, Film and the Practice of Painting*.

74   The talk was reproduced in the *Listener* on 3 January 1952.

75   In the *Listener* for 18 December.

76   7 July 1955.

77   In so doing, he remarked that Bacon had told him that he had never taken photographs. This appears to be contradicted by recent evidence from Martin Harrison and Margarita Cappock.

78   Lucie-Smith was still saying much the same 26 years later. In the book which accompanied the exhibition 'The New British Painting' which opened in Cincinnati towards the end of 1988 he wrote, 'Bacon has perhaps suffered from too much rather than too little acclaim.' He saw Bacon as a mixture of 'the sublime, the excessive, the outrageous and the slightly ridiculous'.

79   Compiled by Krzysztof Cieszkowski.

CHAPTER 7

1   Reliance for the history of the Festival has been placed on *A Tonic to the Nation*, ed. Mary Banham and Bevis Hillier, London, 1976.

2   The letter from Morrison to Clark inviting him to join the Council is in the Clark Archive in the Tate, under reference TGA 8812.1.4.151. It is dated 18 March 1948.

3   Local artists were in some cases commissioned to produce works. For example, in Belfast John Luke was commissioned to paint a large mural on the tympanum of the dome of the City Hall, representing the history of Belfast. A book was published in 1951 called *The Arts in Ulster. A Symposium* edited by Sam Hanna Bell, Nesca Robb and John Hewitt, to coincide with the Festival. Exhibitions of various different types of pictures were held around the country. For example, the Southampton Art Gallery held a show of The Camden Town Group; the Shipley Art Gallery in Gateshead showed 'Contemporary Artists of Durham County'; the Williamson Art Gallery in Birkenhead showed Philip Wilson Steer; and the Women's International Art Club had a show at the RBA Galleries in London.

4   The minutes are in the Arts Council Archive held at the V&A Archive Centre near Olympia. The Art Panel Minutes have not yet been catalogued.

5   1902-1984, he was a painter and stained-glass designer, but also a muralist and pen and ink draughtsman. He ended up doing a large mural for the South Bank.

6   The reason for the large size requirement seems to have been that the Arts Council, and Philip James in particular, wanted the artists to create pictures which would not be the usual sizes generated by artists and sold through their dealers in the expectation that they would end up on the walls of private homes, but rather that they would appeal to the perceived new buyers, such as companies, hotels, churches, municipal bodies, office canteens and so on. Accordingly, many letters were sent out by the Arts Council inviting people from such organisations to come to the viewing. Not many seem to have made purchases.

7   William Roberts, for example, simply sent a curt letter, dated 17 March 1951, saying he was not able to contribute after all. Craxton began work on his picture, but then got an offer to design the set and costumes for the ballet, *Daphnis and Chloë* at Covent Garden. Realising that he couldn't do both, he chose to accept the ballet commission, as it interested him more. (Information supplied to the author by John Craxton in June 2005.)

8   Of course, the Academy included architects and sculptors as well as painters.

9   There must have been relevant shows at various places outside London in private galleries. For example, the Crane Gallery in Manchester had the interesting idea of holding three shows of some of the same artists as the City had seen in the 60 paintings exhibition. As an antidote to the impression that the country's galleries must all have been heaving with modern British art in May 1951, it is worth noting that the Tate also thought it appropriate to show 52 leaving portraits from the Provost's Lodge at Eton, a curious choice at a time of such high-profile Festival-related events.

10   The Arts Council papers for these exhibitions are held in the V&A archive centre under reference ACGB/121/14-16.

11   The private lenders were: Richard Addinsell, Sir Colin

Anderson, Thomas Balston, J.L. Behrend, Howard Bliss, Sir Kenneth Clark, Alec Clifton-Taylor, Miss B. Dawson, H.S. Ede, Max Ede, A. Emery, Brinsley Ford, Mrs Charles Grey, Mr and Mrs F.W. Halliday, Forrest Hewit, Mrs Image, Mrs Cazalet-Keir, Dr Laing, Edward le Bas, Stanley Lief, Mrs Naomi Mitchison, R.D.S. May, Mrs Elsie Myers, Mrs Margaret Nash, Mrs C. Neilson, Eric Newton, Ben Nicholson, Victor Pasmore, Roland Penrose, Robin Pitman, C.S. Reddihough, AJ. McNeil Reid, Ceri Richards, H.M. Roland, John Rothenstein, Mr and Mrs Samuels, Sir Osbert Sitwell, Miss Helen Sutherland, D.W.Tooth, the executrix of the late Edward Wadsworth, Miss Lucy Wertheim and Godfrey Winn. The institutional (public) lenders were heavily weighted towards the North: Bradford City Art Gallery, the British Council, the CAS, the Ferens Art Gallery, Hull, Hanley Museum and Art Gallery, the Harris Museum and Art Gallery, Preston, Leeds City Art Gallery, Southampton Art Gallery, the Tate, the Walker Art Gallery, Liverpool and the Whitworth Art Gallery, Manchester. The private galleries lending were: the Hanover, the Lefevre and the Redfern.

12 It may, on this basis, have been a source of wry amusement to Mr Baxandall when he asked Peter Watson for the loan of his Bacon and he – on 11 March 1951 – refused, without giving a reason. In the end, the Bacons in the show came from the Hanover Gallery, the CAS and Colin Anderson. One suspects the latter was the main member of the subcommittee pushing for Bacon, since he was an early supporter, having caused the CAS to buy its first Bacon as early as 1946.

13 He was invited to do the selection by letter dated 13 November 1950.

14 On 20 June 1951 Robert Buhler, having viewed the exhibition, wrote in to the Arts Council asking for his picture to be removed. He didn't give a reason and it isn't clear whether it was removed.

15 While those born in Ireland did not feature, unless one counts Bacon, at least Gillies and Hunter got in from Scotland. Pasmore got into both Anthologies because of his extraordinary change of style in 1947-1948 from dull 'Euston Road' style to even duller abstract. In this regard it may be worth noting the extremely disparaging – and entertaining – comments by William Johnstone, who knew Pasmore well. Johnstone was Principal first of Camberwell College of Art and then of the Central School. In his autobiography *Points in Time* he noted that Pasmore was not known for being very bright. Also, 'despite all his efforts to be "modern" Victor Pasmore still remains the same decorative painter of good taste, a "drawing room" artist. I am positive that if he had stuck to his Hammersmith paintings his work would have attained much greater depth and profundity; instead of an imitation of the work of other abstract artists, his painting would always have been his own'.

16 Of the private lenders, quite a large number were the artists themselves. This list includes Vanessa Bell, Buhler, Coldstream, Dodgson, Gillies, Gowing, Grant, Le Bas, Moynihan, Napper, Pasmore, Potter, Rogers, Townsend and Weight (together with Ethel Walker's executors, she having recently died). There is a critical letter in the Arts Council files from a member of the public asking why it was necessary to borrow so many pictures from the artists themselves, since this effectively amounted to the Arts Council giving the artists the opportunity to offer their work for sale.

17 See the minutes of the 18th meeting of the Art Panel of the Arts Council, held on 9 May 1950, in the Arts Council archives.

18 Bilbo's entry in Buckman hints at the perversity of this choice by describing him as 'huger-than-life'. His work apparently 'mixed Expressionism, naivety, humour and the bizarre'. One can safely say that his name did not trouble the art critics to any material extent over the years of this study. His dates were 1907-67 and he was German.

19 W.O. Grey is either fictional or so obscure that he doesn't even merit a mention in Buckman.

20 1909-89. Famous for his work with the World Wildlife Fund and for painting birds.

21 1898-1991. A difficult artist to place, her work often appears in auction catalogues. Buckman's opening description can perhaps be left to speak for itself: 'Painter, stage-set and costume designer, writer and noted horsewoman.'

22 Under reference ACGB/121/387(2).

23 One hopes that the shock didn't kill him, but he did die in 1950.

24 In a letter of 15 June 1951.

25 In a letter of 26 February 1951.

26 It is instructive – and revealing – to get a glimpse of Clark's far-reaching influence in all areas of the British art scene at this time. When he wanted something like this, it would appear that he tended to get it.

27 'I have personal reservations about this, for my comments were never meant to be shouted from the housetops. But, after all these years, my casual remarks can perhaps be allowed to stand as a minor testimony to a point-of-view of that period.'

28 I have to show my prejudices by saying that I agree with that. My feeling is that Nicholson is one of the great painters of the 20th-century British art scene.

29 It is noteworthy that the jaded reviewer picks out for comment the artist whose work he is less familiar with.

30 In the context of the tiresome 'Tate Affair'.

31 Curiously, the *Sunday Times* thought that Chadwick's mobile dominated the show.

32 I don't know if this review was written by Alan Clutton-Brock but, if so, there was a certain conflict of interest since he had been one of the three judges. The reviewer, whoever he was, was certainly neutrally complimentary about the five winners chosen by the judges.

33 In file 121/387(2).

34 Thomas Wade Earp (1892-1958) had been educated at Magnus Grammar School, Newark, and Exeter College, Oxford. He had written poetry in his youth and was to write books on Van Gogh, Augustus John, French painting and Frank Dobson, as well as translating Stendhal. The only recreation listed in his *Who's Who* entry (for 1948) was 'silence'.

35 Interestingly, no mention of Bacon.

APPENDIX

MEMBERS OF THE BRITISH AND IRISH ART WORLDS 1945-51

Throughout this book many names have been mentioned and this Appendix provides brief biographical details of those who made up the British and Irish art worlds. Few artists' details are provided, except where they had some sort of rôle which took them beyond the 'mere' act of creation. So, for example, there are no entries for artists like Bacon or Freud, but there are entries for those who engaged in some way with the art establishment (Moore, Coldstream, Lowinsky, Lord Methuen, Edward Le Bas and Sutherland for example) or who enjoyed judging their fellow artists as journalists (such as Ayrton, Heron and Wyndham Lewis). Insofar as artists are mentioned in this Appendix, therefore, it will not be because of their artistic achievements.

In other words, the people whose names are set out in this Appendix were the 'Art Establishment'. They took the views and decisions which led to painters' work being successful or not.

Between them, in only slightly varying permutations, they formed the committees which decided to buy art for various institutions; and as individuals many were amongst the most prominent buyers of modern British and Irish art at the time.

And what summary of this world can be deduced from the 166 names (153 men and 13 women) set out in this Appendix? The predominance of male, public-school (26 from Eton alone and 7 from Winchester) and Oxbridge (68) educated individuals is what the facts tell us. That was what the art world was dominated by in post-War England (undoubtedly to a lesser extent in the very much smaller art worlds of Ireland and Scotland). Whenever – if ever – the predominance of that type materially altered, it was not during the period 1945-51.

PART A

KEY INDIVIDUALS

Sir Colin Anderson 1904-80. Eton and Trinity College, Oxford. Extremely important patron of modern British art. See further details in Chapter 3.

Brynmor Anthony 1886-1966. Llanelli and University College, Aberystwyth. Academic administrator. Member of the Executive Committee of the CAS for Wales.

Leigh Ashton 1897-1983. Winchester and Balliol College, Oxford. Knighted in 1948. His particular interest was Chinese art. Director of the V&A from 1945-55. Member of the Fine Arts Advisory Committee of the British Council. Member of the Art Panel of the Arts Council. Old friend of Kenneth Clark

and had, indeed, been best man at Clark's wedding. His obituary was in the *Times* on 17 March 1983.

Gladys Barnard 1887-1972. Joined the Castle Museum, Norwich in 1904, curator 1937-51. Wrote a brief guide to the art collection. Member of the Art Panel of the Arts Council.

David Baxandall 1905-92. KCS, Wimbledon and London University. Worked at the National Museum of Wales 1929-41 and became Director of Manchester City Art Galleries from 1945-52. Then became Director of the National Galleries of Scotland. He published a book on Ben Nicholson in 1962. Father of art historian Michael Baxandall. Obituaries in the *Guardian* (11 November 1992) and the *Independent* (28 October).

Viscount Bearsted 1882-1948. Second Viscount. Eton and New College, Oxford. Trustee of the Tate from 1938-42 and of the National Gallery from 1936-43.

Clive Bell 1881-1964. Marlborough and Trinity College, Cambridge. His name is associated with two things: membership of the Bloomsbury Group and a distinctive form of art criticism. Produced innumerable books and lived at Charleston in Sussex. Member of the Fine Arts Advisory Committee of the British Council.

John Berger 1926–. St Edward's, Oxford, Chelsea School of Art and Central School of Art. Painter, novelist and art critic.

Douglas Percy Bliss 1900-84. Watson's College, Edinburgh and Edinburgh University. Painter and wood engraver. Studied at the RCA. Friendly with Bawden and Ravilious and wrote a book about the former. He was for a time the London art critic of the *Scotsman*.

Howard Bliss 1894-?. Rugby and Trinity College, Cambridge. Art collector, particularly favouring Hitchens. Member of the Committee of the CAS.

Anthony Blunt 1907-83. Marlborough and Trinity College, Cambridge. Became Director of the Courtauld Institute in 1947. Blunt's heavy presence in the art world need not concern us here too much, because his interests in and influence on contemporary art of the time were minimal. It perhaps does not reflect too well on his taste for contemporary art that he seems to have particularly favoured painters of the Euston Road School. In this he resembled Kenneth Clark. Member of the Fine Arts Advisory Committee of the British Council.

Professor Tom Boase 1898-1974. Rugby and Magdalen College, Oxford. He was Director of the Courtauld and Professor of the History of Art at the University of London 1937-47. Moved up to being President of his old college from 1947-68; was a trustee of the National Gallery 1947-53 and of the British Museum 1950-69; and was a member of the Advisory Council of the V&A 1947-70. Member of the Fine Arts Advisory Committee of the British Council.

Thomas Bodkin 1887-1961. Clongowes Wood and the Royal University of Ireland. Director of the National Gallery of Ireland in 1927 and then first Director of the Barber Institute of Fine Arts in Birmingham in 1935, where he was to remain until 1952. Commissioned by the Irish State to write a *Report on the state of the arts in Ireland*, which was published in 1949 and helped lead to the creation of the Irish Arts Council. His collection of pictures was sold at auction in 1959. His obituary was in the *Times* on 25 April 1961.

James Bomford 1896-1979. Epsom College. Stockbroker, then farmer. Extremely important patron of modern British artists, especially Bacon. See further details in Chapter 3.

Tancred Borenius 1885-1948. Born in Finland. Became Professor of History of Art at University College, London in 1922 and was editor of the *Burlington Magazine* from 1940-45.

Oliver Brown 1885-1966. St Paul's School. Became a partner in the Leicester Galleries in 1914. Member of the Art Panel of the Arts Council. Highly important figure in British art of the period covered by this book.

Lillian Browse 1906-2005. Art dealer. Helped to found Roland, Browse and Delbanco.

Sir William Burrell 1861-1958. Wealthy shipowner. Left enormous collection of art objects to the City of Glasgow in 1944 but although the bulk of his collection was handed over in 1944, he continued to acquire works of art for the rest of his life. For almost half a century he spent on average per annum the incredible sum of £20,000 on art. In 1948 he spent over £60,000. He was at one time a trustee of the Tate and of the National Gallery of Scotland 1923-46.

Frances Byng-Stamper ob. 1969. Sister of Caroline Lucas. Created an art gallery in Lewes in Sussex in 1941 and established the Miller's Press there in 1945. Had previously lived at Manorbier Castle in Wales. Member of the Executive Committee of the CAS for Wales for over 30 years.

Thelma Cazalet-Keir 1899-1989. From a wealthy political background. Conservative politician. Art collector. Member of the committee of the CAS.

Sir Wynne Cemlyn-Jones 1888-1966. Shrewsbury and London University. A founder member of the Executive Committee of the CAS for Wales.

Sir Kenneth Clark 1903-83. Winchester and Trinity College, Oxford. Perhaps the dominant figure of the British art world during our period. See Chapter 3.

Alan Clutton-Brock 1904-76. Eton and King's College, Cambridge. Became an art historian, art critic of the *Times*, trustee of the National Gallery and Slade Professor of Fine Art at Cambridge. One of the three judges for '60 Paintings for '51'. His father, Arthur Clutton-Brock, had also been art critic of the *Times* and was one of the founders of the CAS.

Colonel Gerald Coke 1907-90. Eton and New College, Oxford. Member of the Fine Arts Advisory Committee of the British Council. Merchant banker.

William Coldstream 1908-87. Attended Slade. Visiting teacher at Camberwell from 1945-49 and Slade Professor of Fine Art, 1949-75. Trustee of the Tate and of the National Gallery. Member of the Art Panel of the Arts Council.

Maurice Collis 1889-1973. Rugby and Corpus Christi College, Oxford. Wrote extensively about his own life, publishing his Diaries 1949-69 and two volumes of autobiography, The Journey Up and The Journey Outward. He knew well a number of the artists covered in this book, especially Topolski, Peake, Lowry and Scottie Wilson. Began to write art criticism for the Observer in January 1945. He was writing for Time and Tide at the time and carried on doing so until 1951. Pieces by him also appeared (in 1947) in *Harper's Bazaar* and in *La France Libre*.

Winifred Coombe Tennant 1874-1956. Patron of Welsh artists. See *Winifred Coombe Tennant: a life through art* by Peter Lord.

Douglas Cooper 1911-84. Wealthy art historian and collector, of Australian origins. Enjoyed controversies. Papers now in the Getty Research Library in California.

Samuel Courtauld 1876-1947. Rugby. Wealthy art collector. Trustee of the Tate and the National Gallery. Member of the Art Panel of the Arts Council.

Trenchard Cox 1905-95. Eton and King's College, Cambridge. Member of the Art Panel of the Arts Council, Director of the Birmingham Museum and Art Gallery from 1944-55. Took over from Leigh Ashton as Director of the V&A 1956-66.

Earl of Crawford 1900-75. Twenty-eighth Earl. Eton and Magdalen College, Oxford. Trustee of the Tate 1932-37; of the National Gallery 1935-60; and of the British Museum 1940-73. Member of the Standing Commission on Museums and Galleries 1937-52; Chairman of the Trustees of the National Galleries of Scotland 1952-72; Chairman of the Royal Fine Arts Commission 1943-57; and so on.

Hugh Crawford 1898-1982. Painter, mural artist and designer. Studied at Glasgow School of Art, the Central School and St Martin's. On the staff at Glasgow from 1925-48; at Gray's School of Art, Aberdeen from 1948-54; and then principal of Duncan of Jordanstone College of Art, Dundee from 1954-64.

Geoffrey Crawshay 1892-1954. Wellington College and University College, Cardiff. A great social benefactor in Wales. Member of the Executive Committee of the CAS for Wales.

Anthony Cronin 1928-. University College, Dublin. Irish writer, poet and critic. Personal friend of Colquhoun and MacBryde.

Stanley Cursiter 1887-1976. Kirkwall Grammar

School and Edinburgh College of Art. Keeper of the National Galleries of Scotland 1930-48.

Leonard Daniels 1909-98. Painter, particularly of portraits. Had studied at the Regent Street Polytechnic and the RCA. Head of Painting at Leeds College of Art. Principal of Camberwell. In 1965 became President of the National Society for Art Education.

Robin Darwin 1910-74. Eton and Cambridge University. Studied at the Slade. Sufficiently well-known as an artist in his own right that he had a solo exhibition at the Leicester Galleries in April 1946. Great-grandson of Charles Darwin and a great-great grandson of Josiah Wedgwood. His appointment as Principal of the Slade was announced in the *Times* on 2 September 1947 and he took up his position on 1 January 1948. In the Journal of the Royal Society of Arts for 5 February 1954 there appeared the text of a speech which he had given to the Society on 20 January 1954 called 'The Dodo and the Phoenix: the Royal College of Art since the War'. This described how run-down and ramshackle the college was in 1948 and how much effort had gone into improving and modernising its facilities.

Gwendoline Davies 1882-1951. Member of the Executive Committee of the CAS for Wales. She and her sister, Margaret, were immensely rich collectors, especially of works by Impressionist painters. Margaret particularly also bought 20th-century British art by such people as John, Herman, Stanley Spencer, Paul Nash, Cedric Morris, Kyffin Williams, Frost, Piper, Sickert, Hitchens and Wyndham Lewis. They together bequeathed 250 works to the National Museum of Wales in 1951 and 1963, having already given works in 1940. See Fairclough, op. cit.

Margaret Davies 1884-1963. Sister of Gwendoline.

Bernard Denvir 1917-94. Merton College, Oxford. Distinguished art critic, art historian and writer. First editor of *Art News and Review* from 1947.

Edward O'Rorke Dickey 1894-1977. Wellington and Trinity College, Cambridge. Studied at the Westminster School of Art. Member of the Art Panel of the Art Council. First curator of the Minories Gallery in Colchester. His obituary was in the *Times* on 17 August 1977.

Campbell Dodgson 1867-1948. Winchester and New College, Oxford. Joined the British Museum in 1893 in the Department of Prints and Drawings and became Keeper in 1913, retiring in 1932. He had a large collection of modern prints and drawings. He married a daughter of the famous Warden Spooner of New College. Member of the Fine Arts Advisory Committee of the British Council.

Sean Dorman St Columba's College, Rathfarnham, and Worcester College, Oxford. Dorman was an Anglo-Irish Protestant. He was also editor of monthly magazine, Commentary. His autobiographies are called *Limelight over the Liffey* and *Portrait of my Youth*.

Thomas Earp 1892-1958. Magnus Grammar School, Newark, and Exeter College, Oxford. Art critic for the *Daily Telegraph*. Had written poetry in his youth and was to write books on Van Gogh, Augustus John, French painting and Frank Dobson, as well as translating Stendhal. The only recreation listed in his *Who's Who* entry (for 1948) was 'silence'.

Wilfrid Evill 1891-1963. Admitted as a solicitor in October 1919 and began work in Finsbury Square in the City. Great collector of the work of contemporary British artists. Member of the committee of the CAS.

Ian Fleming 1906-94. Painter and printmaker. Studied at the Glasgow School of Art, where he taught 1931-48. After Hospitalfield, he went on to become Principal of Gray's School of Art in Aberdeen 1954-72.

Brinsley Ford 1908-99. Eton and Trinity College, Oxford. According to one obituary, led 'a life of civilised indolence'. He was in fact something of an old-fashioned art connoisseur. Heavily involved with the National Art Collections Fund. Wealthy art collector. Director of the *Burlington Magazine* 1952-86. Chairman of the National Art Collections Fund 1975-80.

Sir Cyril Fox 1882-1967. Christ's Hospital and Magdalene College, Cambridge. Director of the National Museum of Wales 1926-48. Member of the Executive Committee of the CAS for Wales. Primarily an archaeologist.

Zoltan Lewinter Frankl 1894-1961. Great collector of modern Irish art. Based in Northern Ireland.

George Furlong 1898-1987. Clongowes Wood and UCD. He was Director of the National Gallery of Ireland 1935-50. Previously an Assistant Keeper at the National Gallery in London under Kenneth Clark.

Richard Gainsborough 1896-1969. Magdalen College, Oxford. His second wife was the artist Eileen Mayo. Founder of the *Art News and Review* in 1949. His *Times* obituary was on 17 September 1969.

William Gibson 1902-60. Westminster and Christ Church, Oxford, at both of which he was a contemporary of Philip Hendy, and keeper of the National Gallery from 1939. He wrote occasional art criticism (e.g., for *Britain Today*). According to his obituary in the *Times* he liked to live without telephone, wireless or, where possible, electric light.

Mary Glasgow 1905-83. Central Newcastle High School and Lady Margaret Hall, Oxford. Founding Secretary of CEMA in 1939 and first Secretary General of the Arts Council, which she left in 1951. There are frequent mentions of her in 'Artist Unknown. An alternative history of the Arts Council' by Richard Witts. Her autobiography is called *The Nineteen Hundreds – A Diary in Retrospect*. Her obituary was in the *Times* on 2 November 1983.

Theodore Goodman Art critic in Dublin. Brother of well-known lawyer, Lord Goodman.

Nigel Gosling 1909-82. Eton. Had a long career at the Observer, where he started in 1950. He became art critic in 1962 and stayed in that position until 1975. He was also ballet critic from 1955-82. He had been at Eton with David Astor, who became the proprietor of the paper in 1948. Gosling's art journalism was later published under the title *Prowling the Pavements: selected art writings 1950-1980*.

Barbara Ayrton Gould 1886-1950. Notting Hill High School and University College, London. Labour MP. Mother of artist, Michael Ayrton. Member of Art Panel of the Arts Council.

Duncan Grant 1885-1978. St Paul's. Artist. Member of the Art Panel of the Arts Council.

Eric (Peter) Gregory 1887-1959. Bradford Grammar School. Great art collector. Proprietor of publishing house Lund Humphries.

Geoffrey Grigson 1905-85. Wrote poetry and many books on many different subjects, including art.

Allan Gwynne-Jones 1892-1982. Bedales. On the staff at the Slade from 1930-59. Trustee of the Tate.

Lord Harlech 1885-1964. Fourth Baron. Eton and New College, Oxford. Member of the Arts Council (until 1948), trustee of the National Gallery 1927-34 and 1936-41, of the Tate 1933-38 and of the British Museum 1937-47. Member of the Fine Arts Advisory Committee of the British Council.

Robert Harling 1910-2008. Owen's School and the Central School of Arts and Crafts. Typographer, graphic artist, designer, editor and novelist. Editor of *Image*.

Philip Hendy 1900-80. Westminster and Christ Church, Oxford. Director of the National Gallery. Member of the Art Panel of the Arts Council. Slade Professor of Fine Art, Oxford.

Patrick Heron 1920-99. Little formal education. Attended Slade. A tendentious art critic, whose work appeared in *The New English Weekly*, the *New Statesman and Nation* and *Art News and Review*, amongst other places. Minor artist.

John Hewitt 1907-87. The Methodist College, Belfast and the Queen's University of Belfast. Poet. Appointed art assistant at the Belfast Museum and Art Gallery, eventually becoming Deputy Director. He was a member of the Arts Council of Northern Ireland from 1943-56.

Arthur Hind 1880-1957. City of London School and Emmanuel College, Cambridge. Art historian, curator and watercolour painter. Keeper of prints and drawings at the British Museum 1933-45, having worked there since 1903. Slade Professor of Fine Art at Oxford 1921-27. Member of the committee of the CAS.

George Hoellering 1897-1980. Hungarian born. Film producer. Involved in the early years of the ICA.

Geoffrey Holme Art critic. Editor of *The Studio*.

Tom Honeyman 1891-1971. Trained at Glasgow University as a doctor but later changed direction and joined Reid and Lefevre as an art dealer. Director of Glasgow Art Gallery from 1939-54. His particular interest was in modern French paintings. His autobiography is called *Art and Audacity*. In 2006 the Glasgow Art Gallery at Kelvingrove acquired an attractive portrait of him by the Scottish Colourist Leslie Hunter, painted in about 1930. Member of the Fine Arts Advisory Committee of the British Council.

The Revd Walter Hussey 1909-85. Marlborough and Keble College, Oxford. Patron of modern British art, although largely operating as such outside our period. Whilst Vicar of St Matthew's, Northampton,1938-55 he commissioned music from Britten and Tippett, sculpture from Moore and a picture by Sutherland. It is thought that this enlightened attitude to church patronage encouraged the creation of the atmosphere which led to the form of the patronage for the interior of Coventry Cathedral in the 1950s. Later, outside the scope of this study, Hussey moved on to become Dean of Chichester Cathedral. There he was to commission a set of copes designed by Ceri Richards, an altar frontal by Cecil Collins, an altar tapestry from Piper, a stained-glass window from Chagall and music by Bernstein and Walton.

Robin Ironside 1912-65. Painter and writer. Assistant keeper at the Tate 1937-46. Member of the committee of the CAS.

Philip James 1901-74. Sherborne and University College, London. Director of Art at CEMA and then at the Arts Council from 1942-58. Member of the Fine Arts Advisory Committee of the British Council.

Arthur Jeffress 1904-61. American art collector and dealer (based in London). Provided financial backing for Hanover Gallery.

William Johnstone 1897-1981. Scottish artist. Studied at Edinburgh College of Art. Principal of Camberwell 1938-46; Principal of the Central 1947-60.

Percy Jowett 1882-1955. Painter, especially of landscapes. Attended Leeds College of Art and the RCA. Became Principal of the RCA. Member of the Art Panel of the Arts Council. Exhibited widely, with a series of one-man shows at the St George's Gallery in the 1920s. His obituary was in the *Times* 7 March 1955.

Viscount Jowitt 1885-1957. First Viscount; later first and only Earl. Marlborough and New College, Oxford. Lord Chancellor. Trustee of the Tate and of the National Gallery.

Sean Keating 1889-1977. Studied at the Dublin Metropolitan School of Art, where he was taught by Orpen. President of the RHA from 1949-62.

Sir Gerald Kelly 1879-1972. Eton and Trinity Hall, Cambridge. President of the RA from 1949-54.

Lord Keynes 1883-1946. Eton and King's College, Cambridge. Economist. First Chairman of the Arts Council, his interest in the arts was focused on opera and ballet.

Rex Nan Kivell 1899-1977. New Zealander. Director of the Redfern Gallery for over 50 years, according to his *Times* obituary on 21 June 1977.

Eardley Knollys 1902-91. Winchester and Oxford. Painter. In 1945 bought a house called Long Crichel in Dorset, together with Desmond Shawe-Taylor and Eddie Sackville-West. Raymond Mortimer and Pat Trevor-Roper later acquired an interest. Founded the Storran Gallery in London. Member of the committee of the CAS.

James Laver 1895-1975. The Liverpool Institute and New College, Oxford. Prolific author on a wide variety of subjects. Published an autobiography in 1963 called *Museum Piece*. When the War finished he returned to his pre-War job at the V&A as Keeper of Prints and Drawings. (He was an Oxford contemporary of Leigh Ashton, who was by then the Director of the V&A.) A large obituary was published in the *Times* on 4 June 1975.

Edward Le Bas 1904-66. Minor painter. Harrow and Pembroke College, Cambridge. Member of the committee of the CAS and of the Art Panel of the Arts Council.

John Lehmann 1907-87. Eton and Trinity College, Cambridge. Writer. Founded Penguin New Writing and published there reproductions of the work of various young British artists, such as Craxton, Colquhoun and Vaughan.

Wyndham Lewis 1882-1957. Rugby and the Slade. Artist, critic and writer. Art critic for the *Listener*.

Dr Robert Lillie 1907-77. Scottish art collector. His papers in the National Library of Scotland include correspondence with a number of people mentioned in this book, including Cursiter, Rothenstein, Gabriel White and David Baxandall.

Major Alfred Longden ob. 1954. Durham School, he was a medallist at the Royal College of Art. He was an extremely experienced art administrator and was Director of Fine Art at the British Council 1940-47 and a member of the Art Panel of the Arts Council. His *Times* obituary, on 21 September 1954, described him, rather damningly, as 'essentially an organiser'. After the British Council he became Director and Curator of the Wernher Collection at Luton Hoo.

Thomas Lowinsky 1892-1947. Eton and Trinity College, Oxford (the same combination as the later Sir Colin Anderson and Brinsley Ford), and then at the Slade. Member of the committee of the CAS and of the Art Panel of the Arts Council. He was an unusual, independent artist and, another coincidence, ended up living at the Old Rectory in Aldbourne, the same village in Wiltshire as Jimmy Bomford.

Caroline Lucas ob. 1967. Studied art in Paris, Rome and London. At one time had a studio in 77 Bedford Gardens. Established art gallery in Lewes in 1941 with her sister Frances Byng-Stamper. Founded the Miller's Press in 1945.

D.S. MacColl 1859-1948. Glasgow Academy, University College School and Lincoln College, Oxford. Painter and art critic. Keeper of the Tate 1906-11 and of the Wallace Collection 1911-24. Trustee of the Tate.

Duncan Macdonald ob. 1948. Director of Reid and Lefevre. Great supporter of various contemporary British artists.

Neville MacGeough Bond 1907-86. Eton and King's College, Cambridge. Prominent Northern Irish collector of modern British and Irish art. Lived at the Argory.

Thomas MacGreevy 1893-1967. Trinity College, Dublin after serving with the British Army during the First World War. Interestingly, like his predecessor, George Furlong, he also had a connection with the National Gallery in London during Clark's time, working there as an occasional lecturer from 1935-41. Close friend of Samuel Beckett.

Colin MacInnes 1914-76. Well-known novelist who wrote *City of Spades* (1957) and *Absolute Beginners* (1957), as well as many other novels. He was also later to write, jointly with Bryan Robertson and with an introduction by Kenneth Clark, what is still the main book on the Australian artist, Sidney Nolan. What is perhaps less well known is that he was a grandson of Burne-Jones, his mother was the novelist, Angela Thirkell, and he was himself a painter, having attended the Euston Road School. On the staff at Camberwell from 1946-48. His name crops up in various parts of the art world from time to time. For example, he helped to select pictures from the British Council Collection to tour Canada in 1952/3 under the heading 'Five Contemporary British Painters'.

Sir Eric Maclagan 1879-1951. Winchester and Christ Church, Oxford. Vice President of the Society of Antiquaries; President of the Museums Association 1935-36; Chairman of the National Buildings Record; Director of the V&A 1924-45. Member of the Fine Arts Advisory Committee of the British Council.

James Manson 1879-1945. Alleyn's School. A painter. Director of the Tate from 1930-38. Member of the Executive Committee of the CAS for Wales.

Sir Stanley Marchant 1883-1949. Royal Academy of Music. Fellow of Pembroke College, Oxford. Chairman of Council of Royal School of Church Music. Member of Art Panel of the Arts Council.

Sir Edward Marsh 1872-1953. Westminster and Trinity College, Cambridge. Civil servant. Long serving member of the committee of the CAS.

Member of the Fine Arts Advisory Committee of the British Council. Trustee of the Tate. His life is dealt with in truly staggering detail in a biography of over 700 pages by Christopher Hassall.

Roger Marvell Post-War art critic of the New Statesman and Nation.

Stewart Mason 1906-83. Uppingham and Worcester College, Oxford. Director of Education for Leicestershire from 1947-71. Worked with Alec Clifton-Taylor and Rex Nan Kivell (and later Bryan Robertson) to create large collection of modern British art, which was used for Leicestershire schools.

Vincent Massey 1887-1967. Born in Toronto, he was at Balliol 1911-13 and became High Commissioner for Canada in the UK 1935-46. He was Chairman of the National Gallery 1943-46. Member of the committee of the CAS. Back in Canada he chaired the Royal Commission on National Development in the Arts, Letters and Sciences 1949-51. His autobiography is *What's Past is Prologue* and Claude Bissell has written two volumes of biography of him, *The Young Vincent Massey* and *The Imperial Canadian*.

Denis Mathews 1913-1997. Highgate School and the Slade. Painter, printmaker and critic. He had a solo exhibition at the Leicester Galleries in 1947.

Freddie Mayor 1903-73. Founder of the Mayor Gallery.

A.J.L. McDonnell 1904-64). Australian. London-based art adviser (from 1947) to the wealthy Felton Bequest of the National Gallery of Victoria. He was permitted to spend the large amount of £2,000 p.a. on contemporary British art without reference to Melbourne. One of the judges of '60 Paintings for '51'.

Edward Mesens 1903-71. Belgian artist and dealer. Ran the London Gallery.

Lord Methuen 1886-1974. Fourth Baron. Eton and New College, Oxford. Artist. Member of the Committee of the CAS. Trustee of the Tate and of the National Gallery.

Michael Middleton Art critic for the *Spectator* from May 1946.

Tom Monnington 1902-76. Painter, who had studied at the Slade, whose staff he joined in 1949. Member of the Art Panel of the Arts Council. Became President of the Royal Academy in 1966.

William Montagu-Pollock 1903-93. Marlborough and Trinity College, Cambridge. He was a senior member of the Diplomatic Service. His father was a baronet. Member of the Fine Arts Advisory Committee of the British Council.

Henry Moore 1898-1986. Sculptor. Member of the Art Panel of the Arts Council. Trustee of the National Gallery and of the Tate.

Sir Owen Morshead 1893-1977. Marlborough and Magdalene College, Cambridge. Librarian and Assistant Keeper of the Royal Archives at Windsor

Castle 1926-58. Member of the Fine Arts Advisory Committee of the British Council. His obituary appeared in the *Times* on 3 June 1977.

Raymond Mortimer 1895-1980. Malvern and Balliol College, Oxford. Writer and critic. Member of the committee of the CAS.

Rodrigo Moynihan 1910-90. Painter. Member of the Art Panel of the Arts Council. Professor of Painting at the RCA 1948-57.

Sir Alfred Munnings 1878-1959. Framlington College. Painter. President of the Royal Academy 1944-49. Published three volumes of autobiography.

Grant Murray 1877-1950. Principal of the Swansea College of Art 1910-43 and Director of Glynn Vivian Art Gallery in Swansea 1910-50. Member of the Executive Committee of the CAS for Wales.

Ernest Musgrave 1902-57. Director of Temple Newsam Gallery in Yorkshire. Member of the Art Panel of the Arts Council.

Eric Newton 1893-1965. Artist, art historian and critic. Art critic for the *Manchester Guardian* and 1947-51 for the *Sunday Times*. Member of the Art Panel of the Arts Council. There is a 1943 portrait of him by Barnett Freedman in the National Portrait Gallery.

Benedict Nicolson 1914-78. Eton and Balliol College, Oxford. Son of Sir Harold Nicolson and Vita Sackville-West. Deputy Surveyor of the King's Pictures under Kenneth Clark 1939-47 and editor of the *Burlington Magazine* thereafter.

Peadar O'Donnell 1893-1986. St Patrick's College, Dublin. Member of the IRA. Editor of the *Bell* 1946-54.

Sean O'Faolain 1900-91. The Presentation Brothers Secondary School, Cork and at the National University of Ireland. Founder member and editor of the *Bell*. Irish short story writer. Later Director of Irish Arts Council 1957-59.

Earnan O'Malley 1898-1957. Irish art critic, writer and collector. Member of the IRA.

Roland Penrose 1900-84. Leighton Park School and Queens' College, Cambridge. Painter, writer and collector. Helped to found the ICA.

Hugo Pitman 1892-1963. Eton and New College, Oxford. Stockbroker. Member of the committee of the CAS.

Sir Ernest Pooley 1876-1966. First and last baronet. Winchester and Pembroke College, Cambridge. Appointed Chairman of the Arts Council in succession to Lord Keynes, in 1946. Held the post until 1953.

A.E. Popham 1889-1970. Dulwich and University College, London. Member of the committee of the CAS. Succeeded Arthur Hind as keeper of prints and drawings at the British Museum in 1945 and published his great *Drawings of Leonardo da Vinci* in the same year. Retired in 1954 and embarked on a new career at the age of 65, cataloguing print collections for auction houses and scholars.

Arthur Power 1891-1984. Born in Guernsey, he came to Ireland at an early age with his father who was in the British army. He later inherited a large house called Bellevue near Waterford. Served in the British Army in the First World War. Lived in Paris about 1919-30, becoming friendly with James Joyce and Modigliani. After the sale of Bellevue in 1940, he lived in Dublin, painting and writing. He also wrote for the Waterford News. He was made an honorary member of the RHA. His autobiography is called *From the old Waterford House.*

Beatrice Proudfoot ?-? Controlled Aitken Dott (the Scottish Gallery) 1940-50.

Herbert Read 1893-1968. Leeds University. Art critic. Member of the Fine Arts Advisory Committee of the British Council and of the Art Panel of the Arts Council.

Hon Sir Jasper Ridley 1887-1951. Eton and Balliol College, Oxford. Chairman of the Tate trustees.

Bryan Robertson 1925-2002. Battersea Grammar School. Curator of the Whitechapel 1952-68.

Earl of Rosse 1906-79. Sixth Earl. Eton and Christ Church, Oxford. Even the Irish arts world in a Republican age could not escape the post-war influence of Etonians which so pervaded the institutions of the British arts world.

John Rothenstein 1901-92. Bedales and Worcester College, Oxford. Director of the Tate; member of the Fine Arts Advisory Committee of the British Council; member of the Art Panel of the Arts Council; member of the committee of the CAS.

Gordon Russell 1892-1980. Campden Grammar School. Designer, his name being linked during the War with 'Utility Furniture', which was intended to be furniture which was well designed, affordable and mass-produced. Chairman of the Board of Trade Committee on Design from 1943-47, when he became Director of the Council of Industrial Design. Later became the first chairman of the Crafts Council. Member of the Fine Arts Advisory Committee of the British Council and of the Art Panel of the Arts Council.

John Russell 1919-2008. St Paul's and Magdalen College, Oxford. Wrote for the *Sunday Times* for many years from 1951 and then moved to New York and wrote for the *New York Times*. He also found time to write a large number of books on a wide variety of subjects including Bacon, Ben Nicholson and Henry Moore.

Earl of Sandwich 1874-1962. Ninth Earl. Winchester and Magdalen College, Oxford. Trustee of the Tate

1934-41. Member of the Fine Arts Advisory Committee of the British Council and of the Art Panel of the Arts Council.

Randolph Schwabe 1885-1948. Painter, illustrator and designer. Studied at the RCA and the Slade. Had been Professor at the Slade since 1930. His grave, in the Churchyard Extension of Hampstead Parish Church, is marked by the statue of a girl by sculptor Alan Durst.

Hugh Scrutton 1917-91. Charterhouse and King's College, Cambridge. Director of the Whitechapel Art Gallery. (Later Director of the Walker Art Gallery, Liverpool.)

Lady Sempill (Cecilia Dunbar-Kilburn) Died 1984. Had married the 19th Lord Sempill in 1941 after the death of his first wife (who had been Lavery's daughter). Studied at the Royal College of Art in the 1920s and had won a travelling scholarship to the Far East. During the later 1930s she had run a shop called Dunbar-Hay, selling the best of British design. Collected modern pottery by such as Lucie Rie, Bernard Leach and William Gordon, much of it remaining in Craigievar Castle in Aberdeenshire. Member of the committee of the CAS. Her knowledge of modern crafts is reflected in the fact that she was the CAS buyer for their Pottery and Crafts Fund in 1945/6. (I am particularly grateful to Lady Sempill's daughter, Janet Forbes-Sempill, for the information in this note.)

Edward Sheehy Art critic of the *Dublin Magazine*.

James Sleator 1885-1950. Painter. Studied at the Dublin Metropolitan School of Art and was heavily influenced by the teaching of Orpen. President of the RHA.

Sir Donald Somervell 1889-1960. Harrow and Magdalen College, Oxford. Made a Lord Justice of Appeal in 1946 and a Law Lord in 1954 as Baron Somervell of Harrow. Fellow of All Souls. Trustee of the Tate.

Lilian Somerville 1905-85. Abbot's Hill. Married to the composer, Horace Somerville. She was also a painter, as well as an administrator, and had studied at the Slade. Member of the Fine Arts Advisory Committee of the British Council, and of the Art Panel of the Arts Council.

John Steegman 1899-1966. Clifton and King's College, Cambridge. Keeper of the Department of Art at the National Museum of Wales since 1945. Previously worked at the National Portrait Gallery. Lectured for the British Council on British art on many occasions and acted as an art adviser to Margaret Davies in her later years. Member of the Fine Arts Advisory Committee of the British Council and of the Executive Committee of the CAS for Wales.

Sir John Stirling-Maxwell 1866-1956. 10th baronet. Eton

and Trinity College, Cambridge. He had been Chairman of the Royal Fine Art Commission for Scotland and also a trustee of the Scottish National Galleries. He was a founder member of the National Trust for Scotland in 1931. He lived at Pollok House, which was given after his death to the City of Glasgow and opened to the public.

Graham Sutherland 1903-80. Epsom College. Artist. Tate trustee.

Denys Sutton 1917-91. Uppingham and Exeter College, Oxford. Art critic. Editor of *Apollo* 1962-87. Member of the Fine Arts Advisory Committee of the British Council.

David Sylvester 1924-2001. University College School. Art writer, known for his obsessive promotion of Francis Bacon.

Basil Taylor 1922-75. Tonbridge and Wadham College, Oxford. Attended the Slade. Worked at the BBC 1945-51 and 1949-50 was Secretary of the National Art Collections Fund. Member of the Fine Arts Advisory Committee of the British Council. Expert on Stubbs. Wrote on art occasionally for the *New Statesman* and the *Spectator*. His obituary was in the *Times* on 12 July 1975.

Viscount Tredegar 1893-1949. Second Viscount. Eton and Christ Church, Oxford. Member of the Fine Arts Advisory Committee of the British Council. Member of the Executive Committee of the CAS for Wales. A notorious eccentric, his *Times* obituary, on 28 April 1949, is headed 'A modern dilettante'. His love of animals extended to a pet macaw which he allowed to perch on his shoulder. Perhaps this was a characteristic of the Welsh upper classes at the time: there is a photograph in the Tate Archive of Cedric Morris with a pet macaw on his shoulder.

Sir Leonard Twiston-Davies 1894-1953. Charterhouse and Liverpool University. He was a great archive collector. Member of the Executive Committee of the CAS for Wales. President of the National Museum of Wales in 1947.

Victor Waddington Art dealer, initially in Dublin and subsequently in London.

Lord Howard de Walden 1880-1946. Eighth Baron. Eton. Trustee of the Tate 1938-46. Chairman of the Executive Committee of the CAS for Wales 1937-46.

Nevile Wallis Art critic for the *Observer* and writer.

Allan Walton 1891-1948. Harrow. Architect and painter, attending the Slade and the Westminster School of Art. Director of the Glasgow School of Art 1943-45. Member of the Fine Arts Advisory Committee of the British Council, and had just been appointed Professor of textile design at the RCA when he died.

Alan Ward ?-? Member of the committee of the CAS. Married to John Rothenstein's sister, Rachel.

Ellis Waterhouse 1905-85. Marlborough and New College, Oxford. Described in his *Times* obituary, on 9 September 1985, as perhaps the most distinguished art historian of his generation. Member of the Fine Arts Advisory Committee of the British Council and of the Art Panel of the Arts Council. Editor of the *Burlington Magazine* in 1946; Reader in Art History at Manchester University in 1947; Director of the National Galleries of Scotland in 1949. Became Director of the Barber Institute, Birmingham, 1952.

Francis Watson 1907-92. Shrewsbury and St John's College, Cambridge. Art historian and museum curator. Trustee of the Whitechapel Art Gallery. Assistant keeper at the Wallace Collection. Member of the Art Panel of the Arts Council. Director of Visual Arts at the British Council.

Peter Watson 1908-56. Eton and St John's College, Oxford. Important art patron. See further details in Chapter 3.

Duke of Wellington 1885-1972. Seventh Duke. Eton. Surveyor of the King's Works of Art 1936-43 and trustee of the National Gallery 1950-59. Member of the Fine Arts Advisory Committee of the British Council.

Sir Charles Wheeler 1892-1974. Sculptor. President of the RA 1956-66. Knighted in 1958. Trustee of the Tate.

Leo Whelan 1892-1956. Painter. Attended the Dublin School of Art under Orpen. Represented the RHA on the Board of Governors of the National Gallery of Ireland and on the art advisory committee of the Municipal Gallery of Modern Art in Dublin.

Eric White 1905-85. Wrote innumerable books about music and eventually became the Arts Council's first literature director.

Gabriel White 1902-88. Downside and Trinity College, Oxford. Member of the Art Panel of the Arts Council. The influence of Trinity men on the art world during our period must be a coincidence, but it included Anderson, Clark, Ford and Lowinsky – as well as White. In fact Trinity was, under the presidency of Blakiston at this time, notoriously sporty and keen on undergraduates from the grander public schools.

James White 1913-2003. Belvedere College. Tenth director of the National Gallery of Ireland 1964-80 and the author of a number of books on Irish artists. There is a striking portrait of him by Irish artist Edward Maguire.

Bill Williams 1896-1977. Manchester University. Knighted in 1955. Editor-in-chief of Penguin Books 1935-65. Executive member of both the British Council and the Arts Council. Became Chairman of the Art Panel of the Arts Council.

John Witt 1907-82. Eton and New College, Oxford. Solicitor, eventually becoming Senior Partner of Stephenson Harwood. Trustee of the National Gallery for 14 years. Member of the Fine Arts Advisory Committee of the British Council.

PART B
KEY INDIVIDUALS IN KEY PURCHASING INSTITUTIONS

THE ARTS COUNCIL – MEMBERS OF THE ART PANEL

Sir Colin Anderson Eton, Trinity College, Oxford Member of the Fine Arts Advisory Committee of the British Council; member of the committee of the CAS; trustee of the Tate.

Leigh Ashton Winchester. Balliol College, Oxford. Member of the Fine Arts Advisory Committee of the British Council; Director of the V&A.

Gladys Barnard Curator of Castle Museum, Norwich.

Oliver Brown St Paul's. Director of the Leicester Galleries.

Thelma Cazalet-Keir Conservative MP. Member of the committee of the CAS.

Sir Kenneth Clark Winchester. Trinity College, Oxford. Member of the Fine Arts Advisory Committee of the British Council; Slade Professor of Fine Art, Oxford University; member of the committee of the CAS; director of the National Gallery; trustee of the Tate; member of the committee of the Royal Fine Arts Commission; member of the committee of the NACF.

William Coldstream Artist.

Samuel Courtauld Rugby. Trustee of the Tate and of the National Gallery.

Trenchard Cox Eton. King's College, Cambridge. Director of Birmingham Museum and Art Gallery.

Barbara Ayrton Gould Notting Hill High School. University College, London. Labour MP. Mother of artist, Michael Ayrton.

Duncan Grant St Paul's. Artist.

Sir Philip Hendy Westminster. Christ Church, Oxford. Member of the Fine Arts Advisory Committee of the British Council; director of the National Gallery; Slade Professor of Fine Art, Oxford University.

Philip James Sherborne. University College, London. Member of the Fine Arts Advisory Committee of the British Council; director of Art at the Arts Council.

Percy Jowett Principal of the RCA.

Lord Keynes Eton. King's College, Cambridge. Chairman of the Arts Council.

Edward le Bas Harrow. Cambridge. Member of the Committee of the CAS.

Major Alfred Longden Durham. Art director of the XIV Olympiad; director of Fine Art Department of the British Council.

Thomas Lowinsky Eton. Trinity College, Oxford. Member of the committee of the CAS.

Sir Stanley Marchant Royal Academy of Music. Fellow of Pembroke College, Oxford. Chairman of Council of Royal School of Church Music .

Tom Monnington Brunswick School. University College, London. Later PRA.

Henry Moore Trustee of the Tate.

Rodrigo Moynihan Professor of Painting at the RCA 1948-57.

Ernest Musgrave Director of Temple Newsam Gallery.

Eric Newton Art critic.

Edward O'Rorke Dickey Wellington. Trinity College, Cambridge. Staff Inspector for Art, Ministry of Education.

Sir Ernest Pooley Winchester. Pembroke College, Cambridge. Chairman of the Arts Council.

Herbert Read Member of the Fine Arts Advisory Committee of the British Council.

John Rothenstein Bedales. Worcester College, Oxford. Director of the Tate; member of the Fine Arts Advisory Committee of the British Council; member of the committee of the CAS.

Gordon Russell Campden Grammar School. Member of the Fine Arts Advisory Committee of the British Council.

Lilian Somerville Member of the Fine Arts Advisory Committee of the British Council.

Ellis Waterhouse Marlborough. New College, Oxford. Reader in History of Art, University of Manchester; fellow of Magdalen College, Oxford.

Francis Watson Shrewsbury. St John's College, Cambridge. Director of Visual Arts at the British Council. Trustee of the Whitechapel Art Gallery.

Gabriel White Downside. Trinity College, Oxford.

Bill Williams Manchester University. Editor-in-chief of Penguin Books.

THE BRITISH COUNCIL – MEMBERS OF THE FINE ARTS ADVISORY COMMITTEE

Leigh Ashton Winchester. Balliol College, Oxford.

Sir Colin Anderson Eton. Trinity College, Oxford.

Clive Bell Marlborough. Trinity College, Cambridge.

Anthony Blunt Marlborough. Trinity College, Cambridge. Professor of History of Art, University of London; director of the Courtauld Institute; surveyor of the King's pictures.

Professor Tom Boase Rugby. Magdalen College, Oxford. President of Magdalen College, Oxford; Trustee of the National Gallery; Professor of the

History of Art in the University of London; Director of the Courtauld Institute.

Sir Kenneth Clark Winchester. Trinity College, Oxford.

Colonel Gerald Coke Eton. New College, Oxford. Merchant banker.

Earl of Crawford Eton. Magdalen College, Oxford. Trustee of the Tate; trustee of the National Gallery; trustee of the British Museum; Chairman of the trustees of the National Galleries of Scotland; Chairman of the Royal Fine Arts Commission; Chairman of the National Art Collections Fund.

Campbell Dodgson Winchester. New College, Oxford. Keeper of the Department of Prints and Drawings of the British Museum.

Lord Harlech Eton. New College, Oxford. Trustee of the Tate; trustee of the National Gallery; trustee of the British Museum; President of the National Museum of Wales.

Sir Philip Hendy Westmister. Christ Church, Oxford.

Tom Honeyman Queen's Park School. Glasgow University. Director of Glasgow Art Gallery.

Philip James Sherborne. University College, London.

Sir Eric Maclagan Winchester. Christ Church, Oxford. Director of the V&A.

Ernest Makower

Sir Edward Marsh Westminster. Trinity College Cambridge. Trustee of the Tate; chairman of the CAS.

William Montagu-Pollock. Marlborough. Trinity College, Cambridge. Counsellor, HM Foreign Service.

Sir Owen Morshead Marlborough. Magdalene College, Cambridge. Librarian, Windsor Castle; fellow of Magdalene College, Cambridge.

Herbert Read Crosley's School. Leeds. Writer on art.

John Rothenstein Bedales. Worcester College, Oxford.

Gordon Russell Campden Grammar School. Member of Council of Industrial Design.

Earl of Sandwich Winchester. Magdalen College, Oxford. Member of the committee of the CAS.

Lilian Somerville

John Steegman Clifton. King's College, Cambridge. Keeper of the Department of Art, National Museum of Wales.

Denys Sutton Uppingham. Exeter College, Oxford. Art critic.

Basil Taylor Tonbridge. Wadham College, Oxford. Secretary of the National Art Collections Fund.

Viscount Tredegar Eton. Christ Church, Oxford. Member of the Executive Committee of the CAS for Wales.

Allan Walton Harrow.

Ellis Waterhouse Marlborough. New College, Oxford. Reader in History of Art, University of Manchester; fellow of Magdalen College, Oxford.

Duke of Wellington Eton. Trustee of the National Gallery.

John Witt Eton. New College, Oxford. Trustee of the National Gallery.

CONTEMPORARY ART SOCIETY – MEMBERS OF THE COMMITTEE

Sir Colin Anderson Eton. Trinity College, Oxford.

Howard Bliss Rugby. Trinity College, Cambridge.

Thelma Cazalet-Keir Member of the Arts Council.

Sir Kenneth Clark Winchester. Trinity College, Oxford.

Wilfrid Evill

Arthur Hind City of London. Emmanuel College, Cambridge. Slade Professor of Fine Art, Oxford University; keeper of Prints and Drawings, British Museum.

Robin Ironside Artist.

Edward le Bas Harrow. Pembroke College, Cambridge. Artist.

Thomas Lowinsky Eton. Trinity College, Oxford. Artist.

Vincent Massey Balliol College, Oxford. Trustee of the Tate. Chairman of the National Gallery.

Lord Methuen Eton. New College, Oxford. Trustee of the Tate and the National Gallery.

Raymond Mortimer Malvern. Balliol College, Oxford. Literary editor of the New Statesman and Nation.

Hugo Pitman Eton. New College, Oxford. Trustee of the Tate.

Arthur Popham Dulwich. University College, London. Keeper, Department of Prints and Drawings, British Museum.

Sir John Rothenstein Bedales. Worcester College, Oxford.

Lady Sempill

Alan Ward

PART C: SCHOOLS ATTENDED BY KEY INDIVIDUALS

ETON
Sir Colin Anderson
Viscount Bearsted
Alan Clutton-Brock
Colonel Gerald Coke
Trenchard Cox
Earl of Crawford
Robin Darwin
Brinsley Ford
Nigel Gosling
Lord Harlech
Sir Gerald Kelly
Lord Keynes
John Lehmann
Thomas Lowinsky
Neville MacGeough Bond
Lord Methuen
Benedict Nicolson
Hugo Pitman
Sir Jasper Ridley
Earl of Rosse
Sir John Stirling-Maxwell
Viscount Tredegar
Lord Howard de Walden
Peter Watson
Duke of Wellington
John Witt

WINCHESTER
Leigh Ashton
Sir Kenneth Clark
Campbell Dodgson
Eardley Knollys
Sir Eric Maclagan
Sir Ernest Pooley
Earl of Sandwich

MARLBOROUGH
Clive Bell
Anthony Blunt
Walter Hussey
Viscount Jowitt
William Montagu-Pollock
Sir Owen Morshead
Ellis Waterhouse

RUGBY
Howard Bliss
Professor Tom Boase
Maurice Collis
Samuel Courtauld
Wyndham Lewis

PART D: OXFORD COLLEGES ATTENDED

TRINITY
Sir Colin Anderson
Sir Kenneth Clark
Brinsley Ford
Thomas Lowinsky
Gabriel White

BALLIOL
Leigh Ashton
Vincent Massey
Raymond Mortimer
Benedict Nicolson
Sir Jasper Ridley

CHRIST CHURCH
William Gibson
Sir Philip Hendy
Sir Eric Maclagan
Earl of Rosse
Viscount Tredegar

MAGDALEN
Professor Boase
Earl of Crawford
John Russell
Earl of Sandwich

NEW
Viscount Bearsted
Colonel Gerald Coke
Campbell Dodgson
Lord Harlech
Viscount Jowitt
James Laver
Lord Methuen
Hugo Pitman
Ellis Waterhouse
John Witt

PART E: CAMBRIDGE COLLEGES ATTENDED

TRINITY
Clive Bell
Howard Bliss
Anthony Blunt
John LehmannSir Edward Marsh
William Montagu-Pollock
Edward O'Rorke Dickey
Sir John Stirling-Maxwell

KING'S
Alan Clutton-Brock
Trenchard Cox
Lord Keynes
Neville MacGeough Bond
Hugh Scrutton
John Steegman

Part F: Key individuals at key Public Institutions

(a)   **Directors of the National Gallery**
Sir Kenneth Clark
Sir Philip Hendy

(b)   **Director of the V&A**
Leigh Ashton

(c)   **Director of the Tate**
Sir John Rothenstein

(d)   **Trustees of the Tate**
Sir Kenneth Clark
William Coldstream
Allan Gwynne-Jones
Lord Harlech
Viscount Jowitt
Henry Lamb
Vincent Massey
Henry Moore
John Piper
Hugo Pitman
Sir Jasper Ridley
Sir Donald Somervell
Graham Sutherland
Sir Charles Wheeler

(e)   **(i) Chairmen of the Arts Council**
Lord Keynes
Sir Ernest Pooley

        (ii) Directors of the Arts Council
Philip James

(f)   **Presidents of the Royal Academy**
Sir Alfred Munnings
Sir Gerald Kelly

(g)   **Director of the Whitechapel**
Hugh Scrutton

(h)   **Directors of the National Gallery of Ireland**
George Furlong
Thomas MacGreevy

Art Schools

(i) The Slade (Professors)
Randolph Schwabe
William Coldstream

(ii) The Central
William Johnstone

(iii) Royal College of Art
Professors: Gilbert Spencer
Rodrigo Moynihan

Principals: Percy Jowett
Robin Darwin

(iv) Camberwell
William Johnstone
Leonard Daniels

BIBLIOGRAPHY

Paul Addison *Now the War is over. A social history of Britain 1945-1951*, London, 1985

Dawn Ades and Andrew Forge *Francis Bacon*, London, 1985

Eileen Agar *A Look at my Life*, London, 1988

Ronald Alley *William Scott*, London, 1963; *Graham Sutherland*, London, 1982

Colin Anderson (introduction) *The Private Collector: an exhibition of pictures and sculpture selected from the members of the Contemporary Art Society's own collections*, London, 1950;

Colin Anderson (foreword) *Seventeen Collectors*, London, 1952

William Anderson *Cecil Collins: the quest for the great happiness*, London, 1988

Julian Andrews *London's War: the shelter diaries of Henry Moore*, Aldershot, 2002

Michel Archimbaud *Francis Bacon: in conversation with Michel Archimbaud*, London, 1993

Bruce Arnold *Mainie Jellett and the Modern Movement in Ireland*, New Haven and London, 1991; *Jack Yeats*, New Haven and London, 1998; *A concise history of Irish Art*, London, 1977

Ruth Artmonsky *The school prints: a Romantic project*, London, 2006

Arts Council *An Exhibition of Paintings of the French School. Bomford Collection*, London, 1945

Arts Council *C.E.M.A. Collection of Oil Paintings, Water Colours and Drawings*, London, 1945

Arts Council *British Painters 1939-1945*, London, 1946

Arts Council *Contemporary British Art from the collections of the Arts Council and the British Council*, London, 1949

Arts Council *Some recent purchases of the Contemporary Art Society*, London, 1949

Arts Council *Some recent purchases of the Contemporary Art Society*, London, 1951

Arts Council *Paintings and Drawings from the Sir Edward Marsh Collection*, London, 1953

Arts Council *William Johnstone*, London, 1981

Arts Council *Landscape in Britain 1850-1950*, London, 1983

Arts Council *Edward Burra*, London, 1985

Sylvia Backemeyer *Making their Mark: art, craft and design at the Central School*, 1896-1966, London, 2000

Caroline Bacon and James McGregor *Edward Bawden*, Bedford, 2008

Denys Val Baker *Britain's Art Colony by the Sea*, 1959

Mary Banham and Bevis Hillier (ed) *A Tonic to the Nation: the Festival of Britain 1951*, London, 1976

Noël Barber *Conversations with Painters*, London, 1964

Leland Bardwell *A restless life*, Dublin, 2008

Cyril Barrett *Irish Art 1943-1973*, Cork, 1980

Pamela Beasant *Stanley Cursiter, a life of the artist*, Orkney, 2007

Jack Bedlington *Young Artists of Promise*, London, 1957

Belfast Museum and Art Gallery *Reports of the Committee 1945-1952*, Belfast, 1953

Belfast Museum and Art Gallery *The Lewinter-Frankl Collection*, Belfast, 1958

Keith Bell *Stanley Spencer*, London, 1999

John Berger *About Looking*, London, 1980

Jeffrey Bernard *Reach for the Ground*, London, 1996

Oliver Bernard *Getting over it: an autobiography*, London, 1992

Roger Berthoud *Graham Sutherland*, London, 1982

Anthony Bertram *Paul Nash. The Portrait of an Artist*, London, 1955; *A Century of British Painting 1851-1951*, London, 1951

Claude Bissell *The young Vincent Massey*, Toronto, 1981; *The Imperial Canadian: Vincent Massey in office*, Toronto, 1986

Eileen Black (ed) *Drawings, paintings and sculptures of the National Museums and Galleries of Northern Ireland*, Belfast, 2000

Jonathan Black *Edward Wadsworth: form, feeling and calculation. The Complete Paintings and Drawings*, London, 2005

Douglas Percy Bliss *Edward Bawden*, Godalming, 1980

Thomas Bodkin *Report on the Arts in Ireland*, 1949

Patrick Bourne *Anne Redpath, 1895-1965*, Edinburgh, 2004

Alan Bowness *The Conditions of Success. How the modern artist rises to fame*, London, 1989

Alan Bowness *William Scott: Paintings, drawings and gouaches, 1938-71*, Tate Gallery, London, 1972

Alan Bowness (introduction) *Decade 40's. Painting, Sculpture and Drawing in Britain, 1940-1949*, Arts Council, London, 1972

Andrew Brighton *Francis Bacon*, London 2001

Brighton Art Gallery *The Wilfrid Evill Collection*, Brighton, 1965

Roger Bristow *The Last Bohemians. The Two Roberts – Colquhoun and MacBryde*, Bristol, 2009

Andrew Brown *Robert Colquhoun*, Kilmarnock, 1981

David Brown (introduction) *Allan Gwynne-Jones*, Cardiff, 1982

Oliver Brown *Notes from Exhibitions*, London, 1968

Lillian Browse *The Duchess of Cork Street: the autobiography of an art dealer*, London, 1999

Iain Buchanan et al. *Frances Hodgkins: paintings and drawings*, London, 1995

David Buckman *The Dictionary of Artists in Britain since 1945*, Bristol, 1998

John Burke and Sir John Bernard Burke *Burke's Peerage, Baronetage & Knightage 1949*, London, 1948

George and Arthur Campbell *Now in Ulster*, Belfast, 1944

Peter Cannon-Brookes *The British Neo-Romantics 1935-50*, Cardiff, 1983

Margarita Cappock *Francis Bacon's Studio*, London, 2005

Roger Cardinal *The Landscape Vision of Paul Nash*, London, 1989

Miranda Carter *Anthony Blunt: his lives*, London, 2001

Andrew Causey *Paul Nash*, Oxford, 1980

Andrew Causey *Paul Nash. Writings on Art*, Oxford, 2000

Andrew Causey *Edward Burra: complete catalogue*, Oxford, 1985

Elizabeth Cayzer *Changing Perceptions: milestones in twentieth century British portraiture*, Brighton, 1999

Thelma Cazalet Keir *From the wings*, London, 1967

Edward Chaney and Christine Clearkin *Richard Eurich (1903-1992): visionary artist*, London, 2003

William Chappell (ed) *Well dearie! The letters of Edward Burra*, London, 1985

Sarah Jane Checkland *Ben Nicholson: the vicious circles of his life and art*, London, 2000

Kenneth Clark *Another Part of the Wood: a self-portrait*, London, 1974

Kenneth Clark *The Other Half: a self-portrait*, London, 1977

Kenneth Clark 'The New Romanticism in British Painting', *Art News*, February 1947

Kenneth Clark (introduction) *Paintings of Graham Bell*, London, 1947

George Kitson Clark *The Critical Historian*, London, 1967

W.B. Cleaver *Contemporary Art Society for Wales. 50th Anniversary Exhibition*, Cardiff, 1987

David Coke (ed) *Hans Feibusch: the heat of vision*, London, 1995

William Coldstream (foreword) *The Slade 1871-1971*, London, 1971

Cecil Collins *The Vision of the Fool and other writings*, Ipswich, 1994

Judith Collins and Robin Hamlyn *Within these shores. A selection of works from the Chantrey Bequest 1883-1985*, London, 1989

Maurice Collis *Stanley Spencer*, London, 1962

Maurice Collis *Diaries 1949-1969*, London, 1976

Maurice Collis *The Journey Outward: an autobiography*, London, 1952

Maurice Collis *The Journey Up: reminiscences, 1934-1968*, London, 1970

Alex Comfort *Art and Social Responsibility: lectures on the ideology of romanticism*, London, 1946

Susan Compton (ed) *British Art in the 20th Century. The Modern Movement*, London, 1986

Becky Conekin *The Autobiography of a Nation. The Festival of Britain*, London, 1976

Douglas Cooper *Alex Reid and Lefevre, 1926-1976*, London, 1976

Richard Cork *David Bomberg*, New Haven and London, 1987

Riann Coulter 'Hibernian Salon des Refusés', *Irish Arts Review*, Autumn 2003

Crane Kalman Gallery *Alan Lowndes. Paintings 1948-1972*, n.d.

Anthony Cronin *Dead as Doornails: a chronicle of life*, Dublin, 1976

Diana Crook *The Ladies of Miller's*, Lewes, 1996

Ruth Dalton (foreword) *Sculpture: an open air exhibition organised by the London County Council in association with the Arts Council of Great Britain*, 1951

Amanda Davidson *The sculpture of William Turnbull*, Much Hadham, 2005

Hugh Davies *Francis Bacon: the early and middle years, 1928-58*, New York, 1978

Russell Davies *Ronald Searle*, London, 1990

Dan Davin *Closing Times*, London, 1975

Bryony Dawkes and Robert Meyrick *Radical Visions. British Art 1910-1950*, Cardiff, 2006

Bernard Denvir 'Art Collectors and their Collections – Evill', *The Studio*, 137 (February 1949)

Nicolette Devas *Two flamboyant fathers*, London, 1966

Terence de Vere White *A Fretful Midge*, London, 1957

Frances Donaldson *The British Council: the first fifty years*, London, 1984

Sean Dorman *Limelight over the Liffey*, Fowey, 1983

Sean Dorman *Portrait of my youth*, 1995

Janet Dunbar *Laura Knight*, London, 1975

Geoff Dyer *Ways of Telling. The Work of John Berger*, London, 1986

Margot Eates *Paul Nash. Master of the image*, London, 1973

Paul Edwards *Wyndham Lewis. Painter and Writer*, London, 2000

Patrick Elliott *William McCance 1894-1970*, Edinburgh, 1990

Anthony Emery 'A new Oxford Movement', *The Studio*, January 1951

England & Co *Benjamin Crème*, London, 1992

Oliver Fairclough (ed) *Things of beauty. What two sisters did for Wales*, Cardiff, 2007

Brian Fallon *An age of innocence. Irish Culture 1930-1960*, Dublin, 1998

Brian Fallon *Edward McGuire*, Dublin, 1991 *Irish Art 1830-1990*, Belfast, 1994

Daniel Farson *The Gilded Gutter Life of Francis Bacon*, London, 1993

Daniel Farson *Sacred Monsters*, London, 1988

Daniel Farson *Never a Normal Man*, London, 1997

Daniel Farson *Soho in the Fifties*, London, 1987

William Feaver *Art News*, September 1985, volume 84

William Feaver *Frank Auerbach*, New York, 2009

William Feaver and Paul Moorhouse *Michael Andrews*, London, 2001

Denise Ferran *William John Leech. An Irish painter abroad*, London, 1996

Ian Finlay *Art in Scotland*, London, 1948

Fischer Fine Art Limited *The British Neo-Romantics*, London, 1983

Clive Fisher *Cyril Connolly: a nostalgic life*, London, 1995

Boris Ford (ed) *The Cambridge Guide to the Arts in Britain. Volume 9: Since the Second World War*, Cambridge, 1988

Andrew Forge *The Slade, Motif*, 6 (Spring 1961)

Andrew Forge (introduction) *Helen Lessore and the Beaux Arts Gallery*, Marlborough Gallery, London, 1968

Brian Foss *War Paint: Art, war, state and identity in Britain 1939-1945*, New Haven, 2007

Robert Fraser *The Chameleon Poet: a life of George Barker*, London, 2001

Christopher Frayling *The Royal College of Art. 150 years of art and design*, London, 1987

Allen Freer *John Nash*, Aldershot, 1993

Paul Fussell *Abroad. British literary travelling between the Wars*, Oxford, 1980

Edward Gage *The Eye in the Wind. Scottish Painting since 1945*, London, 1977

Iain Gale *William MacTaggart 1903-1981*, Edinburgh, 1998

Matthew Gale *Francis Bacon: Working on Paper*, London, 1999

Matthew Gale and Chris Stephens (eds) *Francis Bacon:* London, 2008

Margaret Garlake *New Art, new world: British art in postwar society*, New Haven and London, 1998

Margaret Garlake (ed) *Artists and Patrons in post-War Britain*, Aldershot, 2001

Martin Gayford 'John Craxton at 70', *Modern Painters*, vol 5, part 3 (Autumn 1992)

Andrew Gibbon Williams *William Roberts: an English Cubist*, Aldershot, 2004

Andrew Gibbon Williams and Andrew Brown *The Bigger Picture: a history of Scottish art*, London, 1993

Mary Glasgow *The Nineteen Hundreds: a diary in retrospect*

Mark Glazebrook (introduction) *John Armstrong 1893-1973*, London, 1975

John Gledhill *Matthew Smith. A catalogue raisonné of the oil paintings*, Farnham, 2009

Jacqueline Golden and T. McCann (eds) *The Dean Hussey Papers – a catalogue*, Chichester, 1997

Mel Gooding *Patrick Heron*, London, 1994 *Gillian Ayres*, London, 2000 *Ceri Richards*, Moffat, 2002

Jean Goodman *What a go! The Life of Alfred Munnings*, London, 1988

Nigel Gosling *Prowling the pavements: selected art writings 1950-1980*

Ted Gott, Laurie Benson and Sophie Matthiesson *Modern Britain 1900-1960. Masterworks from Australian and New Zealand Collections*, Melbourne, 2007

Paul Gough *Stanley Spencer. Journey to Burghclere*, Bristol, 2006

Nicolette Gray *The Paintings of David Jones*, Hatfield, 1989 *Helen Sutherland Collection: a pioneer collection of the 1930's.* Arts Council, London, 1970

Tony Gray *The Lost Years. The Emergency in Ireland 1939-1945*, London, 1997

Tony Gray *Mr Smyllie, Sir*, Dublin, 1991

Lynne Green *W. Barns-Graham: a studio life*, Aldershot, 2001

Alastair Grieve *Constructed Abstract Art in England*, New Haven and London, 2005

Geoffrey Grigson *John Craxton*, London, 1948

Geoffrey Grigson (introduction) *Ten decades: a review of British taste, 1851-1951*, Arts Council, London, 1951

Douglas Hall *20th century Scottish painting*, Arts Council, 1963

Douglas Hall *Art in exile. Polish painters in post-War Britain*, Bristol, 2008

Douglas Hall and Michael Tucker *Alan Davie*, London, 1992

Nigel Vaux Halliday *More than a bookshop: Zwemmer's and art in the 20th century*, London, 1991

Michael Hamburger *A Mug's Game: intermittent memoirs, 1924-1954*, Cheadle, 1973

Michael Hamburger *String of Beginnings*, London, 1991

James Hamilton *25 from 51. Paintings from the Festival of Britain*, Sheffield City Art Galleries, Sheffield, 1978

Martin Hammer *Bacon and Sutherland*, New Haven and London, 2005

Martin Hammer *Graham Sutherland. Landscapes, War Scenes, Portraits 1924-1950*, London, 2005

Sam Hanna Bell (and others) *The Arts in Ulster. A symposium*, London, 1951

William Hardie *Scottish Painting 1837 to the Present*, London, 1990

Meirion & Susie Harries *The War Artists: British official war art of the twentieth century*, London, 1983

Martin Harrison *Transition. The London art scene in the Fifties*, London, 2002 *In Camera: Francis Bacon. Photography, Film and the Practice of Painting*, London, 2005

Martin Harrison et al. *Francis Bacon. A terrible beauty*, Dublin, 2009

Michael Harrison *Alan Reynolds*, Kettle's Yard, University of Cambridge, 2003

Keith Hartley *Scottish Art since 1900*, London, 1989

Christopher Hassall and D. Mathews *Eddie Marsh. Sketches for a composite literary portrait of Sir Edward Marsh, KCVO, CB, CMG*, London, 1953

Christopher Hassall *Edward Marsh, patron of the arts. A biography*, London, 1959

Geoff Hassell *Camberwell School of Arts & Crafts, its students and teachers, 1943-1960*, Woodbridge, 1995

Chili Hawes (ed) *Gerald Wilde, 1905-1986*, London, 1988

Josef Herman *The Journals*, London, 2003

Frank Herrmann *Sotheby's. Portrait of an auction house*, London, 1980

Robert Hewison *Under Siege. Literary Life in London 1939-1945*, London, 1977

Robert Hewison *In Anger. Culture in the Cold War 1945-1960*, London, 1981

John Hewitt *Art in Ulster 1557-1957*, Belfast, 1977 *Colin Middleton*, Belfast, n.d.

Tristram Hillier *Leda and the Goose. An autobiography*, London, 1954

Tom Honeyman *Art and Audacity*, London, 1971

Justine Hopkins *Michael Ayrton: a biography*, London, 1994

John House *Impressionism for England. Samuel Courtauld as Patron & Collector*, London, 1994

Arthur Howell *Frances Hodgkins. Four vital years*, Rockliff 1951

Robert Hughes *Nothing if not Critical: selected essays on art and artists*, New York, 1990

Robert Hughes *Frank Auerbach*, London, 1990

Hunt Museum *Jack B. Yeats. Master of Ceremonies*, Limerick, 2004

Leonard Huskinson *A loan exhibition in memory of Fred Hoyland Mayor*, Mayor Gallery, London, 1973

Walter Hussey *Patron of Art: the revival of a great tradition among artists*, London, 1985

Paul Huxley (ed) *Exhibition Road. Painters at the Royal College of Art*, Oxford, 1988

James Hyman *The Battle for Realism: figurative art in Britain during the Cold War, 1945-60*, New Haven and London, 2001

James Hyman *Derrick Greaves From Kitchen Sink to Shangri-La*, Aldershot, 2007

Brian Inglis *West Briton*, London, 1951

Institute of Contemporary Arts *Forty years of modern art 1907-1947*

Institute of Contemporary Arts *A selection from British Collections*, London, 1948

Institute of Contemporary Arts *Robin Ironside Painting since 1939*, London, 1947

Philip James (foreword) *60 Paintings for '51*, Arts Council, London, 1951

Philip James (foreword) *British Painting 1925-1950, First Anthology*, Arts Council, London, 1951

David Fraser Jenkins *Portrait of the Artist: Artists' portraits published by 'Art News and Review' 1949-1960*, London, 1989

David Fraser Jenkins (ed) *John Piper*, London, 1983

David Fraser Jenkins *John Piper: the forties*, London, 2000

David Fraser Jenkins and Frances Spalding *John Piper in the 1930's. Abstraction on the Beach*, London, 2003

David Fraser Jenkins *Paul Nash. The elements*, London 2010

Nevill Johnson *The other side of six*, Dublin, 1983

Penny Johnson and Judith Collins *Adventure in art. Modern British art under the patronage of Lucy Wertheim*, Salford, 1991

William Johnstone *Points in Time, an autobiography*, London, 1980

Donald Jones *Stewart Mason: the art of education*, London, 1988

Geraldine Keen *The Sale of Works of Art. A study based on the Times-Sotheby Index*, London, 1971

Alice Keene *The Two Mr Smiths: the life and work of Sir Matthew Smith, 1879-1959*, London, 1995

Brian Kennedy *Dreams and Responsibilities. The State and the Arts in Independent Ireland*, Dublin, 1991

S.B. Kennedy *Irish Art and Modernism 1880-1950*, Belfast, 1991

S.B. Kennedy *Paul Henry*, New Haven and London, 2003

S.B. Kennedy *The White Stag Group*

Peter Khoroche *Ivon Hitchens*, London, 1990

James King *Interior Landscapes. A Life of Paul Nash*, London, 1987

James King *The Last Modern. A Life of Herbert Read*, London, 1990

Kunstmuseum Wolfsburg *Blast to Frieze. British Art in the 20th century*, Ostfildern-Ruit, 2002

Aziz Kurtha *Francis Newton Souza. Bridging Western and Indian modern art*, India, 2006

Andrew Lambirth *Eileen Agar. An eye for collage*, Chichester, 2008

Bruce Laughton *William Coldstream*, New Haven and London, 2004

James Laver *Museum Piece, or the education of an iconographer*, London, 1963

James Laver (foreword) *Contemporary British Paintings and Drawings, Australia 1947-1948*, London, 1947

Jane Lee (introduction) *Anthony Gross*, Oxford, 1989

James Lees-Milne *Midway on the waves*, London, 1985

Leicester Galleries *From Gainsborough to Hitchens. A selection of paintings and drawings from the Howard Bliss collection*, London, 1950

Michel Leiris *Francis Bacon. Full Face and in Profile*, Oxford, 1983

Michel Leiris *Francis Bacon. L'art de l'impossible. Entretiens avec David Sylvester*, Geneva, 1976

Mervyn Levy *Carel Weight*, London, 1986 *Ruskin Spear*, London, 1985

Wyndham Lewis *The demon of progress in the arts*, London, 1954

Jack Lindsay *Paintings and Drawings by Leslie Hurry*, London, 1950

Philip Long *John Maxwell 1905-1962*, Edinburgh, 1998

James Lord *A gift for admiration: further memoirs*, New York, 1998

Peter Lord *The Visual Culture of Wales. Imaging the Nation*, Cardiff, 2000

Peter Lord *Winifred Coombe Tennant: a life through art*, Aberystwyth, 2007

Michael Luke *David Tennant and the Gargoyle Years*, London, 1991

Andrew Lycett *From diamond sculls to golden handcuffs. A history of Rowe and Pitman*, London, 1998

Norbert Lynton *Ben Nicholson*, London, 1993 *William Scott*, London, 2004

Norbert Lynton (introduction) *British Painting 1940-1949*, London, 1966

Julian Machin *Adrian Ryan. Rather a rum life*, Bristol, 2009

Colin MacInnes (introduction) *Contemporary British Drawings, Canada 1948-1949*, London, 1948

James MacIntyre *Three Men on an Island*, Belfast, 1996

James MacIntyre *Making my mark*, Belfast, 2001

Julian Maclaren-Ross *Memoirs of the Forties*, London, 1965

Michael Macleod *Thomas Hennell*, Cambridge, 1988

Duncan Macmillan *Scottish Art in the 20th Century*, Edinburgh, 1994

Anne Madden *Seeing his way: Louis le Brocquy, a painter*, Dublin, 1994

Mary Major and June Rose *Vision Splendid. Theodore Major 1908-1999*, Chichester, 2008

John Malkin *Robert Colquhoun 1914-1962*, Kilmarnock, 1972

David Manson *Jacob Kramer. Creativity and loss*, Bristol, 2006

Arthur Marwick *Culture in Britain since 1945*, Oxford, 1991

Vincent Massey *What's past is prologue. The memoirs of the Right Honourable Vincent Massey*, London, 1963

Mayor Gallery *A loan exhibition in memory of Fred Hoyland Mayor*, London, 1973

Kenneth McConkey *A Free Spirit. Irish art 1860-1960*, London, 1990

E.H. McCormick *Portrait of Frances Hodgkins*, Auckland, 1981

A.J.L. McDonnell (introduction) *Eleven British Artists, Australia 1949*, London, 1949

John McEwen *William Gear*, Aldershot, 2003

Ross McKibbin *Classes and Cultures. England 1918-1951*, Oxford, 1998

Robert Medley *Drawn from the life: a memoir*, London, 1983

David Mellor 'A taste for tragic excellence', *Adam*, vol. 1974-75

David Mellor *The Barry Joule Archive. Works on paper attributed to Francis Bacon*, Dublin, 2000

David Mellor et al. *Recording Britain. A pictorial domesday of pre-War Britain*, London, 1990

George Melly *Don't Tell Sybil. An intimate memoir of ELT Mesens*, London, 1997

George Melly *It's all writ out for you. The life and work of Scottie Wilson*, London, 1986

Robert Melville (introduction) *Graham Sutherland*, London, 1950

Robert Melville (foreword) *'In our View'. Some paintings and sculpture bought by Hans and Elsbeth Juda between 1931-1967*, Graves Art Gallery, Sheffield, 1967

Robert Meyrick *John Elwyn*, Aldershot, 2000

John Milner *Kenneth Rowntree*, Aldershot, 2002

Dom Moraes *My Son's Father. An autobiography*, London, 1968

Dom Moraes *Never at home*, New Delhi, 1992

Richard Morphet and Denys Hodson *The Swindon Collection of Twentieth Century British Art*, Swindon, 1991

Richard Morphet *Cedric Morris*, London, 1984

Desmond Morris *Animal Days*, London, 1979

John Moynihan *Restless Lives. The Bohemian World of Rodrigo and Elinor Moynihan*, Bristol, 2002

Peter Murray (compiler) *Illustrated summary catalogue of the Crawford Municipal Art Gallery*, Cork, 1991

National Galleries of Scotland *John Maxwell, 1905-1962*, Edinburgh, 1963

National Museum of Wales *Contemporary Art Society for Wales. 50th Anniversary Exhibition*, Cardiff, 1987

Christopher Neve *Leon Underwood*, London, 1974

Christopher Neve 'Shared Studios', *Country Life*, 10 May 1984

Christopher Neve *Unquiet Landscape. Places and Ideas in 20th century English painting*, London, 1990

Eric Newton *In my view*, London, 1949

Tom Normand *Wyndham Lewis the artist. Holding the mirror up to politics*, Cambridge, 1992

Mark O'Brien *The Irish Times. A history*, Dublin, 2008

Robert O'Byrne *Hugh Lane 1875-1915*, Dublin, 2000

Padraic O'Farrell *The Ernie O'Malley story*, Dublin, 1983

Simon Ofield 'Wrestling with Francis Bacon', *Oxford Art Journal*, vol. 24, 2001

Paul O'Keeffe *Some sort of genius: a life of Wyndham Lewis*, London, 2000

Cordelia Oliver *Joan Eardley, RSA*, Edinburgh, 1988

Susan Owens *Watercolours and Drawings from the Collection of Queen Elizabeth the Queen Mother*, London, 2005

William Packer (introduction) *Roy Turner Durrant 1925-1998*, London, 2008

Parkin Gallery *Artists of the Colony Room Club. A tribute to Muriel Belcher*, London, 1982

Carol Peaker *The Penguin Modern Painters*, London, 2001

Fiona Pearson *Joan Eardley*, Edinburgh, 2007

Antony Penrose *Roland Penrose. The friendly Surrealist*, London, 2001

Roland Penrose *Scrap-Book 1900-1981*, London, 1981 'Cyril and Peter: complementary opposites', *Adam*, vol. 1974-75

Michael Peppiatt *Francis Bacon. Anatomy of an Enigma*, London, 1996 *Francis Bacon in the 1950's*, New Haven and London, 2006

Michael Peppiatt *Francis Bacon. Studies for a Portrait*, New Haven and London, 2008

John Piper *British Romantic Artists*, London, 1942

Kenneth Pople *Stanley Spencer*, London, 1991

Paul Potts *Dante called you Beatrice*, London, 1960

Arthur Power *From the Old Waterford House*, London, n.d.

Alan Powers *Art and print: the Curwen story*, London, 2008

The Public Catalogue Foundation *Oil Paintings in public ownership in the Government Art Collection*, London, 2007

Alan Pryce-Jones 'The kind sad benefactor', *Adam*, vol. 1974-75

David Pryce-Jones *Cyril Connolly. Journal and Memoir*, London, 1983

Robert Radford *Art for a purpose. The Artists' International Association 1933-1953*, Winchester, 1987

Priaulx Rainier 'Personal Recollections', *Adam*, vol. 1974-75

Geoffrey Raynor (and others) *Artists' Textiles in Britain, 1945-1970*, Woodbridge, 2003

Herbert Read *The Meaning of Art*, London, 1931

Herbert Read *Contemporary British Art*, London, 1951

Herbert Read (introduction) *The Gregory Memorial Exhibition*, Leeds City Art Gallery, 1960

Herbert Read (preface) *Exposition internationale de peintures modernes*, Paris, 1946

Gerald Reitlinger *The Economics of Taste* (3 vols.), I, *The rise and fall of pictures prices 1760-1960*, London, 1961

Maurice Rheims *Art on the Market: thirty-five centuries of collecting and collectors from Midas to Paul Getty*, London, 1961

Jasper Ridley (foreword) *The Tate Gallery's wartime acquisitions*, National Gallery, 1942

William Roberts *Five posthumous essays and other writings*, London, 1990

Bryan Robertson *Robert Colquhoun*, Whitechapel, 1958

Bryan Robertson *John Craxton. Paintings and drawings 1941-1966*, Whitechapel, 1967

Bryan Robertson *British sculpture and painting from the collection of the Leicestershire Education Authority*, Whitechapel, 1967

Bryan Robertson 'The Younger British Artists', *The Studio, March 1946*

Bryan Robertson *Ceri Richards*, Tate Gallery, London, 1981

Bryan Robertson and Ronald Alley *David Carr: the discovery of an artist*, London, 1987

Leonard Robinson *Paul Nash. Winter Sea: the development of an image*, York, 1997

W.K. Rose (ed) *The letters of Wyndham Lewis*, London, 1963

Alan Ross (ed) *Keith Vaughan. Journals 1939-1977*, London, 1989

Alan Ross *The Colours of War: war art 1939-45*, London, 1983

Alan Ross *Time was away: a journey through Corsica*, London, 1948

Peter Rossiter *Martin Bloch. A painter's painter*, Norwich, 2007

John Rothenstein *Autobiography 1: Summer's Lease: 1901-1938*, London, 1965

John Rothenstein *Autobiography 2: Brave Day, Hideous Night, 1939-1965*, London, 1966

John Rothenstein *Autobiography 3: Time's Thievish Progress*, London, 1970

John Rothenstein *Edward Burra*, London, 1973

John Rothenstein *John Nash*, London, 1983

John Rothenstein *Modern English Painters* (vols. 1, 2, 3), London, 1984 (revised)

John Rothenstein (introduction) *Matthew Smith. Paintings from 1909-1952*, Tate Gallery, London, 1953

John Rothenstein *Robin Ironside*, New Art Centre, London, 1966

Michael Rothenstein *Looking at Paintings*, London, 1947

Royal Academy *The Royal Academy Illustrated 1951*, London, 1951

Royal Academy *Stanley Spencer RA*, London, 1980

Ken Russell *A British Picture*, London, 1989

John Russell-Taylor *Edward Wolfe*, London, 1986

John Ryan *Remembering how we stood: Bohemian Dublin at the mid-century*, Dublin, 1975

Edward Sackville-West *Graham Sutherland*, London, 1943

Martin Salisbury (ed) *Artists at the Fry: Art and design in the North West Essex Collection*, Cambridge, 2003

Scottish Arts Council *One city a patron. British art of the 20th century from the collection of Southampton Art Gallery*, Edinburgh, 1985

Hugh Scrutton (introduction) *British Painting 1925-1950, Second Anthology, Arts Council*, London, 1951

Meryle Secrest *Kenneth Clark: a biography*, London, 1984

Wilfried Seipel et al. (eds) *Francis Bacon and the tradition of art*, Milan, 2003

V. Sekules 'The ship-owner as art patron: Sir Colin Anderson and the Orient Line 1930-1960', *Journal of the Decorative Arts Society*, 10 (1986), pp 22-33

Shambles Art Gallery *A poet's pictures. A selection of works of art collected by John Hewitt (1907-1987)*, Antrim, 1987

Michael Shelden *Friends of Promise: Cyril Connolly and the World of Horizon*, London, 1989

Richard Shone *The Century of Change: British painting since 1900*, Oxford, 1977

Richard Shone *Robert Colquhoun 1914-1962 and Robert MacBryde 1913-1966*, Mayor Gallery, London, 1977

Frank Shovlin *The Irish Literary Periodical 1923-1958*, Oxford, 2003

Kirsten Simister *Living Paint. J.D. Fergusson 1874-1961*, Edinburgh, 2000

Andrew Sinclair *War Like a Wasp: the lost decade of the forties*, London, 1989

Andrew Sinclair *Arts and Cultures: the history of the 50 years of the Arts Council of Great Britain*, London, 1995

Bill Smith and Selina Skipwith *A history of Scottish Art*, London, 2003

W. Gordon Smith *W.G. Gillies: a very still life*, Edinburgh, 1991

W. Gordon Smith *Philipson. A biography of Sir Robin Philipson*, Edinburgh, 1995

Theo Snoddy *Dictionary of Irish Artists. 20th Century*, Dublin, 1996

Michael and Margaret Snow (eds) *The Nightfisherman. Selected Letters of W.S. Graham*, Manchester, 1999

Peter Somerville-Large *1854-2004. The Story of the National Gallery of Ireland*, Dublin, 2004

Frances Spalding *The Tate, a History*, London, 1998 *British Art since 1900*, London, 1986

Frances Spalding *Dance Till the Stars Come Down. A biography of John Minton*, London, 1991

Frances Spalding *20th Century Painters and Sculptors*, Woodbridge, 1990

Charles Spencer *Alfred Wolmark 1877-1961*, Ferens Art Gallery, Kingston upon Hull, n.d.

Gilbert Spencer *Memoirs of a painter*, London, 1974

Hilary Spurling *The Girl from the Fiction Department: a portrait of Sonia Orwell*, London, 2002

Susan Stairs *The Irish Figurists*, Dublin, 1990

Jon Stallworthy *Louis Macneice*, London, 1995

Derek Stanford *Inside the Forties: literary memoirs 1937-1957*, London, 1977

Chris Stephens *Peter Lanyon: at the edge of landscape*, London, 2000

Chris Stephens *Bryan Wynter*, London, 1999

Jane Stevenson *Edward Burra: Twentieth-century eye*, London, 2007

Alice Strang *Consider the lilies. Scottish painting 1910-1980*, Dundee, 2006

Miranda Strickland-Constable *Leeds' paintings. 20th century British art from Leeds City Art Gallery*, London, 1980

Douglas Sutherland *Portrait of a decade. London life 1945-1955*, London, 1988

David Sylvester *Interviews with Francis Bacon*, London, 1999 (reprint)

David Sylvester *Looking Back at Francis Bacon*, London, 2000

David Sylvester *About Modern Art: critical essays, 1948-96*, London 1996

Tate Gallery *London Group. 1914-1964. Jubilee Exhibition, Fifty years of British art*, London, 1964

Tate Gallery *Forty years of modern art 1945-1985*, London, 1986

Tate Gallery *Within these shores. A selection of works from the Chantrey Bequest 1883-1985*, London, 1989

John Russell Taylor (introduction) *Morris Kestelman*, Boundary Gallery, London, 1989

Gesa Thiessen *Theology and Modern Irish Art*, Dublin, 1999

David Thompson (introduction) *Ceri Richards: a retrospective exhibition*, Whitechapel, 1960

Rosalind Thuillier *Graham Sutherland Inspirations*, Guildford, 1982

Ruthven Todd *Fitzrovia and the road to The York Minster*, London, 1973

John Tongue 'Scottish Painting', *Horizon*, May 1942

William Townsend *The Townsend Journals: an artist's record of his times, 1928-51*, London, 1976

Julian Trevelyan *Indigo Days*, London, 1957

Ben Tufnell *Cedric Morris and Lett Haines. Teaching art and life*, Norwich, 2002

Ben Tufnell (ed) *Prunella Clough*, London, 2007

Fred Uhlman *The making of an Englishman: an autobiography*, London, 1960

Ulster Museum *The MacGeough Bond Collection*, Belfast, 1966

Nicholas Usherwood *The imaginative impulse. Julian Trevelyan 1910-88*, Reading, 1998

Stefan van Raay et al. *Modern British Art at Pallant House Gallery*, London, 2004

Philip Vann *Patrick Hayman. A voyage of discovery.* South Bank Centre, London, 1990

Peter Vansittart *In the Fifties*, London, 1995

Hugo Vickers *Cecil Beaton: the authorized biography*, London, 1985

Brian Walker *Dancing to History's Tune. History, myth and politics in Ireland*, Belfast, 1996

Dorothy Walker *Louis le Brocquy*, Dublin, 1981 *Modern Art in Ireland*, Dublin, 1997

John Watney *Mervyn Peake*, London, 1976

J.R. Webster *Ceri Richards*, Welsh Committee of the Arts Council of Great Britain and the National Eisteddfod of Wales, 1961

Angela Weight *Leonard Rosoman. A war retrospective 1939-1945*, Imperial War Museum, London, 1989

R.V. Weight *Carel Weight: a haunted imagination*, Newton Abbot, 1994

Anthony West *John Piper*, London, 1979

Sir Charles Wheeler *High Relief: the autobiography of Sir Charles Wheeler, sculptor*, London, 1968

Gabriel White *Edward Ardizzone: artist and illustrator*, New York, 1980

James White *National Gallery of Ireland*, London, 1968

The Whitechapel Art Gallery *Centenary Review*, London, 2001

John Willett (introduction) *Alan Lowndes. Paintings 1948-1972*, London, n.d.

Paul Willetts *Fear and Loathing in Fitzrovia*, Stockport, 2003

Kyffin Williams *A Wider Sky*, Llandyssul, 2006

Clair Wills *That neutral island: a history of Ireland during the Second World War*, London, 2008

Michael Wishart *High Diver*, London, 1977

Michael Wishart 'Peter and others', *Adam*, vol. 1974-75

Richard Witts *Artist Unknown. An alternative history of the Arts Council*, London, 1998

Barnaby Wright et al. *Frank Auerbach. London Building Sites 1952-1962*, London, 2009

H. Harvey Wood *W. MacTaggart*, Edinburgh, 1974

J. Wood Palmer (introduction) *Three Young Collectors*, Arts Council, London, 1952

Adrian Wright *John Lehmann. A pagan adventure*, London, 1998

Malcolm Yorke *Mervyn Peake: my eyes mint gold, a life*, London, 2000

Malcolm Yorke *The Spirit of Place: nine neo-romantic artists and their times*, London, 1988

Malcolm Yorke *Matthew Smith: his life and reputation*, London, 1997

Malcolm Yorke *Keith Vaughan: his life and work*, London, 1990

Malcolm Yorke *The Inward Laugh. Edward Bawden and his circle*, Huddersfield, 2005

Michael Yoss *Raymond Mortimer: a Bloomsbury Voice*, London, 1998

Philip Ziegler *London at War*, New York, 1995

INDEX